AGAINST YOUTH VIOLENCE

D0782852

Studies in Social Harm series

Series editors: **Christina Pantazis**, University of Bristol,
Simon Pemberton, University of Birmingham and
Steve Tombs, The Open University

The Studies in Social Harms series seeks to understand the production of harm within contemporary society. The series offers comparative and international perspectives to understand the distribution of harm and combines new theory and empirical research.

Forthcoming in the series:

Border Harms and Everyday Violence
Evgenia Iliadou, June 2023

Out now in the series:

The Harms of Work
Anthony Lloyd, October 2019

Labour Exploitation and Work-Based Harm
Sam Scott, April 2018

Harmful Societies
Simon A. Pemberton, March 2016

Environmental Harm
Rob White, September 2014

Find out more at

bristoluniversitypress.co.uk/studies-in-social-harm

AGAINST YOUTH VIOLENCE

VIOLENCE

A Social Harm Perspective

Luke Billingham and Keir Irwin-Rogers

BRISTOL
UNIVERSITY
PRESS

First published in Great Britain in 2022 by

Bristol University Press
University of Bristol
1-9 Old Park Hill
Bristol
BS2 8BB
UK
t: +44 (0)117 374 6645
e: bup-info@bristol.ac.uk

Details of international sales and distribution partners are available at bristoluniversitypress.co.uk

British Library Cataloguing in Publication Data
A catalogue record for this book is available from the British Library

ISBN 978-1-5292-1405-5 hardcover
ISBN 978-1-5292-1406-2 paperback
ISBN 978-1-5292-1407-9 ePub
ISBN 978-1-5292-1408-6 ePdf

Cover design: Bristol University Press
Front cover image: Getty/Sergey Ryumin
Bristol University Press use environmentally responsible print partners.
Printed and bound in Great Britain by CMP, Poole

Contents

Series Editors' Preface

We are delighted with the addition of *Against Youth Violence* to the Studies in Social Harm series. Billingham and Irwin-Rogers provide a piercing social harm analysis that offers fresh insights into a pressing and much debated issue. In doing so, the authors successfully: dissect the true scale and nature of youth violence in the UK, revealing its disproportionate impact on already marginalized communities; locate youth violence in a complex aetiology of injurious forms of poverty, exclusion and insecurity; and detail the construction of the policy issue and current policy approaches that have done little to ameliorate the situation, and have in some instances produced unintended but demonstrably harmful consequences. Readers will find an engaging and insightful account of youth violence that is accessible to those unfamiliar with the social harm approach or from non-academic backgrounds. This does not detract from the weight of the academic argument, it just speaks to the skill with which complex issues are presented throughout.

We wish to use this preface to the book to highlight and reflect on the aspects of Billingham and Irwin-Rogers's analysis that extend beyond the immediate confines of the pages of this book. We note contributions to the definition and causal analysis of social harm, as well as specific contributions to the violence literature.

First, for those unfamiliar with the social harm literature, what we might or might not consider to be harmful lies at the heart of much that has been written to date on the topic. For critics of the approach, with little social consensus for the term, 'social harm' is considered to be relativist in nature. However, as Hillyard and Tombs (2004) first suggested in *Beyond Criminology*, and as Billingham and Irwin-Rogers themselves recognize, the open-ended nature of the definition and its continued application and refinement, promote meaningful and productive analysis of harm that more effectively captures the complexity of social injury in contemporary societies. The social harm definition offered by the authors, grounded within human needs theories, seeks to extend existing approaches to capture subjective dimensions of harm. Billingham and Irwin-Rogers offer a sophisticated picture of harm that captures the psycho-social aspects of 'mattering' and the harm that can result when our own significance and self worth is uncertain. While these harms may have previously been considered as 'objective' states (Pemberton, 2015) which might be accurately measured, the authors provide a framework that allows them to consider how injurious subjectivities of shame, anger, insecurity and so on might be more thoughtfully incorporated into future definitions of harm.

Second, in highlighting the interrelated harms that young people experience, Billingham and Irwin-Rogers carefully unpick the many layers of injury that sit behind acts of interpersonal violence. Inevitably the role of the structural arrangements upon which contemporary societies are based – as both generative contexts of harm and instances of ongoing and various injuries – highlights a critical issue for the social harm approach. In this respect, the 'structural' proves problematic, in so far as it is often interchanged within these analyses, both as a determining causal factor and an identifiable injury. The point is that 'social harm' might dissolve into a never-ending 'tautology' where the same structural feature is both the 'social' and the 'harm' simultaneously. Billingham and Irwin-Rogers offer a neat way out of this conundrum with their 'inherence' and 'directness' criteria, which allows for structural features to be assessed for direct or diverse effects, as harm or generative context – an approach which may prove very instructive for future analyses of social harm.

Third, Billingham and Irwin-Rogers's use of 'mattering' illuminates the processes that underlie violence and effectively bridges the actions of individuals and the contexts that surround them. It is here that the book makes a considerable contribution to the violence literature. 'Mattering' – feeling that you are significant and your life has purpose – fills an important explanatory lacuna in the extensive quantitative literature that repeatedly demonstrates the link between inequality and violence (for example, demonstrating that societies with higher levels of inequality have higher levels of violence; Wilkinson and Pickett, 2009), explaining the pernicious impact of marginalization on our sense of self-worth. Similarly, it adds further context and depth to Gilligan's (1997) seminal work that identifies the roots of violence in the experience of shame and status; 'mattering', the authors here suggest, provides the complex backdrop to these emotions, connecting shame via self-worth to the processes of marginalization. The contribution that 'mattering' might make to the analysis of social harm extends beyond the immediate concerns of the book. At present, empirical work on the issue of social harm focuses on the macro-determinants of harm, often focusing on harm as an event, rather than the actors involved. 'Mattering' offers a means to understand the ways that the generative contexts of harm come to impact on individuals, and how these feelings are wrestled with, navigated and can become all-consuming. Consequently, 'mattering' allows us to explain seemingly 'self-destructive' forms of agency, whereby the 'victims' of poverty and social exclusion are often implicated in their own demise by dominant liberal frames espousing personal responsibility; in turn, this allows us to understand the impacts of the inequitable distribution of resources and opportunities as key factors in individuals' choices and behaviours.

Beautifully and engagingly written, empirically rich, and theoretically and conceptually ground-breaking, *Against Youth Violence* significantly contributes to debates around violence reduction – with sustained policy-relevance – but also moves forward the current state of thinking around what constitutes social harm, how we theorize this, and how we understand it ontologically. But it makes for grim reading; Billingham and Irwin-Rogers persuasively locate youth violence within a dysfunctional society that has disinvested in services, education and social security benefits and in doing so cut adrift large numbers of young people. Youth violence, to paraphrase Dorling (2004), reflects to us more about the organization (or disorganization) of our societies than it tells us about the individual actors involved. Yet as Billingham and Irwin-Rogers observe, the scale of this violence lies within our collective control; violence reduction is premised on the creation of a less harmful society, one based on a more equitable share of resources and respect, and where young people 'matter'. Ultimately we could design out the shame, humiliation and exclusion that drives this violence – this is our choice; one that this book advocates powerfully.

Christina Pantazis
Simon Pemberton
Steve Tombs

References

Dorling, D. (2004) 'Prime suspect: murder in Britain' in P. Hillyard, C. Pantazis, S. Tombs and D. Gordon (eds) *Beyond Criminology: Taking Harm Seriously*, London: Pluto Press, pp 178–91.

Gilligan, J. (1997) *Violence: Reflections on a National Epidemic*, New York: Vintage.

Hillyard, P. and Tombs, S. (2004) 'Beyond criminology?' in P. Hillyard, C. Pantazis, S. Tombs and D. Gordon (eds) *Beyond Criminology: Taking Harm Seriously*, London: Pluto Press, pp 10–29.

Pemberton, S. (2015) *Harmful Societies: Understanding Social Harm*, Bristol: Bristol University Press.

Wilkinson, R.G. and Pickett, K. (2009) *The Spirit Level*, London: Allen Lane.

List of Figures, Tables and Boxes

Figures

Tables

Boxes

About the Authors

Luke Billingham is a youth and community worker for Hackney Quest, an independent charity based in North East London. Alongside this, he is a Research Associate on the ESRC-funded Public Health, Youth, and Violence Reduction project, based in the Open University. In 2020, he co-authored the Youth Violence Commission final report with Keir Irwin-Rogers and Abhinay Muthoo. In a voluntary capacity, he is involved with a number of criminal justice charities, including as a trustee for Haven Distribution, which provides books for people in prison.

Keir Irwin-Rogers is Senior Lecturer in Criminology at the Open University. His research centres on the health and well-being of children and young people, focusing in particular on social harm in young people's lives. Keir was lead criminologist to the cross-party parliamentary Youth Violence Commission and co-authored its final report. He has given evidence to numerous parliamentary committees and is passionate about improving policy and practice to enhance the safety, health and well-being of children and young people.

Preface and Acknowledgements

The roots of this book lie in a chance encounter back in December 2018, when the authors met in London at an event commemorating the 18th anniversary of the death of Damilola Taylor. As the event drew to a close, we spoke briefly and arranged to spend an afternoon together at Hackney Quest, the youth centre where Luke has worked since 2016. That afternoon, we discussed a range of topics, including the work of the cross-party parliamentary Youth Violence Commission, on which Keir was lead criminologist, and which Luke would later join as co-author of its final report.

Since then, we have worked together closely, not only on this book, but writing journal articles, book chapters and blogs, attending academic and practitioner conferences and, most latterly, on a three-year ESRC-funded project exploring public health approaches to violence reduction. Daily and varied contact over e-mail, phone, Zoom and WhatsApp has resulted in our becoming close friends as much as we are colleagues. We now share as many photos and videos of our own children as we do messages about our work and research.

The relationship we have developed has enabled us to have open and frank conversations about often very difficult and sensitive topics. While our views converge on a great many things, there have also been periods of (in)tense disagreement – we've included a footnote in Chapter 2 which summarizes our argument about the value of virtue ethics, for instance. These disagreements could of course have been avoided had we chosen to write separately. However, we believe this book has benefited in numerous ways from the bringing together of two rather different perspectives – one from someone who has worked primarily as a youth worker, and one from someone who has worked primarily as an academic researcher. In part, such benefit lies in what we hope will be the book's broad appeal, to an intended audience that includes practitioners, policy makers and academics. The book reflects a degree of both professional and academic knowledge and experience that it would have lacked were either of us to have approached the task of writing it alone.

We share a passion for seeking to improve children and young people's lives – in different ways, both of our careers and our voluntary commitments are dedicated to that goal. We co-wrote this book in the hope that it might contribute to that aim by bringing together insights we have each gained from our research and practice with young people. The book presents what we hope could be a fruitful way of considering their lives, and working towards their improvement.

This book would not have been possible without the support of a great many people, to whom we are grateful and indebted. Jack Reynolds provided brilliant research assistance which greatly enriched the book, particularly Chapter 6. Gavin Hales undertook much of the statistical analysis which forms Chapter 1. Ciaran Hughes created the infographics and diagrams found throughout the book – his graphic design work has improved the appearance of the book significantly. Randol Contreras, Lynne Copson, Tony Ellis, Gordon Flett, Faith Gordon, Simon Haines, Steve Tombs and James Wintrup all provided very helpful feedback on various parts of the book at different stages of their development, enabling us to improve it substantially. Our anonymous peer reviewer also provided very helpful comments. Of course, all the book's remaining errors, inaccuracies, vulgarities and failed attempts at humour are the sole responsibility of the authors.

Thank you to Ali Fraser, Fern Gillon, Susan McVie and Tim Newburn who are working with us on the PHYVR (Public Health, Youth and Violence Reduction) research project. Many of the ideas developed in this book have benefited from our conversations together, perhaps especially from our (often quite heated!) discussions about criminological literature. It is important for us to emphasize, though, that this book was written prior to the PHYVR project data analysis – this book is not based in any way on findings from that project.

Aside from these joint acknowledgements, we would each like to offer some individual thanks.

Luke would like to thank all of the young people and parents that he has worked with over the past decade. I won't name you here, but you know who you are, and I have learned an enormous amount from your wisdom, resilience, courage and challenge. Our conversations have enriched my perspective on the issues discussed in this book more than any academic study ever could. I'd like to thank all my current and former colleagues at Hackney Quest and Reach Children's Hub: I've gained so much from your expertise, experience and support. Through the course of my work I've been lucky enough to meet a number of bloody brilliant young adults from across London – some of whom weren't yet any kind of adult when I first met them! – from whom I've learned a lot. I mention them here to thank them, but also to suggest to readers that they look out for these names, because they are all trailblazers and community leaders to watch out for: David Adesanya, Athian Akec, Ameerah Amushan, Georgina Appeagyei, Thaddaeus Brown, Joshua Dickinson, Emmanuel Haffner, Diana Hysenaj, Jordan Isaacs, Ranae Kaira, Kaitlene Koranteng, Yolanda Lear, Leo Lukeman, Reece Lukeman, Kadeem Marshall-Oxley, Cheyanne McDonald, Samira Monteleone, Daniel Ocitti, Emmanuel Onapa, Renee Oyeleye, Nicholas Oyeniyi, Alvin Owusu, Shah Rahman, Rajat Singh and David Smith. I'd also like to thank the fellow-travellers and 'professional pals' who've provided me with brilliantly enriching discussion, support and mentorship over the years: Mohammad Abdullah, Deji Adeoshun, Franklyn Addo, Toyin Agbetu, Padraig Cotter-Boston, Shaun Danquah, Matt Ellis, Suzanne Fraser, Tim Head, Hussein Hussein, Jordan Ignatius, Jermain Jackman, Annmarie Lewis, Peter McDonald-Smith, Hannah Millar, Deborah Murphy, Huan Rimington, Hannah Sender, Dami Solebo, Chelsie Sparks, Nick Stanhope, Ashar Smith, Lisa Stepanovic, Frank Sweeney, Ciaran Thapar, Emma Winch, Ruth Woolsey and Ned Younger. Lastly, and probably not least, I'd like to thank my family: my parents, who always seem to have done a decent job; my brother, whose immense pedantry has, I reluctantly admit, probably sharpened my thinking; my daughter Emma (two months), who suggested a number of vital improvements to the manuscript; and my partner, Flossie, without whose boundless support, care and patience I could never have written a word.

Keir would like to thank the many children and young people who have given up time to share their views and experiences in research that he has conducted over the past decade. Thanks also go to the adults working with children and young people who have kindly and generously supported various projects over the years. I am deeply grateful to all those I worked with as part of the cross-party parliamentary Youth Violence Commission. Thanks in particular to Gary Trowsdale, a connector of unparalleled spirit and enthusiasm, for getting me involved in the Commission, and for everything that you do to support young people. Thank you to my parents, for your endless support and encouragement. Thanks to Caroline, for your patience and love, and for being a wonderful mother to our two children. Finn (two years) and Grace (six months), you've been delightful distractions and the cause of a degree of sleep deprivation that has made the task of writing this book incalculably more difficult – thank you both from the bottom of my heart.

Introduction: Against Youth Violence and Against 'Youth Violence'

A harmful society

For far too many children and young people, Britain is a harmful society in which to grow up. Across the country, social harms of various kinds blight the lives of our youngest generations – they are harmed by institutions, policies, norms, systems, organizations, services, adults and, in some cases, one another. This book explores the harms that affect young people in today's Britain, in the hope that they could be more effectively reduced and prevented (see Box 0.1 for our definitions of young people and of Britain).

One particularly contentious, divisive and visceral form of harm is physical interpersonal violence between young people. Whether labelled 'youth violence', 'serious youth violence', 'gang violence' or – when a blade is used – 'knife crime', the violence which occurs between young people is a source of national consternation. It is neither a simple 'moral panic' nor an uncontainable epidemic. It is a type of harm which requires urgent attention and immediate action. It is also the case that it already attracts substantial attention and prompts widespread action, and that some of this attention and action can be, in itself, a source of further harm.

We need both to take seriously the violence which is inflicted on some young people by a tiny minority of their peers, and to place that violence in a wider perspective: in the context of the many other harms which damage, diminish, degrade and demoralize too many young lives. These harms are significant in themselves. Their importance is not restricted to the role they may (or may not) play in encouraging other social maladies. There are, though, connections that can be drawn between harmful social circumstances and violent individual actions. We need to hold individuals responsible for the acts of violence that they commit, *and* to acknowledge that there are social, cultural, economic and political conditions which 'predictably breed violence' (Currie, 2016, p 89). Explanation is not exoneration. The

1

communities which experience the greatest concentration of social harms are also those affected by the highest rates of interpersonal violence. If we are to reduce violence, we need to better understand how social context affects people's behaviour – suggesting neither that actions are automatic responses to material circumstances, group norms or cultural imperatives, nor that they spring entirely from individual choice.

These are all matters which we address in this book. We seek to provide some fruitful exploration of a handful of questions:

- How much interpersonal physical violence is actually being committed by young people? What are the patterns and trends associated with this violence, and how does it compare to violence perpetrated by adults? (Chapter 1)
- Specifically in the context of children and young people's lives, what is a helpful way to conceptualize social harm? (Chapter 2)
- How might the concept of 'mattering' help us to understand young people's lives? (Chapter 3)
- What are some of the most significant and damaging forms of social harm in young people's lives, and what are their effects? (Chapter 4)
- How might the experience of social harm contribute to young people's propensity to commit acts of interpersonal physical violence against one another? (Chapter 5)
- Which kinds of response to 'youth violence' can be harmful, and why? (Chapter 6)
- Given all of these questions, how might we reduce social harm and violence in young people's lives? (Conclusion)

We hope that this book may be of interest to all those who are invested in bettering the lives of children and young people. We hope that, in some way, this book can contribute to that process of bettering, by suggesting some helpful ways to look at harm, at violence and at how young people construct meaningful lives.

Why are we 'against youth violence'?

We are 'against youth violence' in three particular senses, which we introduce later. However, there also is plenty that we are 'for'. Through the course of the book, we write far more about what we consider to be a helpful perspective on young people's lives (Chapters 3–5) than we do about the views which we are 'against' (mostly in Chapter 6); we have not intended to produce a work of pure deconstruction or critique. As the following sections introduce the ways in which we are 'against youth violence', we will touch upon many of the themes, ideas and problems which are further explored in the rest of the book.

Box 0.1: 'Young people' and 'Britain'

Young people

The term 'young people' is used throughout this book. Generally, we follow the United Nations (2018) definition of 'youth' and use the term to refer to people between 10 and 24 years of age. In places, we will refer to 'children and young people', by which we mean those aged 0–24.

We use the term 'young people' in this book to reflect the fact that interpersonal violence can affect any young person, regardless of their sex, gender, age, ethnicity and class. It is important to note, however, that the vast majority of young people to which this book refers are working-class young men and boys, who are disproportionately involved in violence between young people, for reasons which we examine. This is of course not to suggest that young women and girls are unaffected by violence between young people – a growing body of research has examined the involvement of young women and girls in violence, as well as the ways that they can be harmed by the violence or coercion of young men (see, for example, Batchelor, 2011 and Young, 2011 on violence among young females, Totten, 2003 on girlfriend abuse among violent young men, Iyere, 2020 and Havard et al, 2021 on young girls' exposure to traumatic or harmful experiences due to young men's involvement in violence).

Britain

Through much of the book we refer to 'Britain', a landmass composed of three nations: England, Scotland and Wales. While these nations share many similar characteristics and challenges, there are also some significant differences between them. All are subject to governance from Westminster, although Scotland and Wales both have devolved powers. In certain places, we refer more specifically to England or to England and Wales, often due to the geographic coverage of the data presented. Due to the location of much of our research and professional experience, and to the city's disproportionate levels of violence between young people, we focus especially on London in much of the book.

Against youth violence as a reality: we want there to be less violence between young people

A small number of young people in Britain commit acts of physical interpersonal violence against other young people. It is vitally important that we understand the true scale and nature of this problem, and place it in the context of other forms of violence and harm in young people's lives. It is not a problem which should be exaggerated, sensationalized or glamourized. But, notwithstanding these caveats, it remains the case that our society should vastly improve its capacity to prevent and reduce violence between young people.

We both know parents who have lost children to violence at the hands of a peer. Having each worked with young people in different capacities, we have seen the devastation that one young death causes to a community – the pain and trauma can ripple through friendship groups, families and neighbourhoods. In many cases, the mothers and fathers, brothers and sisters, school friends and teachers, professionals and neighbours who grieve for a lost young person killed by violence can never fully 'process' the bereavement. The violent curtailing of a young life is always an immeasurable loss, because no one can ever quite know what that person would have gone on to do, achieve or be. Grieving for a murdered child can stir complex pain and anguish; unbearably raw feelings of despair, horror, guilt, shame and fury. We must prevent more young people, more families and more communities from experiencing this. Writing of her own experience of grieving for her nephew, Nico Ramsay, who died in 2016 after being stabbed, Joy White (2020, p 109) explains that she has difficulty imagining what this kind of grief must feel like for Nico's peers: 'if, with all my years of life experience, I struggle to make sense of what happened, wrestle and resist feelings of anger, helplessness, sadness and rage, then what do you do with those feelings if you are a young adult?'

The fear and despair which can permeate whole communities affected by violence between young people can also devastate lives. The perceived threat of imminent physical danger can hang over a neighbourhood. It can restrict where people feel able to travel or to spend time, it can cause a near-permanent state of uncomfortable anxiety and it can prompt intense mutual suspicion and distrust, even among close companions. It can be a common refrain among parents who feel the emotional strain of living in such communities that their favourite sound in the world is their child's house key turning in the lock, confirming their safe return (Billingham et al, 2018, p 39). Children approaching adolescence in these communities can be deeply frightened of their own impending teenage years, assuming – rightly or wrongly – that they will inevitably feature violence and danger. They can fearfully anticipate having to make terrible decisions between rival groups of their peers, or having to negotiate the horrible catch-22 of choosing between the illusory safety of gang membership, on the one hand, and the potentially fragile solitude of avoiding affiliation with any local grouping, on the other. A single violent incident can cause terror to reverberate through a borough, town or city, marring lives far beyond those directly connected to the events.

Precisely due to the importance and the weight of this issue, reducing violence is not a task to undertake with jerking knees or ideological blinkers. We hope that some of the ideas and discussion that follow may aid the development and implementation of more effective policies and practices to reduce levels of violence between young people. We do not attempt to present a comprehensive blueprint for reform, particularly as we have made a series of policy recommendations to the United Kingdom (UK) government elsewhere, through our work with the cross-party parliamentary Youth Violence Commission (Irwin-Rogers, Muthoo and Billingham, 2020). Neither do we seek to identify which specific programmatic interventions are 'best' for reducing violence. We offer what we consider to be useful ways of looking at and thinking about the problems of social harm and violence in young people's lives, and – in the final chapter – we make broad suggestions about the kinds of changes that are needed if our society is to become a less harmful place for children, young people and families.

Relevant power-holders in Britain certainly appear to see levels of violence among young people in our society as not just a 'condition' – a state of affairs which exists – but a 'problem' – an issue which requires political attention and action (Kingdon, 1993, p 42; see Chapter 6). We agree. Violence between young people is a political problem which requires a serious response. But there is significant contention and disagreement about what kind of problem violence is, and the lenses through which it should be viewed. Violence can be seen as a moral failing of individual character, as a signal of 'troubled' families or as an issue with more structural and historical determinants. We can focus with microscopic intensity on the particular young people who have committed acts of violence, scrutinizing them with a moralizing, demonizing, criminalizing eye, or we can bring the lens outward, situating violence that occurs between young people within the context of other violence and other harm in their lives, considering the ways in which the social and economic arrangements of our society make such violence more likely. This leads us to the next sense in which we are against youth violence: we are doubtful about the value of 'youth violence' as a descriptive label, as it currently seems to function more as an individualizing, magnifying lens than it does as a concept to encourage reflection on the wider societal conditions and issues with which violence between young people is inextricably tied.

Against the connotations of 'youth violence' as a descriptive label: we want there to be less misconception about young people and violence

We think that the term 'youth violence' has developed enormously unhelpful associations, but we have no interest in policing anyone's language. Though we do think that the phrase in itself has some inherent implications which are misleading, our bigger objection is to the current and contingent connotations which can become attached to it. In general, the context and consequence of language is more important than its precise content. Discussions around 'youth violence' can mobilize the term in a way which demonizes, stigmatizes, pathologizes, patronizes or stereotypes young people, and in a way which generates profound misconceptions of violence, young people and harm. Whether or not the two-word concept of 'youth violence' has now become inseparably attached to these damaging effects is a difficult question to answer. We are more concerned about the extent and nature of the damage than we are about the strength of the semantic adhesion. If the words continue to be used, but to tell a far more nuanced and accurate story, with the unhelpful connotations stripped away, that would be more of a positive development than if people found alternative words to portray exactly the same misguided assumptions.[1] We are labouring this point for an important reason: we would hate for this book to do little more than increase people's scepticism about the phrase 'youth violence', while doing nothing to challenge actual misconceptions. We most certainly do not wish for it to encourage the kind of concept-snobbery or label-pedantry which is all too common in politics, academia, the public sector and the charity sector: the form of holier-than-thou self-aggrandizing in which it is pronounced that a certain term must now be abandoned, as if this marks one out as uniquely enlightened or progressive, and as if this act of linguistic disposal will inevitably produce profound societal change.[2]

It is one of the primary objectives of this book, then, to describe and dismantle many of the damaging distortions which seem to have now become associated with the term 'youth violence'. Through the chapters that follow, we will explore many of these fallacies in detail – here we will just provide a brief overview of some of the most mendacious muddles and bunkum binaries that are disfiguring the discussion about violence between young people. When laying this out in this section, we make liberal use of caricature and straw men, and provide only scant references. In the body of the book, particularly in Chapter 6, we will more thoroughly examine many of these misconceptions, sketching how they have developed since the Victorian era. Here we indulge in a cursory, introductory salvo. We start with the more inherent problems with the phrase, working outwards towards those looser connotations which can (and too often have) become more contingently associated with it.

Firstly, and somewhat unavoidably, the idea of 'youth violence' both narrows and blurs focus. It refers broadly to violence involving young people, tending to centre attention on the violence which is perpetrated by young people against other young people, but it could also be taken to include violence perpetrated by young people against adults – it is unhelpfully imprecise in this regard. Despite this imprecision, the frequent circulation of the concept can narrow our sense of who is involved in violence: if our concern about acts of violence comes to be dominated only by those which are committed by the young, it can nudge our gaze away from other forms of violence which are more common, such as street-based violence between adults (usually between men), domestic violence between adults (usually committed by men against women) and violence perpetrated by adults against children and young people. It can also imply that violence between young people is some discrete, bounded problem, which can be isolated from other kinds of violence and harm and from other connected issues, such as education, welfare, drug policy, racism, child maltreatment and so on. It can seem to position 'youth' as a 'bounded receptacle for blame' (Cottrell-Boyce, 2013, p 202). At worst, if it saturates our understanding of violence, the concept of 'youth violence' can skew our perspective, leading us to instinctively assume that any report, coverage or research about violence must involve young people. When we see news headlines or article titles referring to violence in Britain, for instance, there may be a tendency for this to conjure images of violent young people on the street, rather than violent adults in the home, despite the far greater frequency of the latter.

The narrowing and skewing of our attention can work in the other direction, too: leading us not just to associate all violence with youth, but all youth with violence. The political potency of 'youth violence' as a fundamental problem of our age can lead both to profound misconceptions about the proportion of young people involved in violence[3] and to the colonization of other aspects of youth experience – as if the only matters of concern are those which can be tied to the issue of violence; as if all problems in young people's lives should be defined by their (potential) connection with violence.

Moving on to the conceptual associations of the term, the phrase 'youth violence' can suggest that the violence denoted is of a youthful character: 'youth' can seem adjectival, describing the *nature* of the violence, rather than just who is involved in it, suggesting that youthfulness is inherently criminogenic. Whether violent acts committed by young people are somehow affected in their nature by the age of the perpetrators is questionable – a physical assault undertaken by a 28-year-old, for instance, may not differ very much from one undertaken by a 17-year-old. Of course, some might say that a 28-year-old is still young, and this is another problem: the category of 'youth' can be so vaguely defined that it is used with great plasticity, especially by those with an interest in overstating the extent of 'youth violence'. Aside from its vagueness, the word 'youth' can also by itself have certain connotations; it can be associated with uncontrollable, anarchic, hyper-hormonal, threatening, heavily group-based forms of behaviour or attitude. It now has pejorative overtones, whether used in the singular or plural: describing an individual as a 'youth' in contemporary Britain has inevitable connotations of yobbishness, while referring to 'the youth' as a group can seem to designate them a problematic generational mass. Given all of this, the term 'youth violence' can imply that there is something inherent in youth itself which is somehow always potentially violent, aggressive or uncontainable, and therefore – at worst – every young person is a potential perpetrator in waiting.

As a product of how it narrows and skews focus, and of its conceptual implications, 'youth violence' can also become associated with the idea that violence is not only perpetrated by individual young people, but is somehow self-generated by today's youth. Young people form a separate, distinct community, and it is within this hermetically sealed world that violence is fostered. It is nothing to do with adults, institutions, structures, systems, politics or economics: violence is a self-spawned property of youth. This misguided perspective can have biological or cultural assumptions attached to it – violence between young people can be seen as a 'natural' outgrowth of adolescent risk taking and boundary testing, or it can be seen as a feature of life which is incubated within particular, apparently self-contained youth cultures. In the latter case, at the extreme, an especially simplistic form of cultural determinism can suggest that, out of nowhere, young people develop norms and values which valorize violence and discredit peacefulness, as if this malicious cultural creativity occurs in a vacuum. This view appears evident in some policy reports, such as that produced by the Centre for Social Justice back in 2009, which mutilated the work of Elijah Anderson (2000) to suggest that youth violence and gang crime in Britain was caused by a vicious 'code of the street' which nigh-on necessitated violence among young people in certain neighbourhoods (Centre for Social Justice, 2009). The report failed to attend sufficiently to Anderson's rich account of how the complex, ambiguous street codes which he observed in his study of inner-city Philadelphia were developed as an alternative means for young people to live a meaningful life, in the face of their considerable economic immiseration and social stigmatization. Anderson carefully details the ways in which wealth has been magnetized away from these places, and dignity stripped from their inhabitants, as the generative context for understanding how young people then construct meaning for their lives individually and collectively, mobilizing the few resources they have – including violence – to achieve some sense of significance, self-respect and status. We would argue, with Anderson, that it is equally as important to understand how power, resources and esteem have been torn from a community as it is to understand how their cultural innovation in the face of this harmful inequity may contain destructive social conventions. This does not mean that culturally coded violence is justifiable, but it does mean that it is impossible to understand such violence without its wider socio-historical context, and that there is little value in any attempt to narrate any subculture as if insulated from this context.

The term 'youth violence', then, can encourage us to train our lenses downwards from on high, so that we can observe young people below us. Like the late 19th century authors studied by Griffin, we can 'view young people from the perspective of an outraged but respectable bourgeoisie' (1993, p 100). Casting our eyes onto the youth beneath us implies a kind of ennobled disdain, as though we are looking down on something entirely detached and degenerate. Their violence is a distant spectacle, we can absolve ourselves of any responsibility to consider how it may be connected to our society's structural features. Viewed in this way, young people can seem 'at once fascinating, incomprehensible and intimidating' – a phrase used by Sharpe to describe how 'poorer urban brethren' were viewed by better-heeled members of Victorian society (Sharpe, 2016, p 412). As this suggests, the demonization of young people – especially those experiencing poverty – has a long history. Golding and Middleton (1982, p 10) argue that this 'minimally informed mythology about the monstrous underworld of the wretched poor' goes back at least to the 16th century in Britain.

More specifically in relation to violence involving young people, Pearson (1983) traces a significant trend in British political life across many centuries, in which the mythological belief repeatedly takes hold that society has been 'suddenly plunged into an unnatural state of disorder' (Pearson, 1983, p ix), caused by the uniquely unruly habits of younger generations, who 'soar to new heights of insubordination and depravity' (Pearson, 1983, p 208), disturbing the pristine social peace which pre-existed them, and signalling a period of inexorable decline. He wrote this in the 1980s, in a biting critique of the simplistic 'law-and-order' agenda which remains influential to this day. He did not intend to suggest – and neither do we – that violence among young people is trivial, nor that it is some perennial, inevitable problem which we therefore need not worry about: he was equally scathing about both 'ageless mythologies of historical decline' and 'the equally pernicious social doctrine that nothing ever changes' (Pearson, 1983, p 223). We should not hesitate in any era to examine the precise extent and nature of violence and harm, but we should studiously avoid rehearsing any of the damaging and lazy mythological notions which abound all too frequently in discussions of 'youth violence': that this latest generation of young people are worse than any which has come before, that their violence has sprung from nothing, that we have never seen violence like it, that they manifest or cause all of society's ills or that their behaviour signifies an irreversible decline in our country's morality and culture. Too often, this mythology supports the age-old habit of focusing our fury on those with the least power and the scarcest wealth, while the preponderance of harms caused by those with the most of both goes relatively unnoticed.

If the concept of 'youth violence' can become attached to the demonization of young people, it is important to note that not all young people are demonized equally. Pearson (1983, p 224) articulates this point forcefully, criticizing the 'dishonourable tradition of British belly-aching against the "racial degeneration" of the common people and its supposed manifestation in "unprecedented" violence'. Demonization is almost invariably racialized. When he was writing in the 1980s, Pearson identified 'black muggers' as the major folk devil of the time, but he also explored the many other groups who were deemed to be 'foreign' defamers of the orderly 'British way of life' in other eras, from discharged Legionnaires to Irishmen (Pearson, 1983, p x). In more recent times, many researchers have raised concerns about the frequent stereotypical association of 'youth violence' with young Black men – for instance, Hallsworth and Brotherton (2011, p 8) describe 'a highly racial discourse that panders to fears of the black criminal other'; Gunter (2017, p 225) critiques the 'news-media images that portray black youth as intrinsically criminogenic and violent'; and Williams and Squires (2021, p 38) scrutinize the 'narrative of "knife crime" as a young, Black, male, pathology'. The statistics on ethnicity and violence paint a complex and contested picture: across Britain, it is significantly more common for White young people to be involved in violence than young Black people (Thapar, 2021, pp 181–2), while in cities such as London, there is evidence that young Black people are disproportionately affected by violence (see Chapter 1; Webster, 2015; Nijjar, 2018; Williams and Clarke, 2018; Pitts, 2020; Bhattacharya et al, 2021; Thapar, 2021). Whatever the exact statistical reality may be, the problem of youth violence (and its sister problem of gangs, especially) is too often simplistically and xenophobically associated with blackness. This is frequently blended with the vacuous cultural determinism touched upon earlier, to suggest that violence is some essential feature of inherently violence-inducing 'Black culture' (Hallsworth and Brotherton, 2011; Williams and Squires, 2021). The 'racialising discourse' of whiteness in Britain can also distinguish between different categories of White people, according to presumed moral status or ethical worth, meaning that poorer and non-British White people are racialized as 'less than White', inferior, subhuman or lumpen, especially those who are affected by violence (Tyler, 2013, p 187). The racializing and racist tendency to blame a 'foreign' Other for the alleged downfall of our society seems, unfortunately, to be alive and well in many discussions of youth violence.

Lastly, the concept of 'youth violence' seems to encourage a great number of false dichotomies. As a supposedly isolable subcategory of crime, it attracts simplistic 'takes' of all kinds, which too often involve commentators coming down squarely on one side of an artificially constructed binary. Young people are described superficially as either powerfully immoral perpetrators or blameless, vulnerable victims; their violence seen either as a freely chosen choice or as a fully determined product of their environment – they are demonized, pathologized and patronized in turn. Involvement in violence is seen as the consequence of either brutal exploitation or boundless enthusiasm, as entirely motivated by drugs or money, or solely as a means of shoring up insecure self-identity. It is all about gangs, or gangs do not exist. Behaviour is guided by overwhelmingly forceful group norms and cultural imperatives, or is a mere reflection of individual psychological difficulties. Violence is caused by mysterious, unknowable forces, or by easily tabulated risk factors. Young people are just the same as adults, guided by similar kinds of drives and concerns, or they are a fundamentally different subsection of humanity, which we could not possibly hope to understand or empathize with. The subcultures that they form are grounded in their passionate rebellion against mainstream society, or they are hyper-conformist bundles of consumers. With all due respect to Billy Bragg, asking 'which side are you on?' in relation to any of these binaries is not the most helpful contribution to be made to better understanding young people's lives.

Like any concept, the notion of 'youth violence' structures our attention. We fear that it can obscure far more than it illuminates, particularly as its mobilization seems to have become all the more febrile in 21st Century Britain. In this book, we will tend not to use the phrase, referring instead to 'violence between young people', or – more generally – to 'violence affecting young people'. As outlined at the outset of this section, though, it is misconceptions and misunderstandings that we seek to challenge, more than specific words used. There is a way of thinking about and looking at violence between young people which takes it as a discrete problem, detached from wider societal issues, encouraging us to cast our critical gaze downwards onto young people as Others, deemed to be the sole origin of their own mutual viciousness. If your aim is to find violent young people, and to find reasons to blame them, and them only, for their violence, you will probably find ways to see, speak and write about the issue on those terms – you will tend to find what you're looking for (White, 2013, p 178). Too often, the idea of 'youth violence' seems to encourage this kind of approach.

In this book, we instead look upwards and outwards from the perspective of young people, seeking to explore the various kinds of social harm which press down on their lives, the ways in which they construct a sense of meaning for their lives individually and collectively in the context of this harm, and how this may all connect to the problem of physical interpersonal violence. We also explore, historically and analytically, the more misguided ideas about 'youth violence' sketched in this section, as well as drawing out how and why they are harmful. Rather than seeking to find and describe violence between young people as if it is possible to understand it on its own terms, we intend to explore broader questions about harm in young people's lives. This involves an examination of the systems, policies, institutions and agencies which structure possibilities for children, young people and families, define and constrain their resources, and enrich or diminish their dignity.

Given the inextricable link between social harm and immense economic inequality in Britain, our approach involves considering political economy as much as sociology and psychology. The single most defining feature of our society's development over the past fifty years has been the continued magnetization of power, privilege and prestige towards those who already enjoy the greatest proportion of those resources, and the ongoing concentration of pain, pressure and powerlessness among those communities and those lives which are already structurally diminished. This parallel enrichment and immiseration forms the structural background of young people's lives today. And in fact, as we go on to argue throughout the book, inequality is not a distant 'background' feature of anyone's experience: its symptoms and its harmful effects intrude on children and young people's everyday lives.

We do not intend to write fatalistically about people's lives, nor deny their complex humanity: we regularly see for ourselves young people's considerable ingenuity, talent, passion, resilience and strength in the face of adverse circumstances. We do believe, however, that we should strive to create more equitable societies in which all children and young people grow up within social conditions which enable them to develop and express these capabilities, and to flourish. Alexander (2000, p 226) rightly highlights the temptation to write about young people's lives as if they are 'simply about constraint or simply about creativity'. Our focus on social harm (and structural harm in particular) does entail greater attentiveness to constraint than creativity – we write extensively of the ways in which various kinds of harm limit, restrict and damage young people's lives – but in our discussion of mattering (in Chapter 3 especially) we hope to have done some degree of justice to the richness of young people's inner lives, and to the complexity of their agency. Young people are never passive recipients of social injury, but that does not reduce the importance of investigating the most prominent forms of social harm which diminish their lives, in order to hold accountable those people and those structures with the greatest responsibility for causing them.

Against the sensationalization and industrialization of 'youth violence': we want there to be less exploitation of young people's suffering

The kinds of harmful misconception about young people and violence outlined in the preceding section do not come from nowhere. It is worth asking a simple question in relation to it: who benefits? As Canning and Tombs have argued: 'Harm is always linked to benefit, whether this is for identifiable agents, institutions and interests, or for maintaining or exacerbating existent, unequal power structures' (Canning and Tombs, 2021, p 7). Unfortunately, there seems to be a sizeable cohort of power holders – certain media moguls, politicians, charity bosses and senior police officers, for instance – whose interests are served rather well by the continued proliferation of simplistic portrayals of young people and violence. At worst, young people's suffering is both misrepresented and exploited to boost careers, swell funding coffers and enhance the punitive discretion of authorities. Sensationalized and superficial accounts of 'youth violence' can engender the kinds of rage, disbelief and incredulity which regrettably generate clicks, increase newspaper sales, affect the polls, exacerbate authoritarian instincts and secure votes. This problem is the focus of Chapter 6, where we look at the history of sensationalizing and simplistic portrayals of young people, crime and violence, seeking to explore where they have come from, what drives their proliferation, what they look like in the present and why they are harmful.

We do not wish to rehash lazy narrations of a simple moral panic,[4] nor to suggest that all those engaged in discussion of 'youth violence' must be motivated by cynicism and self-interest. There is much sincere, empathetic and sensitive conversation about and reporting on violence between young people, and it is certainly a positive thing if more adults are concerned about the welfare of children and young people. All the more reason, we would argue, to critique the forms of coverage and discussion about youth violence which are harmful and exploitative. A helpful litmus test for any portrayal of issues affecting young people, we suggest, is whether its overall impact is to devalue and denigrate young people, or to uphold their dignity and moral worth – regardless of which specific individual behaviours are the focus. Two different accounts of the same act of violence between young people can be equally honest and damning about the viciousness and disrespect for human life that was involved in the incident, while carrying quite different ramifications: one could dismiss young people as merely a menace to be managed, while the other could reckon with the nuanced complexity and difficulty of growing up in 21st century Britain. One could be motivated by a kind of distant, armchair disdain, a nose-holding peer down at people, neighbourhoods and communities who are deemed worthy only of curious horror, while another could be shot through with genuine compassion and concern. Much of Chapter 6 is dedicated to the analytical exercise of discerning the origins and nature of a particular, connected set of harmful perspectives on young people and violence, which continue to circulate to this day and which tend to centre on a series of 'bounded receptacles for blame': 'youth', gangs, (Black) youth culture, dysfunctional families and the 'culture' of poverty. These ideas have highly significant effects on contemporary policing and punishment, and on the practices of public and charity sector agencies, as we will explore in Chapter 6. At worst, they both sensationalize and exploit young people's suffering.

Structure and style

Though the foregoing discussion contains references to the content of each chapter, in this section we provide a more comprehensive breakdown of the book's structure. While both authors worked with one another on each of the chapters, Chapters 1 and 2 were primarily authored by Keir Irwin-Rogers, and Chapters 3, 5 and 6 by Luke Billingham. The Introduction, Chapter 4, and the Conclusion were equally contributed to by each of us.

Chapter 1 provides a detailed analysis of the latest available data on physical interpersonal violence, and violence between young people in particular. Though we are not naïve to the stark limitations of data on this issue – and crime data more generally – we recognize the vital importance of laying the ground for all that follows by giving as clear a picture as we can of the actual extent and nature of violence in today's Britain. Given that our primary objective is to put 'youth violence' in its place, in proportion and in perspective, we need to begin with an account of how much of this violence is occurring, where it is happening and how it compares to other kinds of violence (data limitations notwithstanding).

Chapter 2 offers a working definition of social harm, particularly in relation to the lives of children and young people. Beginning with a literature review which covers the development of the concept since the turn of the millennium, we then offer a conceptualisation of social harm which we use throughout the remainder of the book.

Chapter 3 focuses on the concept of 'mattering', which we believe to be a helpful conceptual tool for understanding young people's thoughts, emotions and actions. The idea of mattering centres on the ways in which people seek to establish a meaningful sense of their significance and consequence – both their importance to other people and their influence on the world around them. We also discuss recent and ongoing social changes and global processes which may be making it more difficult for individuals to develop a secure sense of mattering in today's world.

Chapter 4 brings together our concepts of social harm and mattering to consider the lives of young people in contemporary Britain. We examine some of the most significant and damaging forms of social harm which affect young people in this country today, using both quantitative and qualitative data, and discuss the nature of their effects, including on young people's sense of mattering. Composite case studies are included in order to bring to life the ways in which multiple forms of social harm can cumulatively diminish young people's lives.

Chapter 5 draws together the themes of the preceding chapters, exploring the theoretical and empirical connections between social harm, mattering and violence, through discussion of relevant literature from a range of disciplinary perspectives. Although not presenting anything like a comprehensive theory of violence between young people, it is an attempt to explain how social harms (and harmful social structures in particular) can affect the subjectivity of young people (and their sense of mattering in particular) in a manner which can make certain forms of action, including interpersonal physical violence, more likely. The chapter explores how certain kinds of social harm can cumulatively constitute 'social conditions which predictably breed violence', particularly due to the pernicious effects of social harm on young people's sense of mattering.

Chapter 6 is about responses to 'youth violence' which we deem to be harmful. In particular, we focus on three tendencies: the tendency to demonize young people; the tendency to punish and control young people in ways which are ineffective, disproportionate and counterproductive; and the tendency to engage in unhelpful forms of 'child-saving'. We first trace a brief history of youth demonization since the 1800s, before then exploring modes of punitive state action which appear to feed off and reinforce particularly prevalent forms of demonization, and modes of action in the public and charity sectors which appear to exploit and sensationalize the suffering of young people.

The Conclusion brings together the main themes and ideas explored in the book. After briefly summarizing our main arguments, we describe a 'near-future dystopia', in order to dramatize the dangerous and damaging tendencies that we have identified through the course of the book. The bulk of the chapter is then dedicated to an exploration of the changes that we believe are necessary if we are to substantially improve the lives of children and young people in this country. After introducing the 'four Rs' of recognition, resources, risk and (state) retribution, and arguing that a more equitable distribution of each should be a central political goal, we go on to describe the more specific changes to policies, systems and institutions that we believe are needed, ranging from the education system to youth provision to the criminal justice system.

As is perhaps implied by this rundown, the chapters of this book can reasonably be regarded as discrete essays, as well as constituent parts of a (hopefully) coherent overall argument. We are aware that different readers will be engaging with this book for a variety of reasons, often focused on quite specific areas of interest, and that this may lead a significant proportion to read only a small number of chapters which most directly appeal. Afflicted as we can both be by an odd kind of academic guilt when we do this ourselves, we would like to encourage readers to be as selective as they wish – we will not be offended, and, unless you are a friend or colleague, it is exceedingly unlikely that we will ever find out.

As this Introduction has hopefully demonstrated, we have tried to write this book in an accessible style, so that it is suitable for general readers, school pupils and university students, as well as seasoned academics and researchers. We are aware that this runs a significant risk: it may well come across a tad too plain speaking for the academic, and a bit too theoretical for the general reader. Such is life.

The Nature and Scale of Interpersonal Violence in Britain

Introduction

To best make sense of interpersonal violence and address it, we need an accurate picture of the nature and scale of the problem. When asked about levels of violence in society, however, people consistently overestimate its prevalence and (often wrongly) perceive things to be getting worse – something commonly referred to as 'the perception gap' (see Roberts and Hough, 2005; Mohan et al, 2011). There are many potential causes of the perception gap, including sensationalist, agenda-driven media reporting (Peelo et al, 2004; Humphreys et al, 2019) and the 'law of small numbers' – people's tendency to generalize from a small number of cases (Tversky and Kahneman, 1971). This is particularly important, given the political nature of interpersonal violence. Violence – and crime more generally – frequently dominates media, political and public discourse. Crudely put, money and political capital can be made from distorting the reality of violence and framing it in certain ways (something we discuss at length in Chapter 6).

This chapter provides an insight into the nature and scale of interpersonal violence based on the best available empirical data at the time of writing.[1] We would like to stress that it is primarily descriptive. It presents an account of what violence looks like currently and historically, but it does not generally attempt to provide explanations for what is observed. As such, the chapter serves two main functions. First, it reveals key aspects and trends concerning interpersonal violence, which we hope readers will find interesting and useful in and of itself. And second, it provides an essential grounding for the arguments and analysis that we develop in the remainder of the book. The chapter is structured is as follows:

- We begin by outlining the different data sources drawn upon in this chapter, discussing their main strengths and limitations.
- Next, we explore what violence looks like at a national level in England and Wales.
- Finally, as much of this book focuses on England's capital city, we provide a more detailed insight into interpersonal violence in London.

Sources of data: strengths and limitations

The following sections draw on three main sources of data:

1. police recorded crime;
2. hospital admissions data;
3. the Crime Survey for England and Wales.

For present purposes, it is incumbent upon us to consider briefly some of the key strengths and weaknesses of each of these data sources. For a more detailed discussion of the various ways of measuring violence (and crime more generally) see, for example, Mosher et al (2010).

Police recorded crime

One of the most common sources of evidence used to make claims about the nature and scale of interpersonal violence is police recorded crime (PRC) data. On the face of things, PRC seems to offer a highly useful data source. The harmful nature of violence should in theory compel people – particularly victims – to report instances of violence to the police, who in turn will record it and expend resources identifying and apprehending the suspect(s). In practice, however, we know that a significant amount of violence is not reported to, or recorded by, the police. There are many reasons for this, including regional variation in the effectiveness and efficiency of police recording practices (Baumer, 2002; Goudriaan et al, 2006), a lack of trust in the police and low perceptions of police legitimacy (Kochel et al, 2013; Boateng, 2018), and the fear of potential responses and repercussions, at the hands either of state authorities or of perpetrators of violence themselves.

People's propensity to report cases of violence is influenced both by factors related to those involved in the case, as well as by the nature and location of the offence. So, for example, we know that domestic violence (Cheng and Lo, 2019), violence involving younger people (Hart and Rennison, 2003) and violence in deprived areas (Bottoms et al, 1987; Berg et al, 2013) are all particularly under-reported and under-recorded. The strongest predictor of a crime being reported to the police is the perceived seriousness of the offence (Tarling and Morris, 2010). In relation to violence, this is most obviously the case in relation to homicide, where offences are almost invariably reported and recorded (Skogan, 1977). There is good evidence, however, to suggest that many violent incidents that do not involve loss of life are likely to escape the attention of the police. A report by the Mayor's Office for Policing and Crime (2019), for example, indicated that just 44 per cent of young victims reported the offence to the police, and that low levels of confidence in the police meant that reporting was especially low among young people from Black, Asian and minority ethnic backgrounds. Therefore, while we can expect a high degree of accuracy from PRC regarding homicides, PRC involving levels of violence that result in less severe injury are likely to represent significant underestimates of the true scale of interpersonal violence.

Hospital admissions data

Hospital admission records are another useful source of data on interpersonal violence. To some extent, this data does not suffer from the same level of reporting bias associated with PRC. While certain people are more or less likely to report certain offences to the police, it might reasonably be assumed that there are fewer barriers to people being admitted/admitting themselves to hospital to receive medical attention for injuries resulting from incidents of interpersonal violence. Evidence generated by the parliamentary Youth Violence Commission, however, indicates that some young people attempt to avoid attending hospital, even in cases involving relatively severe injury (Irwin-Rogers, Muthoo and Billingham, 2020). One the main reasons for this is the perceived need to avoid attracting the gaze of authorities, which can lead to young people being negatively labelled (as gang members, for example) and/or receiving an enhanced level of attention and surveillance from public and third sector organizations, the latter of which increasingly operate violence reduction interventions in major trauma centres in England and Wales (see, for example, Wortley and Hagell, 2021).

This point should not be pushed too far. We are confident that the vast majority of young people who are severely injured by interpersonal violence do attend hospital in cases where treatment is needed. Nevertheless, it remains important to note that many incidents of violence do not result in a level of injury severe enough to warrant admission to hospital, despite the violence being of a serious nature (for example, involving the use or presence of a knife). As with PRC, hospital admissions data is likely to capture a more accurate picture of interpersonal violence involving relatively severe injury, but presents an incomplete account of violence involving less severe levels of harm.

Crime Survey for England and Wales

Victimization surveys have been designed and implemented in large part to address some of the limitations associated with the data sources outlined earlier;

the Crime Survey for England and Wales (CSEW) (formerly the British Crime Survey) is one such example. Beginning in 1982, the intention of the CSEW has been to provide a nationally representative picture of crime that is more accurate than that based on police records. Although the precise methodology has changed a number of times since its inception, the survey involves a multistage stratified random sample that asks around 36,000 randomly selected people from randomly selected households about cases where they (or in some instances their household) have been a victim of crime in the last 12 months. Although the measures taken to contain the spread of COVID-19 meant that the most recent survey was conducted by telephone, ordinarily it has involved conducting interviews in respondents' homes. While there is some variability, around three-quarters of households invited to take part in the survey agree to participate year on year. Before January 2009, only those aged 16 and over were eligible to take part in the survey. Since this time, however, children aged 10–15 have also been invited to participate.

While the CSEW can in many ways be seen as providing more accurate and reliable estimates than other sources of data, it cannot straightforwardly be taken to measure and represent the true picture of the prevalence of all forms of violence (and of crime more generally) in England and Wales. Common critiques of victimization surveys include:

• Sampling error, which occurs when a sample is not representative of the broader population. This presents less of an issue for relatively prevalent types of crime, but can be more problematic for relatively rare events (which includes serious interpersonal violence) where the effects of sampling error can be substantial (see Lynch, 2006). High nonresponse rates are of particular concern in relation to serious violence between young people, because there are good reasons for suspecting young people involved in violence are more likely than other members of the general population not to give up their time to be interviewed about their experiences of crime. The quarter of people who decline to participate in the CSEW, therefore, might disproportionately contain those young people involved in or affected by violence. Victimization surveys can attempt to lessen the effects of nonresponse by weighting or imputing data, but both of these approaches make the assumption that persons in the sample have the same (or very similar) victimization experiences as others in the general population who share similar demographic characteristics.
• Systematic variation in the propensity of certain groups to report certain types of crime, including an increased likelihood that well-educated respondents will report minor assaults compared to less well-educated respondents (Taylor, 1983; Gove et al, 1985).
• Systematic variation in the way certain groups (based on, for example, age, race, sex, gender or social class) might interpret key terms such as 'threaten', 'use force' and 'use violence' (Mosher et al, 2010).

- The imperfection of people's memories and their ability to recall with accuracy historical events and incidents.
- The potential for people to feel unable or unwilling to provide truthful answers to questions that may be sensitive (Turner, 1972).
- The potential for people to fabricate incidents in the hope that this might somehow drive desired policy changes designed to tackle crime (Coleman and Moynihan, 1996).

★★★

In summary, it is clear that the CSEW, police data and hospital data all have their own unique set of strengths and limitations. By bringing these sources together, we hope the following sections will present a useful insight into key features and trends concerning interpersonal violence. While we will not continue to labour the point throughout the chapter, it is important to remain mindful of the potential biases and limitations of the lenses into the scale and nature of interpersonal violence that are provided by each of these sources of data.

Interpersonal violence in England and Wales

Taken as a whole, the CSEW indicates that levels of interpersonal violence in England and Wales have been declining since the mid-1990s. As Figure 1.1 indicates, a sharp decline in rates of violence took place during the late 1990s and early 2000s, followed by a steady decline thereafter. While there

Figure 1.1: Annual trends in rates of violence in England and Wales, 1981–2020

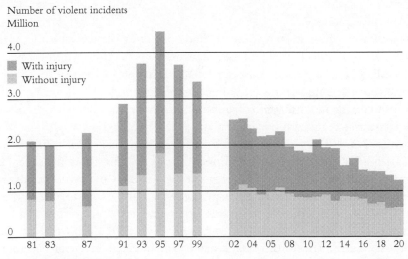

Source: CSEW (ONS, 2021a)

Figure 1.2: Victims' perceptions of offender characteristics in incidents of all violence, England and Wales, 2009–10 and 2019–20

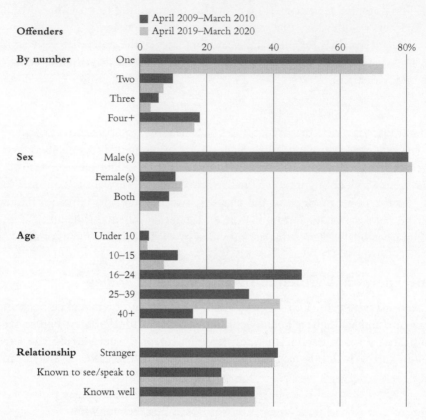

Source: CSEW (ONS, 2021a)

have been exceptional years where small increases in violence appear to have taken place – 2010–11 and 2014–15, for example – the overall trend is clear. The CSEW also suggests that the percentage of people saying that they were worried about being a victim of violent crime declined from around one in five respondents in 2002/03 to around one in ten respondents in 2015/16 (the latest year for which data is available; see ONS, 2017).

Figure 1.2 displays data gathered over the ten-year period 2009–10 to 2019–20 concerning victims' perceptions of the characteristics of perpetrators of violence. It reveals that the vast majority of violent incidents involved a single perpetrator – 73 per cent in 2019–20, up from 67 per cent in 2009–10 – and that the vast majority of perpetrators were male – 82 per cent in 2019–20, up from 81 per cent in 2009–10. Notably, there has been a significant shift in the perceived age of perpetrators of violence, with the share of violence committed by those aged 16 to 24 declining

Figure 1.3: Offences involving the possession of a knife or offensive weapon, resulting in a caution or sentence, England and Wales, 2007–20

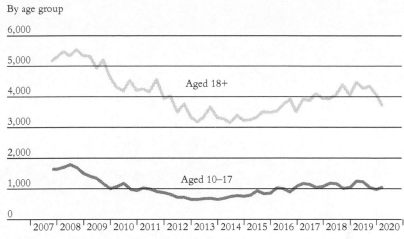

Source: House of Commons Library (2021)

from 49 per cent in 2009–10 to 28 per cent in 2019–20. Over the decade, and on the whole, the share of violent incidents committed by those under 24 (children and young people) fell from 61 per cent in 2009–10 to 38 per cent in 2019–20. Although there has been some year-on-year variation, in general terms, data from the CSEW indicates that around two in five violent incidents involve a stranger, two in five involve someone who is known well to the victim and the remaining one in five involve someone known by sight or to speak to.

Violent offences involving the use of weapons – and knives in particular – have come to dominate media and political discourse over the past couple of decades (see, for example, Cowburn, 2020). Figure 1.3 shows that the number of offences involving the possession of a knife or offensive weapon resulting in a caution or sentence declined between 2007 and 2013, before gradually increasing thereafter. Although there is some variation, the data indicates that around three to four times as many of these offences are committed by those aged over 18, compared to 10- to 17-year-olds.

Given the potential for these statistics to be shaped by police enforcement practice, it is useful to note that data on hospital admissions in England for assault with sharp objects reveals a similar trend. Figure 1.4 shows that the number of finished consultant episodes for assault by a sharp object reached its peak in 2006/07 before declining until 2014/15. Thereafter there was a steady increase, disrupted in 2020/21 by what one might reasonably assume was the impact of the spread of COVID-19 and the associated measures restricting people's movement outside of the home.

Figure 1.4: All hospital admissions in NHS hospitals in England for assault with sharp objects, 1998–2021

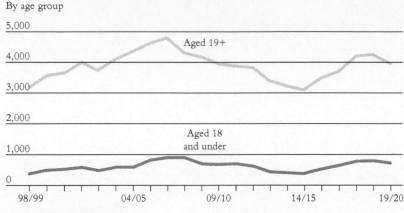

By age group

Source: NHS Digital (2021)

Figure 1.5: Number of police recorded offences involving a knife or sharp instrument, year ending March 2011 to year ending March 2020, England and Wales (exc. Greater Manchester Police)

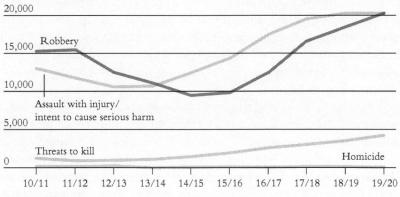

Source: ONS (2021c)

The rise in police-recorded offences involving a knife or sharp instrument between 2014/15 and 2019/20 can largely be attributed to a rise in the offences of robbery and assault with injury/intent to cause serious harm (see Figure 1.5).

As is to be expected, rates of homicide are far lower than rates of violence involving less severe injury. As such, only a very small fraction of the overall population of England and Wales are perpetrators or victims of homicide. For example, according to the last national census (which

Figure 1.6: Police force-level data on rates of knife (points/blades) offences per 100,000 population, year ending March 2020

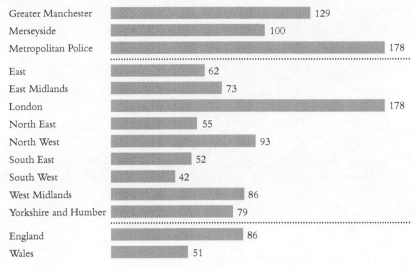

Greater Manchester	129
Merseyside	100
Metropolitan Police	178
East	62
East Midlands	73
London	178
North East	55
North West	93
South East	52
South West	42
West Midlands	86
Yorkshire and Humber	79
England	86
Wales	51

Source: ONS (2021c)

was conducted in 2011), there were 6,658,636 young people between the ages of 16–24 living in England and Wales (NOMIS, 2021). In the year the census was taken, a total of 180 young people aged 16–24 were convicted of homicide (ONS, 2021b), which equates to less than 0.003 per cent of the youth population.

Violence, and particularly violence that involves knives or sharp instruments, appears to be concentrated in urban areas (see ONS, 2021a; Figure 1.6).

Police force areas with the highest rates of knife and sharp instrument offences – Greater Manchester, Merseyside, West Yorkshire, West Midlands and London – all contain some of the country's largest and most densely populated cities (Manchester, Liverpool, Leeds, Birmingham and London). London in particular is an outlier, as it is in the context of other sources of violence-related data. For example, with 148 homicides in 2019/20, the police force area of London had the highest number of homicides compared to other police force areas (this has also historically been the case). Its rate of homicide in 2019/20 – 16 homicides per million of the population – is among the highest in the country (see ONS, 2021b). There are reasonable grounds, therefore, for focusing our analytic gaze in particular on London in this book, above and beyond the fact that our research over the past several years has been based in and around this city. Let us now, then, take a closer look at violence in the country's capital.

Figure 1.7: Homicide victims recorded by the Metropolitan Police, 2003–20

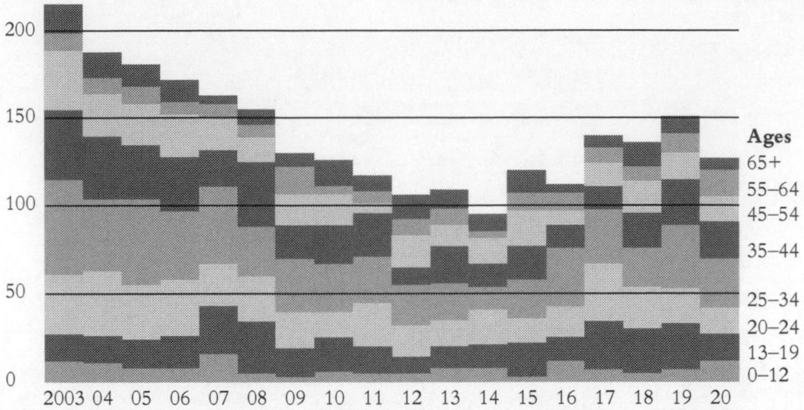

Source: MPS (2021a)

Interpersonal violence in London

Data on homicides that have been committed in London shows a similar temporal pattern to much of the data outlined in the previous section (Figure 1.7). After a period in which the number of homicides declined (the years preceding 2013/14), there was then a general rise thereafter. The peak of this rise in 2019 (152 victims), however, remained well below the previous peak in 2003 (216 victims).

With some relatively minor variation, the proportion of homicide victims falling into various age groups has remained broadly similar throughout the period 2003 to 2020. Every year without exception, in absolute terms, more people aged over 25 (adults) are murdered than those aged under 25 (young people and children). However, over the period 2003–20, the rate of those murdered was highest in the age group 20 to 24. A similar pattern emerges when looking at those who were proceeded against for homicide by the Metropolitan Police Service (MPS) (Figure 1.8).

The data in Figure 1.8 shows that there was a general decline from 2004 to 2013 in the number of persons proceeded against for homicide, before a gradual (although inconsistent) rise thereafter. While there were more people aged over 20 proceeded against each year compared to those aged 10 to 19, this again should be considered in the context of the number of people falling into these two age groups. According to the 2011 census, there are around 928,524 people aged 10 to 19 living in London. This compares to 6,171,113 people aged 20 years and over (ONS, 2013). Combining this information with the number of people proceeded against for homicide, the rate of those proceeded against is significantly higher for the younger age group. For example, in 2020, 0.0082 per cent of young people aged 10 to 19 were proceeded against for homicide, compared to 0.0025 per cent of

Figure 1.8: Persons proceeded against for homicide by the Metropolitan Police, 2003–20

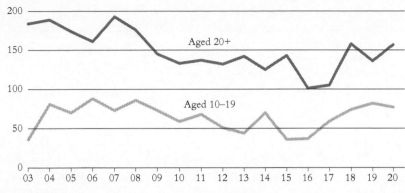

Source: MPS (2021a)

those aged 20 years and over. To reiterate a point made earlier, this shows that only a very small fraction of the population is involved in homicide, either as victims or as perpetrators. Nevertheless, it remains the case that young people aged 10 to 19 are more than three times more likely to be proceeded against for homicide compared to those aged 20 and over. A similar pattern can be found every year between 2003 and 2020.

Much political and media attention has been centred on the perceived links between race and violence (see, for example, Gunter, 2017; Phillips, 2018; Pitts, 2020). This is a complicated issue that is difficult to unpack, partly because of the complex overlap between race and social class (see, for example, Messerschmidt, 2013; Spigner, 1998) and partly because of significant regional variation (see, for example, Williams and Clarke, 2016). Homicide data for London broken down by age and ethnicity shows that Black people are murdered at disproportionate rates compared to White and Asian people (Figure 1.9).

The number of Black, White and Asian homicide victims declined in the years preceding 2014. Between 2014 and 2020, however, a divergent pattern emerged whereby the number of White and Asian homicide victims remained at broadly similar levels, while the number of Black homicide victims rose, both for those aged 0 to 19 and 20 years and over. Drawing on the 2011 census data, the rate of Black homicide victims aged 0 to 19 in London in 2020 was approximately four times higher than that of White homicide victims; for those aged 20 years and over, the rate was approximately five times higher (MPS, 2021b; ONS 2013).

MPS data on young people (aged 10–19) in particular reveals that there was a marked decline in the number of people proceeded against for offences of violence against the person over the period 2015–19 (Figure 1.10). While the number of young people proceeded against for homicide increased year

Figure 1.9: Homicide victims recorded by the Metropolitan Police by age and ethnicity, 2003–20

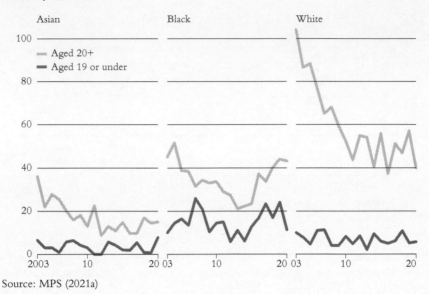

Source: MPS (2021a)

Figure 1.10: 10- to 19-year-olds proceeded against by the Metropolitan Police for violent offences, 2015–19

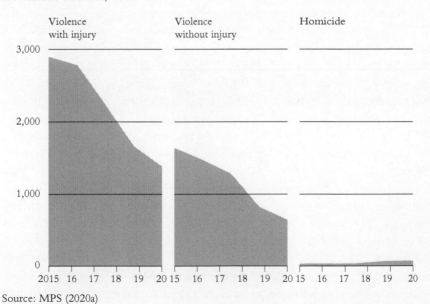

Source: MPS (2020a)

Figure 1.11: Teenagers charged with homicide by the Metropolitan Police, number of teenage suspects charged per case, 2017–20

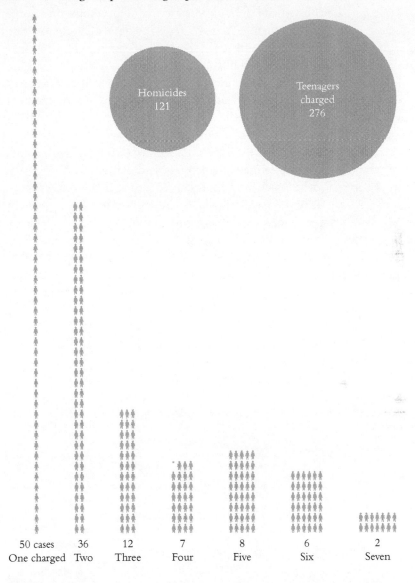

Source: MPS (2021b)

on year during this period, this was accompanied by a sharp reduction in the number of young people proceeded against for the offences of violence with and without injury.

Closely related to the discourse around race in London, another common narrative thread concerns the role of 'youth gangs' in violence (see, for example, Harding, 2014; Odling, 2021). It is difficult to obtain accurate and reliable data on the proportion of violence linked to gangs in London, in large part because of the difficulty of ascertaining whether or not gang affiliation played a central role in any single incident of violence. Simply because someone is 'gang affiliated' does not mean that any instance of violence they may be involved in is necessarily 'gang related'.

This problem sits on top of a more fundamental issue about how, and indeed whether, it is possible to categorically define someone as a 'gang member' or 'gang affiliated' (see Williams, 2015). According to data from the MPS, just 2.5 per cent of knife crime offences were gang-flagged between the years 2009 and 2020 (MPS, 2020b). This accords with other data obtained via Freedom of Information requests, which revealed that in 2017, for example, just 0.4 per cent of violence with injury and 7 per cent of knife crime with fatal or serious injury was gang-flagged by the MPS. The highest percentage of MPS gang-flagged violent offences are for homicide: in 2017, 10 per cent of homicides in London were gang-flagged (see Irwin-Rogers et al, 2019).

Connected to this, over the period 2017–20, the average number of suspects charged per homicide allegedly committed by teenagers was 2.3, and most homicides in which the suspects were teenagers involved multiple people being charged (Figure 1.11; and see Young et al, 2020 for a critical discussion of 'joint enterprise' – a set of legal principles that enables more than one individual to be charged for a single criminal offence – also discussed in Chapter 6).

Figure 1.12: Knife crime with injury recorded by the Metropolitan Police, 2011–20

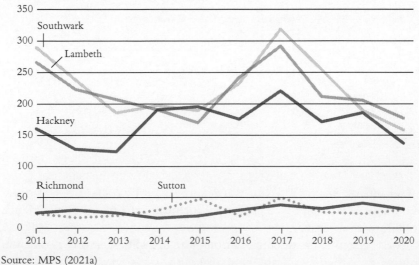

Source: MPS (2021a)

Figure 1.13: Persons proceeded against for homicide by the Metropolitan Police, totals for the period 2003–20

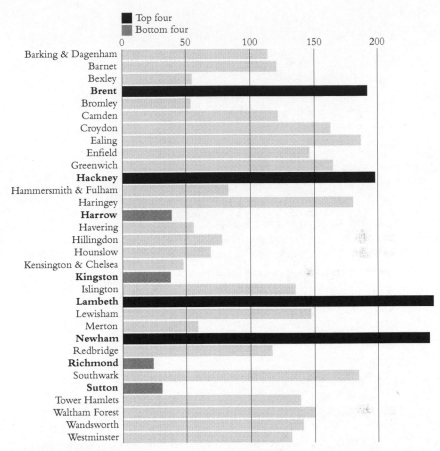

Source: MPS (2021b)

Among the most striking disparities in the data is the difference in levels of interpersonal violence by London borough (Figure 1.12). Over the decade 2011–20, some boroughs have consistently experienced relatively low levels of knife crime with injury recorded by the MPS. Other boroughs, such as Southwark, Lambeth and Hackney, have experienced fluctuating and higher levels of violence. A similar pattern of violence by borough is found when looking at the number of people proceeded against for homicide (Figure 1.13).

While the link is not direct and straightforward, there is a clear connection between socioeconomic deprivation and London boroughs containing the highest and lowest number of persons proceeded against for homicide. Richmond, Sutton, Kingston upon Thames and Harrow, for example, are

Figure 1.14: Hackney gun crime and knife crime totals by Safer Neighbourhood Team name, 2018–20

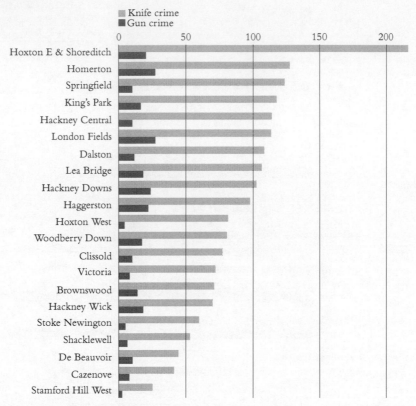

Source: MPS (2021b)

all located in the bottom ten boroughs in the index of multiple deprivation (IMD, a measure of relative deprivation for small areas); Lambeth, Newham, Hackney and Brent, on the other hand, are all found in the top ten (Ministry of Housing, Communities and Local Government, 2019).

Finally, significant variation in levels of violence can be found within boroughs, as well as between them. In Hackney, for example, Stamford Hill West, Cazenove and De Beauvoir are the three wards with the lowest levels of recorded knife crime, and they are also in the least deprived six of Hackney's wards. Homerton, Springfield and King's Park, on the other hand, are in the top six most deprived (Figure 1.14).[2]

Similar patterns are repeated at the ward level for other London boroughs. In Haringey, for example, Highgate, Stroud Green and Fortis Green, all of which are in the least deprived six wards of the borough, have the lowest levels of reported knife crime. The top three wards for recorded knife crime – Tottenham Green, Tottenham Hale and Northumberland Park – also make up three of the top four most deprived wards.

Conclusion

In this chapter we have sought to present an insight into the nature and scale of interpersonal violence, based on the best data available at the time of writing. The data we have presented, however, is inevitably selective. It provides neither a comprehensive picture of all forms of interpersonal violence, nor an insight into all of the many different ways of making sense of the forms of violence included within its scope. In addition, and to reiterate a point made at the outset of the chapter, there are numerous limitations and caveats associated with the data sources that we have drawn upon.

Despite this, it is important not to let the perfect be the enemy of the good. It is better to attempt to shed some light on key aspects and trends associated with certain forms of interpersonal violence that are most pertinent in the context of this book, than to shy away from the task altogether due to its potential enormity and the many data imperfections and limitations. With this in mind, the key features and trends in interpersonal violence that we think can and should be drawn from the data already presented are as follows:

- Taken as a whole, levels of interpersonal violence in England and Wales have been declining since the mid-1990s.
- The vast majority of interpersonal violence is committed by men.
- The vast majority of interpersonal violence involves a single perpetrator.
- Since 2015, adults (those aged 25 and over) have been responsible for a higher percentage of interpersonal violence in England and Wales than children and young people (those aged 24 and under).
- Since 2015, offences involving the use of knives in England and Wales have increased, as have hospital admissions for assaults involving sharp objects.
- In absolute terms, there are more victims and perpetrators of homicide in London aged over 20 than under 20, but under-20s as a group have a higher rate of homicide victims and perpetrators.
- There has been a general increase in the number of homicides in London since 2014, but the number of homicides in each of the seven years from 2014 to 2020 remains below the previous peak in 2003.
- The vast majority of interpersonal violence in London is not flagged as gang related.
- Knife crime, gun crime and homicide are generally concentrated in the most deprived boroughs of London, and in the most deprived wards of these boroughs.

Although there are some indications that levels of interpersonal violence are in decline – see, for example, Figures 1.1 and 1.7 – we are not claiming that there has been a general reduction in crime more broadly. On this issue, we would draw readers' attention to the work of Hall and Winlow (2015). They argue that it is more accurate to see crime as being in a state of mutation rather than decline, with huge volumes of harmful activity now taking place online. It remains the case, however, particularly in relation to interpersonal violence resulting in severe levels of injury and fatality, that current and recent levels are below the peaks seen in previous decades.

While this initial chapter has presented data on the scale and nature of some forms of interpersonal violence, it has not focused on what we consider to be its causes – we explore this issue in Chapter 5 in particular. Before we do so, however, the following two chapters explore and develop the conceptual and theoretical frameworks which underpin our analysis in later chapters. The next chapter focuses on a concept that we think holds significant value in making sense of children and young people's lives, and one that is increasingly capturing the attention of those working in various disciplinary fields: social harm.

2

Developing an Approach
to Social Harm

Introduction

In the early 21st century, an edited collection was published with the title *Beyond Criminology: Taking Harm Seriously* (Hillyard et al, 2004). The book played a central role in drawing people's attention towards the concept of social harm. In the years that followed, an increasing number of academics – many of whom might traditionally have called themselves 'criminologists' (and many who would not) – have been turning to social harm as a means of moving beyond some of the limitations and shortcomings associated with the concept of crime. In this chapter, we develop an approach to social harm that we believe holds value in the context of making sense of children and young people's lives.

This and the following chapter outline the conceptual and theoretical lenses that are applied throughout the remainder of the book (Chapter 3 explores the concept of 'mattering'). Its structure is as follows:

- First, we consider the critiques and limitations associated with the concept of crime.
- Second, we provide an overview of some of what we perceive to be the key debates and points of contention in the social harm literature.
- Third, we develop and outline our own approach to the concept of social harm.
- Fourth, we attempt to pre-empt and respond to some of the potential limitations and drawbacks associated with our approach to social harm.

Before we begin, a couple of caveats. For readers unfamiliar with the concept of social harm, there are better places to start than this chapter. For an in-depth account of social harm and its associated field of zemiology, we would recommend reading Canning and Tombs' (2021) *From Social Harm to Zemiology*. While this chapter attempts to provide a gentle introduction to the topic and help readers get to grips with a number of key and ongoing debates, it is far from comprehensive in its scope.

Our primary goal is to provide readers with a basic grasp of a conception of social harm that we believe will make good sense to people working with children and young people, as well as to children and young people themselves. Indeed, the potential for its practical application has been paramount in our thoughts throughout. For this reason, we have been relatively pragmatic about some of the choices we have made concerning the nature and scope of our conception of social harm. Depending on readers' backgrounds and interests, we anticipate that some are far more likely than others to be more or less sympathetic about our inevitable skirting of certain issues (such as the reason for our preferring a particular framework of needs over others). In this regard, we recognize that ultimately all choices are trade-offs. We believe the choices we have made have helped us to develop an approach to social harm that benefits from relative simplicity and practical applicability, and we hope this is reflected in the analytical traction that it has enabled in subsequent chapters of the book.

Why not simply focus on 'crime' in children and young people's lives?

To appreciate the potential value of the concept of social harm in making sense of young people's lives, we need to consider some of the limitations associated with the concept of crime.

Firstly, it is necessary to consider how and why certain forms of behaviour come to be considered as 'crime'. There are no intrinsic characteristics of behaviour that necessarily lead it to be defined as crime. Instead, crime is constructed in particular societies by particular groups and individuals. This invariably involves the disproportionate influence of powerful groups and individuals over the law-making process that defines what is and isn't counted as crime. Behaviours that constitute crime are therefore liable to shift over time and vary across space. Homosexuality, for example, was classified as a crime in England and Wales up until the provisions of the Sexual Offences Act 1967, and it is still defined as a crime in many places around the world. What constitutes criminal behaviour in one place and time, therefore, may not constitute it in another. In short, the definition of what is and what is not a crime – conceptualized as behaviour that violates the criminal law – is inherently political, and therefore liable to being shaped by powerful groups with vested interests. Consequently, although some crimes are common across countries around the world, the concept of crime itself lacks any firm foundation beyond it encapsulating behaviour that violates the criminal law.

Secondly, and relatedly, 'crime' includes many petty acts that involve little (if any) harm, and it excludes many acts or omissions that generate severe harm (Hillyard and Tombs, 2005). The former includes behaviours such as possession of small quantities of cannabis for personal use or the inability to pay minor fines. The latter includes acts or omissions on the part of corporations or states, including, for example, workplace injuries or the selling of arms to countries known to be engaging in forms of warfare which involve significant civilian deaths.

Thirdly, crime is organized closely around the notion of intent or the guilty mind. Consequently, behaviours that are committed with intent to cause harm are typically treated more severely than those that are committed with indifference or general disregard. While this might appear to make sense when stated in abstract terms, when applied in concrete cases it can lead to very harmful behaviours being treated more leniently than those that are less harmful. Reiman (1998) provides the example of the intentional killing of a single individual, and compares it to a mine executive who cuts corners around health and safety, leading to the deaths of numerous employees. Although the mine executive intended to kill no one in particular, he would nevertheless be conscious of the fact that his actions were likely to harm someone, and perhaps a great many people. Challenging the higher moral culpability that the law attaches to acts of intention, Reiman argues that acting with indifference to a potentially lethal and generalized threat should be considered at least as serious – if not more so – as acts with a more confined and specific intention.

Fourthly, the concept of crime serves to support the status quo and undermine what could be welcome challenges to existing power relations in numerous ways. For example, to reiterate a point made earlier, the individualizing nature of the criminal law leads the law enforcement apparatus to focus squarely upon individual and street-level acts, rather than on the (often much more) harmful consequences of decisions made by powerful actors in the suites and corridors of state and corporate offices (Hillyard and Tombs, 2004). In addition, the role of institutions in generating serious harms is overlooked or downplayed at the expense of a myopic focus on individual responsibility and blame. Consider, for example, the 2008 financial crisis, which inflicted serious harm on millions of people around the world. Some individuals received criminal convictions for their role in bringing about the crisis, but these convictions were arguably too few and too lenient (Shichor, 2018). This aside, however, it is notable that the overarching institutional framework and economic system remained unscathed – existing arrangements were protected and propped up and 'business as usual' continued.

It is true that some of the pain and suffering in children and young people's lives comes about because of acts that are currently considered criminal – acts such as serious interpersonal violence perpetrated by one young person against another. The limitations associated with the concept of crime, however, mean that the adoption a 'crime lens' would provide only a limited insight into many of the things that play a significant role in undermining or damaging the quality of children and young people's lives. In short, there are many things that affect children and young people's lives in significant and lasting ways that are not considered 'crime'. It is for this reason that we now turn towards the concept of social harm, which we argue can be a more fruitful lens through which to view the damage that is done to children and young people's lives.

From crime to social harm

There is a voluminous literature on social harm, and debates continue to unfold over its most useful and desirable meaning and scope (see, for example, Yar, 2012; Tombs, 2018; Hillyard, 2019; Rucman, 2019). We do not aim to provide a comprehensive account of these debates in this chapter.[1] Instead, we draw out some of what we consider to be the key areas of controversy to help explain and justify our approach to social harm.

In the early 2000s, Hillyard and Tombs (2004) pioneered a categories approach to defining social harm. Commenting on the difficulties associated with defining precisely what is meant by social harm, Hillyard and Tombs (2004, p 19) expressed their desire for the term to 'embrace a wide range of events and conditions that affect people during their life course'. From here, they proceeded to outline four types of social harm:

- Physical harms, which include premature death or serious injury from things such as workplace and traffic 'accidents', exposure to pollutants or lack of adequate food or shelter.
- Financial/economic harm, which covers poverty, and various forms of fraud, mis-selling and misappropriation of funds.
- Emotional and psychological harm, such as depriving a child of love and consistent care or the harm associated with non-physical domestic partner abuse.
- Cultural safety, which includes 'notions of autonomy, development and growth, and access to cultural, intellectual and informational resources generally available in a given society' (Hillyard and Tombs 2004, p 20).

Although recognizing the potential for their approach to be open to charges of relativism, Hillyard and Tombs (2004, p 20) mount a pragmatic defence, arguing that 'a social harm approach is partially to be defined in its very operationalisation, in its efforts to measure harm'. Copson (2016, p 88) has argued that while social harm approaches of the kind advocated by Hillyard and Tombs (2004) are underpinned by:

> a commitment to developing a more socially just, safe, and equitable society in which social harm is significantly reduced if not eradicated, the shift towards a language of harm demands a broader policy focus which transcends existing specialisms to address a whole host of issues across institutions, rather than on improvements to the criminal justice system.

A focus on social harm, therefore, encourages a fundamentally different approach to that taken by existing systems of crime and criminal justice – one that centres on joined-up and comprehensive social policies. Pantazis and Pemberton (2009, p 232), for example, point towards Sweden's state interventions 'in the form of universal and generous welfare benefits, healthcare and access to education, planned housing policy, and a commitment to full employment' as examples of impressive harm-reduction social policies.[2]

Copson (2016) warns, however, that there are problems associated with the shift from a discourse of 'crime' to 'social harm'. First, shifting discourses is rarely easy or straightforward. By way of just one example, the attempts of Professor David Nutt to replace the dominant criminal justice suppression and enforcement strategies to recreational drugs with harm-reduction approaches led to his dismissal from the UK government's Advisory Council on the Misuse of Drugs. Advocating alternative discourses, therefore, poses a potentially serious threat to the status and careers of those doing so. Furthermore, Copson reiterates concerns around the extent to which harm is any less socially constructed than crime, pointing towards the risks of majoritarianism and relativism in any attempts at defining and identifying social harms.

To address some these challenges, Yar (2012) draws on the concept of recognition and defines social harm as 'nothing other than *the inter-subjective experience of being refused recognition with respect to any or all of these dimensions of need'* (Yar, 2012, p 59, emphasis in original). A theory of recognition, according to Yar (2012, p 59), has the capacity to ground a theory of social harm because 'it seeks to establish at a fundamental anthropological level the "basic needs" that comprise the conditions of human integrity and well-being (what Aristotelians call "flourishing")'. Based on critical theories of recognition, human basic needs can all be conceptualized as falling within one of the dimensions of love, rights and esteem (see Honneth, 1996, pp 131–9). When each of these forms of recognition is denied, it generates a corresponding form of disrespect: the violation of the body, the denial of rights and denigration of ways of life, respectively. While Copson (2018) has acknowledged the potential contribution of Yar's approach in reconciling harm with crime, she suggests that it might be prone to overlooking harms arising from 'benign neglect'. In other words, this approach avoids imposing any positive duty to assist those experiencing hardship and suffering in cases where these experiences 'do not arise from identifiable events or active interventions' (Copson, 2018, p 42). Moreover, Copson argues that the absence of a positive duty to realize equality means that a recognition-based conception of social harm will not necessarily result in inequalities in the basic structures of society – for example, extreme gaps in distribution of income and wealth – being recognized as harms, as perhaps they should.

Pemberton (2015, p 24) similarly promotes a definition of social harm that maintains the concept's close connection with human need: 'social harm acts *as shorthand to reflect the relations, processes, flows, practices, discourse, actions and inactions that constitute the fabric of our societies which serve to compromise the fulfilment of human needs and in doing so result in identifiable harms*' (emphasis in original). According to this definition, social harms occur when the fulfilment of human needs is compromised – something Pemberton (2015, p 28) conceptualizes as 'constituting either "disablement" or "impediments" to successful human action' which would allow people 'to achieve adequate forms of self-actualisation and social participation'. Pemberton proceeds to distinguish between three main categories of harm: physical/mental health; autonomy; and relational. This approach enables Pemberton to produce a piercing and insightful analysis that exposes a range of social harms associated with different state regimes. He does, however, helpfully acknowledge that by focusing on harm as an event, this can result in neglecting 'the harmed' themselves, distorting the reality of social harm and losing sight of the agency of those who are harmed. We also have reservations about Pemberton's definition of social harm: to what do the 'flows', 'relations' or 'discourse' (which constitute the 'fabric of our societies') refer? While we appreciate the attempt to provide examples of the types of thing that can serve to compromise the fulfilment of human needs, the phrase 'relations, processes, flows, practices, discourse, actions and inactions that constitute the fabric of our societies' seems loose enough to include virtually any aspect of any human society. In other words, the definition excludes little (if anything) in terms of aspects of a given society which are eligible, or ineligible, in defining social harm. Therefore, while we agree that social harms might be generated in any and all of these ways, given that this element of the definition appears to exclude nothing, we would question whether it is useful to include it as part of a basic or starting-point definition of social harm.

This leads us to the first key point about our approach to social harm: from our perspective, the more pertinent feature of social harm is that it must be preventable, by human beings – individually or collectively – in whatever way. As we will explore in the following section, it is for this reason that we place an emphasis on the *preventability* of anything which is deemed to be a social harm.

More recently, Raymen (2019, p 138) has questioned whether any consensus on what constitutes social harm is possible within societies underpinned by postmodern liberal frameworks that lack shared and coherent sets of customs, rules and values. Drawing on Žižek (2000; 2008) and recent work by Winlow and Hall (2013), Raymen (2019, p 139–45) mounts a scathing attack on the 'unspoken collusion' of two mirror-image liberalisms: the economic liberalism of the neoliberal Right and the sociocultural liberalism of the liberal Left. Both of these liberalisms, he argues, are based on a flawed understanding of human beings that overstates their autonomy and encourages a cynical and intense competitive individualism. As part of a move away from individualizing ideologies, Raymen welcomes the integration of the notion of human flourishing into social harm approaches, but argues that this aspect of work on social harm appears relatively underdeveloped. As a remedy, he promotes the use of a three-part concept of virtue developed by MacIntyre (2007) to identify a notion of the good against which social harms can be evaluated.

Raymen suggests that identifying the 'use value' of social practices and social roles has the potential to generate objective reference points for ethics and the study of social harm, before illustrating this potential by exploring a number of concrete examples. For instance, he explains that the social practice of housing in late capitalism has become 'a largely speculative affair, in which it is predominantly used and understood for its exchange value (its external good) as opposed to its use value (its *telos* or internal good)' (Raymen, 2019, p 154). This has resulted in exorbitant house and rental prices, and large numbers of properties sitting empty, functioning not as homes but as private financial assets. He asserts that this is a common pattern that occurs within capitalist systems: external goods – such as private wealth accumulation and the pursuit of status, celebrity and power for the sake of power – are pursued at the expense of the internal good or use value of social practices. Social harm, from this perspective, therefore, would involve any action or inaction that hinders the achievement of the use value of a social practice. Raymen concludes by arguing that the privately defined notions of the good encouraged by liberal capitalism must be replaced by the pursuit of objective and collective goods internal to social practices.

Reflecting on these various points of contention and debate around the concept of social harm, and in a chapter designed to probe the ontological bases of harm, Canning and Tombs (2021, pp 107–9) close by stating four main conclusions about the concept of social harm's state of play:

- There is some agreement that social harm is related to the denial of human needs, albeit that there is no simple theory of needs by which these, or the harmful denial of them, can be recognised.
- Human beings have the capacities towards flourishing and self-realisation, and fulfilling such capacities is intrinsic to being human – so that harm is identified as the absence or stunting of such self-actualisation.
- Self-actualisation and human flourishing require a good society, and that good society is one which must be envisioned, imagined, and brought into being by people pursuing shared goods through social practices across a variety of social fields and institutions.
- A good society must transcend forms of liberalism and capitalism, based upon rights, negative liberties and the proliferation of exchange values, and must instead be characterised by economic and cultural justice. In its absence, more or less social harm will remain.

These conclusions provide a useful springboard from which to introduce our approach to social harm, which we develop and adopt in the following sections and chapters.

Our approach to social harm

As outlined in the Introduction to this book, a central interest of both authors is in better understanding and improving children and young people's lives. To this end, we are interested in developing concepts that aid our ability to effectively navigate different areas of our work. We are keen to avoid the use of esoteric language that appears to obscure more than it illuminates, and we are attracted to concepts that seem to offer the potential to genuinely connect with the people and groups with whom we work. We state this explicitly to highlight that our driving motivation to communicate and work with children, young people, policy makers and practitioners has shaped the type of approach to social harm that we develop and advocate here. We aim for an expansive and pragmatic notion of social harm that has adequate conceptual clarity, empirical applicability and practical utility in the sense of being helpful to those working to support and improve children and young people's lives.

Perhaps the most pivotal question to be addressed in any attempt to define or develop an approach to social harm is the question of what precisely it is against which a harm is or can be committed. A bullet wound to someone's torso, for example, can be conceptualized primarily and in its most immediate sense as a harm against someone's body and physical health. In the longer term, the impact might be wider, potentially affecting a person's mental health and personal relationships. In the abstract, what should a social harm be conceptualized as a harm against? After reflecting on the existing approaches to social harm already discussed, the approach that we develop throughout this book takes the following definition as its starting point:

> The term 'social harm' refers to something that compromises human flourishing in a manner that could have been prevented.

While we think this is a relatively straightforward definition of social harm, we will devote some space in this chapter to explaining how we understand some of its parts. First and foremost, to what does the term 'human flourishing' refer, and why do we think it is important in the context of social harm?

Human flourishing

References to human flourishing can be found across a wide and diverse interdisciplinary literature. While its precise meaning varies, broadly speaking, to say a person is flourishing is to suggest that they are living a life that is good and worthwhile (Alexander, 2018). In this book, we conceptualize human flourishing in two distinct, albeit related, ways:

- As needs fulfilment.
- As subjective well-being.

In crude terms, it might help to think of these as corresponding to:

- What people have or don't have in their lives.
- What people think and feel about their lives.

In short, when a person's needs are fulfilled and when they think and feel positively about their life, they can be considered to be 'flourishing'. Conversely, human flourishing is compromised when a person's needs are unfulfilled or when they have negative thoughts or feelings about their life. Paying attention to these ways of thinking about human flourishing can help us to better understand and improve the lives of children and young people. Each is now discussed in turn.

Human flourishing as needs fulfilment

Needs fulfilment is one useful way of thinking about human flourishing. In short, for lives to be characterized as 'flourishing', certain needs must be fulfilled. Over the course of the last century, countless theories and lists of human needs have been developed. Maslow (1943), for example, offered an archetypal model of human needs, in which he differentiated between eight hierarchically organized stages of need:[3] (1) biological and physiological needs; (2) safety needs; (3) love and belongingness needs; (4) esteem needs; (5) cognitive needs; (6) aesthetic needs; (7) self-actualization needs; and (8) transcendence needs. The basic idea behind Maslow's hierarchical structure is that needs placed lower down in the hierarchy, such as biological and physiological need, must be satisfied before a person can satisfy their higher-order needs.

In contrast to this hierarchical structure, several models of need have subsequently been developed that prefer a non-hierarchical, or horizontal, view of needs, which see each needs category as being relatively independent from the others (see Max-Neef, 1992; Vita et al, 2019). Sites (1990) suggested that there are four core, non-hierarchical needs: security, meaning, self-esteem and latency (rest and recuperation). These needs are grounded in four so-called 'primary human emotions' (see Kemper, 1987): the emotion of fear and the need for security; the emotion of anger and the need for meaning; the emotion of depression and the need for self-esteem; and the emotion of satisfaction (happiness) and the need for latency. While Sites separates these emotions and needs for the purpose of analysis, he highlights that in real life any strict separation is unlikely to hold. For example, people may become fearful when their self-esteem is threatened or their sense of meaning is destroyed; they may become depressed when they are forced to live in a constant state of fear, and so on. Nevertheless, each need is rooted (primarily) by one human emotion.

Some lists contain needs that have clear potential to undermine human flourishing at a group level, such as the need for dominance, deference, aggression and abasement (see Murray, 1938). The satisfaction of one's 'need' for dominance, for example, has the potential to prevent the fulfilment of another's needs, such as the need for freedom. The key point here is not to imply that one list of needs is necessarily superior to any other, but to highlight that with any list of needs there is likely to be potential for one person's need fulfilment to conflict with the need fulfilment of another. This is true of the non-hierarchical list of human needs that we promote in this book (Table 2.1).

The origins of this list of needs lie in the integration of Max-Neef's (1992) 'Matrix of human needs' and Nussbaum and Glover's (1995) 'Basic human functional capabilities'. Max-Neef (1992, p 201) saw human needs as grounded in the 'twofold character' of human beings: as deprivation and as potential. Conceived as deprivation, needs typically relate to the physiological domain, such as the biological need to eat, breathe and avoid excess temperatures of hot and cold. Conceived as potential, however, the scope of human needs expands to include, for example, what engages, motivates and mobilizes people throughout their lives. Based on our work and research, our attraction to the specific list of needs outlined in Table 2.1

Table 2.1: Human needs

Need	Satisfier
Affection	Attachment to persons and things outside of ourselves Caring and loving relationships
Creativity	Access to play Opportunities to apply and develop imagination Artistic expression
Freedom	Absence of restrictions on choices that are personal and definitive of selfhood – for example, marriage, childbearing, sexual expression, speech and employment
Identity	Status Recognition Belonging
Leisure	Recreation Relaxation Tranquillity Travel
Participation	Contribution to and having some control over political, community and social life Availability of meaningful employment
Reproduction (biological and social)	Nurturing of children Male and female fertility Transmission of culture
Security	Enforced predictable rules of conduct Safety from violence and property theft Maintenance of safe distance from crossing critical ecological thresholds Care for the vulnerable, for example, sick people, children, elderly
Spirituality	Engagement in transcendent experiences Access to nature
Subsistence	Food Shelter Vital ecological services (clean air and water) Healthcare Rest
Understanding	Access to information Access to education Early-years stimulation

Source: Adapted from Costanza et al, 2007, p 270

is that there is a strong resonance between many of these needs and the things that appear to matter most in children and young people's lives. We will elaborate further on the precise scope and content of some of these needs when applying the concept of human flourishing in the following chapters.

While we welcome and promote the inclusion of a needs-based understanding of the concept of human flourishing, from our perspective, this can provide at best only a partial or incomplete picture. Take, for example, the security need in the list outlined in Table 2.1. Hypothetically, a person could be living in an objectively safe and secure community – a community affected by only relatively low levels of violence, property crime and pollution, for example – but could subjectively perceive themselves to be highly unsafe and insecure. This mismatch between perception and reality could be the result of any number of factors, including sensationalist media reporting that overhypes levels of violent and property crime, or a climate of populist politics in which electoral candidates exaggerate threats to citizens' safety and security in order to frame themselves as potential saviours. The impact of this mismatch on human flourishing, however, is the same, regardless of the cause: perceiving oneself to be living in a highly unsafe and insecure community will reduce human flourishing, whether or not these perceptions are objectively accurate. An approach to human flourishing based on objectively measured need fulfilment alone would overlook subjective perceptions of fear and insecurity in this context.

It is possible to make the case that human needs could include the need to perceive oneself as being safe and secure, as opposed to being 'objectively' safe and secure in terms of living in a society with a low crime rate, a decent and reliable social welfare safety net and so on. Many studies, however, do not frame human needs in a way that requires the subjective input of those whose needs are being measured and evaluated (see Costanza et al, 2007). Focusing solely on human needs, therefore, would create a definition of flourishing and an approach to social harm that we believe is overly restrictive. Pemberton (2015, p 16) argues that we should 'understand harm as an injurious event insofar as it impinges on the realisation of human potential'. Our argument is that human potential – or, as we put it, human flourishing – can be impinged upon just as much by low levels of subjective well-being as it can by unmet human needs.

Human flourishing as subjective well-being

The second way we propose to think about human flourishing is as subjective well-being, which in simple terms refers to the feelings, thoughts and reflections people have about their own lives.

One commonly used definition has been provided by the OECD (2013, p 10), which describes it as: 'Good mental states, including all of the various evaluations, positive and negative, that people make of their lives and the affective [emotional] reactions of people to their experiences.' The Organisation for Economic Co-operation and Development (OECD) state that their definition is intended to be flexible and inclusive, and sufficiently open to cover the following three main components:

- A person's thoughts and reflections about their life or some specific aspect of it, such as their health or their job.
- A person's feelings or emotional states, which are typically measured with reference to a particular point in time. This includes a person's positive emotions such as happiness, contentment or joy, as well as their negative or unpleasant emotions such as anger, sadness or anxiety.
- A person's sense of meaning and purpose in their life. This could include a person's sense of autonomy, competence and goal orientation (what someone hopes to get out of life).

While there are many other ways of conceptualizing subjective well-being (see Eid and Larsen, 2007; Seligman, 2018), we regard this three-part framework as a fruitful one for making sense of children and young people's lives. While the components are distinct from one another, there is likely to be some connection between them in most cases. So, for example, if a young person lacks a sense of meaning in their life, there are good reasons for suspecting that this might negatively affect their feelings or emotional states. However, the relationship is not necessarily determinative or straightforward – there may be some young people who lack a sense of meaning but remain generally happy, while others may have a strong sense of purpose but experience prolonged periods of depression and sadness.

It is worth noting that Pantazis and Pemberton (2009, p 216) have argued against the inclusion of ideas such as happiness (and, by association, subjective well-being) in any definition of social harm on the grounds that such concepts are 'fraught with difficulties, including ambiguity over their precise meanings, their tendency towards subjective interpretation, and consequently the ability to formulate meaningful policy to address such issues'. There is undoubtedly some ambiguity over the precise scope and content of subjective well-being, as well as challenges in measuring it. By its very nature, it involves subjective interpretation. Nevertheless, the concept of subjective well-being has gained currency in countries around the world, with the UK's Office for National Statistics, for example, formally exploring its potential for informing policy development across diverse domains, including sport and culture, mental health services and human resource policies (see Stone and Mackie, 2013). While we accept the issues raised by Pantazis and Pemberton, we believe the drawbacks associated with *not* taking into account something like subjective well-being in the definition and identification of social harms – as already discussed – outweigh these difficulties.

Summarizing our approach to social harm

Although we have provided what we consider to be a relatively simple starting-point definition of social harm, references to human flourishing can be interpreted in a number of different ways. The literature on human flourishing is vast, with countless books, journal articles and research reports centring on the nature and application of this concept.[4] In the preceding sections we have provided a preliminary insight into what we regard as being the most useful way of thinking about human flourishing as applied in this book, based on the two senses of needs and subjective well-being. This is summarized in Figure 2.1.

Readers may be more or less drawn to one of these two ways of understanding human flourishing than to the other. Our contention is that neither constitutes 'the right way' of thinking about human flourishing, nor is one inherently superior to the other. Each represents a distinct way of understanding human flourishing – one focusing on what people need (needs fulfilment) and the other on what people think and feel about their

Figure 2.1: Conceptualization of human flourishing

lives (subjective well-being). They are not intended to be hierarchical. For example, it is not the case that social harms that compromise people's subjective well-being are necessarily more or less serious than social harms that compromise people's needs. Instead, the relative severity of a particular social harm is to be determined in its concrete context, where different approaches to understanding human flourishing will be more or less pertinent. While both ways of thinking about human flourishing are conceptually distinct, in practice there is likely to be some overlap and interconnection. It is likely that a failure to fulfil a child's basic needs around shelter and food, for example, will also serve to undermine their subjective well-being.

Each of the two ways of understanding human flourishing should be thought of as heuristic categories that are unlikely to map in any straightforward way onto individual or social life, not least because of their potential overlap and interconnection. They are therefore best considered sensitizing or orienting devices which will serve to guide our exploration of social harms in children and young people's lives in the following chapters. In this sense, they constitute starting points and springboards from which we begin our analysis, as opposed to rigid conceptual frameworks through which we force our exploration and analysis of empirical data. It is worth reiterating Hillyard and Tombs' (2004, p 20) suggestion that 'a social harm approach is partially to be defined in its very operationalisation, in its efforts to measure harm'. It is precisely in this spirit that we will continue to develop our approach to social harm in the following chapters, as we present and analyse empirical data that sheds light on various forms of social harm.

Distinguishing 'social harm' from (simply) 'harm'

To recap, according to the definition provided earlier, we are suggesting that social harm occurs when the flourishing of children and young people is compromised in a manner that could have been prevented. The 'social' in social harm refers to the possibility that the harm could have been prevented by the actions of human beings. Following our approach, social harms include those that are preventable at the individual, group, organizational and institutional levels. The genesis of the harm could be natural or social, but insofar as the actions of human beings are able to prevent it, we would regard it as social harm. So, for example, while earthquakes are a natural phenomenon and are not typically caused by human activity,[5] individuals, organizations and societal institutions are able to put measures in place to mitigate the associated risks of harm, such as ensuring that buildings in seismic zones are able to withstand major tremors, developing appropriate emergency communication plans, and ensuring that disaster-management supplies are well-stocked. If individuals, organizations and institutions did not take such measures and this contributed to people's deaths in the case of an earthquake, this would constitute a clear case of social harm.

The ability of societies to significantly reduce or prevent many if not most of the major harms that afflict their populations has increased rapidly in recent decades. This applies to countries in the Global North in particular, which have the capacity to deploy unprecedented levels of resources to meet the needs of their citizens. Indeed, it is much more difficult to identify non-preventable than preventable harms. One example of a non-preventable harm would include a large asteroid colliding with the Earth and wiping out humanity. In this case, it would be impossible for any particular individual, organization or institution to protect people from this type of harm at present. At least in one sense, you might find the extreme nature of this example encouraging. Pause for a moment to consider just how many forms of harm there are, in the early decades of the 21st century, that human beings and the social structures in which we operate, or hypothetically could operate, are capable of preventing. This is not to imply that eliminating *all* forms of social harm is a straightforward exercise, nor that all social harms are *equally* preventable. It is, however, to draw attention to the fact that many social harms, particularly those closely connected to inadequate access to necessities such as housing, food and healthcare, *are* preventable, should those in positions of power deem the reduction of these harms to be political priorities, and should they approach this task with sufficient resources, resolve and intelligence. While this is inspiring, on the one hand, the fact that so many serious social harms still occur is utterly disheartening, on the other. Although a comprehensive analysis of why this is the case is beyond the scope of this book, we do attempt to provide some insights in the following chapters about why certain social harms in children and young people's lives have persisted, both historically and at the time of writing.

Structural harm and interpersonal harm

'Social harm' – as it is framed in the preceding sections – can be understood as an umbrella term that includes both interpersonal and structural forms of harm. Interpersonal harm consists of acts (or acts of omission) committed by one person or group that directly affect another person or group in a manner that compromises human flourishing. The most obvious interpersonal form of harm in the context of this book is the interpersonal violence committed by one young person against another. When a young person physically attacks another, this has the potential to undermine the victim's subjective well-being as well as their security needs – in other words, it compromises human flourishing. If, as we argue in this book, the causes of violence between young people are something that can be understood and addressed, then such violence can also be considered preventable, and hence identified as a form of social harm.

Structural harm, on the other hand, is generated at the level of social structures, such as institutions, systems and policies. While individuals still commit acts (or acts of omission) that facilitate structural harm, the distance between the source and object of harm is often enormous (Canning and Tombs, 2021). So, for example, consider a government that decides to cut resources that are used to fund health and safety regulators. It is plausible – if not inevitable – that cuts of a certain level will result in fewer health and safety inspections, or inspections of a lower level of quality and scrutiny. Subsequent declines in health and safety standards – attributable to either a lack of inspection and enforcement in particular cases, a generalized shift towards businesses 'regulating themselves', or both – are then liable to generate serious harms in the form of personal injury and death. This is not a hypothetical scenario, but one that has been well documented and evidenced: staggeringly, around 50,000 people in the UK die every year because of injuries or health problems that have originated in the workplace (see Tombs, 2016). Another example of a structural harm (and one which we explore further in Chapter 4), is school exclusions. Institutional policies within the national education system mean that many children and young people are removed from mainstream education. Though it may be an individual headteacher who completes the relevant paperwork to exclude a pupil, it is the policy framework of the school and education system which makes that individual act possible, and all too common.[6]

While the origin or source of harm does not determine whether or not something is categorized as a social harm, the approach that we advocate in this chapter does have implications concerning the likely genesis of the most serious and widespread social harms. If the desired goal is to protect and advance human flourishing, we must avoid a myopic focus on the individual and the interpersonal, and shift our gaze outwards, towards the many structural harms that blight the lives of too many children and young people.

Direct and inherent harmfulness

Before we move on to consider some of the potential limitations and drawbacks associated with our approach, one final issue that we would like to address is the extent to which social harms must be directly and inherently harmful. Recall that our definition of social harm states that the term 'social harm' refers to something that compromises human flourishing. Deciding whether something compromises human flourishing, however, is not always straightforward. In some cases, the harmfulness of the thing in question is relatively clear. Consider, for example, a case in which Person A punches Person B in the face, breaking their nose. At least some of the harm here (the broken nose) is direct – it flows in an immediate sense from the punch itself. Moreover, the punch is inherently harmful: the act of a knuckle hitting a nose with significant force in itself causes physical injury, undermining Person B's security needs. We have, therefore, a very clear instance of social harm (or, more specifically, an instance of interpersonal harm, if we employ the distinction outlined in the preceding section).

There are other things of interest to us that are less straightforward, however. Take, for instance, something like globalization. While we cannot provide anything like a comprehensive analysis of the effects of globalization here, it provides an illustrative contrast to the example of 'the punch' as a form of social harm just described. A substantial literature evidences the numerous and varied costs and benefits associated with globalization, which span economic, cultural, political, social and ecological dimensions (see, for example, Issit, 2020; Steger, 2020). So, for example, while globalization has played a central role in the rapid and significant development of many national economies – most recently the 'tiger economies' of East Asia – it has left poorer national economies in Africa, Asia and South and Central America increasingly stunted and marginalized (Intriligator, 2003). Such stunted and marginalized economies have serious adverse implications for human flourishing. To what extent, however, has globalization itself been responsible for these instances of human flourishing being compromised? Many have argued that this is not an inevitable feature of globalization, but has instead been the product of advanced economies pursuing specific sets of exploitative policies as part of the globalization process (Chua, 2003; Sollner, 2014). This raises a difficult question: should globalization itself be classed as a social harm?

In essence, this question requires us to grapple with the thorny problem of causation, which cannot be answered in any straightforward or clear-cut sense. However, we do think it is useful to consider the extent to which the harms associated with our object of interest – in this case globalization – are *direct* and *inherent*. Neither of these issues is binary, in the sense of harm being *either* direct *or* indirect, inherent *or* entirely adventitious. Instead, judgements must be made about the extent of directness and inherence based on the best available theory and empirical data available at the time. The more direct and the more inherent the harm, the more clearly it can be classed as a social harm, and vice versa. We return to this issue in Chapter 3.

Limitations and drawbacks of our approach

The integration of human flourishing into our definition of social harm brings with it all of the critiques and shortcomings associated with this concept and the different ways in which it can be understood. Among these critiques is the argument that what it means to flourish might vary across time and space. This applies most obviously in the context of studies that attempt to compare levels of human flourishing historically and cross-culturally. According to this critique, there are fundamental design flaws in using survey instruments that assume that human needs and domains of subjective well-being should be treated as static and identical, regardless of time and place. It is worth noting, however, that large-scale studies, such as those conducted by Sartorius et al (1993), indicate that people worldwide have a relatively similar understanding of what it means to flourish (see further Sender et al, 2020). Generally speaking, for example, regardless of sex, age and culture, people seem to care about their physical fitness, social integration, psychological stability, the ability to fulfil daily roles and their experience of social support in materially and economically safe environments (Bullinger, 2002). In any case, as already discussed in relation to the operationalization of our approach, we are mindful of the need to be sensitive to the potential for context-specific factors to shape and reshape the way in which we make sense of social harm in children and young people's lives.

One potential drawback of our framing and definition of social harm is that it is overly expansive, so much so that it allows an excessively diverse range of actions and inactions into its scope. Whenever attempts are made to develop a concept or theoretical framework to enhance our understanding of the social world or some aspect of it, parsimony is a useful guiding principle: the simplest approach is the usually the best. For this reason, a case could be made for focusing squarely on one particular way of understanding human flourishing, whether that be through needs fulfilment or subjective well-being. The alternative case, however, is that shutting down different ways of understanding human flourishing by focusing solely on one in isolation from the other would be to limit the extent to which we can fully make sense of and improve the lives of children and young people. Should readers think that one of the approaches to understanding human flourishing is preferable or superior to the other, they are of course free to focus on this approach alone while discarding the other. This may well depend on the particular context in which people are working or researching. While we believe that it is helpful to consider human flourishing in relation to both needs fulfilment and subjective well-being in the context of this book – as well as their potential overlaps and interconnections – we are open to the possibility that this may not be desirable in all contexts.

One way that our approach to social harm might be considered overly open and expansive is in its potential to include what could be considered relatively trivial forms of harm. Pemberton (2015, p 18) has argued that

to be able to identify harm through empirical study, we must first develop a rationale to discern why specific instances of injury or loss are serious enough to be considered harmful. Otherwise we are left with a version of social harm that captures a host of grievances and is unable to distinguish between serious harms and minor personal hardships.

Seemingly in contrast to Pemberton, we consider anything that compromises the flourishing of children or young people to be harmful, and we are not attempting to develop a concept that will capture only the most serious harms that afflict people's lives. Following our approach, certain social harms could be minimal (even trivial) if they compromise human flourishing to a minor extent, or they could be moderate or severe if they involve greater adverse effects. The severity of the social harm in question is to be judged empirically, through reference to the best data available. However, should people deem it desirable for a severity threshold to apply in defining what does or does not constitute social harm, a minor tweak to our definition is possible: the word 'severely', for example, could precede the term 'compromises' to give: social harm refers to something that *severely* compromises human flourishing in a manner that could have been prevented. While this tweak would leave open the task of explicating what precisely the term 'severely' means in this context, it would be one such way of excluding minor personal hardships from the remit of the concept.

One reason for opposing a severity threshold in our definition of social harm is that we consider relatively minor harms affecting very large numbers of children and young people to be potentially as important as relatively severe harms that affect far fewer children and young people. For example, while it is not straightforward to draw comparisons between the overall gravity of severe harm affecting a single individual and minor or moderate harm affecting millions, it seems clear to us that the level of harm as measured at the level of the individual should not be the only factor in determining its overall importance – the number of people affected should be also be factored into any consideration of the seriousness of a social harm. From our perspective, to state that something constitutes a social harm is, in itself, a starting point. Important steps then remain in defining in more precise terms the nature, scope and severity of the social harm, which, following our approach, equates to the ways in which and the extent to which the social harm compromises the flourishing of children and young people.

Conclusion

A social harm approach, conceptualized and operationalized as we intend it, has the potential to act as a sensitizing and orientating device for researchers, policy makers, professionals, practitioners and activists concerned with identifying and addressing all those things that can potentially compromise the flourishing of children and young people. From our perspective, human flourishing can be understood in different ways: as needs fulfilment and as subjective well-being.

While interpersonal violence committed by children and young people against other children and young people is a serious issue – and one example of a social harm – all too often this dominates the attention of powerful individuals, groups and institutions, such as MPs, political parties and the mainstream media, at the expense of attempts to understand and tackle other forms of social harm that afflict these very same children and young people. Interpersonal violence does require urgent attention and action, but so too do many other social harms, particularly given the significant connections that exist between those social harms and the perpetration of violence (see Chapter 5).

As Gilligan (1997, p 186) so eloquently puts it, this applies in equal measure to the way in which interpersonal forms of violence tend to dominate the concerns of the relatively powerless:

> The kinds of assaults that the very poor suffer from the 'criminals' among them (rape, murder, and assault and robbery) are so direct, palpable, and visible, so physically painful, so impossible to ignore, so life-threatening and lethal, that they inevitably distract the very poor from noticing or fighting the more hidden, disguised assaults they suffer from the class system itself.

These hidden and disguised assaults include things such as poverty and inequality, homelessness and insecure housing, unemployment, environmental degradation and pollution, and so on. Social harms such as these can be considered 'calamities that patiently dispense their devastation while remaining outside our flickering attention spans – and outside the purview of a spectacle-driven corporate media' (Nixon, 2013). While interpersonal violence is often spectacular, vivid and horribly tangible, there are countless other social harms that receive far less attention, whose damage is relatively banal, slow, undramatic and in some sense less visible.

A number of significant 'disguised assaults' and 'slow, undramatic' social harms affecting children and young people are discussed in Chapter 4. First, however, we must consider the second of our two key concepts used as analytical tools in this book: mattering. This is the subject of the following chapter.

3

The Importance of Mattering
in Young People's Lives

Introduction

We all want to matter: to be a person of significance and consequence in the world. The concept of mattering has received substantial attention in academic psychology during the 21st Century (see especially Elliott, 2009; Flett, 2018, 2022; Prilleltensky and Preilleltensky, 2021), but its impact on related disciplines – such as social theory and criminology – appears to remain relatively limited (there are exceptions – see, for example, Lewis, 2017). In this chapter, we make the case for the value and helpfulness of the concept of mattering for grasping the internal and external complexity of young people's lives, particularly when it is deployed in a psycho-social mode – reckoning both with the intricacies of inner worlds and with the profound effects of social, economic and political structures. If the concept of social harm is a fruitful tool for considering the factors and forces which have a damaging effect on young people's lives, we believe the concept of mattering is a fruitful tool for understanding the development of their subjectivity (in later chapters, we bring the two lenses together).

This chapter is in two parts:

• First, we undertake a detailed exploration of 'mattering', deploying it as a psycho-social concept which can help us to understand the development of individuals' subjectivity: the connections between a person's inner world and the consequential relationships, social groupings, structures, institutions and systems which make up their outer world.
• Second, we explore the wide-ranging social changes and global processes of the past fifty years which we think may well be making it harder for people to establish a secure sense of mattering.

As in Chapter 2, violence will not take centre stage. This and the previous chapter provide the conceptual and theoretical backdrop for the following chapters, in which we discuss connections between social harm, mattering and violence. Proceeding in this order is in keeping with our wider commitment to avoid defining young people by violence, and to ensure that the attention given to interpersonal physical violence is kept in proportion: if we are to improve the flourishing of children and young people in our society, it is imperative that we do not just look at their lives through the lens of violence. We believe that, aside from the role they may play in illuminating some drivers of violence (discussed in Chapter 5), both the concept of social harm and the idea of mattering can have considerable independent value when considering what life is like for younger generations in today's Britain.

The importance of mattering

Black Lives Matter

Before delving into the concept of mattering, it would be remiss not to mention the most historically important application of the broad idea of mattering in recent times – the Black Lives Matter (BLM) movement. We are not the best-placed academics or people to describe or explain BLM, nor to explicate the exact meaning of mattering as it has been mobilized by the movement (for this, see, for example, Taylor, 2016; Lebron, 2017; Ransby, 2018). But it is clear that the movement has powerfully asserted the dignity, equality and worth of Black people, in a social and historical context in which all too many Black lives continue to be treated as though they are disposable. The movement has eloquently articulated that this is not just the effect of individual attitudes or of societal morals: Black people have been historically, institutionally, systematically and structurally denigrated and harmed for centuries, and this monumental injustice continues in the present.

We certainly do not wish to suggest that our idea of mattering, as expressed in this chapter, must be what everyone else means when they talk about mattering. Lebron suggests that the use of mattering within the BLM movement is largely on an ethical and political register, as a protest against racial inequality and injustice: it represents 'a civic desire for equality and a human desire for respect' in the face of ongoing 'disvaluation of black lives', which are treated as 'inconsequential and disposable' (Lebron, 2017, pp xiii, 44). In our investigation of the term, as laid out in the chapter, mattering is used more as a psycho-social category – a lens through which to explore individual subjectivity as it is buffeted by social forces. That is not to suggest that these two applications of the term are entirely incompatible, and the pages that follow do include discussion of ethnicity, 'race' and racialization. The two applications, however, are clearly distinct, and we are under no illusions that we could do justice here to the richness or force of the ideas mobilized by the BLM movement, which have deep historical roots and wide-ranging cultural resonances (see Lebron, 2017, especially).

Why is the psycho-social concept of mattering helpful?

The concept of mattering is a helpful lens through which to explore subjectivity. It is best viewed as a psycho-social concept, as it attends to 'internally complex, socially situated subjects' who occupy 'often difficult and cross-pressured social circumstances' (Gadd and Jefferson, 2007, p 1), and thus avoids both 'sociological reductionism' and 'psychological reductionism' (Gadd and Jefferson, 2007, p 144).[1] Though most well developed within psychology (especially by Elliott, 2009; Flett, 2018, 2022; Prilleltensky and Prilleltensky, 2021), the idea of mattering is transdisciplinary in its implications. The questions of 'Do I matter? To whom and what, and how?' are social, psychological, philosophical, existential, moral and political; local, global, past and future oriented. Because of this, it is a productive conceptual tool for addressing the complexity of young people's lives, as they are constrained or enriched by various kinds of social forces, and diminished or damaged by various kinds of social harm. The concept of mattering invites us to attend to the inner, individual aspects of life; the visible, relational elements of social experience; and their wider structural determinants, without placing imbalanced emphasis on any one of these dimensions. At the very least, it should encourage avoidance of any kind of unconstructive lens-narrowing: looking at young people's lives as if their psychologies dictate everything, or as if they are passive respondents to social norms, or as if they are just individual nodes within overbearing structural systems.

These remarks are fairly bold in tone – perhaps too bold. Our intention is not to present a grand new theory of subjectivity, but to offer some reflections on how and why the concept of mattering could be a helpful lens through which to look at young people's social experiences, including how they are affected by social harms (see Chapter 4). In this section, we present a detailed exploration of the concept of mattering; in the next section we focus on various recent and ongoing social changes and processes which may be making it more difficult and more complicated for individuals to establish or to maintain a secure sense of mattering.

What does it mean to matter?

> There are young men literally dying to be someone or something, anything but no-one and nothing.
>
> Lee Dema, founder of St Matthews
> youth project, Brixton, London

Psychologists have given the concept of mattering sharp analytical clarity over the past two decades. Gregory Elliott and colleagues, for instance, have defined mattering as 'the perception that ... we are a significant part of the world around us' (Elliott et al, 2004, p 339), and as 'the belief that one makes a difference in the lives of others' (Elliott et al, 2005, p 223). As these definitions imply, mattering relates to two closely entwined and deeply rooted desires: to have a sense of social significance and a sense of material influence. You need to feel you are significant to others, and you need to feel you have some effect on the world. Various terms have been used to denote these two components of mattering. Flett (2018, p 63) describes 'a sense of being connected to other people' and 'a sense of agentic effectiveness', while Prilleltensky (2014, p 151) refers to the two aspects as 'recognition' and 'impact'. Though writing more in a psychoanalytic mode, May (1998, p 35) wrote similarly of the need for both a 'sense of significance' and a 'sense of power'.

As these writers have suggested, we have a deep-seated yearning to matter to other people, and to matter in the physical world; to be a consequential force in both a social and material sense. As Lee Dema puts it, we all want to be 'someone' – a person seen as significant by others – and we all want to be 'something' – an entity with some force or power in the world. The term 'matter' in this latter sense is something of a pun on the meaning of matter in physics, where it refers to a substance which occupies physical space and has a mass: there is an analogy between the feeling of utterly *not mattering*, or being a 'nothing', and feeling as though you do not physically exist – you *are not matter*. The drive to avoid non-existence and the craving to achieve substantial significance are two subtly distinct but equally forceful motivations (see Flett, 2018, 2022).

The quest to matter in this way is fundamental to being human. It has been shown to have great importance across geographical and cultural boundaries (Prilleltensky, 2020, p 16; Flett, 2022, pp 4–5), and its significance is evidenced in the very earliest stages of life. Studies with babies have shown that they become utterly gleeful when they first realize that they can prompt people to change their expression and that they can move objects – they experience what Groos (1901) called 'the pleasure of being the cause' (quoted in Graeber 2018, p 83). If infants are denied causal influence on the world in an unexpected way (if a formerly loose object is glued down, or a formerly responsive parent becomes unresponsive, for instance), this is deeply troubling to them – they can experience what Broucek (1979) called 'the trauma of failed influence'. This can be profoundly damaging: in René Spitz's studies of extreme neglect, he found that infants who are denied the experience of social influence – of their actions causing a response from those around them – literally wither away, physiologically and psychologically (cited in May, 1998, p 40). This reflects the well-evidenced significance of attachment in child development: as decades of research across multiple countries has shown, the nature of early relationships can have lasting effects on our sense of who and what we are. Disordered forms of early attachment to caregivers can lead to entrenched feelings of 'worthlessness' (De Zulueta, 2001, p 45); childhood maltreatment can prompt fundamental doubt about a person's mattering (Raque-Bogdan et al, 2011; Flett et al, 2016; Flett, 2022). These examples help to show how interconnected the two components of mattering can often be, especially in childhood: when seeking to attract the attention of caregivers, an infant is both seeking reassurance of their significance to those important others and exploring the extent of their causal power. Prilleltensky (2020, p 17, 22) suggests that the 'two essential parts' of mattering are always 'interdependent'.

As the reference to early childhood interactions makes clear, mattering is a fundamentally relational concept: we are not atomized selves, whose sense of mattering is wholly individual, independent or bounded. All kinds of human relationships throughout life can leave lasting, potent emotional residues which support, undermine or complicate our sense of mattering (see Flett, 2022, p 18). As Retzinger (1991, p 25) has argued, 'the primary motive of human behaviour is to secure important bonds'. This is an evolutionary inheritance – all humans need social bonds in order to survive (see Clark, 1990) – but it is also an existential imperative: we need strong social bonds to feel assured in our social existence. Consistent, secure, lasting and committed relationships (romantic or otherwise) provide a unique kind of deep recognition, affirming that we truly exist, that we are acceptable, that we are valuable, that we matter. As Pearlin and LeBlanc (2001) observed, people are more likely to matter to others who matter to them – mutual mattering can be a powerful kind of 'reciprocal social exchange' (Flett, 2018, p 45). This has been found to be the case between children and parents, for instance – a child who feels that they matter to a parent is likely to regard that parent as someone who matters to them (Rosenberg and McCullough, 1981). On the other hand, damage and threats to important social bonds can be devastating (Clark, 1990; Retzinger, 1991; Scheff and Retzinger, 1991; Ray, Smith and Wastell, 2003; O'Hara, 2020). A number of writers suggest that a troubled social bond is the essential cause of shame, which can leave us feeling not just 'unloved' but 'unloveable' (Gadd and Jefferson, 2007, p 169); 'reduced and belittled … helpless and passive … devalued' (Ray, Smith and Wastell, 2003, p 124). The most unsettling stirrings of doubt in relation to mattering can come from these impaired bonds and relationships.[2]

An individual's sense of mattering is thus affected by the constellation of relationships and interactions that they experience. As well as being temporal – influenced by a person's past experiences, such as childhood, and their expectations for the future – mattering is cross-contextual, affected by self-perceived significance within different institutions such as family, peer group and school (Flett, 2018). Mattering is supported by secure integration within a social group or institution which tangibly values the person (Schieman and Taylor, 2001; Elliott, 2009, p 37), but dwelling within any kind of social group or institution does not only involve affirmation, of course. Experiences of respectful or disrespectful interactions and relationships, and perceived (lack of) status in social hierarchies within these social settings, will affect one's sense of mattering within them. To use Bourdieu's (1979) language, mattering will be affected by the forms of capital an individual can mobilize within different social fields – if a person displays prized knowledge and behaviour (cultural capital), and establishes valuable connections (social capital), for instance, their sense of social significance within that field will be enhanced.[3] As this all suggests, there is a family of concepts and social experiences which describe different, more specific kinds of social significance and agentic power; these are captured in Figure 3.1.

Figure 3.1: The twin components of mattering: concepts which capture different forms of social significance and agentic power

SOCIAL SIGNIFICANCE	AGENTIC POWER
Being an important feature of the world **as recognized by others**	Being a feature of the world which makes a **difference** to it

Belonging	Agency
Dignity	Competence
Fame	Dominance
Honour	Influence
Individuation (feeling unique)	Instrumental power
Recognition	Mastery
Reputation	Potency
Respect	Self-efficacy
Social and cultural capital	
Social esteem	
Status	

It is not our intention to flatten all these ideas and aspects of human experience into the concept of mattering, as if their only significance is to be found in how they affect some 'deeper' sense of mattering. Each of these concepts is profoundly complex and consequential in itself, and many of their independent intricacies have received substantial academic discussion (for example, see Horowitz, 1983 on honour; Honneth, 1996 on recognition; Bourgois, 2003 on respect – discussed further later on). They do all relate, however, to a person's sense of their presence in the world – how their worth is perceived by others, and the extent to which their existence has an external influence. They represent more granular, specific forms of self-perception; more sharply focused lenses through which to conceive of your significance and power. They also help to further illustrate the close interconnectedness of mattering's twin components. If you enjoy considerable status within a particular social group, for instance, it will likely increase your influence on others within that group, and the extent of your agency in navigating it. If you have achieved a high degree of competence and mastery in how you affect a particular aspect of the world – by being an impressive artist of some kind, for instance – this may tend to increase the degree to which you are respected and recognized.

In Flett's terms, an individual's 'global, overall sense of general mattering' (Flett, 2018, p 7) is affected by their self-perceived significance within all of the various social settings that they experience. Mattering is therefore affected by social experiences which occur at various levels: a person can feel that they matter to particular, identifiable others; to specific institutions or groups; to their local community; to their nation-state; or to the world (see Flett, 2022, pp 16–20). You can feel that you matter in an the immediate, relational, interpersonal way, or you can have a more structural sense of (not) mattering – you may feel structurally devalued or marginalized due to your ethnic heritage, 'race', gender or sexuality, for instance. There is thus a link between a person's internal perception of how much they matter and the structural factors which affect their interactional experiences and their social status within different social fields (Flett, 2018, p 43; see Chapter 4 for examples of structural harms which can diminish the sense of mattering).

As may well be clear from the preceding discussion, the concept of mattering also helps to illuminate the extent to which need fulfilment and subjective well-being – the two central components of human flourishing discussed in Chapter 2 – closely interrelate. The sense of mattering is a form of subjective well-being: it pertains to how a person thinks and feels about themselves and their life. It is also inseparable from identity needs, however; the need to be perceived by others as valid and valued. The concept of mattering helps to illustrate the fact that, though analytically distinguishable, in people's lives the experience of unfulfilled needs and the experience of undermined subjective well-being often go hand-in-hand: for example, denial of affection needs (attachment to persons and things outside of ourselves) or of participation needs (contributing to and having some control over political, community and social life) will negatively affect a person's sense that they are significant and consequential in the world, in a way which will have inevitable repercussions for their thoughts about life, their emotions and their sense of meaning and purpose.

'The terrifying abyss of insignificance' and the problem of over-entitlement: the experience of not mattering and the desire to matter 'too much'

> We are acutely aware of our need to make a difference only when we suspect we do not. In that case, we are faced with a profoundly frightening possibility. We confront the realization that, whatever the truth of our physical presence, we are socially non-existent.
>
> Elliott, 2009, p 40

> [He had] an intense desire to avoid a terrifying abyss of insignificance.
>
> Ellis, 2016, p 58

Social non-existence is horrifying. The sensation of feeling utterly diminished and belittled, to the point that you sense you do not matter, is a psychologically devastating experience – the research is clear on this (see Rosenberg and McCullough, 1981; Schlossberg, 1989; Taylor and Turner, 2001; Elliott, 2009; Ellis, 2016; Flett, 2018). Ellis's use of the term 'abyss' is well chosen, because the dread that can accompany this profoundly troubling state of mind impinges upon our most basic existential insecurities about whether or not we are 'really' in the world. It can be one of the things that we fear the most.

There is a well-researched correlation between feeling you do not matter and suicidal ideation (Flett, 2018, p 111; 2022, p 17). Suicide can, in some instances, demonstrate 'the depth of someone's despair when they feel as though they don't matter at all to anyone' (Flett, 2018, p 7). Suspecting, or knowing, that you have been entirely forgotten represents 'an existential challenge that goes to the heart of one's sense of mattering in the social world' (King and Geise, 2011, p 704). This is an acute example of a much broader problem. The gnawing anxiety of feeling that you do not matter as much as you would like, hope or expect to is a far more common experience than its suicidal extreme, but may be similar in nature if not in extent: any sense of significantly impaired mattering can be psychologically and emotionally troubling.

The sense of not mattering is not an inherently pathological or delusional state, but may relate to an individual's social situation. Flett (2018) provides a number of illustrative examples of people whose social circumstances have left them feeling that they do not matter. He narrates biographies of people who have been abandoned by their families; been left out of their prestigious sports team; been rendered socially invisible due to their ethnicity; been utterly ignored while in prison; suffered 'a clear and unambiguous history of mistreatment and relational victimisation' within their family; and encountered others 'who have minimised, denied, invalidated, or ignored their feelings and emotional experiences' (Flett, 2018, pp 23–7, 43, 40).

On the other hand, Prilleltensky and Prilleltensky (2021) suggest that it is possible to have an over-inflated sense of mattering. They describe this as a kind of entitlement or self-centredness (Prilleltensky and Prilleltensky, 2021, pp 6, 267), in which individuals have an unduly heightened expectation of the recognition, status, influence or potency that they should experience. They suggest that contemporary American culture encourages 'infatuation with ourselves' and that it makes people 'obsessed with feeling valued' (Prilleltensky and Prilleltensky, 2021, p 6). Implied by this is the idea that there are desirable bounds within which the sense of mattering is best kept, and that an individual's estimation of the extent to which they matter may be a better or worse reflection of external reality. Notwithstanding the deeply messy, imprecise and emotive nature of self-perception, it seems right to suggest that an individual's expectations of the significance and agentic power that they *are due* should be kept within reasonable bounds, and that, in addition, it is possible to have a more or less accurate or healthy approximation of the recognition and impact that they *actually have*. No one should believe that they are inherently worthy of more recognition and impact than anyone else, or that other people's lives should revolve solely around the satisfaction of their sense of mattering. Equally, it would be a kind of self-deception to believe that you are widely respected and revered if you are not, or that you have substantial influence over others if you do not, and it would be just as self-deceiving to believe that you have far less significance and agentic power than you actually do. Of course, all of this is difficult to 'objectively' or precisely assess, but it is clearly the case that some people receive more recognition and respect than others, that some people have a greater degree of power and influence in the world and that self-perception can bear an unsteady, fallible relationship with reality.[4]

All of this alludes to the close ties between the sense of mattering and internal emotional struggle, and between the sense of mattering and culture. An individual's 'ideal self' will often be characterized by a perception of substantial mattering, and their 'feared self' by a deadening lack of mattering (see Vigil, 1988, p 425), and both are encultured: masculinity cultures can affect a man's sense of the kinds of recognition and power that they should ideally enjoy, for instance, and the forms of misrecognition or impotence which are to be most deeply feared (this can be highly significant to the emotional drivers of violence, as discussed in Chapter 5). As this implies, it can be psychologically intolerable to experience a considerable distance between your 'ideal self' and your self-perceived 'real self', or to discern substantial proximity between your 'feared self' and your 'real self': much of our activity can be motivated by 'maximising the distance between feared and real identities and minimising the gap between ideal and real selves' (Vigil, 1988, p 425). Our fear that we are a self who does not matter is a complex emotional phenomenon, affected significantly by the culture(s) we inhabit. We explore the cultural and emotional complexities of mattering further in the following section.

The cultural and emotional complexity of mattering

To this point, our discussion has presented a largely social-psychological concept of mattering, centring on the relationship between social interactions, social structures and individual psychology. We would argue, however, that the concept is best used as a *psycho-social* concept, which requires two additional layers of complexity: firstly, a recognition that exactly what it means to matter will vary by culture; and secondly, an acknowledgement of the tensions, contradictions and intricacies within any individual's internal world. We will take these two points in turn.

Precisely what it means to matter is culturally and historically constituted. What can make you socially significant, the forms that significance might take, the kinds of agentic power and efficacy that are possible – as well as how all of these things are culturally interpreted – will all vary over time and by place. The quest to matter is neither a simplistically transhistorical and unchanging feature of human nature nor a novel cultural imperative; like any other deep-rooted psycho-social need, its exact flavour will be different through historical eras and across cultures. We all need to eat, but we can find a vast smorgasbord of different foods, each with its own particular cultural resonances. We all need to matter, but what exactly that entails will be specific to the cultures that we occupy.[5]

Sociocultural constructions of identity are what give mattering its flavour. How you are classed, gendered and racialized within your society, for instance, will affect the precise forms of social significance and agentic power that are plausible for you to experience. When Ralph Ellison (2001 [1947]) wrote of an *Invisible Man*, the nature of his invisibility and his insignificance was shaped by the ways in which he was racialized as Black and gendered as male in mid-20th century America. He was ignored or ridiculed in conversation, while doing his best to make a positive impression, encountering a kind of interpersonal marginalization which reflected his status in society as a whole (Flett 2018, pp

26–7). As Ellison (2001 [1947], pp xxx–xxxii) has described it, his protagonist experienced a kind of 'existential torture' in his 'conscious struggle for self-definition' in a world which 'regarded his life as of lesser value than the lives of whites'. It is not enough to say that this man felt that he did not matter; his society culturally constituted him as a person who mattered less due to the colour of his skin. In a somewhat similar way, the struggle to establish a sense of mattering experienced by young boys growing up in working-class communities is given its content by the constructions of working-class masculinity which circulate in their particular social milieu, and the particular kinds of respect, status, belonging and agency that these make possible (see, for example, Anderson, 2000; Bourgois, 2003; Fraser, 2015; Ellis, 2016). In Bourgois's (2003) work, for instance, he provides a rich portrayal of what 'respect' means within a particular community at a specific time which is unique: the idea of respect – though common in some form across cultures – does not have the exact same cultural connotations anywhere else, or in any other historical period, as it did in a poor Puerto Rican community in East Harlem in the mid–late 1980s, where Bourgois conducted his ethnographic research. To matter as a female means something different to mattering as a male, involving a distinct experience of culturally available forms of social significance and power (see, for example, Young, 2011 on the similarities and differences between male and female experiences of violence as a means to mattering).

The influence of cultural norms on individual subjectivity is not a one-way street: we all have complex relationships with the people, places, groups, institutions and activities in our lives, which alter how their different cultures affect us. The meaning and value that we perceive in ourselves, and the meaning and value that we attach to different aspects of the world, are co-constitutive: if a meaningful life is defined by 'active and loving engagement in projects of worth' (Wolf, 2010, p 32), this will be inextricably tied to the worth that we see in our selves. Our sense of personal mattering will be affected by what becomes significant in our lives – our experience of feeling consequential and worthwhile will be shaped most by those aspects of our lives which come to obtain most importance to us.[6] This is irreducibly emotive: when something or someone becomes significant to us, it is an emotionally charged experience. There is a complex, two-way relationship between the effects on us of the cultural norms embodied by particular people, places, groups and institutions, and the worth, value, meaning and significance that we ascribe to them.

There is power in all of us to resist the ideas and social conventions which we encounter, and we may be more inclined to do so where we experience this encounter as a form of disrespect, denigration or devaluation. Thus, if we feel that we do not matter within a certain social group or institution, it may prompt us to attempt emotional divestment from it – to try to make it less emotionally significant for us. To give an example: my experience within school will be shaped by both how much I perceive myself to matter within that social setting, and its significance to me – my self-perceived worth within the institution will be closely entwined with the value that I deem the institution to have in my life. Of course, emotionally detaching from any social field or any human relationship, such that it has little significance for us and therefore has minimal influence on our sense of mattering, is never just a matter of choice; it will always involve negotiating different kinds of compulsion and necessity (for example, the mandatory nature of school, the financial necessity of work), and may well entail a degree of emotional tear. To use a more holistic example, if my life takes place within and through my family, my workplace, my friendship group, my sports club, the youth work sector, the academic world, and the national culture of Britain, I will experience varying kinds of emotional attachment and detachment, attraction and repulsion, to each of these different social entities, and this will influence how they each affect my global sense of mattering. Flett uses the example of a footballer left out of his team – being left out of the team, and so not mattering to it, was an especially difficult psychological experience for the player because he based his sense of self too much on his status within the club (Flett, 2018, p 26): football was of such importance to him that feeling like a 'nobody' in his team had a devastating effect on his self-concept and sense of mattering as a person.

The sense of mattering within individual self-narratives

As all this will have made apparent, there is considerable introspective complexity in each individual's psycho-social experience of mattering. In the external world, each person is engaged in establishing a sense that their life is in some way consequential for the cosmos: that they are acknowledged, recognized, respected by others within the relationships and social fields which have significance for them, and that they have a tangible effect on their surroundings through agency, efficacy, competence. Internally, each person experiences the existential, emotional and psychological struggles entailed by this quest to matter in the world, constructing stories to make meaning of it all, and of themselves (see McAdams, 1993). In a complicated cultural and social world, people try to work out what is of significance to them, who and what they wish to matter to, and how.

Even before reaching a couple of decades of life, many young people have a lot to choose from. Joey, one of the 'lads' observed by Willis in his classic ethnography of working-class school life, once made this point with a beautifully vulgar eloquence: 'we've been through all of life's pleasures and all its fucking displeasures, we've been drinking, we've been fighting, we've known frustrations, sex, fucking hatred, love and all this lark' (Willis, 1977, p 16). In simpler terms, Duckworth (2002, p 37) quotes the Recorder of Birmingham as having written in a 1855 report on a young person accused of criminal activity: 'he knows much of what is called life'. Young people's lives can be a concatenation of chaotic cultural influences, experiences and emotions.

An individual's particular form of self-understanding is guided by their reckoning of what has worth to them, and what and who they matter to, within all this complexity. As they develop and reflect on their lives and actions, young people take material from the 'collective cultural narratives' that they encounter (whether through imposition or exploration), and adapt them into their 'personal self-narratives' (Munro, 1997, p xi). This provides them with an 'account of the world and his or her place in it' (Munro, 1997, p xii). This will be, as any narrative is, an account of what has meaning: a more or less coherent story pulled together by assigning different degrees of significance to different parts of the flotsam and jetsam of their life, and to different components of their own self (see McAdams, 1993). Their self-narrative will consist of what seems meaningful to them in their complicated life-story, and how they – as the protagonist – have significance to and influence on their family, their school, their community, their society.[7] However much life they have lived, whatever 'pleasures and fucking displeasures' they have experienced and cultural influences they've confronted, they can neither absorb it all nor resist it all; they go through a sifting process of establishing, consciously or otherwise, what does and does not hold value to them; who they do and do not matter to; where and how they are of consequence (see McAdams, 1993, p 11).

If we want to better understand a young person, we can do a lot worse than grappling with how they do this, within the context of the history, social structures and biography which set the parameters of their lives. Some young people will have a self-narrative which is dominated by a global sense of insignificance; by a sense that they lack value in the eyes of other people and they lack material influence in the world, across all aspects of their lives. This is likely to be experienced as shameful, rage inducing. Others will entirely immerse themselves in one particular social field, grouping or institution, perhaps having been repelled from others by belittling experiences, and will thus wholly invest their sense of mattering in that one social entity – they are to be consequential there, or nowhere. More young people, hopefully, will form a self-narrative based on varying experiences of mattering within different social fields, which amounts to a validating – but not aggrandizing – perception of significance and efficacy. In such cases, they will experience the kind of power which May (1998) described as a 'birthright'– a degree of personal importance to others, and a palpable sense of counting in the world as a causal force. Whatever the case may be, a young person's emotions, thoughts and actions can be reduced to neither psychological impulses nor sociocultural imperatives; if the sense of mattering is as important as suggested here, it is reflective of the complex psycho-social 'struggle for subjectivity' (McDonald, 2003).

An insecure society? Social changes and global processes affecting young people's sense of mattering in Britain today

It takes a lot to maintain a sturdy sense of mattering; to establish a secure belief in your significance to others and to the world. There is a gamut of factors which can shake, weaken or destabilize this belief for any individual person, and they arguably have the greatest impact in the lives of the young (see Flett, 2022). We explore just a handful of such factors here, briefly exploring a few macro-scale social changes of the past fifty years which have significantly altered the landscape within which individuals seek to develop a sense of mattering. We argue that these changes can make establishing a firm sense of mattering a more difficult and more complicated endeavour, and may have made the sense of mattering more fragile for many. As we will explain in further detail at the close of this section, they are not inherently harmful in themselves, as they have varied, ambivalent and often indirect influences on different people in different places, but they may be a causal factor in encouraging certain social harms to proliferate (see Chapter 2 on inherence and directness as defining features of social harms).

According to many social thinkers, it is quite easy to feel insignificant in today's world. Prilleltensky (2020, p 31) has suggested that we are living through a 'crisis of not mattering', arguing that there is a 'serious mattering deficit' across the globe. In our previous work (Billingham and Irwin-Rogers, 2020, 2021) we have similarly proposed that there may be grounds for describing the current situation as a 'crisis', due to the extent and range of social processes and social changes which may well be making it more difficult for people to feel consequential.[8] As Kruglanski and co-authors (2014, p 75) point out, 'individual significance loss' can be prompted by 'general economic, social, and political conditions' as much as by more tangible, immediate factors. We will go on to explore the more immediately palpable and direct effects of specific social harms in the following chapter; here we focus on the more imperceptibly pervasive influence of a few particularly important broad-ranging social changes.

As a range of commentators have argued, social, economic and technological changes since the late 20th century have fostered a culture of hyper-individualized insecure competitiveness, complicating people's perception of how they can feel significant and how they can have an influence on the world. It has been argued that 'contemporary postmodern society' renders us 'anxious, insecure subjects' who are unavoidably 'embroiled in a process of constant reappraisal of [our] individual identities' (Ellis, 2016, p 36). Even among those who eschew the idea of postmodernity, preferring somewhat more tentative terms, such as 'late modernity' (for example, Giddens, 1991 Garland, 2001; Young, 2007), there is something of a sociological consensus that we all face heightened ontological insecurity in today's world. It is harder to establish firm ground for our sense of self than it was in less complex, more tightly convention-bound times, due to cultural developments such as the loosened 'grip of tradition, community, church and family' (Garland, 2001, p 89). Thus the prospect of securing social significance is thornier – it is more difficult to establish the recognition that we all need if there are greater and deeper uncertainties about the self which is seeking that social esteem. Central to this difficulty is the rise of expressive and 'competitive' individualism (Gilbert, 2006). As Young put it, even before the turn of the millennium: contemporary capitalist culture 'encourages an ideal of diversity, a marketplace of self-discovery, yet provides for the vast majority a narrow, unrewarding individualism in practice' (Young, 1999, p 47). This kind of individualism is inherently comparative, encouraging a culture of 'invidious comparison' which renders both respect and self-respect more precarious, particularly in a supposedly meritocratic society in which individuals' social standing is thought to flow from their talent and effort (Sennett, 2003, p 94; Somerville, 2009, p 147). Young lays bare the mythology of British meritocracy, describing our political economy as 'casino capitalism', in which – despite claims of equitable wealth and income distribution – there is in fact 'chaos of [financial] reward' (Young, 2007, p 35; discussed further in Chapter 4). Writing about the US context, Prilleltensky and Prilleltensky (2021, p 6) suggest that its 'rampant individualism' promotes unhealthy and unrealistic expectations of the recognition and validation that people are due, as well as encouraging the pursuit of overly individualized, atomized forms of mattering, thus breeding dissatisfaction and resentment.

This pressure to compare ourselves, as much as to conform, is intensified by technological developments. Social media, in particular, can operate as a kind of hand-held panopticon, which people voluntarily expose themselves to, showing the world their life and measuring it against their peers'. Social media collapses time and space (Irwin-Rogers, 2019, p 605), allowing users to project themselves across the globe in a moment, opening themselves up to immense instant approval or overwhelming disdain (or, perhaps just as horrifying, deafening indifference). As Mishra (2018, p 13) has argued, modern technological capitalism creates 'humiliating new hierarchies' within which people engage in a 'commonplace, and therefore compromised, quest for individual distinction and singularity'. A culture of consumerism means that purchasable goods can become key features of these online hierarchies – at its most intense, this culture can suggest that a person's worth primarily pivots on the products they can afford to buy and display (Irwin-Rogers, 2019, p 595). It is not just through social media that contemporary technology influences the means that we have to matter: from credit scores to workplace productivity monitoring, we are constantly subject to the 'classifying, sorting, slotting and scaling' power of algorithmic computing

(Fourcade, 2021, p 8). Fourcade bluntly emphasizes this point: 'algorithms determine the value of each and everyone' (Fourcade, 2021, p 12). In the contemporary world, to feel individually consequential means navigating this intricate web of social forces, which have significantly altered the media through which we can obtain a meaningful sense of mattering.

The wider context for these changes, arguably determining them to an extent, is the rise of a much more globalized form of capitalism, which has both connected the world and eroded many local communities. Globalization can leave us terrifyingly aware of how massive and interconnected the world is, and crushingly conscious of how relatively tiny each individual is within it. Mishra (2018, p 339) writes with characteristic verve of how this means that 'the individual confronts a new indecipherable whole: the globe ... the individual can act satisfactorily neither upon [themself] nor upon the world, and is reminded frequently and humiliatingly of [their] limited everyday consciousness and meagre individual power'. We do not live our lives within the perceptible, comprehensible boundaries of particular communities, but can often feel like a vanishingly small feature of an enormous, boundless social landscape. This unsettling experience is exacerbated by the much-discussed 'death of community' and decline of civil institutions, immortalized by Putnam's (2001) image of individuals 'bowling alone'. Again, this arguably has its roots in changes to the global political economy: Streeck (2016, p 41) suggests that we are living in 'de-socialised capitalism', which amounts to a kind of 'post-social society'. It would be foolhardy to generalize about the effects of these changes across Britain, let alone across the globe, but it is clear that, for some, the sense of significance and influence that they gained from being known, appreciated and recognized within their community has been subject to considerable erosion. One of Ellis's (2016, p 75) respondents captured this with frank despair: 'there's no community anymore. Everyone's suspicious and fearful of each other.'

All of this can engender what Young (2007, p 35) referred to as a 'chaos of identity', and 'discontinuities of personal biography'. The interconnected complexity of the contemporary world means that many of us have highly limited control over our lives (Young, 2007, p 57), and experience 'broken narratives' (Young, 2007, p 39) rather than a coherent, linear sense of self-narrative, which can be profoundly disquieting (see McAdams, 1993). He summarizes the somewhat gloomy predicament that we all face in the current historical conjuncture: 'in no other time has there been such an emphasis on individualism and self-development, yet the building blocks for such a personal narrative are increasingly insubstantial' (Young, 2007, p 209). We have summarized these changes in Table 3.1.

This brief account of profound and interwoven social transformations is of course far from comprehensive, and is inevitably somewhat simplified and flattening – in reality, of course, the pressures that these changes have

Table 3.1: Some significant social changes which may complicate the quest to matter

Category	Forms of change
Technological	Social media and permanent internet connectivity
	Algorithmic forms of personal valuation
Economic	Globalization
	'Casino capitalism'
Cultural	Individualism
	Ideology of meritocracy
	Loosened influence of family, religion, tradition
Social	Erosion of community cohesion
	Atomization

produced have uneven effects on different people in different places, can be resisted and reshaped as much as absorbed and internalized, and in some cases might promote and bolster mattering, rather than undermine it. Their effects are felt very differently in the Global North and Global South, among individuals of different ethnic heritages, 'races', genders and classes. For those living in Britain, they have reconfigured personhood to varying extents. The 'ideal type' of modern individual which these social transformations produce – one with a fragmented, insecure, precarious, competitive sense of self – will be approximated by actual British people to a greater or lesser extent depending on individuals' particular social circumstances.

Age is one important variable affecting how individuals will be influenced by these various social changes. Arguably, these kinds of changes have the most profound effect on those who are experiencing the formative years of personal identity: teenagers. As Vigil has put it, adolescence is a time of inherent 'status crisis' (Vigil, 2003, p 227), a 'marginal period' which involves experimental self-configuration (Vigil, 1988, p 152). Though there is debate about the extent of psychological storm and stress that occurs during the teenage years (McAdams, 1993, p 75), living as a teenager inevitably involves 'struggling to find [your] place in a meaningful social environment' (Lauger, 2012, p 158) – trying to establish both what in the world is significant to you and how you might be significant to the world. The personal insecurity and precariousness which contemporary life can encourage may well be felt with particular intensity by young people. For many, the world is experienced as 'confusing, oppressive and disenchanting' (Brotherton, 2015, p 74). Indeed, there is substantial evidence, from North America at least, that the sense of not mattering is alarmingly common among young people: Flett (2018, p 297) cites numerous, large-scale studies which suggest that up to 50 per cent of young people in various parts of the US and Canada do not feel that they matter to their communities, and around a third don't feel they matter to other people. When discussing the 'crisis of not mattering', Prilleltensky (2020) suggests that this apparent decline in mattering is tied to the kinds of social changes outlined earlier. Flett concludes frankly that 'feelings of not mattering are far too prevalent among adolescents' (Flett, 2018, p 297). To our knowledge, similar studies have yet to be undertaken in Britain, and it would be possible only to speculate on the exact similarities and differences in the social experience of young people on either side of the Atlantic, and how these are affecting each cohort's sense of mattering.

It is vital to distinguish between these planetary-scale, broad social *changes* and the specific, identifiable social *harms* which affect young people's lives in Britain. These global transformations undoubtedly complicate life, and alter the nature of selfhood, but to discern the extent of their potentially harmful effects requires a more fine-grained analysis of their manifestations in daily life. To take globalization as an example: this complex, worldwide social phenomenon undoubtedly contributes to and exacerbates a number of social harms felt in various places across the globe, but to declare globalization itself a social harm would muddle more than it clarified, given the enormous range of processes and effects that it entails. What we could say, for example, is that the nature of the property market in Britain is structurally harmful (see Chapter 4) – many people live in inadequate shelter as a result of its operation – and that this market has been significantly affected by the kind of international capital flows which have been enabled by globalized capitalism. This particular feature of globalization has exacerbated a specific structural harm. Similarly, social media can facilitate and accelerate social harm – enabling humiliating forms of interpersonal interaction which significantly undermine subjective well-being, for instance – but cannot be described as a social harm in and of itself. For some young people, these macro-level social changes may be beneficial rather than harmful, or may form only a background context for their lives, rather than significantly altering their daily reality.

Thus, returning to the inherence and directness criteria for social harms outlined in Chapter 2, we cannot describe the social changes outlined in this chapter as social harms, given the indirectness and diversity of their effects. In the next chapter, we switch our attention to significant social harms which are affecting young people's lives in Britain today, some of which are tied to these broad social changes, others of which are related to them only tenuously, or barely at all. As we will go on to discuss, the social harms described in the next chapter have a range of inherent and direct injurious effects, including a sometimes devastating impact on young people's sense of mattering.

Conclusion

In this chapter, we have sought to make the case for the importance of mattering. The two entwined and deep-seated drives to feel significant to other people and to feel consequential in the world are powerful forces affecting the thoughts, emotions and actions of individuals. In order for a person to flourish, and to achieve a sense of subjective well-being, we would argue that they need to feel that they matter.

There is extensive research evidence which substantiates this, connecting the sense of mattering with a whole host of positive effects, and the lack of mattering with a range of negative ones. It appears that feeling you matter can significantly improve your life, while feeling that you do not matter can be a (literally) dreadful experience.

An individual's sense of mattering will be shaped and flavoured by the cultures they dwell within, and by the self-narrative they form: to whom and to what you seek to matter is closely tied to your (encultured) perception of who and what is worthwhile and significant. Pursuing meaning in life and endeavouring to matter in the world are interwoven quests.

We ended the chapter by sketching some of the global social processes of the past fifty years which we suggest may be making it more complicated and more difficult to develop a secure sense of mattering. These processes may be making it more complex to achieve or to assess either significance or impact.

All of this lays ground for the following two chapters. In the next chapter, we describe a number of social harms which we believe are having a particularly significant negative effect on young people in today's Britain, including on their sense of mattering. We then go on to argue, in Chapter 5, that it can be fruitful to examine the issue of violence between young people through the conceptual lenses of social harm and mattering.

Social Harm and Mattering in Young People's Lives

Introduction

> The scars of inequality, built up over centuries, fester and burn.
>
> Savage, 2021, p 94

Britain has the resources to ensure that all of its children and young people have ample opportunities to flourish, and are protected effectively from significant harm. For too many, this is not the reality. In this chapter we bring together the conceptual lenses of the previous two chapters, exploring the extent and nature of particularly prominent social harms in the lives of young people in Britain, and the effects that these harms have, particularly on their sense of mattering.

We believe that analysing some of the most damaging social harms affecting young people – and in particular those which can be described as structural harms – is valuable for a number of reasons. First of all, it helps to put interpersonal violence between young people in perspective. As illustrated in Chapter 1, it is a relatively small number of young people who are affected by violence from a peer. We will go on to see in this chapter how, compared to those who experience this specific kind of interpersonal harm, there is a far larger proportion of young people who are affected by the deeply injurious effects of other social harms. To emphasize again: this is not to suggest that violence between young people is not important – as we explained at length in our Introduction, and will go on to explore further in Chapter 5, interpersonal physical violence is a devastating form of harm which requires far more effective societal responses. It is to suggest, however, that if we are invested in the improvement of young people's lives, we will not be helped by a myopic, tunnel-visioned focus on street-based violence between young people: we must attend to the myriad other forms of social harm which damage and diminish young lives, particularly those structural harms which result from the nature of various policies, systems and institutions in this country.

Secondly, and moreover, the social harms discussed in this chapter connect in significant ways with the problem of violence between young people. Analysing the effects of social harms on young people's lives helps us to better understand 'the social conditions which predictably breed violence' (Currie, 2016, p 89), because the daily infliction of such harms on young people forms an important aspect of these conditions. Investigating the social harms affecting young people can provide valuable insight into important drivers of their thoughts, emotions and actions, by bringing to light the effects of particular institutions, policies and systems on the social, psychological and existential aspects of their lives – including their propensity to violence. Those communities which experience acute concentrations of social harm, of the kind detailed in this chapter, are also the communities which tend to suffer from the highest rates of interpersonal physical violence (see Chapter 1). We will explore this in greater depth in Chapter 5, but suffice it to say here that this adds another dimension to the importance of understanding social harms in young people's lives: not only are they inherently significant in their extent and their effects, separately from the issue of interpersonal violence between young people, but they also play a considerable role in making such violence more likely, within the lives of particular individuals and within the streets of particular neighbourhoods.

To draw these two points together: analysing the extent and the effects of social harms in young people's lives can help to pierce through the myth that our society is a peaceful, cohesive, just and fair place, aside from anomalous eruptions of crime and violence. This myth very often targets young people and racialized Others in particular as its objects of opprobrium, casting them as the sole disruptors of an otherwise pristine social order. This notion is perpetually reassuring for those who maintain a rose-tinted view of our nation, with its uniquely civil 'Englishness' (see Gilroy, 1982; Emsley, 2005), and has reappeared in various guises for centuries (see Pearson, 1983 for a history; Kotzé, 2019, pp 132–7 for an analysis of a contemporary variant; and Chapter 6 for further discussion of all these themes).

Looking at our society through the lens of social harm, the myth of criminally disturbed immaculacy quickly evaporates. We do not wish to promote a mirror fallacy, that our society is unmatched in its injustice and oppression, but we do wish to take an unflinching look at the historically embedded harms affecting significant numbers of our young people. To use Savage's evocative phrase, structural harms especially bear 'the weight of history' (Savage, 2021, p 21) – policies, systems and institutions are most harmful when they reflect and reinforce the historical accumulation of wealth, power and prestige in some corners of our society, and the concentration of pain, pressure and powerlessness in others. These inequalities amount to societal 'scars', formed through centuries of our history, and in the present, they 'fester and burn' (Savage, 2021, p 94). Effectively addressing these harms – and the related problem of violence – is thus not just a matter of designing the right programmatic interventions for the right individual young people, as if they can be lifted from their socio-historical context into some kind of petri dish; it is a matter of addressing the social history and present condition of those who are structurally belittled (we will return to this point at length in the concluding chapter of this book).

Lastly, drawing attention to both the material and the psycho-social effects of social harms on young people can be a corrective to two different kinds of simplification in academic portrayals of their lives. Firstly, to those accounts which relegate the effects of economic structure, institutions and systems to the explanatory 'background', as if they have only a vague contextual impact on young people; and secondly, to those accounts which refer to 'structural violence' without providing much analytical grip on exactly what that means, or on which specific structures are injurious to young people, and how.

As already touched upon, social harms are not evenly spread across the country. Certain communities experience a substantial concentration of these harms, and some young people's lives are shaped significantly by their cumulative impact. All of the social harms we discuss in this chapter are in some way created, catalysed or exacerbated by the maldistribution of recognition, resources and risk in our society. This maldistribution is social as well as geographical: class, sex, gender, sexuality, (dis)ability, ethnic heritage and 'race' are all vectors of substantial inequality in the prevalence of harm. These themes are explored throughout this chapter, which is focused on five especially significant forms of harm in children and young people's lives: poverty and inequality; declining welfare support; harms of our education system; harms of our labour market; and harms of our housing system. (We intentionally omit the substantial harms of the criminal justice system from this chapter, as they are a central focus of Chapter 6, in which we discuss harmful responses to the issue of 'youth violence'.)

In our discussion of each kind of harm, we describe its extent, nature and origins, and analyse its effects on young people, focusing in particular on how it can diminish their sense of mattering. The chapter also includes three composite case studies, which provide richer accounts of the ways in which multiple forms of social harm can have especially damaging cumulative consequences, drawing attention to the fact that – though analytically separable – these harms are often closely interlinked. Composite case studies can help to illuminate the ways in which various factors influence the biographies of individuals who experience particular life commonalities. They have been used, for instance, to explore the lives of women with HIV (Reyes, 2013), of people who have experienced complex trauma (Briggs and

Cameron 2012) and of people who have particularly complicated difficulties with emotional regulation (Santanello, 2011). For the purposes of this chapter, we blend factual details from a number of young people's lives, to create accounts of 'plausible lives' lived within a particular community. In our case, the community is North East London. Presenting composite case studies in this way allows us to utilize our 'practice experience' of the many different harms which can affect young people in this community (Briggs and Cameron, 2012, p 43), and to explore their cumulative influence on individual lives in the real world, while maintaining the full anonymity of all the young people upon whose biographies we draw.

Poverty and inequality

Poverty has a devastating impact on people's lives around the world. Given children's relative vulnerability compared to adults, and the importance of early years development, the impact of poverty on this group can be particularly acute. The potential effects of a childhood lived in poverty not only include any suffering or degradation endured during these years, but in many cases extend throughout adulthood. When a child is deprived of the resources and experiences that many others are able to take for granted, this can undermine their ability to flourish both as a child and later as an adult. For this reason, the elimination of child poverty should be a central goal for all societies that care about the well-being of their citizens.

Poverty is a social harm because it compromises human flourishing and is preventable, and it is a structural harm because it is substantially determined by the cumulative effects of policy decisions, systemic features of our society and institutional inequities. Our political economy structurally facilitates destitution. As it has developed over centuries, the structure of our economy means that wealth and income have been concentrated in a relatively small number of families and communities, while a significant number of others are left facing considerable scarcity. For those with resources and investments accrued through multiple generations, it is difficult to become poor. For those with very little, a small number of miscalculations can result in abject poverty, while there are vanishingly slim chances of amassing wealth of any significance. Where other economies provide substantial supports for economic security, and work to significantly reduce the chance of any individual or family sliding into destitution (Esping-Anderson, 1991), ours is an economy which enables both extreme impoverishment and unfathomable wealth. As Dorling has put it: 'to inflict poverty on huge numbers of people in an affluent nation state is far from easy, it takes hard work' (Dorling, 2020, p xiv). For a number of decades, British political economy has been characterized by 'redistributing resources, wealth, opportunities and value upwards' (Tyler, 2020, p 163). To use Royce's memorable terms, Britain rivals the US in the capacity of its political economy to continue reliably 'producing poor people' (Royce, 2015, p 7). Poverty is best understood as the product of interlocking problems, baked in by the ways in which societies are organized and power is distributed. While some accuse the poor of making bad choices, the reality is that they face structurally determined 'undesirable alternatives' – their options are shaped in large part by economic, political and social forces which are beyond their influence (Royce, 2015, pp 245–7).

In the depth and breadths of its effects, poverty may well be the most punishing social harm, particularly given that it can operate as a kind of catalytic harm: as well as having significant harmful effects in and of itself, it can accelerate and exacerbate many other forms of harm affecting young people. As Bennett and colleagues have put it, exposure to poverty in childhood both 'creates and compounds adversity' (Bennett et al, 2022, p 496). For that reason, we discuss it at some length in the following section.

The extent and nature of poverty and inequality affecting young people in Britain today

There are two main ways of defining and measuring poverty: in absolute and in relative terms. Both are important, for different reasons. When we talk about someone living in absolute poverty, we refer to that person's household income dropping below levels necessary to maintain basic standards of living. This might involve being unable to afford sufficient food to maintain one's physical health, for example, or adequate housing to be protected from the elements. When we say someone is living in relative poverty, on the other hand, we make reference to thresholds that shift according to the levels of income and wealth of those around them.[1]

The reduction of levels of absolute poverty is necessary for improving people's basic health and security. Without adequate food or shelter, people are exposed to direct and immediate threats to their lives. In its most direct sense, therefore, absolute poverty constitutes the failure to fulfil people's subsistence needs and consequently undermines one of the integral components of human flourishing. Even once these fundamental biological and physiological needs have been met, however, people's lives can be desperately difficult, and their human dignity undermined, if their incomes fall below relative poverty thresholds. This much was acknowledged at least as far back as the late 18th century, when the economist Adam Smith recognized that 'a disgraceful degree of poverty' would include not only being unable to afford 'the commodities which are indispensably necessary for the support of life, but whatever the custom of the country renders it indecent for creditable people, even of the lowest order, to be without' (Smith, 1776, p 865). At the time of writing, Smith held such commodities to include linen shirts and leather shoes. In the UK in 2022, this would arguably include things such as an adequate internet connection and the requisite technology to make use of it, such as smartphones, tablets and laptops. Acknowledging the value of measures of relative poverty, UNICEF (the United Nations Children's Fund) has argued that, of the available measures, 'the most important single guide to, and predictor of, a family's socio-economic status remains its level of household income' (Nastic, 2012). This measure therefore provides substantial insight into the lives of children and young people. In this section, we examine a small sample of the available data on it.

In 2002/03, 29 per cent of children in the UK lived in relative poverty. In 2017/18, the figure was 30 per cent, equating to 4.1 million children (Department for Work and Pensions, 2020a).[2] These rates vary significantly across the country, with numerous pockets of concentrated and severe poverty. In some London boroughs, particularly after housing costs are taken into account, child poverty is exceptionally high (Figure 4.1).

The data in Figure 4.1 illustrates the stark inequality that exists in England's capital city. While around one in five children in Richmond upon Thames live in poverty (a shocking statistic in itself), over half of all children in Newham and Tower Hamlets grow up in poverty when housing costs are taken into account. The situation has become so bad for so many families that the latest Joseph Rowntree Foundation (2022) report into UK poverty has promoted the adoption of additional measures that they refer to as 'deep poverty' and 'very deep poverty' (being in households below

Figure 4.1: Rates of child poverty in the top and bottom five London boroughs, 2017/18

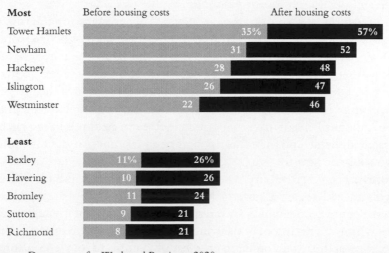

Source: Department for Work and Pensions, 2020a

the threshold of 50 per cent and 40 per cent of the contemporary median income, respectively). Of the total number of children and parents in poverty, the Foundation found that four in ten lived in very deep poverty (Joseph Rowntree Foundation, 2022, p 20).

In addition to measuring poverty solely in terms of income, efforts have also been made to capture something known as 'material deprivation'. To measure this, people are asked to indicate whether they are able to afford certain items, including: 'a warm winter coat for each child', 'fresh fruit and vegetables eaten by children every day', 'outdoor space or facilities nearby to play safely' and 'celebrations on special occasions such as birthdays, Christmas or other religious festivals' (Department for Work and Pensions, 2020b). In 2010/11, half a million children lived with *severe* low income[3] and material deprivation, a figure which had risen to 0.6 million children by 2018/19 (Department for Work and Pensions, 2020a).

The importance of defining and measuring poverty in relative terms was clearly demonstrated by the impact of COVID-19. School closures during the pandemic, for example, required children to learn from home, with teachers providing guidance and support online. However, lack of access to laptops and adequate home internet connections stunted the ability of a significant proportion of school-aged children in the UK to engage with their learning.[4] This has numerous implications for child flourishing. For example, lack of contact with teachers and access to learning materials has clear potential to undermine children's need to develop their understanding of the world around them. How dispiriting it must have been for many children to realize that while the majority of their peers were able to continue their learning through the provision of online materials and support, they – through no fault of their own – were to be left behind. A report published by the Institute for Fiscal Studies revealed that the poorest 20 per cent of children at primary school spent 7.5 hours less time on educational activities during the pandemic compared to the richest 20 per cent (Andrew et al, 2020, pp 8–10). A combination of factors account for this disparity, including the already cited lack of access to technology and the internet, and relatively rich families 'topping up' their children's education through the purchase of private tuition. While secondary school-aged children living in the richest 20 per cent of households spent an average of 40 minutes per day with a private tutor, the average for the poorest 20 per cent of children was less than five minutes. A report by the Child Poverty Action Group (2020) explored the effects of the pandemic on children's subjective well-being and highlighted that those from low-income families were particularly likely to feel anxious and worried about being left behind, while their parents or carers felt guilty and stressed about their children not having access to the educational opportunities available to their peers.

The use of foodbanks serves as another proxy measure or indicator of poverty. A study by Garthwaite (2016) highlighted that 19.3 million people in the UK lived in poverty at some point between 2010 and 2013, and that people on a low income spent over a third of their disposable income on food (see further Loopstra et al, 2015; ONS, 2015). Garthwaite's research with the Trussell Trust also revealed that the number of people given emergency food parcels by the Trust's foodbanks rose from 25,899 in 2008–09 to 1,084,604 in 2014–15 (Garthwaite, 2016, p 36). In December 2020, for the first time in its 70-year history, UNICEF – the UN agency responsible for providing humanitarian aid worldwide – stepped in to help feed children and families in the UK by providing emergency resources in the South London borough of Southwark (Storer, 2020). Low-income families with children are among the most likely to depend on support from foodbanks.

The effects of poverty and inequality on children and young people's sense of mattering

Using a variety of different measures, studies consistently show the negative effects of poverty on children's subjective well-being and life satisfaction (see, for instance, Gross-Manos and Ben-Arieh, 2017; Spruyt et al, 2021). For our purposes here, we focus especially on how poverty can affect young people's sense of mattering. The research is clear: poverty is very often accompanied by a gnawing sense of insignificance and of utter powerlessness – an inability to feel control over your own life, let alone have influence on the world around you (see O'Hara, 2020, p 203). As Ranciere has put it, those experiencing poverty in economies like Britain are 'the category of people who do not count' (cited in Lister, 2021, p 91). Poverty leaves a disturbingly large number of British people, including children and young people, feeling that they do not matter.

Poverty has this effect in a few different ways, for a few different reasons. Firstly, poverty in Britain is inherently shaming and stigmatizing. This is because our culture tends both to 'lionise' wealth (Dorling, 2018, p 249) and to maintain a highly dubious self-image as a self-styled meritocracy (Lister, 2021, p 119). Despite all evidence to the contrary (see, for example, Sayer, 2015; Littler, 2017), Britain remains gripped by a powerful self-perception that those with the greatest wealth and power have earned it, and those with the least have, in the same way, got their 'just deserts'. Inequality is consequently seen as legitimate, and poverty as 'a disease that is self-authorised' (Hallsworth, 2013, p 175). Particularly in our most unequal cities, there is a stark inequity of respect and social esteem accompanying material disparities. In London, the finance sector receives cultural adulation in tandem with its economic power, while the poor are considered of lesser value to the urban economy (Atkinson, 2020). The accumulated, almost ritual exposure to disparaging kinds of political rhetoric, bureaucratic systems, institutional culture and interpersonal interaction can leave those who experience poverty to feel a grating sense of worthlessness (see O'Hara 2020, pp 179, 203). It is a fundamentally belittling experience to live in relative scarcity in sight of extreme wealth, particularly if you are encouraged to view this as a deserved disparity.

Individuals, families and communities are both economically excluded and culturally devalued. Shaming cultural narratives combine with what Wacquant (2008) has called 'territorial stigmatisation' to mean that poorer neighbourhoods experience 'nonrecognition to the point of nonexistence' (McDonald 2003, p 73). Tyler (2013, 2020) has written extensively of these processes as both excluding and humiliating, entailing forms of abjection and stigma which erode dignity, in classed, racialized and gendered ways: mothers receive particular disparagement as the supposed origins of shameful family poverty, young people from poor neighbourhoods who are racialized as Black encounter particularly vicious forms of racist discreditation. Societal disrespect presses down on those who already experience the material hardship of poverty, fostering, at worst, a sense of inconsequential existence.

Compounding this are the policy harms of our ever-diminishing social security system, which can leave people with a pervasive sense of powerlessness. Demeaning social security policies impair rather than enhance agency (Lister, 2021, p 214), and induce shame rather than promote dignity (Lister, 2021, p 212). Tyler (2020, p 59) draws a striking comparison between the recent, brutal stripping back of social security provision for those experiencing poverty and 18th century enclosures, arguing that in both cases people went from holding a dignified status as 'rights-bearing subjects' to being deemed 'undeserving populations'. People in poverty are more often the objects of other people's decisions and actions than the subjects of their own lives – 'more powerful actors control the wages, benefits, services and opportunities available to people in poverty' (Lister, 2021, p 205). They are thus often troubled by a sense of 'inability', and a lack of 'agency or control': they feel 'controlled and dehumanised by the systems and structures which govern access to social and material resources' (Chase and Walker, 2013, pp 740–1). Those who are forced to rely on foodbanks often experience a pernicious sense of humiliation (Purdam et al, 2016). Due to both the cultural and institutional experience of poverty, its shame is manifest 'as a sense of powerlessness and feeling small' (Chase and Walker, 2013, p 740). Poverty is characterized not just by the direct, constraining effects of material hardship, then: our culture, policies, institutions and systems mean that it is a deeply diminishing and disempowering experience.

All of this is felt with particular intensity by children and young people. Research has shown that children are aware of social misrecognition from as young as five years old – particularly those who perceive that they are misrecognized due to their experience of poverty (O'Hara, 2020, p 211; Lister, 2021, p 81). In the transitional period of adolescence, in which teenagers struggle to establish their subjectivity, this sense is perhaps even more acute. Baum (1996) found that young people in poorer, 'discredited communities' were profoundly conscious of their 'discreditation', 'stigmatisation', 'perceived incompetence' and limited 'possibilities for gaining status-enhancing resources'. Irwin-Rogers (2019, p 598), in his study of teenagers' lives in a pupil referral unit, puts it frankly: 'to remain poor was to remain a nobody'. If money is increasingly the measure of all things, and you have precious little of it, it is difficult to evade a sense of personal devaluation.

Lastly, but perhaps most importantly, poverty affects mattering because it can undermine the quality of relationships, particularly those in the home. Arguably the most consequential of relationships, those between parents and children, can be affected by all manner of factors – resource scarcity is one of them (see Garthwaite, 2016). What 'really counts' in parenting is the quality of interactions and the strength of relationship which is established between caregiver and child, which can be significantly strained by profound financial hardship (Golombok, 2000). Poverty can cause discord, confusion, frustration, helplessness, self-doubt and perennial worry, all of which can affect interactions and relationships – there is a well-evidenced connection between poverty and adverse childhood experiences (Walsh et al, 2019). At worst, such difficulties can amount to 'toxic stress' in the home, which can have a damaging effect on child development, even affecting brain architecture (see Franke, 2014). It has been suggested that this form of acute stress is more common in lower-income households (Cox et al, 2018), as may be evidenced by the association between increased child poverty and increased numbers of children taken into care (Bennett et al, 2022). It is clearly not the case that the quality of parental interactions with children correlates simply with income or wealth – the infinitely messy craft of parenting is of course far more complex than that, and there are both wonderfully nurturing and harmfully abusive parenting relationships in households of all economic circumstances. Acute financial hardship is a well-evidenced stressor on these relationships, however (see, for example, Golombok, 2000); it amounts to a substantial difficulty which parents in those circumstances are forced to grapple with and overcome. As Eisenstadt and Oppenheim put it, poverty not only means less money to buy products and services which can help healthy child development, but it is also 'a key factor in parental stress' – they conclude that 'persistent poverty and hardship are particularly damaging' for children (Eisenstadt and Oppenheim, 2019, pp 143–4). A recent review of research on connections between poverty, abuse and neglect similarly concluded that poverty and inequality are key drivers of harm to children (Skinner and Bywaters, 2022).

Poverty, then, induces a structural form of stress: it undermines the subjective well-being of parents, can affect the fulfilment of infants' needs and can damage parent–child interactions and relationships. In the most severe cases, poverty can harm family relationships in a way which has lasting effects – contributing to the experience of attachment problems and childhood trauma which can affect an individual throughout their lifecourse. These experiences can foster the lingering, sometimes lifelong sense of worthlessness which De Zulueta (2001, p 45) identified. All of this is exacerbated when families experiencing poverty are affected by intersecting forms of structural harm: when single mothers' access to support and their self-perception are undermined by misogyny, or when parents of colour lack culturally competent services or experience institutional racism, for instance. The pernicious effects of multiple compounding and cumulative structural harms can be most damaging during the early formative years of childhood. One of these effects can be an entrenched, enduring struggle to matter.

For all of these reasons and more, the structural harms deriving from our radically inequitable political economy can substantially diminish individuals' and communities' sense of mattering. As Lister (2021, p 117) has put it, the experience of inequality and poverty in Britain can leave people feeling that they are worth nothing at all, and 'that "nothing at all" value is a destroying experience'.[5] The composite case study in Box 4.1 covers many of these themes.

Declining welfare support: under-resourced communities and social care systems

The significant degree of inequality between individuals which is produced by our political economy is accompanied by substantial disparities in community resources. Some neighbourhoods are characterized by abundance: well-resourced services and plentiful community institutions which provide wide-ranging forms of support to children, young people, parents and families. In other areas, provision is vanishingly small. This inequality has been significantly worsened by some of the decisions made by successive UK governments since the financial crisis of 2008, which have resulted in the substantial contraction of state support across the country. This has both exacerbated levels of household poverty and inequality discussed earlier and sharply restricted the availability of state-derived care and support to some of the most vulnerable people in society.

How did this come to be? Between 1997 and 2010, New Labour invested extensively in the provision of support and care for those worst affected by another aspect of their policy regime: the continuation of Thatcherite 'free-market' economics, which reliably generates the forms and levels of poverty and inequality discussed earlier. Social policies during this time

Box 4.1: Composite Case Study 1 – The interwoven effects of poverty, inequality and housing issues on Hamza's life

Hamza's young life has been characterized by the harsh constraints of poverty. He is now in his early twenties. His whole childhood, adolescence and early adulthood has been shaped by the restrictions, compromises, sacrifices and strains associated with constant financial pressure.

Hamza's parents moved to Britain as young adults, and struggled to navigate a discriminatory job market. Their work, and thus their income, was perennially insecure. They gave Hamza all that they possibly could when he was a young child, but it was never easy to get food on the table, or to give Hamza all he needed to participate fully in education. Their home was often a place of stress and tension. Hamza's mum, in particular, has suffered from severe depression.

The family moved a number of times in Hamza's childhood, and never had landlords who seemed committed to the effective maintenance or upkeep of their home. Damp and heating issues have been repeated problems wherever they've lived, causing health issues for Hamza and his siblings. Threats of eviction have been common throughout Hamza's life – he's now somewhat accustomed to the sense that having a place to live is a precarious achievement, not any kind of guarantee. When the rent arrears stack up and the financial pressure from creditors intensifies, it still prompts acute anxiety and worry in the household; no one can remain calm when their home is at risk.

From his teenage years, Hamza has always felt it to be imperative that he should achieve academic and career success, in order to earn money for the family. He has deeply internalized a meritocratic vision of life, and dedicates himself to hard work. He achieved average grades at school, and met some supportive teachers, but sensed that most of them had no understanding of his background or situation – the social distance between them and him was palpable. The work Hamza was able to get was poorly paid and exploitative. He battled with the ambiguous emotional consequences of this: on the one hand, his instinct has always been to be conscientious and diligent, on the other, he couldn't help thinking that his employer was taking advantage.

The accumulated strains of this life have led to Hamza suffering from mental health issues for as long as he can remember. This has affected his friendships, academic qualifications and employment. Through sheer effort and bloody-mindedness, he has fought through periods of unemployment and bouts of intensive job seeking to now have a more secure, decent job. But the hours are long, the training is insufficient, the support is inadequate and he is very aware of occupying the lowest-status role in a large, multinational company. Most of his earnings go towards maintaining the family home, and he is gripped by the obligation to keep his job and keep supplementing the household's income, for fear of the hardships that could result without it.

Regardless of the analytical method used to assess the causal roots of the poverty Hamza has experienced, the political economy in which he lives has facilitated his family's hardship. Some will lay blame on structural factors: the unforgiving and exploitative job market, the inadequate benefits system, the corrupt and broken housing market. Others would blame family 'dysfunction', bad choices on the part of Hamza's parents and Hamza himself. But from whatever angle you look at Hamza's situation, his material deprivation has been societally fostered – British society in the 21st century is structured in such a way that the confluence of just a few individual and social factors can result in destitution.

---

sought to alleviate some of the structural harms caused by economic policies. As David Edgar put it, New Labour's attitude was that '["free market"] economics are a given ... all you can do is administer the bruise cream' (quoted in Westergaard, 1999, p 434). Since the fall of Labour in 2010, successive UK governments have continued to frame a particular kind of free market economics as a 'given'. This has involved a blanket refusal to alter the fundamental parameters of the UK's finance-dominated political economy – even after the 2008 financial crisis – and the decision instead to further prop it up with state funding. What has changed, significantly, is that recent governments have also steadily and enthusiastically reduced the application of 'bruise cream'. Alongside reductions in financial support for poorer households, provision for children, young people and families, which is either directly provided by the state or derived from state funding (such as local authority-funded independent youth provision) has been the subject of severe cuts. Benefit spending per head for children dropped 17 per cent between 2010 and 2020 (Eisenstadt and Oppenheim, 2019, p 128). The grants which English councils receive from central government were halved in size between 2010 and 2019 (BBC, 2019). Local authority spending on children's centres and the services delivered through these centres declined from £977 million in 2012–13 to £493 million in 2018–19, a fall of close to 50 per cent (Department for Education, 2020a). Over the same period, the total amount spent by local authorities not only on children's centres but on all services and support for children under five fell from £1.2 billion in 2012–13 to £591 million in 2018–19, a reduction of 49 per cent.

The manifold harms of these policy decisions have been well documented (see, for example, Seymour, 2014; Cooper and Whyte, 2017), and they have undermined the subjective well-being and need fulfilment of millions, particularly as they have simultaneously increased the demand for, and reduced the supply of, mental health services (see McGrath et al, 2016; Cummins, 2018). For our purposes here, though, we will briefly focus on just one dimension of this harm: the ways in which these decisions have weakened supportive relationships outside of the family, and thus undermined young people's sense of mattering. In communities, as in families, relationships require resources, meaning that huge reductions in resources have inevitable implications for the quality of these relationships. We will discuss just two examples, starting with youth provision.

Firstly, between 2010 and 2019, youth services in England and Wales underwent a 70 per cent funding cut (Weale, 2020). This considerable reduction in youth support amounts to a widespread diminishment in the availability of trusted adults with whom young people can establish relationships. As Rodd and Stewart (2009) have argued, strong relationships are the 'glue' of youth work, and can allow young people both to develop a deep sense of their significance and to explore the kinds of influence they wish to have on the world: these kind of relationships within informal, voluntary settings, outside of family and school, can be transformative for a young person's sense of mattering. This is what the youth work funding cuts have removed from many communities.

Secondly, the sharp cuts in funding from national government to local authorities have, by extension, cut the resources available for children's social care, despite the increasing numbers of children and young people who are in the social care system (see MacAlister, 2021, p 7). Though statutory social workers' relationships with children, young people and families of course have a different character to those established between youth workers and young people, they too have been undermined by the policy harms of the post-2010 period. As the need for social care has increased, provision has reduced, causing individual social workers to juggle unmanageable caseloads, while the support they receive via staff supervision has also declined (Cunningham et al, 2021). As Hastings and Gannon (2021) put it, front-line public sector staff, such as social workers, have increasingly become 'shock absorbers' for the disruptions caused by huge state spending cuts. In too many cases, this results in 'stressed, frazzled people performing sub-optimally' (Hastings and Gannon, 2021, p 17). Social workers have been harmed by austerity policies; their subjective well-being has declined. These policies have also meant that social workers have less time and emotional capacity to build meaningful professional relationships with families, as well as a reduced capability to address the effects of both interpersonal and structural harms on children and young people. Compared to their European counterparts, social workers in England are more likely to feel that their job is dominated by procedural tasks, rather than relational work with families, children and young people (Millard, 2021, p 147). These kinds of systemic neglect are most acute for those children and young people who are in residential care, particularly those who dwell in unregulated private children's homes, which make substantial profits but often deliver poor outcomes (Butler, 2021b; Marsh, 2021).

Children and young people feel all of this. They are left more vulnerable to interpersonal harm, particularly within their household, and this is especially concerning given studies which suggest that – depending on age and the precise form of interpersonal harm – between 10 and 25 per cent of children and young people may experience abuse of this kind (Radford et al, 2011; ONS, 2020). More broadly, the social ecology that children and young people live within is less well populated by adults who can help them to recognize their value, to shape the kind of agentic influence they want to exercise and thus to sense that they matter. Too many experience a dearth of nurturing care at home and at school, and so are in great need of the warmth and support which can be provided by a 'third institution', such as a youth or community centre. The policy harms of recent years have hollowed many communities of such institutions, strangled 'collective practices of care' (Tyler, 2020, p 163) and demonstrated a kind of 'systemic carelessness' (Chatzidakis et al, 2020, p 80). For those worst affected by these developments, entrenched material scarcity is combined with intergenerational discord to create an intense need for the extra-familial forms of care, nurture and support which are increasingly absent or inadequate across many parts of the country.

Schools and education

Education is one of the most important elements of childhood and adolescence. At its best, it helps children to make sense of the world around them and their place within it, while also providing the foundations for them to live happy and healthy lives. Of all the institutions that children and young people come into contact with, school is arguably the most consequential. For one thing, it is the only universal institution in society – the only institution that everyone is legally obliged to attend for over a decade (aside from the tiny home-schooled minority) – and thus it holds enormous practical, emotional and relational significance in young people's lives. While precise numbers will vary, most children in England and Wales will have spent around 20,000 hours in formal educational settings by the time they reach their 18th birthday. Considered in this context, schools have the potential to play a vital role in enabling children and young people to flourish. They can be places which support young people's sense of mattering, furnishing them with deeply meaningful forms of recognition and respect and helping them to see the difference that their existence makes to the world. It is our contention, however, that a number of structural features of the education system in England and Wales in fact generate harm, compromising many children and young people's flourishing. In this section, we will discuss a handful of the most pressing issues within the education system in England and Wales at present: provision for those with additional needs; school exclusions; recruitment, training and support of teachers; and students' and parents' relationships with school staff. Each of these will be addressed in turn.

Provision for those with additional educational needs

In far too many cases, provision for children and young people with additional educational needs is inadequate. This harm has been exacerbated by the policy choices outlined earlier – as with other state-funded sources of provision, school funding has been eroded since 2010. Total school spending per pupil in England fell by 9 per cent in real terms between 2009–10 and 2017–18 (Institute for Fiscal Studies, 2019). Students with additional educational needs have seen resources for their support diminish with particular rapidity and severity – a problem which is set to worsen in the coming years (Belger, 2021; Jayanetti, 2021). Many students who require additional support are not even having their needs assessed; those with specific diagnoses do not always receive the provision that they need.

A recent review of this issue by Shaw (2021) has highlighted its many dimensions. Around 15 per cent of children in primary and secondary education in England are identified as having some form of additional educational need, but they 'continue to be marginalised by the education system' (Shaw, 2021, pp 33, 37). Reforms to the Special Educational Needs and Disabilities (SEND) system since 2010 have caused disruption to many children and young people's provision, with many cash-strapped local authorities struggling to manage the transition from 'Statements of Need' to 'Education, Health and Care Plans' (Shaw, 2021, pp 36–7). SEND provision in further education is especially insufficient: both providers and local authorities often lack specialist staff who are able to support students in this stage of their education, particularly, again, due to funding cuts (Shaw, 2021, p 45). Compounding the effects of cuts and reforms, accountability pressures encourage mainstream schools and colleges to prioritize those students who will meet or exceed national averages in exam results – a benchmark which those with additional needs are often the least likely to reach (Shaw, 2021, p 40). Meanwhile, those who attend special schools suffer from the systemic neglect that these settings themselves experience at the hands of central government. The Department for Education's 2019 teacher recruitment and retention strategy, for instance, failed to mention special schools at all (Shaw, 2021, p 43).

Given all of this, it is perhaps unsurprising that young people with additional educational needs are more likely to be unhappy at school and to experience issues with their peers (Shaw, 2021, p 37). Integration into mainstream education can be nominal – many of these students experience segregation and separation, and far fewer direct interactions with teachers, as compared to other pupils (Shaw, 2021, p 39). The educational experience of young people with additional needs is thus affected by multiple forms of harm: there are inadequate resources in the system to meet their educational needs, and they often lack the kinds of relational and interactional support which are central to high levels of subjective well-being. As we go on to explore in the following section, they are also more likely to be excluded from school. It is partly all these factors related to their schooling – alongside others, such as inadequate job opportunities, heightened vulnerability, and the disproportionate poverty experienced by those with additional educational needs (McCluskey et al, 2019, p 17) – which explain why those with additional educational needs are significantly over-represented in our criminal justice system (Prison Reform Trust, 2021).

School exclusions

Given that education provides the foundations for children and young people to enjoy happy and prosperous lives, the exclusion process that removes students from mainstream school is something that merits serious scrutiny. The effects of exclusion can be devastating, affecting not only children and young people's academic progress, but their subjective well-being and the fulfilment of their needs. Exclusion leaves many feeling dejected, angry and isolated, alienating them from institutional authority and emotionally detaching them from mainstream society. Excluded students can, at worst, be left to feel like a discarded irrelevance, rejected by an integral societal institution while simultaneously being taken away from their support network of friends. Irwin-Rogers (2019, p 607) described how one young man's exclusion 'ripped into his already damaged sense of self-worth' – an experience that is not uncommon. It is unsurprising, therefore, that large-scale research has found that exclusions can trigger and exacerbate emotional and mental health problems in children (Ford et al, 2018). Highs level of school exclusion should thus raise considerable cause for concern.

Since 2012, the number of children subjected to fixed and permanent exclusions from mainstream education in England and Wales has been rising (HM Government, 2019). In 2013–14, 6.62 per cent of children in state-funded secondary schools were subjected to fixed-term exclusions. By 2018–19, this had risen to 10.75 per cent, which equated to 199,765 pupils in total (Department for Education, 2020b). The number of permanent exclusions in 2017–18 across all school types was 7,905, up from 4,632 in 2012–13 (Department for Education, 2020c). It is important to note that rates of exclusion vary significantly depending on pupil demographics (Figure 4.2). In summary, the statistics on school exclusions show that male pupils from certain minority ethnic backgrounds who live in socioeconomically deprived households are far more likely to be excluded from mainstream education, as compared to their wider peer group. Numerous explanations have been offered to account for these disparities, including but not limited to:

• The differential treatment of Black and Gyspy, Roma and Traveller pupils by teachers, for example, in the form of lower educational expectations and disproportionately punitive reactions to perceived poor behaviour (Wright, 2010; Bhopal, 2011).

Figure 4.2: Rates of fixed-term exclusion by demographic group

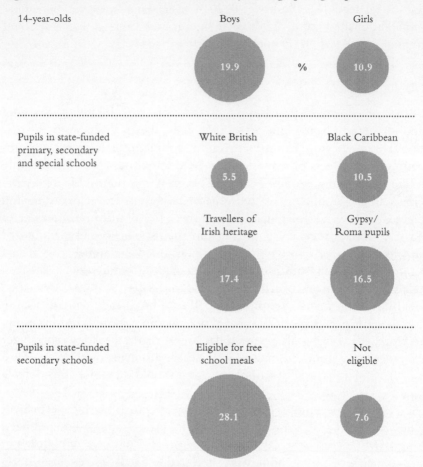

Source: Department for Education, 2020b

- Class discrimination and middle-class privilege, particularly in terms of parents' propensity and likely success in challenging school exclusion decisions (Gazeley, 2012; Kulz, 2015).
- Boys' behaviour being worse and more aggressive on average than girls' behaviour (Smith et al, 2012; Craggs and Kelly, 2017).
- The challenging home lives of children that could involve violence, abuse and living with family members with mental health issues – factors that often aggravate one another and are linked to poverty and deprivation (Evans et al, 2009; Apland et al, 2017).
- Inadequate or non-existent teacher training around special educational needs and cultural diversity (Children's Commissioner, 2013; Gazeley and Dunne, 2013).

School exclusions in England and Wales commonly result in a child being registered with a Pupil Referral Unit or some other form of Alternative Provision (AP).[6] Despite enhanced resources available in these settings, outcomes for pupils in AP are poor. In 2015–16, for example, only 18 per cent of children who were subjected to multiple fixed-term exclusions, and just 7 per cent of children who were permanently excluded, achieved good passes in their Maths and English GCSEs (HM Government, 2019). As one expert witness to the cross-party Youth Violence Commission explained: "Once pushed out, these young people are placed into alternative schools of varying quality. Shorter contact hours … their teachers are twice as likely to be unqualified and temporary … they are basically holding pens before [children] move onto the street" (Irwin-Rogers, Muthoo and Billingham, 2020, p 24). The phrase 'varying quality' is important here – in some cases, AP settings do provide exactly the kinds of specialist support that students need. In many cases, though, as the attainment statistics suggest, students are not gaining the education they are entitled to. Excluded children are often being taught by un(der)qualified teachers, while also often being placed on reduced timetables that inhibit them from making comparable levels of progress to their mainstream peers. It is little surprise, therefore, that school exclusions have been found to catalyse and cement children's disengagement from learning (Evans et al, 2009).

These problems cannot be solved simply by school leaders making decisions to exclude fewer children. Teachers and school leaders face genuine issues in the form of pupil behaviour that disrupts the learning of both the child in question and their peers. Many school exclusions, however, are not being used as an option of last resort, nor are sufficient measures being put in place to support teachers and pupils (Tillson and Oxley, 2020). Several witnesses to the Youth Violence Commission argued that 'substantial extra resources' were necessary to tackle the overuse of exclusions (Irwin-Rogers, Muthoo and Billingham, 2020). While helping to bring down rates of school exclusion is one good reason for providing mainstream teachers with additional resources and support, there are many other reasons for doing so, which are closely related to a current problem in education known as the 'teacher gap'.

Recruitment, training and support for teachers: the 'teacher gap'

For decades, concerns have been raised in England and Wales about the stark differences in levels of educational achievement between children from rich and poor backgrounds. Every year, around one in six children – disproportionately those whose families are living in poverty – leave the formal education system functionally illiterate (Rashid and Brooks, 2010).

According to Allen and Sims (2018, pp 4–6), one of the central barriers to closing the attainment gap between rich and poor children is something that they call 'the teacher gap'. The teacher gap refers to three things: (1) the disparity between what we know about the importance of teachers and how we treat them; (2) the difference between the number of teachers we need, and the number we have; and (3) the difference between the quality of teaching we have, and the quality of teaching we need.

Far from improving teaching quality, many recent educational reforms have created additional obstacles to good practice, such as an ever-increasing list of 'box ticking demands … ceaseless curriculum reform, disruptive top-down reorganisations, and an audit culture that requires teachers to document their every move' (Allen and Sims, 2018, p 4). In areas where teachers deserve and require support – in ensuring workloads are kept to levels that will not lead to high rates of teacher stress and burnout, or through continuous and high-quality learning and training opportunities, for example – there has been abject neglect and failure. Lacking sufficient training and support, and with 72 per cent of teachers describing themselves as stressed (Education Support, 2019), it is understandable that many teachers are finding it difficult to nurture children's creativity and love of learning in the classroom (Cachia et al, 2010). One obvious manifestation of this failure is the shocking rate of teacher retention in England and Wales, well below levels seen in other countries in Europe: a third of those who train as teachers in England and Wales are not working as teachers five years later (Department for Education, 2020d).

This is a damning indictment of the state of the education system in this country. With pupil numbers growing and targets being missed for teacher recruitment and retention year-on-year, the government faces a 'substantial and growing challenge' of ensuring an adequate teacher supply (Worth, 2020, p 6). Staff numbers in secondary schools declined by 15,000 between 2014–15 and 2016–17 (National Education Union, 2018). This equates to an average of 5.5 fewer staff members in each secondary school in England and Wales. Witnesses to the recent cross-party Youth Violence Commission laid bare some of the consequences:

> All schools in this country are cutting, cutting, cutting the whole time, and having to … it's just an impossible situation. And that means for a start in terms of education funding the wraparound services, the pastoral services, the soft skills are the ones that you can't afford.
>
> It's really hard, and the reason is because the staff there, they're scurrying around. They're like headless chickens … too busy … and that's what makes it tough. (Irwin-Rogers, Muthoo and Billingham, 2020, p 23)

Improving the recruitment, training and level of support provided to teachers would bring about a number of important benefits. An encouraging body of research shows that enhancing the quality of teaching practice provides one of the key routes to improving outcomes for children (see Sammons et al, 2007; Hanushek and Rivkin, 2012; Slater et al, 2012; Wiliam, 2016). While good teaching enhances the outcomes of all pupils, it seems to have a particularly positive impact on children from disadvantaged backgrounds. Raising teaching quality thus has the potential to help keep all children engaged in education while simultaneously narrowing the attainment gap (Hamre and Pianta, 2005).

Students' and parents' relationships with school staff

The situation already described is damaging for teachers, ex-teachers and would-be teachers, but it also has serious implications for child flourishing. Undervaluing teachers and providing them with inadequate training and support has adverse effects on teacher–student relationships. This comes at no small cost. While positive teacher–student relationships have been found to have a major and positive impact on pupil behaviour (Obsuth et al, 2017), if these are lacking in schools it can have significant implications for children's subjective well-being, negatively impacting on their attitudes and feelings towards education as well as their wider sense of meaning and purpose in life (Roorda et al, 2011). In worst cases, schools can be places affected by what Brierley (2021) has called 'relational poverty'. Studies in London, for instance, have found that schools can be 'cold and corporate' environments (Thapar, 2021, p 59), which may contain no adult that a pupil would feel comfortable speaking with, even if they were experiencing considerable distress (Billingham et al, 2018). The student-led research organization States of Mind highlighted the urgent necessity and immense value of 'mutual connection or mutual trust' between staff and students, suggesting that this is too often lacking (States of Mind, 2020).

Schools' disciplinary regimes can be actively antithetical to the development of positive relationships between pupils and staff. A recent youth-led research project in London found that schools disproportionately punish those pupils 'who are valued less' (Lunghy et al, 2019, p 21), and Thapar argues – based on his time as a youth worker in London schools – that schools can be 'two-tier' systems in which some pupils are 'left behind and actively demeaned' (Thapar, 2021, p 109). This was certainly the case for 'Osman', a student featured in Kulz's (2017, p 130) ethnography of one inner-London school, who experienced education as an 'increasingly antagonistic landscape where [he] lacked value'. This lack of value can be manifest in particularly punitive formal punishments, such as 'isolation booths' (see Barker et al, 2010), or can be more subtly communicated through the interactions that students have with staff. Gunter (2017, p 182), for instance, detailed the condescending and humiliating encounters that some students experience with teachers, and observed that the resulting confrontations can lead to the students being suspended or permanently excluded.

These cumulative experiences of diminishment can affect parents as well as students. In his own youth work practice, Billingham has directly witnessed patronizing, denigrating interactions with parents in school, and has seen the effect this can have on children and young people. In many cases, it is single mothers who are demeaned in this way, and Bourgois (2003, p 175) has eloquently described how this can feel for the child, writing that no young person 'can stand witnessing the instantaneous transformation of the mother – the authority figure in their lives – into an intimidated object of ridicule'.

Inequalities of harm and mattering in the education system

As the preceding discussion makes clear, young people of different backgrounds do not have an equitable educational experience: many harmful education practices are gendered, classed and racialized. Kulz's (2017) ethnography centred on the reproduction of class and 'race' in the school she studied, for instance, and Gunter (2017) points out that African Caribbean students are often the objects of most humiliation. Alongside disproportionate exclusion rates, factors such as these led a recent Runnymede report to argue that 'racism is deeply embedded in schooling' (Joseph-Salisbury, 2020, p 3). Kulz (2017) suggests that the educational practices she witnessed could only be interpreted in the context of Britain's colonial history, and it is certainly clear that students' contemporary experiences in schools have deep historical roots: the origins of compulsory state-funded education in Britain, developed at the height of the Empire, lie as much in panicked, racialized fears about the 'dangerous classes' as they do in any kind of emancipatory dream for the masses. Mandatory schooling was introduced during a period in which lower-class young people were conceptually grouped with 'savages' in the Empire, sometimes referred to as 'street Arabs' (Duckworth, 2002, p 21; Emsley, 2005, p 180; Lawson and Silver, 2007, p 312), seen as 'almost a race apart' (Gillis, 1981, p 138). If the structural devaluation of some school students is a significant harm in contemporary Britain – as we would contend – it is a historically entrenched one. This history would of course feel distant for many students today, who find school to be a supportive and hugely beneficial experience. For those whose encounters with education are characterized more by diminishment than enrichment, however, it is a history which will feel all too recent. For the students who experience systemic discreditation in the education system, it is difficult not to feel that they matter less than their peers.

As a result of this, no doubt among other factors, some young people emotionally disinvest from their school, or from education as a whole.

It becomes a place of reduced consequence in their lives and their self-narratives, as they seek to establish significance and influence elsewhere. As Bakkali (2019, p 1329) puts it, many young people 'look elsewhere for value and meaningful notions of selfhood'. This was the case for Osman, the student in Kulz's (2017, p 130) study, whose experience of institutional harm in school led him to emotionally detach from education, and invest himself elsewhere. Similarly, for many of the men serving prison sentences for murder who were interviewed by Dobash and Dobash (2020), expulsion from school meant that education became drained of importance – significance was instead found in 'the street, the park, and [with] their pals' (Dobash and Dobash, 2020, p 297). The harms of schooling can be repellent for some students, drawing them towards alternative sources of meaning and mattering. For some, this may have relatively innocuous consequences. For others, it can be hugely dangerous. Composite Case Study 2, in Box 4.2, explores the effects that structural harms in the educational system can have on a young person.

Unemployment and 'marginal work'

Employment can play a crucial role in both enabling and undermining human flourishing. At best, work can be a rich source of meaning, purpose, dignity and value, building an individual's sense that they are of worth and consequence. At worst, a job can cause substantial harm, undermining health and well-being, and leaving a person to feel deadeningly insignificant. Unemployment can of course be even more damaging. For young people, these enriching or harmful experiences of (un)employment can be particularly consequential, as their early endeavours in the labour market can feel like a fundamental part of their entry into the adult world, both reflecting and affecting their orientation towards wider society.

Examining the best available statistics on youth employment in England and Wales shows that the proportion of young people aged 16–24 classified as not in education, employment or training (NEET) was 11.5 per cent in 2020 (Department for Education, 2021). NEET rates vary significantly across the country. During the period October to December 2020, the lowest NEET rate was for young people living in the South East, at 7.9 per cent, and the highest was for young people in the North East, at 13.7 per cent; the rate for London was 11.5 per cent. Trends in the rate of young people classified as NEET differ along the lines of sex. While the NEET rate for females aged 16–24 declined from 15.3 per cent in 2000 to 9.7 per cent in 2020, the trend moved in the opposite direction for young males: the NEET rate increased from 9.3 per cent in 2000 to 13.3 per cent in 2020. In absolute terms, this means that 271,791 females and 390,479 males aged 16–24 were classified as NEET in the final quarter of 2020.

Box 4.2: Composite Case Study 2 – How Tyrell's life has been affected by structural harms in the educational system

Tyrell was labelled from very early on in his educational journey. In his nursery, the staff didn't have adequate training or support to identify additional needs. They interpreted his communication difficulties as straightforward bad behaviour. The health visitor who monitored Tyrell's early development noticed some features of his behaviour which could indicate developmental problems, but these were never communicated to Tyrell's nursery.

Tyrell's mum complained to the nursery about how he was being treated, but she was dismissed as 'emotive'. In the staff room, Tyrell's mum was described as a 'typical loud black mum'. Her concerns were not seen as the expression of justifiable misgivings about her son's formative early years of education, they were just stereotypically over-emotional and over-assertive protests.

In primary school, Tyrell faced similar challenges. The nursery was connected to the primary, and so his reputation preceded him (as did his mother's). His mum repeatedly asked the school about assessing his needs, but, again, her frustration at inaction was interpreted as rudeness.

Tyrell managed to struggle through primary, thanks to staff who were able to dedicate significant time to building a relationship with him, and supporting him. This was not the case in secondary school. On his first day, Tyrell wore the wrong socks. His mum hadn't realized he could only wear the school's branded socks. He was sent home before even starting his first lesson. The school didn't check he had keys, or that anyone would be home. A passer-by found him crying in the street, managed to contact his mum, and took him home.

There were 180 pupils in a year in Tyrell's new school. He was told he could speak to his head of year about any concerns, but he only really saw the head of year when they were barking at students to stay in silence during their thrice-daily 'line-ups'. So he didn't really talk to them.

Fixed-term exclusions quickly accumulated for Tyrell. He was seen as disruptive, and told that he did not have the right attitude for success in the school. Threats began to be made about permanent exclusion. Tyrell felt like every inconsequential infraction of the rules was treated as some great transgression, and he began to resent the school and its staff. His mum tried to encourage him to keep his head down, but struggled to hide her own disdain for how the school was treating him.

In Year 10, Tyrell's youth worker spoke with his mum, and found out about the history of failed attempts to convince schools to assess his needs. Working with the local council's Special Educational Needs advisory service, the youth worker and Tyrell's mum managed to convince the school to pay for an Education, Health and Care Plan assessment. Tyrell's mum was happy, but couldn't help thinking the assessment could have and should have been done about ten years prior.

Before the assessment could be completed, Tyrell was permanently excluded from the school. He brought Vaseline into the school, 'contraband', and was 'disrespectful' to staff when challenged about it. He was told that this was the straw that broke the camel's back.

Tyrell was moved to the one Pupil Referral Unit that served the whole borough. It didn't offer the GCSEs he most enjoyed in mainstream school – the ones that were going to be most important for the BTEC course he wanted to do, and for the career he wanted to get into.

Sliding in and out of worklessness can leave young people feeling infinitely replaceable. They often form 'the most expendable, disposable and exchangeable parts of the economic system' (Bauman, 2000, p 152), or simply do not feel that they are given a chance by employers at all (Billingham et al, 2018). An 'abject feeling of worthlessness' can accompany unemployment for young people (Tyler, 2013, p 200), as they develop an unsettling sense that they are not needed. Those who become subject to the 'workfare' regime in modern Britain, in which increasing numbers are punitively compelled into the workforce, can live a life punctuated by 'various degradation rituals' (Bond and Hallsworth, 2017, p 75; see also Chase and Walker, 2013, p 746). Particularly given the stigma attached to worklessness in contemporary Britain, the experience of unemployment can have profound effects on a young person's sense of recognition and impact, personal significance, and competence. Research has shown that the 'scarring effects' of being out of work are particularly acute among young men and those from working–class backgrounds (Wright et al, 2019).

Even for those who have a job, the world of work can be another institution which undermines, rather than builds up, a young person's sense of mattering. Currie (2016, p 61) describes the deeply belittling effects of what he calls 'marginal work', and emphasizes the effect this can have on young people's sense of themselves, given the importance of 'our place, or lack of one, in the world of productive work'. Ellis (2016, pp 27–8) gives us a sense of what the marginal work undertaken by many young people can look like: 'expendable, low-paid, menial, with a determinate contract length, de-unionized and vulnerable to the whims of a mutative post-industrial economy that may suddenly render them obsolete in the name of "efficiency" or "cost-effectiveness"'. In our 'hourglass' economy, insecure and poorly paid work has proliferated, and youth-led research has found that this work is often 'unrewarding, low-paid and boring' (Lunghy et al, 2019, p 25). The worst kinds of job are little more than 'a long line of daily humiliations' (O'Hara, 2020, p 204), amounting to an 'appalling assault on a person's sense of dignity and self-respect' (Bloodworth, 2019, p 5). A recent paper has analysed the effects of precarious work on young people in Britain using the concept of mattering, concluding that such work 'signals to employees that they are insignificant and disposable, rather than bolstering their sense of mattering' (Soppitt, Oswald and Walker, 2021, p 14).

Precarious work is particularly prevalent among young people. For example, there is a stark disparity between the rates of young people on zero hours contracts, as compared to those in older age groups. In April–June 2020, the rate of employed young people (aged 16 to 24) on zero hours contracts was 10.8 per cent, accounting for around 389,000 young people. This compared to just 1.5 per cent of employed 35- to 49-year-olds on zero hours contracts (ONS, 2021d). Moreover, the general trend is clear: in October–December 2013 the rate of zero hours contracts for employed young people (at just 5.7 per cent) was around half of what it was in 2020. While some young people on zero hours contracts might welcome their associated flexibility, research indicates that the most-reported reason for accepting this type of employment is that it is 'the only work available' (TUC, 2021). The inadequate and relatively insecure nature of young people's employment was compounded by the impact of COVID-19. In the UK, as of May 2020, 33 per cent of young people had either been furloughed or lost their job entirely, compared to 18 per cent of all employees (Gustafsson, 2020).

All of this amounts to a structural harm which undermines both the need fulfilment and the subjective well-being of young people across the country. Unemployment and low-paid work pose a clear threat to young people's subsistence needs, as many struggle to earn enough money to secure a roof over their heads, pay household bills and put food on the table (Galfalvi et al, 2020). The detrimental effects of poor working conditions and low pay on the subjective well-being of young people are well evidenced by a burgeoning international literature, which shows that stress, sleeping problems, anxiety, depression and loss of self-confidence are all commonly reported problems for those in insecure work (Lewchuk, 2017; Apouey et al, 2020). Increasingly, young people find themselves competing against one another to obtain jobs for which they are overqualified, for employment contracts that are short term, insecure or attract very low levels of pay and for 'dead-end' jobs that offer limited if any opportunity for career advancement. The effects of all this on a young person's sense of mattering almost go without saying: whether a data point in an enormous job centre computer system or a casual employee of a gargantuan multinational company, it is easy to feel miniscule and inconsequential.

Housing and homelessness

Property in this country has become something like gold bullion for the wealthy, reliably retaining or increasing its value at a time when rates of profit and returns on investment are declining in many other areas of national economies (Atkinson, 2020). As homes are purchased for profit, particularly in London, harmful effects ripple out through communities. Schelhase (2021) has shown, for instance, how the 'systemic social harms of current housing policies' (Schelhase, 2021, p 450) entail widespread 'inadequate housing conditions', which 'not only affect health outcomes, that is, physical health and mental health, but also educational attainment and opportunities later on in adulthood' (Schelhase, 2021, p 447). These harms derive from international capital flows, national policy making and complex systemic features of the contemporary property market, but their effects have immediate daily potency.

A remarkably high number of children and young people in this country experience homelessness or inadequate housing. In 2018–19, for instance, 71,500 young people in England approached their local authority due to homelessness or risk of homelessness, and over half were not supported into housing (Bowen-Viner, 2021, p 159). The number of children and expected children living in temporary accommodation in England rose year on year from 69,460 in the final quarter of 2011 to 129,380 in the first quarter of 2020 (Ministry of Housing, Communities and Local Government, 2020). The majority of these children live in London – an estimated 90,700 as of 2020. European Union Statistics on Income and Living Conditions (EU-SILC) show that household overcrowding rates are also a significant problem in the UK. For those living in poverty, the highest overcrowding rate was associated with 16- to 19-year-olds, one in four of whom experienced household overcrowding (Eurostat, 2020). Figures from 2010 (the last year in which data was collected) revealed that household overcrowding rates in London vary significantly by borough. Richmond upon Thames and Sutton, for example, had overcrowding rates of just 2.5 per cent and 3.4 per cent respectively, compared to Tower Hamlets' and Brent's overcrowding rates of 11.2 per cent and 12.1 per cent (ONS, 2010).

The effects of all this on young people can be devastating. Those at risk of homelessness or who become homeless often experience forms of trauma which affect attachment and relationship building, emotional regulation, cognition and their sense of self-efficacy (Bowen-Viner, 2021, p 164). In addition, a substantial body of evidence demonstrates the adverse effects that living in temporary and overcrowded accommodation can have on children and young people, which include causing heightened levels of psychological distress, anxiety, depression and difficulty sleeping (Harker, 2007; Evans et al, 2009). The fact that our housing system allows children and young people to grow up without access to decent and secure housing, therefore, marks both a failure to adequately fulfil their subsistence needs and serious neglect of their subjective well-being.

For many young people in inner cities, the most tangible effects of our dysfunctional housing system are felt in their experience of gentrification. This can mean eviction for many, or at least a vertiginous sense that it will not be possible for them to stay in the neighbourhood they call home once they become adults (Billingham et al, 2018, p 56). Even if they are able to remain in their community, some young people experience what Butcher and Dickens (2016, p 800) call 'affective displacement': an undermined sense of belonging, due to feeling progressively displaced by other, wealthier demographic groups. This feeling was powerfully expressed in Billingham, Isaacs and Oyeleye's (2018, p 56) study in North East London: young people reported that they 'don't belong any more', that 'the area is not really ours anymore' and that 'Hackney is no longer the Hackney I grew up in'. Related to this can be a profound sense of political disempowerment: 'they kinda are leaving us behind ... a lot of people are being left behind, if you're not rich, if you're not middle class or above that, the government ain't really helping you' (Billingham et al, 2018 pp 56–7).

Our property market structurally devalues the accommodation needs of great swathes of the population. For some young people, this means a lifetime of navigating insecure housing, the roof above their head and the floor beneath their feet seeming perennially precarious. Those worst-affected by this experience are growing up in major cities such as London, where they can also witness the extravagant luxury of those with eye-watering wealth. To be homeless among mansions is a particular kind of pain, one which is all too familiar for far too many of our young people today.

***

Some young people are barely affected by the social harms considered in this chapter. Those who are most structurally privileged by our political economy and society may live lives free of their influence. For others, though, these harms pockmark everyday social experience. Many individual young people and communities in Britain experience a complex concentration of these harms: a recent analysis of young people's lives in London, for instance, described how interconnected issues related to poverty, housing, (un)employment and reduced public service provision has left young people experiencing 'cycles of insecurity' which sharply diminish their sense of efficacy and agency (O'Loughlin and Sloam, 2022). This historically entrenched form of inequality represents one of the most profound challenges that we face as a society, and has a raft of devastating symptoms, including the increased prevalence of interpersonal violence in some places and among some people (as we will explore in the next chapter). In the following section we present a final, extended composite case study (Box 4.3), which brings to life many of the issues discussed earlier.

Box 4.3: Composite Case Study 3 – A structurally diminished young life, seeking mattering 'on road'

The subject of this composite case study is Mark. Our narrative here will centre on the ways in which Mark's experience of the structural harms outlined in this chapter affected his sense of mattering throughout his young life, and thus reoriented his thoughts, emotions and actions. We will also attempt to approximate in our description the concatenation of cultural influences that any one young person is likely to encounter in 21st century London as they seek to establish what is meaningful to them, and to what and to whom they wish to matter – exemplifying the kind of complex self-narrative formation described in Chapter 3.

Mark is 17. For all of his life his parents have been both resource poor and, closely tied to this, time poor. His father works in security and his mother in care homes. Both are forced to work long, irregular hours to keep the rent paid. Were it not for this financial necessity, they would love to dedicate more of their attention to their children (Mark has a 20-year-old older brother). They provide all the nurture and care that they can, but the pressure of their lives is felt by their offspring as varying forms of emotional absence or discord, depending on the day.

Mark had a largely positive experience of primary school. His school was small, familial, and felt woven into the community. His teacher and the school's inclusion staff got to know his parents, and supported his family in various everyday ways through the years, including helping with food when money was particularly tight. They provided this help in a way which was carefully crafted to convey respect and to maintain dignity.

Once he was in secondary school, life got more complicated for Mark. The school felt huge – it had over 2,000 pupils – and Mark did not absorb the same daily warmth he had experienced in primary education. By his second year of secondary school, his mum became increasingly convinced that he might have additional educational needs. She knew about it from her job, and felt Mark should be assessed, given the extent to which he was struggling with reading and writing, relative to his peers. She wrote to the Special Educational Needs Coordinator (SENCo) multiple times, but didn't get very far, and didn't have the time or headspace to pursue it further. The SENCo at Mark's school was an English teacher who had a 70 per cent teaching timetable and was expected to cater for all the additional needs of the students in the remaining 30 per cent of their time in school.

Around this time, Mark began to feel that he was treated differently in school due to the colour of his skin. Most of the time it was subtle, and he could not put his finger on what exactly was happening, but he felt prejudged, and it seemed to always be students who looked like him and sounded like him who got in most trouble. He became frustrated, experiencing both academic difficulties and increasingly frequent struggles with the school's disciplinary regime. Spells in isolation became more common. There was a 'wall of fame' in a prominent location in the school, celebrating the academic achievements of particular students, which was mentioned by teachers frequently – individualized competition was encouraged actively and intensely. It was painfully clear to Mark that he had precious little hope of ever making that display.

When Mark was in Year 9, the family was forced to move. Their private landlord hiked the rent, saying that he had kept it below market rate for a long time, but now that property prices were rising all across their part of town, the family were naïve not to expect the rent increase. Unable to afford the increased rent, Mark's family was placed in temporary accommodation, thankfully not too far from their previous home, but it was overcrowded, and not in good condition. It was right next to what Mark called the 'trendies market', where every weekend he saw wealthier local residents buying meals and clothes which he thought were inconceivably expensive.

Mark's behaviour in school became more disruptive. Staff knew of the family's difficulties, so made a referral to social care, who allocated a family support worker to them. Dedicated though she was, Mark's family was one in an ever-increasing list of 'cases'. Once, when struggling to identify better housing options for the family, the worker became frustrated with Mark, who she felt was being critical of her. She told him all about the extent of her caseload, in something of a desperate diatribe. It was wounding for Mark to hear this – he had thought she deeply cared about his family, but this made him doubt it.

His first fixed-term exclusion was for breaching what seemed a particularly pedantic rule, but the school said it tipped them over the edge, into the belief that his behaviour was intolerable. Mark's mum had to stay off work for the three days he was excluded. She was reprimanded by her boss and her pay was docked. At the reintegration meeting in school, Mark's mum was stressed and upset. She raised the issue of additional needs, again arguing that an assessment should be done. The deputy head was dismissive, and he advised her not to become so 'confrontational'. Mark noticed his mum shrink in her chair.

When he reached 15, Mark spent increasing amounts of time outside of the home. It was too small to spend much time in, without getting into some kind of argument with his brother or parents. He became close with a group of friends on his block. They kicked a ball about in the cage, spoke about girls, sent funny memes to one another on social media and shared dreams for the future.

Mark knew he wasn't headed to achieve well in his GCSEs. Having had a couple more fixed-term exclusions, his emotional engagement with school was diminishing. He felt disrespected and like none of the staff really knew him; his peers felt similarly. He didn't want to disappoint his parents, so kept his head down as much as possible, but he wasn't going to exert himself towards a goal which seemed futile, especially given his ongoing struggles with literacy.

He wanted to make money more than he wanted good grades. He pounded the labyrinthine passages of Westfield shopping centre in Stratford, CV in hand, willing to take any job going. He was nervous doing this, but felt it was what he should do. In most of the shops he was treated with indifference; in some with outright bafflement; in a few with disdain. Mark knew how he could make money, quite quickly and quite easily, and he knew the boys on his estate to speak with. One of his mates, who went to the local Pupil Referral Unit, could get him an introduction, and then he'd be 'in'. He resisted this option as long as he could, but eventually he relented. Mark felt like he'd entered a different kind of community within his community, one he'd always been equally tempted by and wary of. He quickly developed bonds with the boys he started dealing drugs for and with – bonds which felt meaningful. It seemed clear who was on the fringes and who was on 'top' within the group, and how the messy quest for respect could be navigated within it. The group's collective sense of significance and potency was sharpened by their rivalry with those occupying neighbouring blocks. Mark took home his earnings and gave much of it to his mum. His parents sometimes argued about whether this should continue, but they needed the money.

Mark's life became increasingly spent 'on road' (Gunter, 2017), among both his old friends from the cage and the newer group of associate-'colleagues' he'd met through dealing. He felt invested in this world, and it became a significant 'arena for recognition and approval' (Vigil, 1988, p 230), particularly because it was a place of 'strong emotional attachments' with 'surrogate kin' (Vigil, 1988, pp 159, 168). He felt that he'd made a decision, consciously or otherwise, to take this path. In his developing self-narrative, other aspects of life had been drained of value; in his view of the world, his real place was here among his peers: the rest of his existence, as he saw it, was relatively colourless, bereft of emotional heft, of thrill, of meaning. On road is where he felt he could matter – this is where he could be socially valued, form meaningful bonds and be a consequential agentic force.

In among all this, Mark is grappling to establish which ideals and principles could help guide his life. One of Mark's favourite songs is called 'Normal', by Potter Payper, which reflects this struggle. The lyrics are somewhat list-like; a description of all the things that the artist considers to be usual and unusual in his community, producing a rich account of common experiences and drives in marginalized young people's lives. This includes him saying 'I blow smoke like "fuck feds"/It's normal/I stay with some bad boys they'll call on you'; 'Donny opened his mouth/That ain't normal'; 'You can bang or get banged on/It's normal' – Mark recognizes and sympathizes with these anti-authority sentiments, and what feel like narrations of fairly common incidents that he'd seen locally himself. Some other lyrics from the song, which are different in tone, also resonate with Mark: 'We lay on them bunk beds'; 'They just tryna keep mouths fed'; 'Trying to get this money. ... Better keep that for your mum's sake'; 'Owning your own house ... that ain't normal'. These tales of poverty accompany images of capitalistic striving, of the kind Mark has engaged in: 'We struggle for success/Break bread when we cut cheques'; 'Money truer than religion'; 'Rap game like the trap game/No difference/Everyone trying to make a living'. In the video for the song, this last line is accompanied by black-and-white footage of a trading floor, seemingly Wall Street or the London Stock Exchange. Talk of valour in fighting is illustrated with an image of Mohammed Ali. And then, when discussing people 'bumping heads', there are shots of stags in the wild; when discussing people just needing to get 'mouths fed', it's a pack of lions on-screen. The refrain, sung by Maverick Sabre, includes '"I'm never gonna walk away/I pray to see another day/Lord I know that I've been sinning/But I'm trying to walk away'. Sabre grips the bars of an estate football cage as he sings: he's trapped and wants to get away, but is loyal to his area. Religion is dismissed – there's also a shot of a Bible discarded on the floor – but he talks of sinning and praying. Animal instincts, capitalistic desires, poverty and financial necessity, rebellion and anti-authority sentiment are all woven together in what is 'normal'.

Though he would be unlikely to put it this way, Mark likes the song because it contains more wisdom about the kaleidoscope of shifting motivations and hopes that push and pull young people in marginalized communities than any earnest tract about hapless gangs of consumerist fiends or any romantic tale of rebellious outcasts. Having been brought up Catholic, Mark has an ambiguous relationship with religion, like the singers seem to. The song seems to powerfully depict how a person can try to reject and dismiss a certain worldview and conceptual universe, yet still be stuck in its language and its principles. Religion is cast aside, but, as repeatedly emphasized by Sabre, there's substantial turmoil caused by reflection on sin. Mark knows of this feeling. Religions are broad creeds with which people have complicated, tense relationships. This can produce highly contrasting motivations – Catholicism alone has produced both staunch conservatives and socialist liberation theologists; it has acted as both a social anaesthetic and 'the ideological underpinning for countless rebellions' (Scott, 1990, p 68). Capitalism has a similarly ambiguous force on individual actions, encouraging both the outrageous profiteering of the most hedonistic drug dealers and the quiet diligence of those who work for low pay with incredible discipline – proletarian exponents of the Protestant work ethic, perhaps, which Weber (2010 [1905]) famously argued was key to the birth of modern Western capitalism. Among Mark's friends, he sees both: one of his mates is now a store manager at a local card shop, earning a fraction more than when he worked the tills; another spends most of his time making much larger sums of money through illicit means while displaying his latest purchase of designer goods over various social media platforms.

We'll leave Mark there. Hopefully, this composite case study has provided an illustration of the themes explored in this chapter. Young people like Mark strive to matter within the worlds that are significant and meaningful to them. They endeavour to be recognized and respected by the people whom they value, and seek to feel that they are consequential: that their thoughts and actions make a difference, in some perceptible way. They do not passively absorb cultural or ideological influences – such influences are never 'unproblematically internalised' (Kashima, 1997, p 16). In any young person's complex self-narrative, they ascribe meaning and worth to different aspects of their experience, in a constant process of working out, which is never fully worked out. They form themselves differently within the different parts of their social ecology; they are a different person at home, at school and with peers. Their attempts to make sense of and to matter in these different settings are frequently in tension: a young person like Mark wants to maintain the love and pride of his parents, but knows that to earn similar forms of social significance 'on road' would necessitate quite different kinds of speech, gait, appearance and action. In Mark's case, all of these considerations, thoughts and emotions are shot through with the daily effects of structural harms: it would not be possible to account for his attitudes, decisions or beliefs without reference to their everyday influence. His experience of harms in the past and in the present repels and attracts him to certain places, people and ideals, affects his global sense of mattering and has embedded within his emotional subconscious forms of frustration and anger, shame and pride, hope and despair which play a formative role in shaping his choices.

Harm and subjectivity, structure and agency

> Structural inequalities do not exist 'out there', but are part of our internal worlds, entrenched in the fine grain experiences of those on the margins … a messy amalgamation of structural inequalities and contradictions operate continuously in their lives, working to devalue these young people and inhibit the development of meaningful selfhoods.
>
> Bakkali, 2019, pp 1317, 1329

Bakkali is drawing attention to a crucial point here, reinforcing the driving argument of this chapter. What he refers to as 'structural inequalities' and 'contradictions' broadly adhere to our definition of structural harms, and one of our central contentions – echoing Bakkali – is that structural harms are not some 'background' feature of young people's lives, some inert context for their agency: such harms do not exist 'out there'. Structural harms directly intrude on people's everyday existence, disfiguring their days and altering their life trajectories, contributing to their routine social suffering. Structural harms do not overwhelm individual agency, or remove the moral responsibility from young people for their actions, but we will have little hope of understanding or explaining those actions if we do not attend to the influence of structural harms on their daily lives. These kinds of harm are not just impediments which young people encounter in their temporal present: structural harms from earlier in life are carried by young people in their psychological architecture, and the anticipation of such harms in the future can be a significant influence on young people's choices and actions. As other theorists have put it, these harms are 'seamlessly woven into the fabric of everyday life' (Kotzé, 2019, p 83), and can be 'silent', appearing normal or even natural (Vorobej, 2008, p 93).

In this chapter we have sought to demonstrate that, as well as a descriptive concept which helps us to identify what is injurious to people, social harm can be an analytical tool for understanding their lives. When brought into connection with the concept of mattering, analysing the effects of social harms on young people can provide us with a different perspective on their experiences and actions to that found within more orthodox sociological, anthropological or criminological approaches. We do not intend to suggest that looking at young people's lives through a social harm lens is 'better' than the alternatives, but we do wish to argue that it can illuminate aspects of young people's experience which can be somewhat neglected within other theoretical traditions. It is not a matter of mutual exclusivity: investigating social harms can be compatible with and complementary to other forms of analysis.

Academic accounts of human action, including those centred on the lives of young people, tend to involve a theory of structured agency – an explanation of how individual actions are encouraged, enabled, constrained and channelled by social structures. Discussions about the most fruitful ways to theorize the relationship between social structure and agency have been ever-present in social theory at least since the mid-1850s, when Marx made his famous remark that people make their own history, but not in circumstances of their own choosing (Marx, 1978 [1852], p 595).

Structure/agency approaches to explaining human action can have two limitations which we would argue may be addressed by incorporating social harm analysis of the kind expounded earlier. Firstly, they can tend to provide somewhat 'cold' explanations for how social structures enhance, inhibit or direct individual agency, and are less well-equipped to aid understanding of how social structures can be harmful – how they can undermine people's subjective well-being or restrict access to basic human needs, for instance. To take three particularly influential thinkers as brief examples: in Giddens' (1986) account of how social structures affect action through constraining social 'rules' and enabling social 'resources'; in Bourdieu's (for example, 1979) account of how social structures influence behaviour through their internalisation into individuals' deeply held habitual ways of life (or 'habitus'); and in Foucault's (for example, 1977) more complex account of the various insidious means through which discourses shape individual subjectivities, a powerful causal framework is presented which helps to explain how social structures guide actions, and how those actions cumulatively reproduce social structures. They are less helpful, however, for providing insight into harmful experiences.

This is an external rather than an internal critique: none of these theorists sets out to explain or describe harm, as they all – in different ways – tended to avoid explicit normative judgements about what constitutes the 'good life' or human flourishing (though Habermas, 1987 provides a case for Foucault's 'cryptonormativism' – compare Isenberg, 1991; Kolodny 1996; King 2009). Like many ideas which refer to the most important features of human life, the concept of harm is intrinsically both descriptive and evaluative (Sayer, 2005, p 215; Pemberton, 2015, p 33; see Chapter 2). Deciding what does and does not constitute harm inevitably involves ethical and metatheoretical judgement, but it can also pave the way for careful analytical accounts of how specific harms affect individuals' thoughts, emotions and actions. Such accounts can reckon with the internal and external complexity and richness of any individual's life, thus going beyond descriptions of how their agency was structurally guided, the latter of which can imply an inert form of causal nudging, seeming to flatten the psycho-social depth of real people.

A focus on the interactions between harm and action immediately necessitates a 'warmer' account of human life, including the ways in which various social harms can prompt causally significant emotions such as rage and shame, or foster life-altering experiences such as denigration or recognition, which can shape an individual's sense of mattering. If we look at human lives by investigating the complex, interwoven effects of various interpersonal and structural harms on people's inner worlds, relationships and actions, we can develop a richer account than if we focus our analysis only on the 'cold' causal dynamics of structure and agency.

The second relevant limitation of structure/agency accounts of subjectivity and action is that they tend to involve the prioritization and foregrounding of one level of analysis, be it the level of immediate interaction, of group behaviour or of national political economy. Such accounts often describe a number of social forces at different scales, ranging from interpersonal relationships to national trends, but then focus their analysis overwhelmingly on one particular level: on the significance of micro-level interactions between individuals within groups, meso-level analysis of areas or neighbourhoods or macro-level explanation of political economy, for instance. To give examples from the criminological literature, writers such as Katz (1988) and Collins (2008) explicitly focus on individual actions and interactional dynamics, arguing for the causal priority of these levels of analysis over the structural 'background'. Criminologists who have focused in different ways on the phenomenon of gangs, on the other hand, such as Hallsworth (2013), Pitts (2013) or Harding (2014), tend to focus on the neighbourhood level, recognizing the importance of both socioeconomic structures and individual psychologies, but tending to relegate these to the theoretical background; as Stephen Crossley (2017, p 67) has put it, they can tend to focus on 'the intricacies of "street life" to the detriment of a longer or "thicker" construction of the factors and forces that influence that "street life"'. Theorists whose work mobilizes a wider historical and social scope, such as Young (2007), by contrast, can seem to portray macro-level social forces as of predominant causal significance, relative to more granular levels of social existence.

There are numerous examples of sophisticated 'multi-level analysis' within criminology (see Fraser, 2017), which provide compelling accounts of the complex interactions between social structures at different levels and scales, and how these affect individual and group agency (these are explored further in Chapter 5). Even these, however, can tend to foreground the actions of individuals within the context of proximal norms: when describing how and why young people behave the way they do within particular places, it is local cultural codes and ways of being which are given primacy. In such accounts, individual young people strategically negotiate the social rules and resources of their neighbourhoods, as these have been shaped by higher-level historical change at the levels of the city, the nation and the globe, but the specific derivation of these rules and resources seems to be bracketed out once the analysis 'zooms in' on individual and group actions. Young people's experience within different social fields is explored, including the ways in which they make meaning of and ascribe significance to particular actions, attitudes and dispositions, but less attention is paid to the particular ways in which identifiable systems, institutions and structures harm or enrich their lives on a daily basis.

By contrast, approaches which mobilize the concept of social harm as an analytical tool can explore the daily effects of both interpersonal harms – the harmful interactions within a person's biography – and of structural harms – the harmful institutions, systems or policies affecting a person, which will have their origins in the depths of history or in the immediate past, in the local vicinity or in global processes. Social harms neither fade into an explanatory background nor entirely overwhelm individuals' agency; the concept invites us to explore in detail how various different kinds of harm penetrate into neighbourhoods, institutions, social groupings and inner worlds, and the different kinds of effects this can have. To use Bakkali's language once more, these harms are never 'out there', but are of daily significance, as our account of 'Mark' illustrated. If social harms at different scales become an object of analysis in themselves, rather than just a secondary concern, or a somewhat flattened context for action, it becomes possible to explore in more granular depth how such harms have come to be, and how they are sustained, as well as the cumulative effects that they have on individuals and communities.

We do not wish to dismiss the value of more conventional structure/ agency explanations, but to suggest that the concept of social harm could prove a fruitful complementary lens through which to examine young people's lives, providing insights which complement structure/agency accounts. The felt influence of different social harms on an individual life will be varyingly immediate and interpersonal or slow and systemic; obvious and tangible or subtle and pernicious. The explosive damage of a near-fatal gunshot and the gradual, cumulative denigration of institutional prejudice are harms which could feature in the same individual life, inviting a careful, nuanced analysis of how each kind of social injury can affect that life, be it the person's health, emotional make-up, life trajectory or sense of mattering. As touched upon in Chapter 2, some social harms are blatant, others are 'calamities that patiently dispense their devastation while remaining outside our flickering attention spans' (Nixon, 2013, p 6). Such harms 'often go unseen', as they are 'deeply embedded in our everyday lives' (Canning and Tombs, 2021, p 114). If Contextual Safeguarding helps us to see the risks of interpersonal harm which exist beyond the family – in schools, neighbourhoods, peer groups and online (see Firmin, 2020) – a wider social harm lens could help us to see the institutional, systemic and policy harms which can have equally devastating effects on young lives (recent research on Contextual Safeguarding has incorporated an exploration of structural harms – see Wroe, 2021, especially). Approaches which interrogate structural harm could at best provide more critical purchase and psycho-social depth than structure/agency accounts, while avoiding the somewhat hyperbolic vagueness of accounts which describe structural 'violence' (for example, Žižek, 2009).

Returning to the example of 'Mark', it is conceivable that an academic explanation of the same life could be proffered in which all of the social harms he experienced are represented as little more than matters of background context; a study could focus, for instance, on the norms and values of the local semi-organized criminal group, ascribing primal causal significance to the rituals and conventions that group members create and test with one another, while ignoring the interpenetrating harms which substantially alter their individual and collective lives, intruding on Mark and his peers' daily existence. The opposite kind of account could also be constructed: an explanation of their lives which treats their cultural creativity and agency only as a kind of afterthought, a relatively inconsequential by-product of overwhelmingly powerful political-economic forces, the latter being described only in the abstract, on the macro scale. Our point is not that such accounts would be without value – detailed studies of cultural creation and (inter)national political economy will always be fruitful – but that an analysis of social harms in young people's lives offers a quite different perspective, which could be complementary to these other approaches, and which has arguably been underexplored in criminology, sociology and anthropology.

In the next chapter, we bring these ideas to bear on the subject of interpersonal physical violence between young people. As should be apparent from previous chapters, we believe that this violence is best understood in the context of the other kinds of harm experienced by young people in today's Britain. This is neither to downplay the importance of reducing violence in our society, nor to suggest a simplistic linear causal relationship between violence and other kinds of harm, but it is to stress that the serious violence which occurs between a relatively small number of young people cannot be understood as the product of some bounded 'youth world', nor of atomized 'problem families', as if young people's lives are wholly guided by a set of self-generated ideals, motivations, wants, needs and drives, or by household experiences which derive only from within its walls (we critique these simplifications directly and at length in Chapter 6). In the following chapter we build further on our argument that young people's lives can be helpfully illuminated if viewed as a struggle to matter; a struggle which is affected in many communities by a concentration of social harms.

Relative prevalence of social harms

Before we conclude this chapter, it is worth bringing together some key statistics on different social harms in young people's lives to highlight their relative prevalence (Figure 4.3).

Due to data constraints, neither the jurisdictions nor the age ranges are identical for the six different data points in Figure 4.3. Despite this, the graphic provides a clear visual representation of the relative rarity of violence committed by young people, when compared to other social harms affecting them. If anything, the data displayed could be taken to exaggerate the prevalence of violence, as it shows the rates of young people proceeded against for violence with injury and for homicide in London – a city with one of the country's highest rates of interpersonal violence. To be clear, we present this graphic not to minimize the gravity of interpersonal violence, but to ensure that it is set in an appropriate context: in the UK, social harms such as poverty, unemployment, school exclusion and precarious housing affect many more young people's lives than does serious interpersonal violence.

Conclusion

In this chapter, we have sought to pursue two entwined goals: to identify and describe some of the most significant social harms in the lives of children and young people today, and to vividly portray the extent to which these harms can have substantial effects on children and young people's thoughts, emotions and actions.

We discussed the pernicious effects of poverty and inequality; declining welfare support; harms of our education system; harms of our labour market; and harms of our housing market. All of these harms cause pain, pressure and powerlessness in the lives of children, young people, parents and families, undermining their need fulfilment, subjective well-being and sense of mattering. Through composite case studies, based on real-life

Figure 4.3: Key statistics indicating the relative prevalence of a sample of social harms, 2019

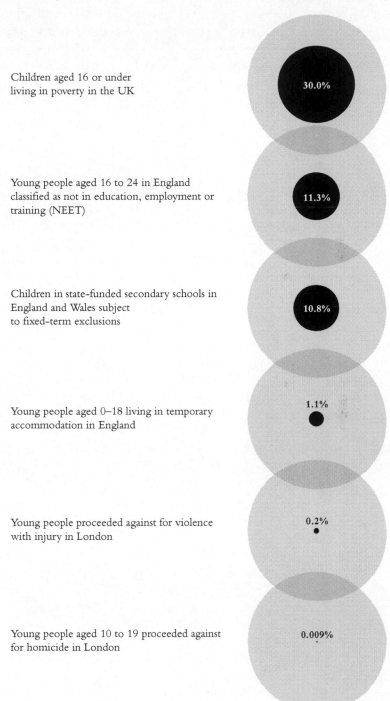

Children aged 16 or under living in poverty in the UK — 30.0%

Young people aged 16 to 24 in England classified as not in education, employment or training (NEET) — 11.3%

Children in state-funded secondary schools in England and Wales subject to fixed-term exclusions — 10.8%

Young people aged 0–18 living in temporary accommodation in England — 1.1%

Young people proceeded against for violence with injury in London — 0.2%

Young people aged 10 to 19 proceeded against for homicide in London — 0.009%

examples, we endeavoured to portray how they have these effects on young lives.

All of this paves the way for the next chapter, in which we will explore in far greater detail how harms such as those described in this chapter affect young people's thoughts and emotions in a way which can – in some cases – precipitate a very particular form of action: interpersonal violence.

5

Social Harm, Mattering and Violence

Introduction

It is perfectly possible – desirable, we would suggest – to both recognize the distortion, exaggeration and demonization which too often accompanies the portrayal of violence between young people (see Chapter 6), *and* to acknowledge that too many young people are committing acts of interpersonal violence against one another. There is no value in being squeamish about this violence. We are not 'against youth violence' because we wish to deny that there is violence occurring between young people, or because we believe there is any worth in being evasive or euphemistic about the brutal reality of this violence when it does occur, or about the gravity of its consequences.

We do believe, however, that it is impossible to get very far in understanding violence between young people if we only train our lenses sharply downwards, on an apparently bounded world of youth. Interpersonal violence of course requires agency – it requires a decision to be made, consciously or otherwise, and an action to be taken. Indeed, violence is not at all easy to undertake, it requires significant emotional and physical exertion: 'violence is hard' (Collins, 2008, p 20). But, following on from our analysis in the previous chapter, we would argue that, in order to understand how interpersonal violence between young people can become possible – to grasp the conditions which make violence more likely in certain places and particular times – we need to attend to the ways in which social harms intrude upon young people's everyday lives.

In Chapter 4, we tended to look upwards, towards the policies, systems and institutions which exert harmful forms of downward pressure on the lives of young people. In our discussion of mattering in Chapter 3, we looked outwards, from the perspective of the young – we began to explore the experience of subjectivity for young people in 21st century Britain. It is largely through the latter perspective that this chapter will proceed, focused on the small minority of young people who engage in acts of serious interpersonal violence.

We mobilize the conceptual tools explored in previous chapters to offer some reflections on the precipitating factors which can contribute to this kind of violence. We seek especially to draw out the plausible connections between social harm, mattering and violence, arguing that the combined social changes and social harms which we outlined in Chapters 3 and 4 create incendiary conditions in some communities, fostering the proliferation of structurally belittling experiences which make violence more likely. These conditions are not universal guarantors of violence: in all British neighbourhoods, interpersonal physical violence between young people remains the preserve of the few, not the many. But this does not mean that the incendiary conditions touch the lives of only those few. Everyone feels the heat, and many catch fire; their flames just burn differently. Self-violence, psychological collapse or – conversely – spectacular acts of cultural creativity, can all be symptoms of the inferno. We can ponder the precise determinants of the various shades of blaze, or we can focus on the social forces which set certain communities alight. We opt for the latter in this chapter, seeking to demonstrate how social harms such as those explored in Chapter 4, which are especially concentrated in poorer communities, can cumulatively form 'adverse social conditions which predictably breed violence' (Currie, 2016, p 89).

Writing in the collective first person, Cusset (2018) has argued that marginalized communities experience 'triple violence': violence 'upon us' from damaging forms of structural constraint and power, violence 'among us' between rival marginalized people and violence 'within us' – the 'psychic ravages' that the marginalized experience (cited in Jouai, 2018, p 95). In part, this book is an exploration of these three dimensions and their connections, though using different terms. Previous chapters have attended to the different forms of social harms visited 'upon' young people (in Chapter 4) and to the psycho-social tension 'within' them (in Chapter 3's discussion of the struggle to matter). In this chapter, we seek to show how those two dimensions of young people's experience are connected with violence 'among' young people. It is clear that the communities in which we find the most social harm – poverty and inequality, especially – are those in which we also find the most physical interpersonal violence: harm 'upon' young people correlates with violence 'among' them (see Chapter 1). The latter can thus often arguably be described as an 'implosion of harm' (Wroe and Pearce, 2022, p 89).

As explored in Chapter 4, there are many ways in which social harms can disfigure and diminish a young person's sense of mattering, and, as we will go on to explore in this chapter, there is a strong case to suggest that battling to matter can be a significant motivational factor precipitating interpersonal physical violence. Though no two violent acts are the same, what we see consistently across many studies of violence is a flawed expression of social presence: violence is a form of self-assertion, be it aggressive or desperate, driven by a yearning to achieve or maintain some kind of social significance, sense of power, or both. For a small minority of young people, violence can become a part of their struggle to matter. Or, more commonly, given what we know about who commits the vast bulk of interpersonal violence (see Chapter 1): for a small minority of young *men*, violence can become a part of their struggle to matter *as a man* (see, for example, Ellis, 2016; Dobash and Dobash, 2020). For them, the entanglement of mattering with masculinity can play a driving role in violence, both against other men and against women, as we will go on to explore.

This chapter is split into two sections:

- First, we briefly recount existing literature which explores different functions of violence, and which identifies the factors which appear to be most commonly associated with violence.
- Second, we provide a detailed account of the ways in which the struggle to matter can be a significant motivational driver in acts of violence, particularly in the context of communities and biographies characterized by a concentration of structural harms. We discuss psychological studies of the connection between mattering and violence, before attending to the additional complexity entailed by a *psycho-social* conception of mattering, including the knotty issue of the role of gangs in violence.

As we stated in the Introduction to this book, our endeavour in this chapter to make violence more *explicable* should by no means be read to suggest that we find violence *acceptable*. Making sense of violence is necessary for its reduction and prevention, but it does not imply exculpation of the violent. Explaining possible or likely precipitating factors for an act is very different to asserting that the actor is not morally responsible for it. Much more needs to be done to ensure that violence is not deemed acceptable, particularly among the young men who disproportionately inflict it. This task requires us to examine those factors which, as things stand, make violence *feel* acceptable – or make non-violence feel unacceptable – for far too many young men. This is the primary focus of what follows.

The functions of violence and the factors most commonly associated with it

The functions of physical interpersonal violence

Psychologists, criminologists, anthropologists and historians typically agree that no violence is truly 'senseless' (for example, Toch, 1972; Katz 1988;

Gilligan, 1997; Adshead, 2001; Batchelor, 2011; Squires, 2011; Sharpe, 2016). Behind every violent act, there is some kind of meaning, purpose or function, even if it may be obscure to the perpetrator themselves. The idea of 'mindless, depraved violence' is empirically groundless (Squires, 2011, p 150); violence is always 'deeply meaningful' (Batchelor, 2011, p 121). In some cases, a motive is relatively clear: violence may occur as part of a robbery, for instance, and it may be evident that the infliction of violence was functionally necessary for the perpetrator to secure the items they wished to steal. In other cases, motivations can be far more psychologically complex and deep seated, involving a greater degree of abstraction: some violent acts have more to do with what the victim represents to the perpetrator, and what the act of violence symbolizes for the perpetrator, than with the observable facts of the situation. As Toch strikingly put it, violence is sometimes 'between two symbols rather than between two real people' (Toch, 1972, p 121). Even where this is the case, the violence is clearly not 'senseless' – it has some sense, even if it would require fairly rigorous psychoanalysis to establish what kind of sense that might be. Though frequently in skewed and convoluted ways, those who commit acts of serious violence often believe their acts to be righteous or virtuous; the realization of some notion of justice (Katz, 1988; Cooney, 1998; Dobash and Dobash, 2020, p 41).

The binary distinction between 'instrumental' and 'expressive' functions of crime can be a helpful starting point for considering the functions of violence, but it begs more questions than it answers, and there is a clear need to go far beyond it if we are to gain any substantial insight. 'Instrumental' motivations relate to quite clear objective purposes, such as obtaining goods or enforcing a contract, 'expressive' ones relate in some way to the assertion of identity. There appears to be some consensus that violence is almost always 'expressive' to some extent: even violence undertaken as part of a highly organized criminal operation, relating to drug markets for instance, tends to involve social motivations, such as the pursuit of status or respect. In their study of people who have committed murder, Dobash and Dobash found that even among acts of violence which seemed driven solely by financial gain, many were 'highly emotional and reputational' (Dobash and Dobash, 2020, p 31). As Hallsworth put it, violence is often 'radically anti-utilitarian' (Hallsworth, 2013, p 130). This is borne out in various forms of statistical analysis: the Home Office has estimated that only 6 per cent of murders are related to organized crime (Hobbs, 2013, p 172; see Chapter 1), while academic researchers have concluded that over two-thirds of violence relates more to social factors than to instrumental issues (Cooney, 1998; Wilkinson, 2001). The significance of non-instrumental motivations is also demonstrated by the different rates of violence that occur in relation to different kinds of drug market: crack and heroin markets are associated with significantly higher rates of violence than other illicit drug markets (Hales, 2021). Hales highlights the importance of 'social reasons' in this, suggesting that the play of reputation, status and respect is especially volatile in these particular markets, which is potentially due to the especially 'expendable', 'vulnerable' and 'disadvantaged' backgrounds of those involved in the most risky roles in those specific trades (Hales, 2021, p 31). When looking at violence, then, we need to take 'a holistic approach to situated agency' (Brotherton, 2015, p 163), going far beyond analytical dichotomies such as the instrumental/ expressive binary. As we go on to explore in the next section, we would suggest that the struggle to matter can be one significant feature of the situated agency at play in many acts of violence.

Factors which have the strongest association with violence

Since time immemorial, there has been discussion about what makes some people more violent than others. Contemporary academic research on the topic has tended to focus on identifying the variables which are most strongly associated with violence, emphasizing the role of factors which operate on different scales, ranging from individual to societal levels. In a recent paper, for instance, Fraser and Irwin-Rogers (2021, p 5) produced the analysis captured in the diagram in Figure 5.1, which is based on international research undertaken by the World Health Organization and by Currie (2016), as well as the recent cross-party parliamentary commission on violence between young people in Britain which reported its findings in 2020 (Irwin-Rogers, Muthoo and Billingham, 2020).

Most individuals who perpetrate acts of serious violence have been influenced by a complex, cumulative combination of many of these factors, on more than one of the four levels indicated in the diagram – it is the dynamic interrelation between factors throughout a person's social ecology which has the most significant effect on increased propensity to violence (Fraser and Irwin-Rogers, 2021, p 5).

A few points are immediately apparent from Figure 5.1. Firstly, most obviously, the diagram includes factors which relate to very different kinds of problem: substance abuse, attitudinal proclivities and deficiencies in the education system, for instance, are social issues which differ greatly not just in their nature but in the kinds of human experience that they relate to – these three factors alone relate to physiological, psychological, institutional, political, cultural and economic problems. Secondly, it is notable how many of the factors identified in the diagram, across all four levels, have featured in the previous chapter of this book as social harms which affect significant numbers of young people in Britain: educational issues; household status and discord; poverty and inequality; lack of relationships with trusting adults; housing problems; child maltreatment; weak welfare provision; discrimination, prejudice and oppression. As we argued in Chapter 4, these

Figure 5.1: Factors associated with interpersonal physical violence

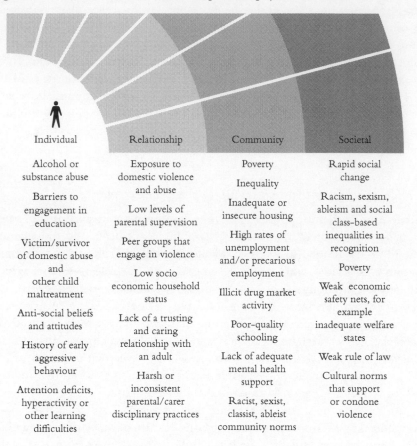

Individual	Relationship	Community	Societal
Alcohol or substance abuse	Exposure to domestic violence and abuse	Poverty	Rapid social change
Barriers to engagement in education	Low levels of parental supervision	Inequality	Racism, sexism, ableism and social class-based inequalities in recognition
Victim/survivor of domestic abuse and other child maltreatment	Peer groups that engage in violence	Inadequate or insecure housing	
	Low socio economic household status	High rates of unemployment and/or precarious employment	Poverty
Anti-social beliefs and attitudes	Lack of a trusting and caring relationship with an adult	Illicit drug market activity	Weak economic safety nets, for example inadequate welfare states
History of early aggressive behaviour		Poor-quality schooling	
Attention deficits, hyperactivity or other learning difficulties	Harsh or inconsistent parental/carer disciplinary practices	Lack of adequate mental health support	Weak rule of law
		Racist, sexist, classist, ableist community norms	Cultural norms that support or condone violence

Source: Adapted from Fraser and Irwin-Rogers, 2021, 2021, p 5

are forms of interpersonal and structural harm which are hugely damaging in and of themselves, in part due to their effects on children and young people's sense of mattering. This diagram makes clear that these harms can also be important features of the social conditions which are predictably breeding violence, as indicated by international research.

In what remains of this chapter, we will focus on these connections between social harms, the sense of mattering and violence. We do not present a grand theory of violence which attempts to explain any and all violence through these concepts. Despite some common determinants, such as those already identified, each act of violence is the product of a unique, complex cocktail of causes. What we seek to do in this chapter is to explore why and how the psycho-social struggle to matter may act as a kind of mediating factor between social harms, on the one hand, and the interpersonal violence committed by a small minority of young people (almost always young men, predominantly in a handful of urban areas), on the other. We know there is a correlation between the experience of social harm and the perpetration of interpersonal violence. We also know that there are some specific experiences, such as school exclusion, which both correlate with violence and have been shown to diminish a young person's sense of mattering. In the sections which follow, we explore the ways in which the struggle to matter may be implicated in the complex motivational environment which precipitates violence. This will not account for all the specificities, contingencies and complications involved in any individual act of violence, but we hope it may be a helpful explanatory lens through which to see how harmful social conditions can, in some cases, promote a kind of psycho-social tension which can increase the propensity to violence – especially in young men. In the course of our analysis, we will make use of both theoretical and empirical literature, from both the recent past and previous periods, focused on both the British context and – where relevant – the US. Not all of this literature directly refers to the concept of mattering. Our point is not that all of this literature has been unknowingly discussing mattering 'all along', but that the lens of mattering can add helpful richness, depth and complexity to existing accounts of violence, and can also be a helpful means to bring together ideas about violence from different eras and disciplines.

Social harm, the struggle to matter and the propensity to engage in violence

> Violence gives one a sense of counting, of mattering, of power. This in turn gives the individual a sense of significance. No human being can exist for long without some sense of his own significance. Whether he gets it by shooting a haphazard victim on the street, or by constructive work ... he must be able to feel this I-count-for-something and be able to live out that felt significance. It is the lack of this sense of significance, and the struggle for it, that underlies much violence.
>
> May, 1998, pp 36–7

In this section, we explore the role that the struggle to matter can play in the perpetration of violence. Mirroring how we structured our discussion of mattering in Chapter 3, we will explore the connections between mattering and violence in two steps, first looking at them through a *psychological* lens, before attending to the added complexity entailed by a *psycho-social* lens. In the former, we mostly (though not exclusively) mobilize literature from developmental and social psychology which explains the connections between an individual's experience of (not) mattering and their likelihood of committing violence. In the latter, we mostly mobilize anthropological and community research which helpfully complicates the picture by attending to the (often harmful) roles of gender, racialization, class and political economy in the relationship between mattering and violence. Through these two steps, we show how the struggle to matter can play a significant role in the situated agency of those who commit violent acts.

Through all this, we seek to add substantiation and illustration to May's point cited at the beginning of this section. In his words, to sense that you matter is to 'feel this I-count-for-something', and the urge to achieve this can be at play in different ways in different acts of violence, involving both of the two components of mattering: both social and causal significance; both recognition and impact. In some cases, it is a dire lack of one or both which can precipitate violence: attempting to obtain some kind of status, respect or reputation which you feel is sorely lacking, or striving to overcome some shameful sense of impotence, can both be drivers of violence. Echoing Lee Dema's words quoted in Chapter 3, it is striking how common it is in the literature on violence for perpetrators to be described as desperate to be 'someone' or 'somebody', and to escape the terror of being a 'nobody' or 'no one' (see, for instance, Vigil, 1988; Gilligan, 1997; Anderson, 2000; Lalander and Sernhede, 2011; Contreras, 2013; Ellis, 2016). In other cases, it can be the eagerness to maintain or to express a sense of mattering which can be at play: a keenness to protect an existing sense of social value, or to physically demonstrate an enlarged sense of power and agentic effectiveness. Undertaking acts of violence can, for some, provide a kind of psychological thrill, due in part to how it can experientially affirm a sense of mattering: in the moment of violence itself, the person can feel a palpable growth in their social importance among others (particularly if there is an audience, and if violence is a valued competence among their group – see Collins, 2008; Ellis, 2016). They can enjoy an intoxicating kind of potency in their domination of, or at least in their infliction of visible physical injury upon, another person. The concept of mattering can thus be a helpful tool for approaching both the motivational drivers and the phenomenology of violence, as we endeavour to demonstrate in the next section.

To reiterate: we do not mean to suggest that social harms are important only due to the role that they can play in making violence more likely, nor do we intend to suggest that the only significance to be found in the concept of mattering is in its relation to violence. As we hopefully made clear through preceding chapters, the various forms of harm and the particular sense of mattering that each young person lives with in this country are profoundly consequential issues in and of themselves, regardless of the role they may play in encouraging or exacerbating violence. The concepts of social harm and mattering do not need their relevance to the problem of violence to provide them with their importance; but we would argue that they can help to significantly illuminate that problem – as we hope to illustrate in what follows.

The psychology of mattering and violence

Violent escapes from insignificance, agentic impotence, shame and humiliation

A wide range of psychological studies have found that feeling you do not matter can play a significant role in the complex causal chains which lead to different forms of violent act (for example, Marshall, 2004; Elliott, 2009; Elliott et al, 2011; Chiodo et al, 2012; Kruglanski et al, 2014; Jasko et al, 2016; Edwards and Neal, 2017; Lewis, 2017; Flett, 2018). Jasko and colleagues, for instance, conclude from their study of 1,500 violence perpetrators that 'the use of violence can be in part predicted by a set of conditions that evoke a common psychological state of personal insignificance' (Jasko et al, 2016, p 13). There is substantial research literature connecting the struggle to matter with what Retzinger (1991) has called 'violent emotions'.

Where a lack of mattering does contribute to a proclivity to violence, this may sometimes lead to violence against the self, rather than towards others: Flett (2018, p 111) outlines the strong links that have been established between the sense of not mattering and self-harm, including suicide. Gender plays an important role here: there is some evidence to suggest that the experience of not mattering is more likely to prompt violence against others in men, and more likely to encourage self-violence or self-harm in women (May, 1998, pp 24–6; Flett, 2018, p 111).

Interpersonal violence, then, can be driven by kinds of psychological and emotional experience which appear to be especially intolerable to men. Both causal and social insignificance can be drivers of such intolerable experience: the sense of being unable to substantially affect the world around you or of being inconsequential to others can play a prominent role in precipitating violence. Centring on the former, Arendt put the point bluntly: 'impotence breeds violence' (Arendt, 1970, p 54). She argued that 'severe frustration of the faculty of action' was violence inducing (Arendt, 1970, p 73), and this connection between agentic impotence and violence has been frequently reiterated in more recent examinations of violence (for example, Gilligan, 1997, p 127; May, 1998, p 53; Žižek, 2009, p 69; Hobbs, 2013, p 176). Focused on young men in particular, Ellis (2016, p 107) cites numerous studies which found that feeling 'devoid of a sense of personal agency' can be a significant catalyst of their violence. In a recent essay on violence, Rose (2020, p 5) suggests that 'no human is spared confrontation with the limits of their own power'. As we will go on to explore further in the following section, though, some people experience far tighter constrictions on their power, and some people find this constriction more insufferable than others.

The urge to escape unbearable impotence is often entwined with the other aspect of (not) mattering – the need to escape a sense of social non-existence or insignificance. Currie (2016, p 60) suggests that violent acts can represent 'a desperate ... demand for respect and recognition' – they do not just function as personal proving grounds for the ability to assert one's power on the world, but can also be cries for social significance; a means for forcibly acquiring meaningful acknowledgement from others. This aligns with Toch's analysis of violent men, many of whom he suggested are engaged in violence either as a means to develop desirable kinds of self-image, which made them likely to *initiate* violence, or to defend an established self-image, which made them likely to violently *respond* to slights or provocations (Toch, 1972, p 141; see also Dobash and Dobash, 2020, p 58). As touched upon in Chapter 3, Vigil wrote similarly of the role that violence can play in helping men to feel that they approximate their 'ideal self' (Vigil, 1988, p 425). Using violence in this way appears to be more common among those who have experienced particular forms of childhood relationships – insecure attachment, violence in the home and/or early trauma can make a sense of worthlessness and inefficacy more likely, and can increase an individual's vulnerability to related feelings of shame and humiliation (for example, De Zuleta, 2001, p 56; Reece, 2021; Levell, 2022).

This connection between the sense of not mattering and emotions of shame and humiliation, as well as the latter's fundamental role in the psychology of violence, is borne out extensively in research. It seems clear that having a self-concept which involves feeling that you do not matter is closely tied with experiencing shame and humiliation. Kruglanski et al (2014, p 74) suggest that 'a loss of significance' and 'humiliation' are identical or inextricable experiences by using them interchangeably. Their study also suggests a correlation between feeling shame and feeling insignificance, as well as highlighting a link between those feelings and acting violently: 'the degree to which they felt shame in the last few weeks, and the frequency of their recently feeling insignificant were ... significantly correlated with engaging in violent actions' (Kruglanski et al, 2014, p 83). It seems intuitive that feelings of not mattering, shame and humiliation will very commonly co-exist: feeling that you are not significant and/or have no causal power, and so you do not 'count in the world', is likely to be accompanied by intense shame and humiliation. Ellis (2016, p 110) alludes to this by writing of 'shame-inducing marginality'.

Gilligan's (1997) abiding thesis is that, among all of the violent men he ever worked with clinically, shame was always a significant feature of their emotional lives, and always seemed causally connected to their violence (see also Gray et al, 2021, p 9). He writes at length about the 'personal insignificance and worthlessness' felt by these men (Gilligan, 1997, p 183), again suggesting a link between the experience of not mattering and a dangerous sense of shame and humiliation. (Like many writers, he tends to use shame and humiliation interchangeably.[1]) The causal link that he establishes between these particularly painful emotions and the perpetration of violent acts has been substantiated by a large number of more recent studies and ethnographies. Reflecting on his clinical work with young people in North London who have been involved in violence, Reece (2021) suggests that his clients frequently relate violent incidents to 'feelings of helplessness, being out of control, shame or worthlessness'. In an ethnographic account of almost identical themes, Ellis (2016, p 41) places great significance on the experience of humiliation in his portrayal of the life of 'Darren', a young man from the North of England. He writes that Darren had a 'painfully humiliating encounter' which contributed to a 'transformation within him': 'As Darren explained himself, he was "a nobody", but in the aftermath of this event he emerged from its shadow determined to become "somebody"' (Ellis, 2016, p 41). Darren's humiliation left him desperately, dangerously eager to assert his social presence. In a similarly rich account of one young English man's violence, Harris (2017, p 527) writes that 'Daniel' adopted 'a veneer of self-sufficiency to mask and defend against intolerable feelings of terror, shame and envy. ... Real or perceived slights gave rise to him unleashing his anger and hostility on those nearest to him who threatened to harm his fragile state.' Feeling shamefully insignificant can cause an aggressive, unpredictable brittleness.

Shame, humiliation and insignificance are potent emotional drivers in the interactional dynamics of violence, affecting both how an individual perceives other people and how they view themselves in relation to those others. Shame is experienced as a kind of 'attack coming from the other' (Retzinger, 1991, p 48), and the perceived source of shame tends to be seen as powerful, active and substantial (Ray, Smith and Wastell, 2003, p 124), while the person experiencing shame or humiliation feels little and insubstantial – as Katz (1988, p 27) put it: 'humiliation drives you down, in humiliation, you feel suddenly made small, so small that everyone seems to look down on you'. This shameful sense of relative insignificance – that you are small and impotent while the other is large and powerful – is key to understanding the skewed, subconscious notion of justice which can be a motivational force in violence: as Katz (1988, p 312) goes on to write, perpetrator-defined 'righteous slaughter' involves 'taking humiliation and turning it into rage' (see also Dobash and Dobash, 2020, p 70). Reece (2021) describes how it is necessary in much of his clinical work to help those who have perpetrated violence 'to get in touch with the pervasive feelings of shame and humiliation ... to limit the natural urge to project the shame onto others'. Returning to Toch's point referenced earlier in this chapter – if violence can be viewed as occurring between two symbols as much as two people, what the victim often symbolizes for the perpetrator is a pernicious sense of shame and diminishment: with or without substantial grounds, a violent man frequently views others as 'sources of possible humiliation and challengers of his worth' (Toch, 1972, pp 121, 102). This feeling can be mutual: violence is of course not always simply inflicted on a victim by a perpetrator, but can be entered into by two or more active combatants, in a parallel play of attempted violent dominance and humiliation. Even in clearer cases of one-sided violent agency, the person violently enforcing humiliation on another can often be motivated by their own previous experiences of similarly humiliating domination (Ellis, 2016, p 102). As this suggests, there can be a close symmetry between the emotional drivers and the emotional experience of violence.

Potency, domination and recognition in the phenomenology of violence

Violent acts are often driven by a deeply felt desire to escape a punishing sense of insignificance, shame and humiliation, then. For some people, enacting violence is experienced as a fulfilment of that escape: as a gratifying expression of potency and a reassuring guarantor of recognition.

Achieving the violent domination of another can be darkly pleasurable, especially where it represents the reassertion of power in someone who felt its shameful lack. Violence has been described as having an 'intoxicating' quality by multiple researchers (for example, Wilkinson, 2001; Hallsworth, 2013). Hallsworth, for instance, suggests that violence can entail the felt 'acquisition of power', which is an especially 'intoxicating medium' for those who 'otherwise have little of it' (Hallsworth, 2013, p 147). Flett (2018, p 64) connects this directly to mattering, referencing 'the sense of power and mastery inherent in dominant interpersonal behaviour'. This sense of power is more or less ubiquitous in writing on the emotional phenomenology of violence (for example, Katz, 1988; Anderson, 2000; De Zuleta, 2001; Contreras, 2013; Ellis, 2016). Enjoying the powerful agency inherent in violence has long been associated with masculinity: Jouvenel wrote in the early 1900s that 'a man feels himself more of a man when he is imposing himself and making others the instruments of his will' – it gives him 'incomparable pleasure' (quoted in Arendt, 1970, p 36). Interestingly, however, studies of violence in young women have identified something similar: the young women studied by Batchelor (2011, p 12) suggested that 'exhilaration, pleasure and power' were key to their experience of violence, and Robinson and Ryder (2013, p 432) found that the violence of girls in their study was 'an existential response to powerlessness'.[2]

In the experience of enacting violence, as much as in its psychological precipitation, the twin components of mattering are tightly entangled.

Gilligan and De Zuleta use identical language to one another when describing the feelings of 'pride and power' which can accompany acts of violence (Gilligan, 1997, p 182; De Zuleta, 2001, p 56), alluding to this close connection between obtaining a sense of power in the world and experiencing a kind of social pride. It is not enough to feel powerful; violence obtains its real emotional heft when that power gains social ratification, from either victim or 'audience'. Anderson conveys this dynamic with victims vividly in his accounts of a violent stick-up: the perpetrator wants the victim 'to recognise him and to acknowledge his power resources ... he wants his possession of that power to be recognised' (Anderson, 2000, pp 127–8). Collins provides a complementary account of how this pleasure of observed violent power can play out with different kinds of audience. When there is anyone directly witnessing violence, they can form a 'reputational goldfish bowl' (Collins, 2008, p 369) for the perpetrator, and even those whose violence is enacted alone, like hitmen, can enjoy 'special kind of reputational pride', the 'prestige of pure violent competence' (Collins, 2008, p 439). A hitman might seem to be a solitary being, but 'he is operating in a social community whose respect he cares about' (Collins, 2008, p 440). The play of social recognition and respect can be of great felt importance to those engaging in violence, even those who seem to be characterized by a cool professionalism. Brookman et al (2011, p 21) found in their study of 118 violence perpetrators that gaining a 'formidable reputation and status and respect' was centrally important for them. In her study of English young men who became violent in their teenaged years, Lewis writes of a subtly different, more relational kind of social significance, suggesting that violence can entail 'compelling someone to care for them', and making themselves 'a matter for concern' (Lewis, 2017, pp 1327–8). In a variety of ways, then, violence can enforce both social acknowledgement and emotional response from others, both reflecting and affecting the felt social significance of the combatants. Violence can be an immensely powerful, hugely destructive means to experience a kind of mattering, even if only fleetingly.

The psycho-social connections between social harm, mattering and violence

So far, so psychological. As emphasized in Chapter 3, however, the idea of mattering is most fruitfully understood as a *psycho-social* concept – a tool for reckoning with the interplay of 'internal' psychological complexity and 'external' social complexity. Though it is clear that the experience of mattering, and its lack, can play an important driving role in the individual and interactional psychology of violence, contenting ourselves with this level of analysis would not be consistent with the kind of approach we advocated for in Chapter 4. What we promoted there, and will pursue in this section, is a more holistic approach to situated agency (to borrow Brotherton's phrase once more) which recognizes the effects of interwoven social forces in young people's lives, and especially the consequential influence of harmful social structures.

The complex play of significance, power, domination, shame and humiliation described above does not occur in some kind of structural vacuum, in which isolated social interactions are the only causal forces, or in which these interactions are only affected by the emotional urges of atomized individual combatants. All individual and collective actions are affected by social structures – by norms, values, traditions, institutions, systems, policies; some of which may have structurally harmful effects – which constrain what is practically possible, define what is socially meaningful and ignite fiery emotional forces. Along these lines, in his critique of the 'zoomed-in' interactional focus of Collins (2008), Contreras makes the point that the psychological drives which enable violent acts are 'informed and sustained' by 'race, class and gender' in particular (Contreras, 2013, p 168). The split-second calculations, tensions and emotions within physically violent interactions are galvanized and vitalized by the structural predicaments of those who are violent.

If mattering plays a role in both the causal precipitation and the immediate phenomenology of violence, then, this can be understood only with reference to the manifold social forces and structural harms explored in previous chapters. The struggle for mattering experienced by any individual will be given form and flavour by the complex combination of these factors in their society, community, family and biography. We need to grasp the immediate psychological energies at play in acts of violence – as we have already done – but this cannot be detached from understanding the wider social processes which catalyse, mobilize and maintain those energies.[3] In particular, understanding how a young person could feel psychologically driven to violence, or could find the perpetration of violence psychologically tolerable, requires attentiveness to the everyday impact of structural harms, especially those which have a pernicious effect on the sense of mattering (see Chapter 4).

The diminishment felt by young people who experience such harm is daily and cumulative, as opposed to operating as either a vague 'background' constraint or an infrequent 'foreground' disturbance. It is not just experienced in moments, but carried through life. In line with Bakkali's (2019) idea of 'munpain', structural belittling is felt as ongoing erosion, abrasion or pressurizing force. It is not a harm which stabs like a knife or punches like a fist; it inflicts its social injury more like scraping sandpaper or a gently tightening vice, leaving people to feel the slow but steady wearing away or shrinkage of their dignity, worth and power.

This daily diminishment can have all manner of consequences, including the incitement of violent emotions, and can play a role in the situated agency of violence, which often involves some kind of socially meaningful assertion of significance and power, as we have seen – a kind of violent reach for mattering. We develop this perspective in the remainder of this chapter by bringing in different examples of these phenomena from anthropological studies and community research, aiming to show how this literature both can contribute to and can be enriched by the ideas of mattering and structural harm. In so doing, we address connections between harm, mattering and violence on three levels: the socio-historical, the biographical and the peer group.

'In search of respect' and in search of mattering: violence in structurally belittled communities

If violence were a matter only of individual psychology (or pathology), detached from societal influences, it would not be concentrated in particular communities at specific times in the way that it is (see Chapter 1). Research which investigates such communities draws attention to the intersecting forms of structural diminishment which affect their inhabitants, creating the kind of incendiary social conditions which ignite violent emotions. Community-level studies also draw out how the particular, localized operation of class, gender and 'race' infuses the agency of those who resort to violence. Common in this literature is an account of the ways that individuals and groups mobilize violence to acquire, compete over or maintain specific forms of socially meaningful significance and power: various concepts of respect, status and social or symbolic 'capital' are nigh-on ubiquitous in these studies (see, for example, Bourgois, 2003; Deuchar, 2009; Densley, 2013; Harding, 2014; Fraser, 2015), serving to represent the idiosyncratically classed, gendered and racialized kinds of mattering which are possible and desirable within particular milieus.

The predicament of living in these communities involves daily exposure to the kinds of structural harm which can erode a person's sense that they are recognized and valued, consequential and potent. Interwoven struggles for meaning, mattering and money in such places are tense and urgent, and can be both individual and interpersonal, solidaristic and competitive, caring and violent. Among some residents of marginalized neighbourhoods at some times, people support one another and collectively campaign for improvements in their conditions; for the social respect and power that they are due. In others, there is a violent internal struggle for material and moral resources. As we will go on to explore, the anthropological and community research which centres on these processes illustrates the play of structural harms, mattering and violent emotions within particular places at particular times, helping to demonstrate the value of these conceptual lenses for understanding how particular kinds of socio-historical condition can generate higher rates of violence.

Respect is often the central concept in sociological, anthropological and community literature on violence. Respect is political, economic, racialized, gendered and classed in complex ways within each society, affecting individuals' and groups' opportunities to obtain a sense of social worth and power, in a way which has profound consequences for their psychology, emotions and actions, including proclivity to violence. As Squires (2009, p 259) has put it, notions of respect are always 'psychologically nuanced, subtle, flexible and negotiated – and also potentially lethal'.

Bourgois's seminal study *In Search of Respect* (2003), discussed briefly in Chapter 3, has become something of a template for anthropological investigations of respect and violence in particular communities. He provides an eloquently analytical account of the particular meaning of 'respeto' for the poor and working-class Latin American community in East Harlem which he lived among in the 1980s, suggesting that it combined specific notions of autonomy, community and self-assertion within a dynamic social hierarchy shaped by age, kinship and gender (Bourgois, 2003, p 324). This specific kind of respect was the product both of the socio-historical predicament of the community – including the effects of structural harms such as racism, poverty, drugs policy and unemployment – and of the particular kinds of cultural creativity which the community engaged in. The culturally specific forms of worth and significance, power and potency to be won by the acquisition of this respect made it enormously consequential: negotiating the play of 'respeto' in the community involved both profound demonstrations of love and devastating acts of violence. This idea of respect also gave shape to the particular experience of structural harms endured by members of the community, including the 'deep humiliation' they frequently encountered in the service economy job market (Bourgois, 2003, p 143) and their common experience of school as a 'hostile, alien institution' (Bourgois, 2003, p 175). Bourgois's account thus vividly conveys the connections between the particular structural harms which press down on a community, the idiosyncratic forms of mattering which vibrate with consequence within it and the intense emotional experiences which can result – including those which directly precipitate violence.

A number of studies in England have similarly centred on the consequential role of (dis)respect in the prevalence of violence in particular places in specific historical moments. To take a lesser-known example, Gaskell (2005) shows how the racialized political disempowerment of a predominantly British-Asian East London community was felt by its young people as 'disrespected citizenship', and that seeking out 'alternative routes to gain respect' involved engagement in violence for some of them (Gaskell, 2005, p 1). Their structural position in relation to democratic politics and their daily experience of racism amounted to a starkly diminished sense of both social significance and power, felt as a kind of disrespect. Interestingly, Gaskell suggests a close conceptual link between shame and respect: 'Respect derives from the primary emotion shame in that it has been understood, interpreted and can therefore be (re)articulated by young people themselves as (dis) respect' (Gaskell, 2005, p 154). The young people she studied were highly familiar with the idea of respect and it was a term which had rich significance for them, and this may, on a deeper level, also reflect the intense, inverse importance of shame. More recent English studies undertaken by young people themselves in London and Manchester have echoed this emphasis on both societal disrespect and the complex interweaving of power, respect and violence (for example, Lunghy et al, 2019; Reclaim, 2020). Research undertaken by young people in North London who have themselves been involved in (or affected by) violence concluded that 'respect, recognition, pride, power' are potent features of it, especially for those whose structural position limits their access to these social resources (Lunghy et al, 2019, p 3). They refer to many of the structural harms outlined in Chapter 4, such as poverty and issues in the education system, arguing that those who 'are consistently looked down on' are compelled to 'find [their] own ways to be respected or powerful' (Lunghy et al, 2019, p 27). The concentration of structural harms in their community manifests itself in this daily sense of being 'consistently looked down on' – cumulatively belittled – in a way which can energize violence.

Class and gender, political economy and patriarchy

The intersection of class and gender in marginalized communities can have a shaping influence both on the particular kinds of structural diminishment felt by their inhabitants and on the culturally valued forms of mattering sought by them. The specific, localized workings of political economy and patriarchy can thus be significant factors in the social incitement of violence. In unequal societies, especially those which purport to be 'meritocratic', the struggle to matter can be inseparable from the struggle for money: both earning and spending money each entails potently symbolic kinds of recognition, and the accumulation of wealth substantially determines freedom of action. Commenting on the fundamental importance of economic inequality in the US, Katz (1988, p 46) and Anderson (2000, p 68) both suggest that wealthier young men have greater and more diverse means to express their worth and value, and to escape humiliating kinds of insignificance. From Australia, White (2013, p 150) writes of business executives not needing physical means to 'exert their power and will', but highlights the profound harm that can result from the exercise of their financial power. Those from poorer and more stigmatized backgrounds have fewer alternatives, meaning that violence can feel both more necessary and more socially recognized as a way to assert power and to force the respect of others. Examining the British context, Hallsworth demonstrates the additional complexities of gender in this: dominant ideals of masculinity remain heavily tied to 'control and power over things and people' in the UK, and while wealthier men can 'own and control things like power and resources', men from poorer backgrounds can in some cases rely upon 'violent assertion' as a 'power resource', as they 'resolve the predicament of a power deficit by mobilising violence' (Hallsworth, 2013, p 150, 168; see also Tomsen, 2008; Ellis, 2016). Young goes further, suggesting that, for as long as we have a political economy which structurally excludes or denigrates many men, and for as long as we have a 'culture of machismo' among such men, some of them will resort to 'the mobilization of one of their only resources, physical strength', to achieve 'masculine powers and respect' (Young, 2007, p 12). Vast economic inequality is a structural harm which, when combined with certain ideals of masculinity, can leave many men feeling a desperate urgency in their struggle to attain some tolerable degree of social value and potency, and can leave them to reckon – consciously or otherwise – that violence is one of the few means they have to mobilize in this struggle.

Our political economy is not just unequal, of course – it constitutes a humiliating hierarchy, in which the relative immiseration of the poor is structurally necessary for the enrichment of the wealthy. Poverty and class are inherently relational: as Young (2007, p 31) put it, 'the ghettos of the rich are dependent on the work of the poor'. This structural connection between the poor and wealthy, combined with Britain's meritocratic culture and its tendency to 'lionise wealth' (Dorling, 2018, p 249), means that the experience of poverty in the UK amounts to 'structural humiliation' (Sayer, 2005, p 161; Young, 2007, p 54; White, 2013, p 190 – also discussed in Chapter 4). This does not just affect people's self-perceived social worth and significance: those with and without wealth also have fundamentally different experiences of agentic power, of how they can act upon the world, either casually enjoying or desperately seeking the control and power which characterizes hegemonic masculinity. Rose may be right that 'no human is spared confrontation with the limits of their own power', but those limits look, feel and *are* profoundly different for people occupying different positions in our political economy.

To the wealthy and powerful, the world tends to feel and to be highly malleable: to a significant degree, they can go where they want to, eat what they want to, hire and fire whom they want to, create new products using their extensive capital, dominate other people. They are far more likely to experience the world as something they can shape and control, or at least smoothly navigate. They can enjoy a tangible kind of social magnitude, expanding themselves across space and time, palpably sensing that their name and their influence will reverberate through neighbourhoods and down generations. Though they may of course remain dissatisfied and eager for more, their structural power can enable them to pursue what Becker describes as 'natural yearnings for self-expansion' (Becker, 1973, p 156).

To those with neither wealth nor power, the world can feel stubbornly immutable, immune to their influence, controlled by those who dominate them, infinitely bigger than them. They can experience a belittling combination of geographical and social immobility – life lived within a claustrophobic cul-de-sac. Structural diminishment can make them deeply aware of their 'cosmic insignificance' in space and time, within an 'indifferent universe' (Wolf, 2010, p 28). In her study of young African Caribbean men in East London, White articulated this point starkly, arguing that they have been 'rendered out of time and out of place' (White, 2020, p 4).

This is the vitally significant political and economic context for the psychologically intoxicating experience of violence discussed earlier: violence can be a way of shattering this structural sense of impotence, giving its perpetrator a tangible sense of causal power, and of asserting themselves in space and through time. Violence can help young men to 'carve out spaces of control' (Sibley, 1995, quoted in Fraser, 2015, p 195), and can give 'a sense of writing history' (Body-Gendrot, 2005, p 12).

Through a wide variety of studies, violence is tied to a metaphorical desire for size – the desperation to 'look big' (Brookman et al, 2011, p 25), to 'feel big' (Renold and Barter, 2003, p 101), to develop '"large" identities' (Wilkinson, 2001, p 233).[4] If, in normal life, you feel miniscule, the world completely impervious to your influence, being able to assert yourself violently on an individual or neighbourhood can bring a revivifying sense of potency and prominence.[5] Even if violence is tied to instrumental ends, such as stealing, the emotional experience of it is more tolerable or even pleasurable if the perpetrator's life has been characterized by the 'mundane pain' of structural diminishment, particularly if this has affected them since childhood (see De Zuleta, 2001), and especially if this has been combined with interpersonal harm from a similarly early age (see Levell, 2022).

The desire to matter, to be both 'someone' and 'something', is common across places and times, but the forms of 'someone' or 'something' that an individual can be are shaped by the particular history, culture and socioeconomic position of their neighbourhood. The search for respect can be tense, complex, frightening and desperate in communities whose structural predicament induces something like a localized crisis of mattering. If we wish to understand why and how particular areas can see far higher rates of violence between young people during particular times, we need to attend to the kinds of harm and diminishment, significance and power which circulate in them. We cannot grasp the nature or drivers of the violent emotions which fire up within particular interactions without understanding these wider socio-historical influences. The structurally derived and socially meaningful forms of insignificance and impotence which affect particular individuals and communities are felt as a punishing daily reality. As the studies cited earlier all testify, the harms of the job market, of schooling, of inequality and of poverty are not in the 'background' of anyone's life – they are grinding, cumulative experiences which can contort personalities and enflame the most dangerous varieties of shame and rage. They do not guarantee violence, but they shape practical possibilities and energize cultural and emotional responses which make violence more likely. They can also, through time, deepen the strength of relationship that an individual develops with their own capacity for violence.

The 'singular quest for significance' and the role of violence within complex individual self-narratives

As already explored, it is not just geographical place which can affect rates of violence, but also place in time: the prevalence of violence in any community is affected by historical factors, such as economic changes and entrenched, institutionalized forms of racism. Parallel to this, the increased proclivity to violence in any individual can be understood only in relation to their biography, and the ways in which personal self-narratives can form around violence. As explored in Chapter 3, any individual's sense of mattering is affected by which aspects of their life come to feel most valuable, worthwhile and consequential to them. The experience of mattering is psycho-socially complex because of this interplay between an individual's emotional investment in what is of significance to them *in* the world, and their sense of personal significance *to* the world. The kinds of cultural norm discussed earlier, such as ideals of masculinity, are not simplistically internalized, but come to obtain their significance when an individual emotionally invests in them. Institutions like schools are monumentally important to some individuals' understanding of their worth, but others emotionally detach from such institutions, seeking other sources of meaning in the world, and other places through which to matter to the world. For some, violence becomes an important feature of self-narrative: it can become something which is deeply meaningful, and one of the few personal competences through which to achieve a kind of significance – to both win recognition and exert agentic power.

Violence can come to obtain particular value for those who experience it as a kind of necessity. Jasko and colleagues (2016, p 3) write of this in psychological terms, finding that the twin need for 'meaning and mattering' can be of such intensity that its frustration 'can foster a powerful experience that overshadows alternative pursuits and redirects individual psychological resources to the singular quest for significance'. As already demonstrated, this frustration is shaped by social, historical, economic, political and cultural influences across the lifecourse. The resultant 'singular quest for significance' can be a key driver of violence (Jasko et al, 2016). The biographical trajectory of violence is similarly portrayed elsewhere: individuals are far more likely to become attached to violence as a means to matter if they have 'lived for a lifetime on a diet of contempt and disdain' (Gilligan, 1997, p 109); if they have experienced 'the stresses of lives lived with limited resources, limited opportunities, and limited chances of dignity and respect' (Currie, 2016, p 80). In some institutional settings, violence can become a uniquely potent tool in the quest for some kind of significance. In their study of violence in 14 British children's homes, for instance, Renold and Barter found that there were few other ways in which boys could acquire reputation or self-worth (Renold and Barter, 2003, p 104).[6] Physical interpersonal violence is very rarely used by those with plentiful options; it becomes a capacity of importance mostly to those who have very few other means to define or to assert themselves (see White, 2013, p 136). This does not mean that people always require immense provocation before resorting to violence; it can also mean that individuals become accustomed to the use of violence as a way to resolve even apparently trivial challenges to their sense of mattering, so focused are they on the 'singular quest' to build or maintain it.

Ellis (2016) brings all of this to life in his study of the role that violence played in individuals' self-narratives in a particular post-industrial British neighbourhood. The violent young men in his study are 'purveyor[s] of complex, contradictory and often inconsistent narratives on their lived experiences' (Ellis, (2016, p 34). They assign significance to various different features and memories from different points in their biographies in a complicated and paradoxical way. But one thing is consistent: in their self-narratives, violence oozes with meaning. The violence that they have been exposed to or the victim of, and the violence they have perpetrated, are of great significance to how they make sense of and convey their personal stories. Violence featured prominently in their self-narratives not only due to its frequency in their lives but because of how much importance it had to them: it seems as though every physical encounter had incredibly high emotional, psychological and existential stakes. If violence, and your competence in enacting it, are of great significance to you, a lost fight does not just result in a bloody nose or a bruised rib, it can be a crushingly humiliating and belittling experience, leaving you desperate to reassert your place in the world. Violence 'made sense' to the young men, it was how they could go about becoming 'recognised and feared as "somebody"' (Ellis, 2016, p 57). The stultifying socio-historical context of the neighbourhood drove this attachment to violence: Ellis describes those he studied as 'fearful ... marginalised men, attempting to negotiate the wreckage of the post-industrial landscape with the few resources at their disposal' (Ellis, 2016, p 142).

Young men's attachment to violence as a means to significance, mastery and power can be entwined with patriarchal norms and forms of domination. Ellis (2016, p 103) writes that the men in his study were obsessed with 'maintaining paternalism, protection and proprietary over female intimates'. The young men craved the power to both protect and control women in their lives, as a defining feature of who they were as men. Invested in this conception of masculinity, a failure to exert this form of influence over women would raise terrifying, humiliating questions about their powerlessness and impotence. This can drive both protective forms of violence, enacted against other men due to the perceived threat they represent to a female, and aggressive forms of violence against women seen to be challenging a young man's sense of control. In the very different context of New York, Miller (2008) draws attention to how these gendered forms of violent victimization affect African American women in particular. Though there are important distinctions, the drivers of violence between young men bear similarities with those which can lie behind the violent abuse of women (see, for example, Totten, 2003; Rose, 2020; Havard et al, 2021 for further analysis of young men's violence and coercion against women).

Anthropological studies from the US echo Ellis, in drawing attention to the ways in which violence can come to play an important role in individuals' pursuit of meaning and mattering. In Anderson's (2000) study of street culture in inner-city Philadelphia, he highlights how much meaning violence had to his subjects: 'Their very identity, their self-respect, and their honour are often intricately tied up with the way they perform on the streets during and after [violent] encounters' (Anderson, 2000, p 76). Writing of his own experiences growing up in a similar neighbourhood to that studied by Anderson, Contreras says that 'as a marginal teenager, any respect felt good, especially if it was linked to masculinity and violence … it made me "somebody" too … utter marginality … created the potential for deadly status-seeking violence on the street' (Contreras, 2013, pp 59, 182). Contreras felt that he did not matter in American society, and – like the men studied by Ellis – it was a particular combination of marginality and masculinity that increased his attachment to violence.

The public character of violence can heighten its significance for young people: Gaskell (2005, p 133) concludes that 'Fighting, for the young men, was a highly visible and celebratory "spectacle", and one that young men themselves placed great importance on' (see also Jasko et al, 2016, p 14). Especially for those who experience their lives as a toxic and chaotic mixture of powerlessness, confusion, exploitation, fear and humiliation,[7] violence can become the part of their self-narrative which they have the greatest hold on – it can make sense to emotionally invest in your capacity for violence if very little else seems to make sense or to have meaning. Harris (2017, p 529) describes Daniel's life as approximating this extreme image, and stresses how difficult it then was for any professional to help Daniel 'construct a subjectivity less centred on violence'. If violence feels like one of the only things in life through which you can both understand and affect the world, it will obtain substantial prominence in your everyday struggle to make meaning of your biography.

Nihilistic violence

Implicit in this is the problem of nihilistic violence. If the world is drained of meaning, and the experience of living within it offers precious little hope for personal significance, a kind of mutually reinforcing external and internal valuelessness can result, in which it seems that there is no value in either internal self or external world – including other people. Vigil has evocatively portrayed this devastating social experience, suggesting that the most violent young people are those who suffer from a kind of 'soul death' or 'psychosocial death' as a result of the harm and trauma they have lived through, leaving them with a sense of 'personal worthlessness' which prompts them to doubt 'why anyone else should be worth anything' (Vigil, 1988, p 166; 2003, p 237; see also Seal and Harris, 2016, pp 122–3). Adshead (2001, p 16) describes a similar phenomenon as 'a literally "unspeakable" sense of nothingness'.

For some young people growing up in marginalized British communities, historical and structural conditions can generate this dangerous sense of nothingness. White suggests that some young men in East London live on a 'nihilistic plane' in which 'no-one cares and nothing matters': for them, she writes, 'there is nothing to win and nothing to lose, it is a zero-sum game ... life – even their own – has little value' (White, 2020, pp 24, 94–7). Also writing about London, Thapar quotes his friend, Suki, who says that violent young people there 'have no immediate reference point for what a good life can be. They have no value for themselves and, in turn, no value for others. Society has told them they're of little value' (Thapar, 2021, p 170). The drill artist Skengdo put it to Thapar this way: 'there ain't nothing here for anyone ... they give us everything we need to destroy ourselves' (Thapar, 2021, p 171–2). East London-based youth worker and activist David Smith provides a more fleshed-out description of this process. In defining what he calls 'unintentional suicide', he said that young people who engage in violence:

'don't see no hope in the future. It's not like you're intentionally trying to kill yourself but you do anything, you don't care about the outcome. ... They see no hope in work, in school or anything, so they out here, they don't care. They're risking anything to get their head out of what they're going through'. (Personal correspondence with Billingham)[8]

The harms and diminishments of life in certain places and times in Britain can all but extinguish any sense that the external world has meaning, and the internal self has significance. All of these researchers and young people are clear that these kinds of nihilism do not spring uncaused from some malevolent internal despair or some pathological group culture – to a substantial degree, they are products of the socio-historical predicament young people find themselves in.

To this point, we have explored the connections between structural harm, mattering and violence on two levels: the socio-historical and the biographical. Between the two is the level of analysis which has perhaps enjoyed the greatest prominence in studies of violence involving young people: the level of group behaviours and localized social codes. The search for meaning and mattering is not just characterized by individuals navigating their socio-historical circumstances, it is also a collective endeavour, shaped and guided by local norms, particularly for young people.

Peer groups, gangs and 'violent street worlds': structural harm and violent assertions of mattering among groups of young people

So far, we have intentionally and studiously avoided the word which is perhaps most closely associated with young people and violence in many accounts: gangs. Just as many discussions of gangs start with the issue of violence (Brotherton, 2015, p 162), many explorations of violence start with the phenomenon of gangs. We have resisted this tendency for a variety of reasons, including questions about the proportion of violence which is 'gang related' (see Chapter 1) and the wider problems with gang discourse, which we will discuss further in Chapter 6. For now, suffice it to say that, when exploring the role of collective meaning-making and group formation in relation to structural harms, mattering and violence, the concept of gangs can have limited utility and explanatory value, if proffered as some kind of self-evident 'cause'. The idea of the gang can beg more questions than it answers, standing in for social analysis rather than providing it, especially due to inherent definitional difficulties (see Fraser, 2015, pp 1–30; Shute, 2016). Organized and semi-organized groups of people, including young people, who have a strong sense of attachment to a particular territory and collective identity do of course exist, and in some cases violence is central to their way of being. But to infer from this a simplistic, linear line of causality, that gangs cause violence, would be a profound mistake.

Reflecting the densely complicated and contentious social processes at work in this, different writers have presented quite sharply opposed views: some tend to focus on the organization of people within what they call gangs (for example, Densley, 2013; Pitts, 2013; Harding, 2014), while others place greater importance on the play of cultural norms and imperatives within the social ecologies that young people occupy, suggesting that the nature of their organization into gangs – where such organization does occur – is of lesser importance (for example, Hallsworth, 2013; Gunter, 2017). For some, gangs constitute relatively structured, hierarchical and somewhat domineering kinds of social institution (for example, Harding, 2014), while for others, they are better described as 'chaotic interactional orders' (Hobbs, 2013, p 191).

Denying that gangs ever contribute to violence, or greatly overstating their role, are mirrored and unhelpful simplifications (see White, 2013, p 151). Even critics of gang-focused explanations, such as Hallsworth (2013, p 194), do not seek to deny the existence of gangs. He writes that he does not 'ignore gangs and the harms they do', but seeks to put them in perspective: the 'street world is occupied by many groups who are not gangs and many individuals doing precisely the same kind of things as those perpetuated by gang members' (Hallsworth, 2013, p 194).

The role of gangs in violence is thus complex and contested, as well as – unfortunately – ripe for simplification and sensationalism (see Chapters 1 and 6 for further discussion). In what follows, we further explore the psycho-social connections between structural harms, mattering and violence, attending to this complex role of the peer group and the gang.

Peer groups, gangs, structural harm and violence

Group peer relationships play a substantial role in young people's negotiation of meaning and mattering, particularly when their lives are constrained and constricted by structural harms. All young people deeply invest in bonds with friends, and it is common across the world for peers to become more influential than parents during the teenage years (see Firmin, 2020). But this emotional attachment acquires additional intensity among those who are affected by multiple forms of marginalization and powerlessness. When exploring sources of significance in their lives, forming tight-knit peer groups can be a potent means of establishing collective meaning (Fraser, 2015, p xxx), and such a group can represent an 'alternative forum for autonomous personal dignity' (Bourgois, 2003, p 8). Especially for those who feel the belittling injuries of misrecognition, disrespect and disempowerment within the systems and institutions with which they are obliged to interact – such as school or work (see Chapter 4) – the peer group can come to attain singular importance as a social setting which both enriches the world with meaning and provides an individual young person with a social place in which to feel dignified, worthy, recognized, respected and influential. For those who have experienced 'relational poverty' (Brierley, 2021) across multiple contexts of their lives, the peer group can fulfil the need to feel wanted and accepted (see Gaskell, 2005, p 216; Deuchar, 2009).

In some studies, groups who identify or are identified as gangs play this role. Vigil describes how a gang can become 'a substitute for the many caretakers who have failed' across an individual's lifecourse, becoming 'a crucial haven' for those who 'lamented that they were "nobody" before' (Vigil, 1988, pp 432, 427, 428). In her study of young people in one particular school in North East London, Kulz uses identical language, describing a gang as a 'haven' for one particular student, Osman: 'his [gang] identity became a more amenable, plausible source of value [than school] ... despite the real dangers, his "family" [gang affiliates] offer him recognition' (Kulz, 2017, p 130). Osman's experience of institutional harm in the school, comprised of racist stereotyping and interactional humiliation, led him to emotionally divest from it as a source of meaning and mattering, finding greater existential and ontological solace in a local gang. In their community research in East London, Community Links observed a similar phenomenon, suggesting that deeply marginalized young people are given 'a sense of belonging and purpose by gangs', which form 'a kind of alternative community, offering a sense of stability and belonging missing from their own lives' (Community Links, 2019, p 17).

In such accounts, what becomes apparent is the psychologically tense 'push and pull' which many young people struggle with. Interactions, experiences and cultures bond them to or alienate them from family, state institutions or legitimate employment, and forms of significance, power, excitement and connection can encourage them to emotionally invest in and identify with their peer group. Through time, the different social contexts and different relationships in young people's lives can wax and wane in the importance that they hold: meaning can seem to drain from them or ooze from them for different reasons at different points in life, and the extent to which they represent consequential sources of personal significance will vary. In the transitional period of the teenage years, young people navigate this complex, ever-evolving dynamic of attraction and repulsion in relation to different places and people, and the ideas of mattering and social harm can be helpful lenses through which to explore these processes.

While some writers are keen to emphasize this role of peer groups or gangs in providing relational warmth and care in a systemically careless society (for example, Gunter, 2017), other accounts focus on the central role that violence can play in gangs' negotiation of respect, status, protection, belonging and power. Debate rages about the extent to which gangs are defined by violence (see, for example, Sanders, 1994 for one 'confirmist' view of gangs' inherent violence, and Hallsworth, 2013 for a 'denialist' perspective), and about the proportion of violence between young people which is gang related (see Irwin-Rogers et al, 2019 for a helpful discussion of this issue in London). Those accounts which do centre on the violence of gangs consistently emphasize the interwoven play of money, meaning and mattering as vitally important for understanding how violence happens within and between them.

To take two American examples, in their rich depictions of gang life in different parts of the US from different historical periods, Vigil (1988) and Lauger (2012) show how violence is a consequential 'gang thing', because it earns individuals and groups both significance and power. In the Barrio gangs studied by Vigil, undertaking violence (as well as other 'gang things') allowed individuals to obtain 'respect and recognition as a dependable gang member with *huevos* (balls)' (Vigil, 1988, p 432). Entwined codes of masculinity, loyalty and territorialism placed substantial value on violent competence. Lauger's (2012) work, focused on the gangs of Indianapolis, pivots on the struggle for authenticity and legitimacy among young men whose 'real' gang status is perpetually questioned (Lauger, 2012, p 159). Violence is key to this, 'a defining trait of the real gang', and young people are desperate to adhere to 'real gang' conventions, for fear of being deemed 'wannabes' (Lauger, 2012, p 120). 'Doing gang' means being violent, or at least – subtly different – obtaining a reputation for violence (Lauger, 2012, pp 163, 139). Violence can earn both group recognition and online reputation – Lauger's attentiveness to the role of social media in this seems to have somewhat presaged later research on this issue (see, for example, Storrod and Densley, 2017; Lauger and Densley, 2018; Irwin-Rogers, 2019).[9] To have any kind of social presence within these consequential worlds of gangs – let alone a sense of status or influence in it – an acknowledged capacity for violence was necessary.

Common across both Vigil and Lauger's studies is an account of the classed and racialized forms of structural harm which played a catalytic role in the growth of gangs within these neighbourhoods – both the cultural creativity of gangs and the attraction that they held for young people were closely related to the ways in which these individuals and communities had harmful experiences of the political economy, policies, systems and institutions which they encountered through their biographies.

Ethnographic accounts of gangs in Britain similarly portray the ways in which violence can become an important means to matter within the hyper-localized group norms of gang-involved peers. Gaskell described the gangs she observed in East London as 'social networks whereby power, respect and status can be negotiated', and found that 'violent actions' were essential for young people to 'prove their worth and make their claims for respect' within them (Gaskell, 2005, pp 132, 216).

More recent British anthropological research by Densley (2013) and Harding (2014) has echoed this. In his study of gangs across various parts of London, Densley suggested that 'serious violence is the fastest way to rise to the top' of the gang 'game' – it is an especially effective means to gain 'ratings' and build a consequential 'personal brand' (Densley, 2013, pp 85,

81). In these gangs, violence is a valued skill: recognized 'violence potential' was a sure route to prominence (Densley, 2013, p 118). Harding's account of gang culture in Lambeth, South West London, is remarkably similar: he describes those involved in this culture as 'strategic actors' who pursue 'street capital', mobilizing violence to 'maintain reputation, build name brands, and maintain respect' (Harding, 2014, pp 129, 119). Street capital is built through individual distinction within collective social rules, and violence can accrue 'mega street capital' (Harding, 2014, pp 60, 123). The play of recognition and status is deadly: disrespect, understood as 'violation', is perceived as 'desecration of something sacred, a personal outrage or spoilation of street capital', and can have violent repercussions, because 'those operating in the social field will put their lives at risk to defend their reputation and prevent their street capital from falling' (Harding, 2014, p 113).

Both Densley and Harding illustrate the role that violence plays within the social worlds of gangs in these communities as a crucial means to the higher value of personal and group mattering: though money is involved too, strategic players vie most urgently for the status, respect, supremacy and recognition which they crave. Both also imply that the 'social fields' of gangs are somewhat magnetic, drawing young people into their orbit with substantial force, due in no small part to the social harms in other parts of their lives: Densley, for instance, cites class and ethnic inequality, unemployment, poverty, harm in the home and confrontational policing as key drivers of gang cultures' magnetism (Densley, 2013, p 175).

Of course, it is not just a kind of social magnetism pulling young people into gangs and their violence: coercion and exploitation can play prominent roles (see Pitts, 2013; Children's Commissioner, 2019b; Harding, 2020a). Perhaps the foremost academic to stress this point is Pitts (for example, 2013), who found in his study of three London boroughs that gang involvement was frequently 'involuntary'. Fear and coercion often played significant parts, and Pitts concludes that 'involuntary [gang] affiliation describes most accurately the bind in which increasing numbers of young people in the poorest neighbourhoods in Britain find themselves' (Pitts, 2013, pp 108–9). Like Vigil, Lauger, Densley and Harding, though, Pitts emphasizes the roles that poverty, inequality, social immobility and other forms of structurally derived hardship play in this. He describes, for instance, how poorly paid work can leave parents feeling 'shame and frustration', as they are 'worn down' by forms of economic exertion which earn meagre reward, leaving them with precious little capacity to monitor or prevent their children's gang affiliation – particularly if the local gang seems to offer a greater chance of safety and money for their children than any realistic alternatives (Pitts, 2013, p 111). It is often observed that those young people who live in or attend the lowest-status and most poorly resourced institutional settings, such as children's homes or AP schools, are at greatest risk of violent criminal exploitation, particularly the forms of drug-running which have become known as 'county lines' (see, for example, Children's Commissioner, 2019a and 2019b; Harding, 2020a; Havard et al, 2021; but compare Koch, 2019; Wroe, 2021). However (in)voluntary gang involvement may be, the research is clear that the cumulative effect of structural harms plays a powerful role. Those most vulnerable to the kinds of exploitation that Pitts (2013) describes are those who have experienced intersecting forms of structural harm: for instance, from economic policies which contribute to poverty; from under-resourced child welfare systems which can place young people in unsafe settings; and from educational institutions which can all-too-readily exclude.

Questioning the importance of gangs, stressing the role of 'violent street worlds'

By contrast, for some writers, gangs rarely have much explanatory worth; it is the social and cultural environment of the 'street world' which is the foremost driver of violence, not the 'gangness' of peer groups. Based on their studies of various sites in England, Hallsworth (2013) and Gunter (2017) concur on this. Gunter sums up his position tautly, by stating that violence 'stems not from the formation of inherently pathological gangs but from the ecology of the worlds that many young males inhabit' (Gunter, 2017, p 109). Where Gunter uses the concept of social ecology, Hallsworth (2013) refers to 'violent street worlds', arguing that there is scant evidence for any highly ordered world of gangs anywhere in Britain, but plenty of evidence to suggest a *dis*ordered, 'inherently unstable', 'radically contingent' street culture in many parts of the country (Hallsworth, 2013, p 129). Both authors contend that what encourages street-based violence between young people is not some rigid, hierarchical kind of organized gang code, but a set of cultural imperatives which exert their potent influence in a more diffuse and unpredictable fashion. Gunter describes the power of respect, status and 'badness-honour' within life 'on road' (Gunter, 2017, pp 172, 181), while Hallsworth stresses the importance of three 'street imperatives': pleasure, respect and money (Hallsworth, 2013, pp 142–55). For these writers, gangs are rarely 'a key explanatory variable' (Hallsworth, 2013, p 42): it is not the 'gangness' of young people which causes violence, but the toxic combination of loosely circulating yet hugely consequential social norms on the street, and immiserating structural conditions within wider society. Precarious and low-status work, the steady drift of wealth towards the already-rich, concentrated poverty and depoliticization leave communities 'deliberately dispossessed and disenfranchised', experiencing a kind of 'structural powerlessness' which breeds anger, resentment, alienation and despondency (Hallsworth, 2013, pp 172–6).

Despite the stark contrast in their perspectives on gangs, then, Hallsworth and Gunter share a remarkably similar view to Densley, Harding and Pitts when it comes to the structural predicament of the young people in Britain who engage in violence. The complex but predictable connections between social harms, mattering and violence seem clear: those young people whose lives are interactionally and structurally diminished and belittled, whose needs and well-being are interpersonally and systemically neglected, and who live in communities in which such an experience is common, are far more likely to feel compelled into a 'singular quest for significance', which can – particularly if localized norms are conducive to it – involve violence.

Applying the concepts of mattering and social harm to gang-related accounts of violence between young people

We would contend that there is much to be gained from drawing together this mass of studies on peer groups, gangs, street worlds and violence with our psycho-social idea of mattering and our conception of social harm. In what follows, we summarize the ways in which we think the lenses of mattering and social harm can enrich this literature, given the complexity and contentiousness of these issues. We make the case for this by offering four points in turn, which build upon our discussion of structure and agency, harm and subjectivity in Chapter 4.

Firstly, perhaps most importantly, viewing various analyses of group-based violence between young people through the lens of structural harm in particular helps to draw out the significant explanatory commonalities between them: in different ways, they all 'connect structural marginalisation with agentic violence' (Fraser, 2015, p 43; see also White, 2013, p 179). The combative viciousness of the academic debate in Britain between those who emphasize and those who downplay the role of gangs in violence between young people can obscure substantial areas of consensus between them. Foremost among these is the emphasis they place on the causal importance of structural harms in young people's lives (though they tend not to use the term): they describe the enormous material, moral and emotional consequences of poverty on young people; they decry the effects of both class and race inequality; they discuss the indignities and diminishments experienced by young people within their homes, schools, workplaces and the welfare system; and they provide vivid accounts of a confrontational and belittling criminal justice system (see, for example, Densley, 2013; Hallsworth, 2013; Pitts, 2013; Harding, 2014; Gunter, 2017 – see Chapter 6 for discussion of the last point).[10] However important gang formations may or may not be in promoting violence between young people, those who have immersed themselves most deeply in attempts to understand this violence all seem to agree that the neighbourhood-level drivers of violence – be they described in terms of organized gangs or anarchic street worlds – are energized, sustained and given their explosiveness by harms which derive from national and local policies, systems and institutions.

The cultural creativity of young people in their communities, whether in identifiable gangs or more indeterminate forms of collectivity, is an agentic response to the particular historical conjuncture that they find themselves in: the place of violence and aggression within local social codes and cultures is not the result of 'pure creation', it is a reflection of the political, economic and social positions of those engaged in this collective cultural innovation. Concentrated structural harms of various kinds form lightning rods against which group cultures are defined, formed, created – mutual destructiveness is found most often in those local cultures which have been generated in conditions of substantial harm, and this is no coincidence: violent emotions in individuals and collective viciousness among groups are predictably fostered in places where people encounter multiple and cumulative forms of pain, pressure and powerlessness. Returning to the analogy used at the outset of this chapter, acute accumulations of structural harm amount to incendiary social conditions which set communities alight. Whether the flames are then thrown by organized gangs, who regulate the distribution of flamethrowers, or there is more of a disordered, individualized, chaotic frenzy of fire breathing, the fuel, oxygen and heat originate beyond the neighbourhood. The ingredients which reliably generate mutual interpersonal harm derive from the preponderance of policies, systems, institutions and interactions which engender individual and collective crises of mattering, meaning and material scarcity.

Meanwhile, secondly, the psycho-social concept of mattering helps to complicate some of the simplifications and unhelpful binaries which could be deduced from the literature on gangs and violence between young people. First of all, an unsophisticated interpretation of this literature could amount to the twin suggestions that (a) street socialization goes 'all the way down', whether via group influence or 'cultural imperatives', fundamentally determining the thoughts, actions and emotions of young people; and (b) any gang or group is either a collection of rebels against the mainstream or an assortment of arch-conformists, desperate to achieve conventional goals, such as consumerist hedonism or hegemonic masculinity (albeit through unconventional means.) These two banalizations are related, as (b) tends to require (a) – the simplistic idea that groups of young people form subcultures of either pure rebellion or utter conformity tends to assume that, either way, they are some kind of cultural dupe, entirely absorbing the norms and values of their milieu. The psycho-social idea of mattering, as developed in Chapter 3 and the preceding sections of this chapter, necessitates an exploration of the ever-evolving dynamic between the individual and group culture; the ongoing negotiation between what particular young people bring to their peers and what their peers bring to them. This avoids an over-socialized view of young people, as it involves attending to the biographical experiences of each individual, across time and through all the contexts of their lives, in order to understand the kinds of significance and power they have experienced; to grasp the granular variations in respect, recognition, worth, status, efficacy, mastery, competence and potency that have shaped the sense of mattering that they *bring to* 'the street'. As Sayer (2005, p 191) has argued: 'the personal is not reducible to the social even though the social is a precondition of the personal'.

Giving due attention to the psycho-social complexity of an individual's internal life entails acknowledging the complicated relationship that they have to all kinds of social and cultural influence. To repeat how we made this point in Chapter 3: whatever 'pleasures and fucking displeasures' they have experienced and cultural influences they have confronted, no young person could either absorb it all or resist it all; they go through a sifting process of establishing, consciously or otherwise, what does and does not hold significance to them. In all of this, we put both the gang and the 'street world' back in their place: however much a young person emotionally invests themselves in a gang or in life 'on road', and seeks to feel that they matter to them, the thoughts, emotions and actions that they bring to that struggle can be understood only in the wider context of their biography, in all its complexity. This means putting the proximate social norms of particular social settings in context, rather than ascribing overweening influence to them. In young people's lives, there will always be a number of rival social institutions for their attention, identification and emotional investment, and their navigation of these various local worlds will be profoundly affected by their past experiences. This kind of perspective also entails rejecting any simple binary between involuntary or voluntary gang affiliation: the enthusiasm for gang identification or vulnerability to coercive gang exploitation that any individual young person has will be significantly shaped by their experiences of harm and mattering through their lifecourse, and across various social contexts. The young person who has experienced harm in the home and structural neglect in the care system, and whose need for a safe and engaging educational setting has not been met, for instance, is both more vulnerable to forcible affiliation with a gang and more likely to view a gang as a comparatively reliable, feasible source of meaning, money and mattering.

Thirdly, the idea of mattering helps to ensure that young people's agency is not conceived narrowly as a strategic form of action. In places, the literature on violence between young people can portray the protagonists as calculating players in a structured game, using violence somewhat mechanistically as a tool to obtain material or reputational benefit (see Harding, 2014 on the 'street casino'; Densley, 2013, p 81 on the 'tournament of the most committed'). This approach to understanding young people's actions can seem most pronounced in accounts which draw heavily upon the theoretical framework of Pierre Bourdieu, especially his concepts of field and capital: in the 'field' of the street, young people strategically mobilize their 'sense of the game' to acquire different forms of capital, be it social capital, symbolic capital or 'street capital' (see, for example, Sandberg and Pederson, 2011; Harding, 2014).[11]

While of course there is a strategic component to young people's behaviour as they seek to earn respect, obtain positions of status, get money and spread their reputation, over-emphasizing this 'cold' mode of action can serve to obscure the profound importance of 'warmer' motivations – the relational, emotional and existential aspects of experience which are crucial to understanding anyone's agency, but perhaps especially that of young people (see Alexander, 2000, p 248; Holligan and Deuchar, 2014). This is particularly true of violent action, which may be the form of agency which is least well placed for any kind of cold or mechanistic explanation (see Collins, 2008): as explored earlier, in some way or another, violence is almost always deeply emotional, in both its causes and consequences. Some people are more psycho-socially 'primed' for violence than others, depending on previous experiences, particularly violence in the home, and their emotional effects (see Densley, 2013, p 118; Levell, 2022). Again, the psycho-socially complex concept of mattering can help to keep things in proportion: to an extent, certain aspects of many people's lives may be like a game, and marginalized young people may feel themselves especially forced into strategic activity, but this activity can be understood only through the wider lens of their socio-historically situated biography, including its 'warmer' elements. Somewhat similarly, any approach to understanding violence which attends to the social harms in a young person's life will by necessity involve addressing both its 'colder' and 'warmer' aspects – the way in which harms can both reduce opportunities and resources on the 'cold' side, and involve all kinds of emotional anguish, ranging from terror and trauma to shame and humiliation, on the 'warm' side.

Lastly, as implied by the three points already made, consideration of mattering and harm necessitates a form of 'multi-level' analysis (Fraser, 2017) which does not privilege any analytical level, as it involves attending to the ways in which various interpersonal and structural harms at different scales have affected the kind of self-concept possible for an individual or community. To understand the complexity of any person or group's sense of mattering, you have to attend to history, social structure and biography; to the global, societal, local and familial influences on their material and moral lives. Harms which derive from planetary social changes and from individual interactions, from centuries-old structures and from the immediate present, manifest themselves in the 'munpain' of everyday life (Bakkali, 2019), providing the practical and emotional context for each person's pursuit of mattering and meaning (and money). Returning to Cusset (2018)'s concept of 'triple violence': interpersonal harms 'among' young people can be understood only in relation to the structural harms pressed 'upon' them, and the resultant emotional tension 'within' them. Some gang-related accounts of violence between young people, such as that portrayed in Vigil's (1988) concept of 'multiple marginality', or in Fraser's (2015) rich picture of Glaswegian gangs in the early 21ˢᵗ century, effectively draw together the global and local, past and present. Others, at times, seem to relegate history, politics and economics to the 'background', delving into the apparently bounded minutiae of localized youth cultures as if the latter were somehow buffered from the influence of the former: a 'zoomed in' focus on 'cultural expression' can 'obscure wider processes of inequality and exclusion' (Alexander, 2000, p 241).

To reiterate our argument from Chapter 4: the point is not that mattering and social harm are the only concepts of worth for understanding violence, or even that they are better than alternatives, but that existing ideas of violence between young people may be enriched by the insights that they offer as lenses through which to view these issues. In addition, we would suggest that the crucial importance both of structural harms and of mattering demand that we decentre gangs in our understanding of what fundamentally drives young people's relationships with violence. We would concur with White (2013, p 190) when he states that:

> It is time to go beyond gangs and to address substantive issues of inequality, racism and oppression that lie at the heart of structural humiliation. The personal search for meaning and the struggle to attain respect are difficult and alienating for so many precisely because of the systemic limits and pressures on who they are and what they can become.

This is not to say that gangs do not exist or do not play a role in some young people's violence, but it is to say that they need to be kept in proportion. Policy-level obsession with gangs both can obfuscate the structural conditions affecting communities and can generate harms in itself – particularly when this obsession is reflected in punitive criminal justice and policing practices (see Chapter 6).

Briefly returning to Mark, the subject of Composite Case Study 3 in Chapter 4: if he were to engage in violence against another young person, proximally motivated by some kind of gang culture or street imperatives, would it meaningfully account for his actions if we foregrounded that immediate cause above all else? We would argue that, to have any hope of understanding such behaviour, we would have to attend to the interwoven interpersonal and structural harms which cumulatively diminished him, and to the complex struggle for mattering which both troubled and galvanized him.

Conclusion

Our economy, policy environment and institutions seem adept at fostering pernicious forms of 'violent emotion' in far too many people. Our democratic and meritocratic culture conveys that all should enjoy political voice and moral value, while bestowing vastly divergent quantities of material and reputational reward to different people, with accompanying disparities in power. As we lionize wealth, and structure our economy such that those with the most are able to further hoard, and those with the least are made to further struggle, we exacerbate the hideous levels of inequality in money, power and respect which we know to predictably breed violence. These various forms of harm cumulatively impose corrosive forms of pain, pressure and powerlessness on communities and individuals, fostering inflammable impotent rage.

The resultant feeling is a gnawing, shameful, dangerous sense that they do not matter – that they are neither significant nor consequential. The complex process of building a meaningful sense of individual and collective value and power in the face of this multiple marginality can involve harmful modes of self-assertion. Seeking power, seeking respect or honour, seeking social bonds, seeking dignity, individuals and groups can engage in destructive violence against others or themselves. Better a violent 'somebody' than a 'nobody'.

There is wide-ranging literature painting this picture – from the psychiatric and psychoanalytical work of Gilligan, Retzinger and May, to the large-scale psychological studies of Kruglanski and Jasko; from the US ethnographies of Bourgois, Vigil and Lauger, to the anthropologies of marginalized British communities undertaken by Gaskell, Pitts, Densley, Hallsworth, Harding, Fraser, Ellis and Gunter. Violent physical harm is self-evidently destructive, morally appalling and – barring self-defence – inexcusable. But an excuse and an explanation are two very different things: an excuse is a moral case in search of vindication, an explanation is an empirical argument in service of understanding. To outline the various ways in which social harms can create conditions which predictably breed violence is not to excuse that violence; it is to work towards its prevention.

6

Harmful Responses
to 'Youth Violence'

Introduction

> [Inequality in the violence affecting different communities] is not
> an inevitable fact of urban life or the result of abstract economic
> or technological forces. It is not a reflection of biological or
> cultural deficiencies. It is the result of conscious decisions that,
> while systematically impoverishing some communities, have
> helped to create extraordinary privilege and wealth in others.
>
> Currie, 2020, p 17

Through the course of this book, we have attempted to convey both the
internal and external complexity of young people's lives. In our discussion
of mattering and social harm, we have sought to describe the psycho-social
difficulties that young people can face, particularly those whose biographies
and communities are characterized by a concentration of structural harms.
These are fostered and reinforced by the profound historical maldistribution
of recognition, resources and risk in contemporary Britain, which leaves
some young people to enjoy substantial affluence, freedom, prestige and
safety, and forces others to negotiate a crushing combination of scarcity,
shame, danger and powerlessness. This multifaceted inequality characterizes
our historical conjuncture, and means that, though growing up is never easy,
different young people face very different predicaments when attempting
to establish a sense that they matter – that they are a significant and
consequential part of the world. All young people of course have choice
and agency in how they navigate their lives and in how they seek to secure
a self-perception of mattering. But there are vast disparities in the material
and social resources available to young people and in the structural harms

that they are exposed to, shaped in large part by a young person's social class, gender and racialization. The extent and nature of this problem is hugely important in itself: the structure of our society is harmful to far too many children and young people. There are also good reasons to believe, as demonstrated in Chapter 5, that the issue of violence between young people is closely connected to these societal conditions.

These arguments are not wholly novel – they build upon and echo many other studies of young people's lives and of violence, but we hope that we have offered a fruitful perspective on these issues. In particular, we hope that our account has adequately portrayed the depth and richness of young people's inner lives and how this affects their agency in the face of their socio-historical circumstances. In deploying the concepts of mattering and social harm, we hope to have done some justice to the psycho-social interplay between individual self-narrative and accumulated experiences of policies, systems, institutions, communities, neighbourhoods, peer groups and family.

In this chapter, we explore the harmful consequences of an arguably more powerful, entrenched vision of British society, youth and violence. Throughout the book, we have critiqued certain kinds of simplification and misconception – sometimes by implication, sometimes more explicitly. Our purpose in this chapter is to more directly and more thoroughly examine the origins, nature and effects of what we consider to be harmful perspectives on young people and violence. Though these perspectives have varied over time and in emphasis, a potent central demonizing narrative has run through them since at least the Victorian era. We will also consider the harmful measures used to punish or 'save' young people, which seem to both emerge from and exacerbate this demonization.

There is, of course, a long-established stream of thought and action in this country which has been concerned with societal conditions affecting the welfare of young people, and which has been attentive to the forms of structural harm that we have examined in this book (see, for example, Hendrick, 2015; Goldson, 2020; Muncie, 2021). Our fear, though, is that there is a wave of 'populist punitiveness' (Muncie, 2021, p 11) coming over, and being driven by, various power holders in Britain at present, which repurposes centuries-old myths of our nation and its youth, and which causes most harm precisely to those young people who already experience the kinds of biographical and localized concentrations of harm discussed in Chapter 4. As well as suffering from the historical maldistribution of recognition, resources and risk, then, they are also affected by substantially disproportionate state retribution. Squires observed in 2009 that there appeared to be an 'intensification of youth demonising and disciplining' (Squires, 2009, p 146) – regrettably, we continue to observe similar phenomena today.

The chapter begins with a brief, stylized description of a broad, powerful kind of mythological misconception that we see continually circulating in relation to young people and violence. The rest of the chapter then traces the history and effects of misconceptions of this nature, in three sections, each of which discusses one form of harmful response to 'youth violence' and to young people deemed a problem to society:

- demonize them;
- punish and control them;
- save them.

We do not set out on an extended exercise of discourse analysis, or to track the exact prevalence of certain ideas in historical and contemporary media and political commentary. Instead, our focus is more analytical, drawing out and explaining why particular ideas of youth and violence can be harmful.

Figure 6.1 summarizes different themes which will be covered in this chapter. As the diagram indicates, and as we will go on to explore, there are a number of connected, harmful ideas which have become attached to perceptions of youth violence, and these both feed into and are reinforced by harmful responses to it.

As we have stressed throughout this book, violence between young people is real, and it devastates lives, families and communities. Our goal is not to evaporate the issue into some simple moral panic but, rather, to critique the unhelpful and harmful mythologies and policy responses which exacerbate the harm experienced by young people. Violence between young people is most certainly a problem, but there are more and less helpful ways of problematizing it. In the Conclusion, as well as re-summarizing the arguments we have threaded throughout the book, we will outline a number of responses to the problem of violence between young people which we believe to be more helpful, effective and encouraging, and which amount to reasons for optimism and hope. By contrast, this chapter, by its nature, may well appear to be one-sidedly negative and pessimistic.

A perennial mythology of youth and violence?

Far from the image of structural inequalities and historical concentrations of harm which we have sought to present in this book, age-old mythologies of youth violence tend to be rooted in an ahistorical, organic vision of Britain. The nation is a united whole, a kind of national body which lives as one – 'inherently ordered and just' (Chamberlen and Carvalho, 2022, p 93). The nation's people are brought together by a peaceful national character, rooted in deep respect and deference for the rule of law. Problems of criminality and

Figure 6.1: Mutually reinforcing perceptions of and responses to the 'youth violence' problem

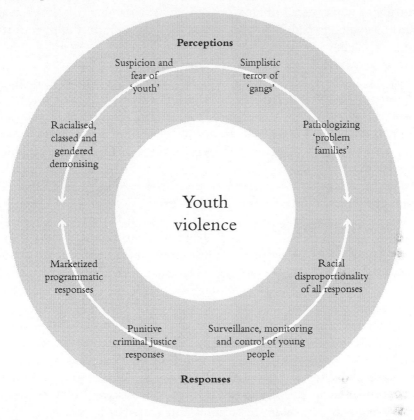

violence arise from different forms of criminogenic pathology – disturbances to an otherwise stable order which originate in various kinds of malevolent dysfunction. These are pathologies of individual character, or families, or (sub)cultures, or 'youth', and they are uncaused, self-generated evils, which are a threat to our otherwise harmonious national existence. To use Currie's phrase from the quote at the beginning of this chapter, they are 'biological or cultural deficiencies'. Implicit – or sometimes explicit – in this story is a racist mythology which imagines that it is foreign elements polluting our organic society.

There is no history in this myth, save for the perpetual nostalgia for a never-real golden era of peace and solidarity, which operates as a kind of static ideal, that is now purportedly lost, or at least at threat, because of the pathologies of younger generations, or of problem families, or of poor people, or of cultural Others. Dangerous classes at home are grouped with assorted 'savages' from abroad, and their young are perceived as either powerfully wilful enemies of society or hapless victims of the pathologies into which they are born, which breed and incubate wickedness. Either all-too-strong independent individuals or entirely crowd-like, swarming collectives, these young people are harbingers of doom: their presence in the present is a signal of decline, an indication that our longed-for mythological near-past is degenerating into a disordered, immoral, frightful future. As this story has morphed and been reconfigured since the early 19th century or longer, it has promoted different kinds of response and solution, broadly oscillating between two main ideas: either punish the young, or save them. Either way, we must be rescued from their danger. As Griffin (1993, p 10) has put it, 'the treatment and management of "youth" is expected to provide a solution to a nation's problems'.

This tale of Britain as a harmonious organic order under threat, especially from its young and from Others, seems to gain its ongoing power precisely from the fact that it is so profoundly ahistorical.[1] If Pearson (2011) is right that ideas of unprecedented youth depravity consistently resurface, with dubious 'perpetual novelty', this can perhaps be partly explained by the two-sided stasis at the core of the organic society myth: it seems to be a static legend – constantly recurring – about an allegedly static order. A cultural ideal which holds that our society was once (and could be again) a perfectly unified whole can be repurposed perennially, ad nauseam, because this dream of fixed harmony always seems just out of reach: we achieved it, but now it is lost; we are clinging on to it, but it is threatened by subversive elements; we could perhaps grasp towards it, were it not for the influence of Others.

The remainder of this chapter substantiates our view regarding the power of this mythology, explores its origins and describes its ongoing effects. In particular, we focus on how young people are demonized, punished, controlled and 'saved', in ways which we consider to be harmful.

Demonize them

In the face of a contentious social problem such as violence between young people, it is inevitable that a wide range of theories will proliferate to explain the nature and causes of the phenomenon. These notions – whether 'lay' or 'expert' – are never random, but draw in different ways upon assumptions and narratives which derive from our cultural history. Neither are they neutral in their effects: the common circulation of particular ideas about any social problem will always be consequential, affecting how certain people and groups are perceived, how leaders of institutions and organizations make decisions and how policies are formulated. In this section, we explore the history and contemporary potency of demonologies about young people and violence which we consider to be particularly entrenched, and especially harmful.

As we will go on to discuss, demonizing particular individuals or groups inherently involves various kinds of simplification and misdirection. It relies on a kind of 'black-boxing' which stands in for explanation: rather than encouraging us to consider the various different factors which could feed into a young person's thoughts, emotions and violent behaviour, it explains all this away with wickedness. We need not examine the matter too deeply; some young people are just evil, or some cultures – which have an allegedly overweening influence on young people – inculcate evil. There is a literal or figurative idea of pathology drawn upon here: individuals or families can be deemed literally pathological, because their genetics or their personalities are deemed physiologically deficient; and certain cultures can be deemed figuratively pathological, because they poison people's morals and generate dysfunction.

We explore these ideas further in this section. After briefly describing the various ways in which demonization is harmful, we discuss the connotations of 'youth' and 'youth violence' in contemporary discourse. We then examine the various ways in which young people have been historically demonized in relation to crime and violence. We conclude the section by returning to the present, to suggest that there is now a particular constellation of very old ideas about young people and the danger that they represent which seems to hold particular potency in today's Britain.

We do not intend to indict particular people or publications for definite cases of demonization. We are more focused on explaining what we would consider to be indic*table*, and why. We seek to explore, historically and analytically, demonizing ideas which have been circulating in British society for many decades and which seem to have maintained their power to this day. We do not see new ideas about young people springing from nowhere, but, rather, to use Golding and Middleton's phrase, the 'recurrent refurbishing of a series of images and beliefs' (Golding and Middleton, 1982, p 59). We aim to identify a few of these images and beliefs, and to describe the particular kind of refurbishment they seem to be undergoing in contemporary Britain.

Why and how is demonization harmful to young people?

It should perhaps go without saying that the demonization of young people is harmful to them, as it amounts to a reduction of all they are to a negative, threatening stereotype which requires management or control. Through this section we will be exploring a variety of forms that the demonization of young people can take and has taken, the various ways in which these are harmful and the reasons why they appear to have deep cultural resonance in this country. To frame this discussion, we briefly outline a few specific ways in which demonization can be harmful, utilizing the conceptualization of social harm which we presented in Chapter 2.

- Misrecognition: Demonization is a form of misrecognition and disrespect, entailing a denial or a stigmatization of young people's individual identities – it is thus harmful to young people's identity needs (see, for example, Tyler, 2020 on the stigmatization of certain youth identities).

- Undermined subjective well-being and mattering: This kind of societal disrespect can negatively affect young people's thoughts and feelings about themselves, including their sense of mattering. It can leave young people perceiving themselves to be of limited value, and their agentic power as either minimal – as they are unable to resist negative influences – or bad – as they are generationally predisposed to use it for ill (see, for example, Matera et al, 2021 on the effects of stereotyping on mattering; see, for example, Söllner et al, 2022 on the effects of age-related stereotypes on well-being).

- Damaged prospects: Negative stereotypes about young people can affect their education and employment prospects – and therefore undermine young people's understanding and subsistence needs – because of how they affect their self-perceptions and employers' and educational institutions' perceptions of young people (see, for example, Fuller et al, 2005; Beck et al, 2006; Pager and Karafin, 2009).

- Labelling and self-fulfilling prophecies: Cultural or institutional labelling of young people as troublesome and dangerous can in some cases make it more likely for them to play out the behaviours that they are reduced to, including 'offending' behaviours (see, for example, Kinsey, 2019; Motz et al, 2020). In this sense, it connects closely to the third component of subjective well-being – young people's sense of meaning and purpose in life.

- Neglect of structural harms: When young people are demonized as self-generating social problems such as violence, this entails a neglect of the wider determinants of their actions. In particular, given the arguments of this book, we are concerned that the demonization of young people could lead to the obfuscation of the structural harms that affect them. If the problems they face are deemed to be produced by their own autonomous, bounded world, this can undermine the case for addressing the structural harms that blight their lives. White (2020, p 51) puts the point in these terms: 'young people in [East London] have been framed as troublesome, but the trouble is structural and institutional'. As should be clear, we would not deny that young people's actions can be troublesome, but if there is a myopic, misguided focus on their actions as if entirely self-generated, this could both (a) lead to a failure to address the structural forms of 'trouble' to which White refers and which we explored in Chapter 4, and (b) lead to a neglect of the connections between structural harms affecting young people and the interpersonal violence which a small number of them commit.

- Encouragement of punitive criminalization and simplistic 'child-saving': demonization of young people can encourage the kinds of punitive criminalization and simplistic 'child-saving' which we explore in the second and third sections of this chapter, each of which can be harmful to young people in a variety of ways in themselves, as we will discuss.

The various forms of demonization which we explore in this section may be harmful in one or more of these ways, either constituting social harms in themselves or exacerbating other social harms. In what follows, we will further explicate how this happens, referring more specifically to particular kinds of demonization.

Connotations of 'youth' and 'youth violence'

> Youth and violence; the words seem inextricably linked … the pictures and words [in media and politics] almost convince us that it is inevitable, this marriage of violence and youth.
>
> Eron and Slaby, 1994, p 1

Before delving into the broad history of demonization, it is worth returning to the implications of the term 'youth violence', briefly surveyed in the Introduction. Both the word 'youth' and the phrase 'youth violence' can have unhelpful connotations. As we made clear in the Introduction, we have no interest in policing anyone's language, or in making grand statements about the need to dispose of particular words, but in our exploration of the various kinds of demonology which can attach to the problem of violence between young people, we start with the associations of both words in the term 'youth violence'.

Different ideas of 'youth' as a problematic generational mass have existed for centuries (see, for example, Gillis, 1981). Youth have been discursively associated with a wide range of negative ideas, such as threat and challenge (Alexander, 2000, p 238); Otherness and strangeness (Griffin, 1993, p 25); 'delinquency' (Griffin, 1993, p 100); crime (Muncie, 2021, p 3); and violence specifically (Eron and Slaby, 1994, p 1). The category of 'youth' has also been tied to various notions of lack or deficiency, and has been represented as fundamentally antithetical to civilization (Griffin, 1993, p 101); corrosive of social trust and community cohesion (Deuchar, 2009, p 95); or hostile to responsibility (Muncie, 2021, p 3). Its inherent attachment to ideas of change and renewal can be cast in a damaging light – the concept of 'youth' has often been associated with upheaval and crisis (Alexander, 2000, p 238; Goldson, 2011, p 3). Seen as an indication of the present and future state of the nation, the condition of our youth is something of a permanent problem, or even a national obsession (Griffin, 1993, p 9; Gunter, 2017, p 233). Contemporary usage of the phrase 'youth violence', then, can bring a lot of connotational baggage deriving from these cultural associations of 'youth'.

According to Google's Ngram Viewer, the proportion of publications written in British English which used the phrase 'youth violence' has grown rapidly since 1970, continuing to increase – though at a slowing rate since around 2007 – into the present (Figure 6.2). There are of course limitations to the validity of this data source,[2] but it does give a general indication of the recent prevalence of this concept in written publications.

The idea of 'youth violence', then, has been on the rise. It can carry with it a range of more or less inherent unhelpful or demonizing connotations. Firstly, by its nature as a noun, it can be a kind of reification, bestowing abstraction and permanence on something which is in fact a complex, diverse, dynamic and changing problem. It can seem a homogeneous or homogenizing category, pulling together all violence involving young people into a discrete group of activities, as if they can all be understood or explained in the same way. Interpreted slightly differently, the 'youth' in the phrase can seem adjectival, not just denoting who committed violence, but describing something about its nature, tied to the ideas of 'youth' surveyed earlier. The phrase 'youth violence' could ascribe a youthful character to violence – it could encourage 'spurious and decontextualized conceptions of youthful brutality' (Brotherton, 2015 p 153). Thus, 'youth' could operate as a kind of self-contained *explanation* for violence – violence can be seen

Figure 6.2: Graph based on a Google Ngram showing the prevalence of the phrase 'youth violence' in published materials written in British English, since 1970

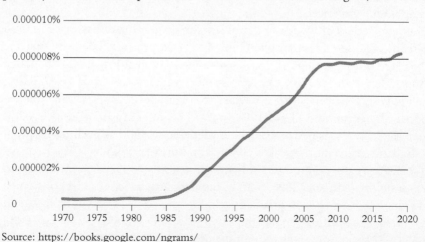

Source: https://books.google.com/ngrams/

as a product of essentially criminogenic youthfulness (see Muncie, 2021, p 65). 'Youth' can operate as a kind of 'bounded receptacle for blame', to use Cottrell-Boyce's (2013, p 202) evocative phrase. Violence can be seen as a self-generated property of youth, rather than the product of complex, interacting socio-historical factors. 'Youth' can become an 'autonomous and criminalised social category' (Alexander, 2000, p 247), seen as separate from the rest of society and in fundamental tension with its moral code.

At worst, then, the growing circulation of 'youth violence' as a concept can consummate the unhealthy 'marriage of violence and youth' referred to by Eron and Slaby (1994). This conflation can lead us to view violence as inherently youthful, and youth as inherently violent, encouraging us to perceive all contemporary youth problems through the lens of violence and criminality (Squires, 2009, p 146), rather than imbuing them with any independent importance. At the extreme, the most simplistic and inflammatory mobilizations of the idea can feed into 'ephephobia' – the generalized fear of young people (Kinsey, 2019, p 2).

To a lesser or greater extent, the various demonizing associations discussed to this point are inherent risks when the term 'youth violence' is used. Though they are tied up with historical narratives about 'youth', they are also quite generic conceptual connotations – products of semantics as much as of cultural history. In the remainder of this section, we go on to explore the more specific, somewhat distinctly British (or even English) kinds of demonology which seem to have become entrenched in our collective consciousness since the early 19th century in relation to violence and young people. We will first travel backwards in time to explore the origins of these demonologies, before then coming back to today, to sketch what appear to be the most prevalent components of youth demonizing in the present: racialized notions of all-powerful subcultures; terror of 'troubled' families; and the peril of gangs and knives. As it circulates today, the concept of youth violence appears frequently tethered to some very old, and very harmful ideas.

Victorian demonologies of youth, crime and violence

Young people have been deemed troublesome by and for their elders since at least the time of Plato (Wallace and Kovatcheva, 1998, p 26). There are good reasons to believe, however, that the forms of youth demonizing which have particular potency in the present are traceable largely back to the Victorian era. As Muncie has put it, during this period ideas about young people, families, crime and violence 'underwent a dramatic reconfiguration in terms that are now familiar with us today' (Muncie, 2021, p 63). The images and beliefs which are undergoing refurbishment and repurposing at present in relation to 'youth violence' are products of 19th century ideas and fears which were energized by historical upheavals of that time – industrialization, urbanization, imperialism and revolution. We explore some of these ideas and fears in the following sections: ideas about criminal responsibility and impressionable vulnerability; colonial fears about savages abroad and at home; fears about family pathology; and fears about the overweening influence of dangerous subcultures.

Victorian conceptions of responsibility and vulnerability, wickedness and weakness

Through the 19th century, different ideas about society, crime and young people were in tension, awkwardly coexisting and vying for dominance. Wiener (1994) distinguishes between two distinct, ideal-typical images of the young criminal which held sway at different times during the Victorian era. In the first, the individual is wilfully evil, a wicked character whose malevolence derives from their self-developed personality flaws. In the second, the individual is vulnerable and malleable, their misdeeds the product of powerful, pathological influences on them, such as their family's moral failings or the depravity of their local culture. What is common between these two images is a notion which remains all too potent today: the idea of some bounded pathological deficiency within a singular criminogenic source, be it character, family or culture.

In Wiener's (1994) view, dominant ideas shifted from the early to the late Victorian period, from the 'wilfully evil' criminal in the early 19th century, to the 'weak impressionable' criminal in the latter part of the century. Of course, these are ideal types, and represent a spectrum of ideas about agency and responsibility, rather than a sharp dichotomy, but Wiener traces a clear move from one end towards the other over the course of the period. Early Victorians tended to see criminals as 'wilful enemies of society' (Wiener, 1994, p 12) who had failed to develop the right kinds of habit and character (Wiener, 1994, p 42). The age was haunted by the 'spectre of instinctualism' – there was a fear that people struggle to contain powerful, dangerous impulses, and that those who fail to develop their character sufficiently will be compelled by these internal forces to commit terrible misdemeanours (Wiener, 1994, p 26). This fear was not generalized to all; it was seen as far more of a problem among the lower orders, and among natives in the colonies (Wiener, 1994; and see later). Individuals were held to be responsible for containing and controlling their instincts, guiding themselves towards morally upright behaviours – 'the age's central myth of the responsible individual' was built on the idea that each person is free to choose good conduct, and must be actively deterred from criminal acts through the existence of harsh punishments (Wiener, 1994, p 48). It was during this period that juvenile delinquency was 'invented' as a category of social problem (Goldson, 2020, p 319). When separate penal facilities were opened for young criminals, though, the institutions were not dissimilar from their adult equivalents, due to the potent notion that all should be held 'fully responsible for their actions', regardless of relative youth (Muncie, 2021, p 55). Throughout this period, then, there was a sense that individuals needed to control their *internally derived* urges and passions: to live a life free of vice and wickedness relied upon nurturing a civilized personality, which would allow you to rise above base instincts.

During the later Victorian period, an alternative view began to proliferate, which placed greater emphasis on *externally derived* habits, preferences and attitudes. The individual criminal was less a self-guiding wicked force, and more of a weak-willed respondent to the guidance of others, vulnerable to the corruption of external influences (Muncie, 2021, p 4). Criminal behaviour manifested moral pathologies which came from various kinds of 'schools of crime', such as working-class culture and problematic families (Wiener, 1994, pp 228, 148). Character was no longer seen as self-formed, but as the product of social environment, and concern was thus redirected from the power of uncontrolled instincts to the no less fearful prospect of children being socialized into crime from a young age. Increased attention was placed on 'bad parents', and on the family as 'the most important nursery of character' (Wiener, 1994, pp 287, 375). There was some awareness of economic influences on people's lives, but the primary concern was with moral and cultural forces, seen to be the pre-eminent shapers of personality (Muncie, 2021, p 57).

Both these visions of the criminal, despite their contradiction, continue to haunt the collective criminological imagination. They each resurfaced in various forms through the 20th century – in Cyril Burt's ideas about 'deficient personality and broken homes', for instance (Muncie, 2021, p 77) – and their influence lives on to this day. Garland has suggested that ideas about crime in the present are defined by an incoherent collision of these two polar opposite images of the individual criminal; what struggles for credence is 'the excluded middle that lies between complete freedom and irresistible compulsion' (Garland, 2001, p 198). There is still a powerful tendency to see those who commit crime through a dubious binary, as either all too wilful or entirely weak willed, as either too self-directed or too deeply influenced by others. Goldson suggests that this binary may be particularly influential in youth justice, in which there has been a somewhat perennial tension between competing conceptions of the young criminal as either a 'needy' individual who should be rescued from negative influences or an unruly 'threat' who should be punished (Goldson, 2020, p 319). Both can rest on a kind of demonization – the difference is in the perceived origin of wickedness: either it is in the young person themselves, through their self-nurtured evil, or the evil has been encouraged externally by, for example, family, gangs or wider culture. Other researchers have similarly commented on the ongoing presence of these old Victorian ideas: Moore, for instance, has argued that the contemporary focus on punitive and exclusionary criminal justice responses is a return to 'the classical liberalism of the early Victorians' (Moore, 2014, p 41), and Fatsis suggests, relatedly, that it is a tenet of current 'neoliberal ideology' that crime is a life-style choice (Fatsis, 2019, p 1309) – again a return to ideas of the wickedly wilful.

The boundaries of Englishness: colonial ideas of savages abroad and at home

Visions of savagery troubled the Victorians. Fears of dreadful impulses and pathological cultural influences were tied to notions of 'race', class and imperialism which developed through the 19th century. Industrialization at this time was also stoking panic about the eradication of pastoral England, with all its legend of organic, cohesive community and oneness. Both at home and abroad, there was deep concern with Englishness, and with a particular image of English civilization. Criminality, and violence especially, was 'un-English' and foreign (Gilroy, 1982, p 92; Emsley, 2005; Cottrell-Boyce, 2013, p 203). Mythologies of a secure, coherent, static English society fed the terror of what could threaten that pristine order. The 'imagined boundaries of Englishness' were carefully marked and marshalled (Williams and Clarke, 2018, p 4), the criminal occupying a stigmatized space beyond its borders.

Crimes were thus committed by 'those not yet brought into the civilised English community'; those from poorer backgrounds who undertook illegal acts were members of the 'rough' working class, 'manifestations of the "other" that helped to define English gentleness' (Emsley, 2005, pp 175, 75). Well-heeled Victorians saw their 'poorer urban brethren' as 'at once fascinating, intimidating and incomprehensible', and viewed their criminal elements as occupying 'a separate moral and physical universe' (Sharpe, 2016, pp 412, 414). For some police officers even into the early 1900s, the East End of London felt like 'a strange and alien land' (Emsley, 2005, p 134). The children and young people who got caught up in criminal groups were often viewed by their moralizing superiors as pitiful victims of these alien lands, who required civilizing. Once they became 'mature Englishmen', they would learn good sense, moderation and restraint (Emsley, 2005, pp 180–1). All of this had very potent colonial undertones – young people's violence in the 1800s was grouped with that of 'savages' in the Empire (Duckworth, 2002, p 21; Emsley 2005, p 180). The use of the term 'thug', for instance, began with media comparisons between garrotting thieves in Britain and the 'Thuggee' sect in India, alleged to have perpetrated similar acts against British soldiers (Emsley, 2005, p 16). Both the prevailing images of colonial subjects as bound into 'naturally lawless' bands, groups and tribes and the manner of their punitive control were paralleled in treatment of domestic 'criminal collectives' (Nijjar, 2018, p 150).[3] As with criminals in Britain, the personalities of colonial natives were seen to be determined by various forms of biological or cultural pathology (Moore, 2014, p 37).

These racist notions are embedded in our national culture. In the early 1980s, Pearson argued that terror of the 'alien interruption of violence' is a 'dominant aspect of the British political culture' (Pearson, 1983, p 209), and many researchers have continued to substantiate this claim into the present (see, for example, Cottrell-Boyce, 2013; Moore, 2014; Williams and Clarke, 2016; Williams and Clarke, 2018; Nijjar, 2018; Bhattacharyya et al, 2021; Williams and Squires, 2021). The English have a deep-rooted tendency to blame their violence on someone else (Pearson, 1983, p x), struggling to come to terms with the fact that the violence in our society is, in fact, all too English. As explored in previous chapters, the problems that we have with interpersonal violence are closely tied to the nature of our political economy and institutions; to our entrenched inequalities of wealth, power and recognition; and to how these manifest as cumulative social harms in particular communities and biographies. Our violence is not unique: as Currie (2016) has demonstrated, our problems with violence are similar to other countries which also have huge inequality; inadequate support for families and welfare; a preponderance of poorly paid precarious work; and an overly punitive criminal justice system. But the particular, idiosyncratic forms that these issues take in our country are closely tied to long-established features of our society – particularly as it has developed since the 19th century. Then and now, our violence is ours.

Pathological families and the pathology of poverty

It seems that the Victorian era was characterized by a peculiar kind of fear for the health of the English national organism, then, and there were plenty of presumed sites of pathology. As well as various Others bespoiling the nation, there were related concerns about the breeding of deviance – the cultures of poor families incubating crime and violence.

We have a long, disreputable history of blaming mothers for societal problems (Pearson, 1983, p 208; Jensen, 2018), and the concerns about parental dysfunction or neglect which grew through the 19th century were tied to this tendency (Wiener, 1994, p 287; Martin, 2008; Muncie, 2021, p 53). Worries about the 'low moral condition' of parents among the lower orders took hold particularly in the second half of the century (Muncie, 2021, p 56), prompting the creation of organizations such as the National Society for the Prevention of Cruelty to Children, which explicitly concerned itself with 'bad parents' (Wiener, 1994, p 287). Concerns centred especially on irresponsible 'slum mothers' (Martin, 2008, p 131). These fears were entwined with emerging ideas about childhood as a period of innocence and dependence, and thus vulnerability to pathological influences. Notions of the ideal family are of course historically and culturally variable, and this was a time when a particular kind of middle-class ideal obtained significant power. Deviations from the ideal were variously seen as biologically or culturally deficient.

Closely bound to these fears of pathological parenting were anxieties about 'cultures' of poverty: apparently self-authored codes of life were seen to perpetuate destitution among the lower classes. The culture-of-poverty myth has circulated in this country, in various forms, for centuries, and the poor have been seen as 'a nuisance, a threat and a burden' throughout our history (Golding and Middleton, 1982, pp 10, 186). Central to this myth is the idea that poverty is caused by the self-generated behavioural habits of the poor, or by their innate inferiority: theirs is a separate, degenerate world, within which scarcity is internally nurtured. Golding and Middleton articulate the core of this mythology in similar terms, arguing that it rests on an image of 'the creation of poverty by and within the world of the poor, a land untouched by any hint of relational disadvantage to the rest of society or to social structures of power and privilege' (Golding and Middleton, 1982, p 239). This idea gained particular potency during the late Victorian era, as it connected with ideas of family pathology, the savagery of the lower orders and the threat of 'foreign' influence, to form a compound peril which resided in the ever-growing inner cities. Social researchers of this time, such as Charles Booth and Henry Mayhew, dedicated themselves to studying these dens of iniquity, seemingly with a considerable degree of nose-holding.

This cocktail of concerns remains potent. Through the 20th century they gained a veneer of scientific validity, in the form of ideas about genetic inferiority which have been popularized by figures such as Charles Murray (for example, Murray, 1999; see Martin, 2008 and Jensen, 2018 for critiques). The 1980s saw growing governmental expression of these worries, which became tied to fears about an allegedly permissive culture, changes to family structures and welfare dependency (Muncie, 2021, p 298). The racialization of these issues also deepened in this era: Gilroy noted the common tendency among power-holders to cite the pathology of Black households, and witnessed increasing panic about the idea that such pathology 'wrought destructive changes on the inner city by literally breeding deviancy' (Gilroy 1982, p 141). These racist ideas hold power to this day (see, for example, Williams and Clarke, 2018, p 5), bound up with the kinds of poverty stigmatization discussed in Chapter 4. Ongoing governmental concern about the state of family life and parenting is evidenced by the steady succession of policy measures brought in since the 1930s to enforce 'responsible parenting', culminating in the 'Troubled Families' agenda of 2012 onwards (Muncie, 2021, p 299), which is explicitly concerned with preventing crime and disorder by assertively intervening in ('turning around') families which are deemed problematic (Newburn et al, 2018; discussed further later on). Critics have highlighted its 'mother-blame' and its 'culturisation of poverty' (Jensen, 2018, pp viii, 122; see also Crossley, 2018).

Dangerous youth subcultures and gangs inculcating criminal habits

Especially in the later Victorian period, when concerns grew about young impressionable minds, the fear was that the wrong sorts of culture and the wrong sorts of peers could send an individual young person down a decidedly delinquent path. Inherent in this was an image of ossified cultural pathology: not of (sub)cultures as made and remade, negotiated and navigated, but as fixed, constant and infinitely shaping, subsuming individual agency. The toxic influence of youth gangs or of criminal subcultures could comprehensively infect the character and actions of young people.

Rebelliousness was seen to spread through culture in both the sociological and the artistic sense of the word: through localized behavioural codes, and through particular forms of artistic expression. 'Fighting gangs' in the late 1800s, such as the notorious Scuttlers, were seen as consisting of youthful rebels rejecting society's norms, initiating their members into subversion (Emsley, 2005, p 35). As well as collectively crafting dangerous group norms, young criminals were also seen as creating and disseminating the 'worst' forms of art. Duckworth (2002, p 31) quotes a clergyman from the mid-19th century who discussed (with some disgust) young people 'listening to tales of murder and singing songs respecting burglars, convicts, highwaymen, etc ... these songs acting on the minds of the ignorant, vicious and excited lads cause them to become more reckless and hardened'. Henry Mayhew (2008 [1859], p 532) similarly bewailed what he observed in lads' lodging houses, where the boys would read each other Jack Sheppard stories: 'it is often this ability to read ... which becomes the instrument of the youth's moral depravity'. A plea for illiteracy, it seems.

These twin terrors remain. As discussed in Chapter 5, and further in this chapter, the figure of the gang continues to cause immense cultural consternation. Entwined with this today are concerns about young people's penchant for peer-produced 'drill' music, which is seen in contemporary Britain, it appears, as our Jack Sheppard stories – as the pre-eminent cultural instrument of the youth's moral depravity (see Fatsis, 2019). The line between artistic expression and criminal activity has become blurred – in 2019 a Metropolitan Police detective said, when commenting on a court case, that drill music can 'amount to gang-related violence' (quoted in Bhattacharyya et al, 2021, p 38). As Alexander has put it, these kinds of attitude display a 'conservative culturalist perspective' which is 'focused on cultural pathology at the expense of structural inequality' (Alexander,

2000, p 238). As in the Victorian era, these perspectives can suggest that cultures are rigid, inescapable forces – their pathological influence 'a fixed and impermeable property of human life', swallowing up individual agency (Gilroy, 1982, p 142). Often implicit in this is a close association between subversive subcultures, crime and Blackness: criminality is perceived to be an 'innate, subcultural feature of black people and black communities' (Williams and Clarke, 2018, p 5). Black youth culture and 'gang culture' are conflated, and seen to be a dangerous 'contagion' spreading through inner-city streets (Bhattacharyya et al, 2021, p 47; see also Williams and Squires, 2021, pp 201–4).

Contemporary conservative fears about rebellious subcultures have a kind of leftist mirror-image in those who lament the supposed ideological ultra-conformity of criminal youth. For some, far from oppositional groups setting themselves up against the norms of mainstream society, young people engaged in crime and violence are ideological dupes, their actions guided in fact by deeply internalized mainstream values. In the wake of the 2011 riots, for instance, ideas of competitive hyper-consumerism gained ground, with some commentators pointing to looting as evidence of young people's consumerist conformity (see, for example, Moxon, 2011). This is at best a simplification (see Jensen, 2013; Newburn et al, 2018), and at worst a return to the 'spectre of instinctualism' which haunted the Victorians – now, rather than emotional impulses, the fear is redirected towards implanted consumerist instincts.

There is something of a parallel between the different Victorian visions of individual will and these different ideas about the orientation of criminal subcultures: subcultures are seen to be composed of either all-too-wilful rebels, actively rejecting society, or all-too-weak conformists, passively absorbing society's ideology.[4] These symmetrical simplifications can be equally demeaning towards young people – in both cases, they are cast as harbingers of criminogenic culture, whether all too subversive or all too mainstream.

Victorian demonologies in an era of Victorian inequality

We have completed our brief tour of the ideal-typical Victorian demonologies which flow into the present. Though alternative ideas of course also circulated, the 19th century was significantly characterized by a set of interwoven fears about youth wilfulness or vulnerability; the depravity of Others; the deficiencies of parents; the degenerate culture of poor people; and the potent, pathological influence of youth subcultures and gangs.

We do not intend to commit some kind of anti-Victorian genetic fallacy: just because these ideas circulated in that period, that does not make them bad. What makes them bad is the way that they demonize, patronize, pathologize and stereotype young people, contributing to the harmful consequences outlined at the outset of this section. The relevance of their Victorian origins is two-fold. Firstly, it is evidence of their deep-rootedness and the powerful grip these ideas have maintained over our collective consciousness – many researchers have suggested that we are somewhat locked in to certain ways of thinking about young people, violence and crime which derive substantially from the 19th century (see, for example, Garland, 2001; Hendrick, 2015; Goldson, 2020; Muncie, 2021). Secondly, the Victorian era is of relevance to thinking about contemporary Britain due to similarities between our time and theirs, particularly in terms of inequality: as Kotkin has put it, for instance, London today is very similar to the 'bifurcated city' it was in Victorian times (Kotkin, 2020, p 135). Kotkin connects these two points, suggesting that similar levels of inequality in the Victorian era and the present may go some way towards explaining the renewed cultural currency now placed on societal stasis and fixity: we have returned, he argues, to a 'static ideal of an ordered society' in which we seek to maintain 'a largely fixed system' (Kotkin, 2020, pp 2, 4). In today's Britain, as in the Victorian era, there is a coterie of highly privileged individuals for whom stasis and fixity – the stretching of the present unchanged into the future – is of clear benefit.

Today's perils: 'Black youth culture', gangs, knives and 'troubled families'

We now have gang culture and youths coming from outside Havering, causing fear on the streets.

Andrew Rosindell, Conservative MP for Romford,
House of Commons, March 2019

Stupid kids and their stupid gangs.

Vernon Coaker, Labour MP for Gedling,
House of Commons, March 2019[5]

The ways that violence between young people is now thought, spoken and cared about are affected by these very old demonologies. Of course, deep concern about violence between young people is wholly justified – as this book should make clear, it is something we share. But concern about a social issue can take different forms, depending on the kind of problem it is seen to be. As the previous chapter illustrated, there is no shortage of thinkers and writers producing sophisticated analyses of what can cause violence between young people: they treat violence as the complex problem that it is, relating it to the socio-historical conjuncture that different groups of young people find themselves in. Too often, though, influential media commentators and power-holders treat violence between young people as a quite different kind of problem, mobilizing culturally entrenched fears about threatening youth to paint simplistic, harmful images of the issue (see, for example, Williams and Squires, 2021). The Victorian terrors discussed earlier have obviously not flowed into the present unchanged, but their influence remains notable: where earlier we explored the contemporary manifestations of these old fears broadly in our culture, in what follows we briefly discuss the far more specific narratives of peril which seem to circulate in relation to young people and violence today.

Researchers who have examined the prominence of different demonologies in the 21st century have highlighted a few particularly common features. Firstly, the extent to which young Black men are singled out for blame is disproportionate at best, racist at worst. Narratives about problematic youth and gang culture rarely stray from alluding to Blackness, and are prone to portraying Black young men as 'inherently criminogenic and violent' (Gunter, 2017, p 225). Despite the fact that, across the country, more violence is committed by young White men than Black men, in the 'national imagination' the latter are too often seen as 'predisposed to criminality and violence' (Thapar, 2021, pp 181–2). When taken proportionally, depending on the dataset, it can appear that Black young men are more likely to be involved in violence in this country (see Chapter 1; Webster, 2015; Pitts, 2020), but this cannot justify the kinds of racist essentializing found by numerous studies (see, for example, Gunter, 2017; Williams and Clarke, 2018; Fatsis, 2019; Williams and Squires, 2021). This essentialism brings us back to Victorian ideas about the biological or cultural pathology of the racial Other, and can also be tied to demonizing portrayals of artforms which are racialized as Black, such as drill music (see Fatsis, 2019; Ekpoudom, 2020). In fact, as emphasized in Chapter 5, the most significant social determinants of violence relate to biography and place, not to 'race' (Goldson, 2011, p 11).

Secondly, closely tied to this, there is an overwhelming focus on gangs. As discussed extensively in the previous chapter, there is an ongoing debate about how to define gangs; the proportion of young people who may be involved in gangs; and the extent to which gang involvement or gang culture plays a causal role in violence among young people. Despite this, many studies have found that a tunnel-visioned focus on gangs is common in media commentary, political discussion and government reports, and that this is often tied to the essentializing ideas about Black young men discussed earlier (see, for example, Hallsworth and Brotherton, 2011; Hallsworth, 2013; Cottrell-Boyce, 2013; Fatsis, 2019; Koch, 2019; Bhattacharyya et al, 2021; Wroe, 2021). Brotherton suggests that simplistic ideas about 'the gang' are the most significant factor encouraging the 'pejorative association between youth and trouble' today (Brotherton, 2015, pp 8–9). References to gangs in relation to violence can operate as a 'substitute for analysis', standing in for explanatory examination by offering up a one-word 'self-explanatory motivation for conflict' (Alexander, 2000, p 21). Despite all the debate and disagreement about the nature and importance of gangs in this country, they have come to obtain 'an absolute ontological status' in policy circles since the late 1990s – treated as a clearly defined political problem and 'amenable to policy action' (Shute, 2016, pp 373–5). Ilan (2015) argues that, in our obsession with gangs, we risk the capture of our 'criminological imagination' by the idea of the 'criminogenic group', which can dilute the attention that we pay to both the psychological complexity of individuals and the macro-scale social determinants of crime (see Chapter 5).

Consternation about gangs has often centred on the issue of 'county lines' – young people from urban areas being exploited into running drugs into more rural territories (see Harding, 2020a; Havard et al, 2021). While protecting young people from exploitation is of course a vital imperative (see Chapter 5), researchers have highlighted the need to balance that imperative with avoiding the gang stereotypes already described, raising concerns that the panic surrounding 'county lines' can exacerbate the disproportionate monitoring and punishment of young people – particularly young people of colour from poorer communities (for example, Koch, 2019; Wroe, 2021).

Often bound up with portrayals of the gang are fears about particular weapons – since around 2008, the focus has been especially on knives (see Williams and Squires, 2021). The phrase 'knife crime' has rocketed in usage since the 1990s (Figure 6.3), despite widespread doubts about its helpfulness (see, for example, Squires, 2009, 2011; Bhattacharyya et al, 2021; Williams and Squires, 2021). A myopic focus on a specific kind of weapon distracts from the social relations and the social ecology of violence, and there has even been suggestion that obsessive media coverage of knives could exacerbate the issue of knife-carrying (Squires, 2011, pp 150, 155), as well as feeding into the over-use of stop and search by police (discussed further later).

Aside from gangs, certain kinds of family are the other apparent incubator of violence. While it is of course vital to attend to the ways in which early childhood life and the nature of relationships within families can support or harm the flourishing of young people (see Chapter 4), what does not help us get any further in our understanding of violence is a simplistic culture of parent-blame. In her recent analysis of this phenomenon, Jensen (2018) shows how contemporary narratives of deficient parenting resemble Victorian images, in which a broad societal crisis is seen to originate in the apparent moral degeneracy of poorer households. The idea of parental irresponsibility having a causal tie to crime and violence among young people has been promulgated through

Figure 6.3: Graph based on a Google Ngram showing the prevalence of the phrases 'youth violence', 'gang violence', 'gang culture', 'knife crime', 'troubled families' and 'gang crime' in published materials written in British English, since 1970

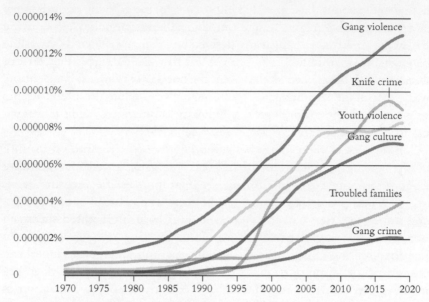

Source: https://books.google.com/ngrams/

the government's 'troubled families' rhetoric – which many have criticized for rehabilitating old stigmatizing ideas about a feckless underclass breeding deviancy (see, for example, Crossley, 2018; Jensen, 2018; Lister, 2021, pp 99–100) – and its 'Troubled Families' programme, which has been of questionable effectiveness (see Jensen, 2018; Muncie, 2021, pp 300–1). Even those who suggest that the Troubled Families programme may have had some positive effects point out that its overall success was undermined by concurrent government policies which 'greatly increased pressures' on families, 'against a backdrop of severe and increasing hardship' (Eisenstadt and Oppenheim, 2019, p 104).

Aforementioned data limitations notwithstanding, the Google Ngram in Figure 6.3 gives a sense of the rapidly increased prominence of phrases associated with these ideas since 1970.

Some contemporary drivers of demonization

It appears, then, that there is an issue of demonization associated with young people and violence in today's Britain. Specifying the exact scale and severity of this issue is beyond the scope of this book – suffice it to say that, on the basis of the research surveyed earlier, there are a number of harmfully simplistic, generalizing and discriminatory ideas about young people and violence that are circulating in our contemporary moment.

A variety of theories have been advanced as to what drives this circulation of demonologies. In line with Kotkin's focus on the cultural consequences of vast disparities of wealth and power, Tyler (2020) suggests that inequality and stigmatization are mutually reinforcing: inequality breeds degrading attitudes towards the most marginalized, and this stigmatization in turn helps to strengthen and solidify the systems which maintain inequality. Echoing earlier studies by Hall et al (1978) and Gilroy (1982), Williams and Clarke (2018, p 5) suggest that we are seeing frequent invocations of crisis at present, and that this encourages the demonization of Others. It is now commonly declared that our society or values are in danger or under threat (or 'broken'), and this leads to a heightened proclivity to fear and marginalize Others as we seek to demarcate the boundaries of our common culture – the boundaries of Englishness – with all the more desperation (see also Williams and Squires, 2021). In their discussion of deeply hardened attitudes towards crime into the 21st century, both Young and Garland point to certain features of 'late modern' society. Young (2007, pp 34–5) suggests that 'punitive anger' and essentializing perceptions of Others are driven by the precariousness of social inclusion in the modern era, and by the terror of the marginalized that this breeds. This leads to more 'disproportionality, scapegoating and stereotyping' in attitudes towards those who have committed crimes, particularly more visible crimes such as violence (Young, 2007, p 41). Along similar lines, Garland (2001, pp 82, 181) argued that late modern society is characterized by growing inequality and declining solidarity, promoting the stigmatization of those deemed to be deviant or troublesome, whose 'perceived worth tends towards zero'. There are a range of economic, cultural and social features of modern Britain, then, which may be exacerbating demonization.

As in any era, today's social attitudes have been affected not only by these broad, sweeping historical trends, but also by specific, spectacular events, and one event in particular – the 2011 riots. Goldson argues that the cultural 'crisis of childhood' which gripped much of the 1990s was in no small part prompted by the murder of James Bulger in 1993, which set in train a period of punitiveness in youth justice which lasted into the 2000s (Goldson, 2011, p 3), during what could be called the 'post-Bulger' period. In the same essay, published the same year as the 2011 riots, but written before them, Goldson suggests that, in more recent years, we had switched to a perceived 'crisis of youth' (Goldson, 2011, p 3). This was certainly consolidated by the urban disturbances of that year. Perhaps we are now in a 'post-riots' period, our cultural fears about young people infused with post-hoc narratives both about the causes of those troubles, and about who is troublesome. Though the riots are now, in 2022, over a decade in the past, the political response which followed them seems to remain influential, centred as it was on a few still-potent ideas: that the riots exhibited 'criminality plain and simple'; that they exemplified failures of parenting; and that they showed the depths of our 'gang culture' problem (Jensen, 2018, pp 1–3; Newburn et al, 2018; Williams and Squires, 2021, p 217). This rhetoric both reflected pre-existing cultural concerns and further encouraged them. These notions of uncaused criminal wickedness, family dysfunction and cultural pathology certainly appear to circulate in present-day discussions about violence between young people, and they also bear striking resemblance to the old demonologies of the 19th century.

Alongside those three purported 'causes' of the riots, there was a fourth major pillar in the political response to the 2011 riots: assertions of the need for more police and more robust policing (Newburn et al, 2018). This brings us to the focus of the next section – the forms of punishment and policing which have developed in 21st century Britain in response to the problem of violence between young people. As already outlined, demonization can be harmful to young people for a range of reasons, but perhaps the most significant is its role in encouraging harsher, more discriminatory and more intrusive forms of punishment and policing.

Punish and control them

> The Home Secretary has increased police funding by more than £1 billion this year, is giving the police more powers to stop and search known offenders, has started recruiting 20,000 more police officers, and is ensuring that those who carry a knife are locked up for longer. We will do everything in our power to end these shocking acts of violence and this senseless loss of life.
>
> Kit Malthouse, Minister of State for Crime and Policing, House of Commons, March 2020[6]

State responses to violence between young people should make society safer. They should allow young people access to the provision that they need to address the individual and social precipitators of their violence. They should form part of a broader agenda to enhance the flourishing of young people and their families. A government which wanted to effectively and sustainably reduce violence would address the adverse social conditions which predictably breed violence; it would attend to the historically sedimented structural harms which are concentrated in particular biographies and communities (see Chapters 4 and 5, and the Conclusion).

In this section, we discuss specific measures undertaken by state agencies in Britain since the early 21st century which purport to respond to the problem of violence between young people but which, in various ways, compound the harm experienced by young people and communities. These measures are concentrated in many of the same communities which experience the most acute accumulations of the structural harms discussed in Chapter 4, thus further exacerbating the adversity and the social suffering of young people living in these areas. Alongside a significant maldistribution of recognition, resources and risk, then, there are also profound disparities in the extent to which different communities are exposed to state retribution. As Currie (2016) has convincingly shown, punitive and ineffective criminal justice systems are one of the major predictors of violence in a society – far from reducing the problem, they can exacerbate it. Policy decisions and institutional practices can deepen the alienation, humiliation and anti-authority sentiment of young people, firing up rather than soothing social antagonism (White, 2013, p 152). Policing and punishment can overlay and reinforce marginalization and social exclusion (Garland, 2001, p 202). We will be exploring these harmful effects, among others, through the course of this section.

It is not all bad. There have been a number of promising initiatives since the start of the century designed to address the problem of violence between young people. Violence Reduction Units (VRUs), for instance, hold significant potential to address localized social determinants of harm and violence (see Irwin-Rogers, Muthoo and Billingham, 2020). We will discuss this and other promising developments at greater length in the Conclusion to this book, which will focus substantially on reasons for hope and optimism regarding the reduction of violence between young people in Britain. We would agree with Edwards, Hughes and Swann when they argue that commentaries which focus only on the 'malign, despotic and oppressive features' of the state's relations with young people are both conceptually and politically limiting (Edwards, Hughes and Swann, 2015, p 205). It is certainly not the case that, when it comes to youth justice in this country, everything is going wrong. The precipitous decline in child and youth imprisonment of recent years, for instance, is a progressive and welcome development (see Bateman, 2015; Goldson, 2015, 2020; Hendricks, 2015; Prison Reform Trust, 2021; discussed further later on).

There is a perennial tension in youth justice between welfarist and punitive principles – between the idea of responding to young people in trouble with measures to enhance welfare and well-being, or to punish and control (see Goldson, 2020). Despite what Scott (2018, p 211) has called the 'punitive trap', in which electoral pressures encourage punitiveness among politicians, there has never been a clear-cut either/or approach by any government: no state regime in Britain has ever been wholly welfarist or entirely punitive in relation to young people (see Hendricks, 2015; Goldson, 2020; Muncie, 2021), and the current government is no exception (see Muncie, 2021, p 402).

Our primary focus in this section, though, is on the ways in which various policies, systems and institutions ostensibly designed to address the problem of violence between young people can be both ineffective – when they either fail to reduce or exacerbate violence – and harmful – when they produce other significant injurious effects. There are signs that recent governments, and especially the current Conservative government of Boris Johnson, are erring towards increased punitiveness. There is a sense of emergency coming out of state rhetoric, tied to a repoliticization of youth justice, alongside indications of heightened 'authoritarian populism' in its approach to crime: there is more fevered condemnation of youth misbehaviour; rapidly expanding measures to control and punish young people seen to have committed misdemeanours 'on the balance of probabilities'; and increased investment in prisons and police as the guarantors of social order (Hall et al, 1978; Goldson, 2020, p 329). As we will discuss later on, an element of this punitive populism appears to be what could be termed an 'obsession with the proximate'. Despite initiatives such as VRUs – which are defined (at least in theory) by a focus on the longer-term, distal causes of violence – governments since 2010 have seemed to be more focused, in both rhetoric and policy, on the more proximate triggers of violence, such as knife-carrying and gang involvement, and on those young people who have already engaged in criminal acts. For instance, despite its purported focus on 'early intervention', the 2018 Serious Violence Strategy was criticized for prioritizing interventions with young people who had already committed offences (see, for example, Hayes, 2018). There is always a risk that heavy-handed measures to address proximate causes can deepen and exacerbate the more distal, entrenched, social determinants of violence: overweening attention to short-term gain can brew longer-term pain.

We explore all of these themes in the following sections, taking different elements of youth punishment and control in turn. Throughout, we will illustrate connections between the ways in which recent governments have sought to punish and control young people, and the kinds of demonization discussed in the preceding section.

Child and youth imprisonment

Since the dawn of the millennium, trends in child and youth imprisonment have exhibited five main features: significantly declining rates of imprisonment; increasing racial disproportionality; worsening conditions; continued ineffectiveness; and a continued governmental commitment to the idea that some children and young people do need to be imprisoned (see Bateman, 2015; Goldson, 2015; Muncie, 2021, pp 398–402; Prison Reform Trust, 2021). The substantial reduction of child and youth imprisonment is to be welcomed, but the scale and extent of harm experienced by those

Figure 6.4: Trends in youth custody numbers and conditions in youth prisons, 2006–20

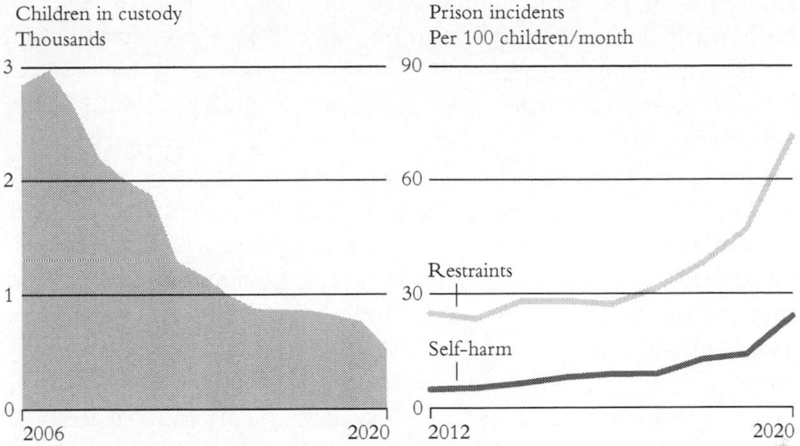

Sources: Youth Justice Board Monthly Youth Custody report August 2020; Youth Justice Statistics 2018–9; Youth Justice Statistics 2019–20

who are imprisoned – coupled with the stark failure of child and youth custody to reduce or prevent crime – remains a cause for deep concern.

The number of under-18s in custody has fallen by 82 per cent since 2006, and as of 2020 there were also 41 per cent fewer 18- to 24-year-olds in prison than there were in 2006 (Prison Reform Trust, 2021, pp 39, 42; Figure 6.4). Various factors have been proffered to explain this decline, including an increased focus on diversionary measures; austerity politics forcing less expenditure on costly incarceration; and the growing range of national and international organizations highlighting the damage caused by child and youth imprisonment (Goldson, 2015; Hendricks, 2015; Muncie, 2021, p 399). Whatever the precise constellation of these forces may be, continued reductions in child and youth imprisonment are a positive development. These reductions have not been as significant for children and young people from Black, Asian or minority ethnic backgrounds, however: as of 2021 these groups represent 52 per cent of the youth custody population, having represented 25 per cent just five years prior (Prison Reform Trust, 2021, p 39), raising urgent questions about why youth custody reductions have been so uneven between those of different heritages.

There remain almost 13,000 children and young people aged between 10 and 24 in prisons, and there is wide-ranging evidence to suggest that they experience significant harm inside. Assaults, restraints and self-harm in child and youth prisons have all more than doubled since 2010 (Prison Reform Trust, 2021, p 39; Figure 6.4). The rate of self-harm in these establishments is now (2021) at a record high (Prison Reform Trust, 2021, p 40). Over the past few years, more Youth Offender Institutions and Secure Training Colleges have been officially deemed unsafe than have been judged safe (Prison Reform Trust, 2021). It does not seem necessary to recall our particular conception of harm in order to elucidate why all of this is incredibly harmful to these children and young people. The policy of continued child and youth incarceration, the nature of the criminal justice system that they encounter and the particular conditions of child and youth prisons are all forms of structural harm which have hugely damaging effects. The self-harm and interpersonal harm that children and young people experience in these prisons clearly relate to the way that these establishments are funded, governed and managed: they have a duty to keep those in their care safe, and they fail to do so.

Youth prisons are also hugely ineffective: 72 per cent of their inhabitants go on to reoffend within one year (Muncie, 2021, p 402) and a wide range of studies illustrate their ongoing failure to address reoffending (Goldson, 2020, pp 182–3). Goldson goes as far as to describe this as a criminological 'fact': child imprisonment 'fails miserably' to prevent or reduce crime (Goldson, 2020, p 182). In their most recent report on this issue, the Prison Reform Trust (2021, p 39) highlight that the rate of crime among children and young people has declined alongside the rate of imprisonment, calling into question whether prison operates as any kind of deterrent. If prison worked as a powerful disincentive to criminal activity, you would expect that its declining usage could prompt increasing crime.

Despite all this, the current Conservative government of Boris Johnson remain committed to the idea that some children and young people need to be imprisoned. Recent measures to address violence between young people, such as Knife Crime Prevention Orders (discussed further later on), for instance, which are specifically targeted at 12- to 18-year-olds, can lead to up to two years' detention (Muncie, 2021, p 371). Back in 2015, Goldson (2015, p 185) maligned then-government ideas about the introduction of Secure Colleges, given what they showed about ongoing government support for child and youth imprisonment. In May 2022, royal assent was granted to (yet) another kind of child prison: Secure Schools (see Lepper, 2022). These have been criticized by many. The Howard League, for instance, has said that they 'threaten repeating the mistakes of the past and expanding the number of children in prison' (Crook, 2016).

It is the children and young people who have experienced acute concentrations of structural harm who are most likely to end up in prison. Imprisoned children and young people are disproportionately drawn from communities which experience significant poverty and inequality, and from those affected by inadequacies in our care and education systems – over half of imprisoned children have been in care and the vast majority have been excluded from school (Prison Reform Trust, 2021, p 40). As Goldson has argued (Goldson, 2015, pp 185–6), combined with the remarkably consistent and deeply harmful failures of child and youth prisons, this makes a compelling case for broader societal change rather than continued use of imprisonment: if we wish to reduce crime and violence among children and young people, we would do better to address the structural harms and inequalities which marginalize and diminish them than to continue insisting on their incarceration. Goldson summarizes the reasons to resist custody as a response to youth crime as follows:

> the adverse social circumstances from which child prisoners are routinely drawn, the damaging conditions and treatment to which they are typically exposed, the failings of penal institutions to deliver in terms of crime prevention, crime reduction and/or community safety, and the enormous expense that child imprisonment imposes on the public purse. (Goldson, 2015, p 185)

A succession of court orders and injunctions

> Police have asked for these orders to help them keep our streets and young people safe, and I will always do everything in my power to ensure they have the tools and powers to cut crime and protect the public.
>
> Priti Patel, Home Secretary, commenting on Knife Crime Prevention Orders, 2021, in Home Office (2021b)

In their public pronouncements on measures being undertaken to reduce violence between young people, 21st century British governments have placed far greater emphasis on various kinds of court order and injunction than they have on youth imprisonment. Despite the many reasons to believe that declining youth custody should be celebrated, it has occurred rather stealthily (Goldson, 2015, p 178), with government preferring to centre attention on the ways in which they are toughening police responses to gangs and weapon-carrying. There has been a growing tendency for state power-holders to reference the extent to which they are listening to the police, and their actions certainly suggest a high degree of engagement with law enforcement agencies. As Hendrick (2015, p 11) has argued, the competition among professional groups to be heard by government, and particularly who 'wins' that competition, are highly significant factors in the development of criminal justice policy. In keeping with late-20th century governments keen to be 'tough on crime' (Hendrick, 2015), it seems that 21st century power-holders have been more sympathetic to the police than to other professional groups, such as social workers, probation officers, youth workers or teachers.[7] This appears to be one reason for the expansion in court orders and injunctions since 2009. We discuss a few of these measures, and reasons to question them, in the following sections.

Gang injunctions

Gang injunctions were made available in the UK following the enactment of the Policing and Crime Act 2009. According to section 34 of the Act, law enforcement agencies can subject a young person to a Gang Injunction if they can prove to a court that, on the balance of probabilities:

- an individual has engaged in or has encouraged or assisted gang-related violence or gang-related drug-dealing activity; and
- it is necessary to grant the injunction to prevent an individual from engaging in, or encouraging or assisting, gang-related violence or gang-related drug-dealing activity and/or to protect an individual from gang-related violence or gang-related drug-dealing activity.

The scope and nature of the prohibitions and requirements that can be imposed through gang injunctions are vast and intrusive. For example, section 35 stipulates that an injunction can prohibit a young person from 'being in a particular place', from 'being with particular persons' (for example, their friends) and from 'wearing particular descriptions of articles of clothing'. According to section 36, the prohibitions and requirements made as part of a Gang Injunction can last up to a maximum of two years.

There are a number of problematic aspects to these injunctions. First, the burden of proof for imposing a Gang Injunction is not 'beyond all reasonable doubt' as with a criminal offence, but 'on the balance of probabilities' – a much lower threshold to satisfy. This means that young people have much less protection against a Gang Injunction being imposed on them than a 'non-gang' member of public has in the case of a criminal conviction. It is likely that – on the balance of probabilities – some of these orders will restrict the freedoms of innocent young people who have not, in fact, encouraged or engaged in gang violence. While the orders themselves do not constitute criminal convictions, the young people subjected to them might subsequently be convicted of a criminal offence and imprisoned if they partake in everyday activities that do not ordinarily constitute criminal law violations – for example, being in certain places, seeing certain friends and wearing certain clothes. Their freedom of association and of action – and with them, their sources of social significance and agency – can be severely diminished.

Given that the consequences of being found guilty of a crime can be severe, there are good reasons to require the trial process to establish that a person has committed a criminal offence 'beyond reasonable doubt'. If the state's role is to protect and serve, rather than attack and oppress, its citizens, then those citizens should rightly demand that state institutions prove beyond all reasonable doubt that people have broken the law before they are punished. It seems reasonable to assume that young people accused of being part of a gang will feel aggrieved that they can be subject to severe prohibitions and requirements following a mere balance of probabilities judgment. This is all the more likely when we consider the nature of some of the potential prohibitions: preventing young people from seeing their friends, for example, who, in many cases, may provide one of only a small number of sources of mattering in young people's lives.

For young people on the receiving end of these injunctions, it is worth considering some of the likely immediate and longer-term consequences. There is a chance that, in the immediate term, an injunction of this kind may reduce the likelihood of a young person perpetrating or becoming the victim of violence (Carr et al, 2017). As with many punitive measures, however, immediate-term efficacy (if there is any) can be outweighed by counter-productivity in the longer term. Gang Injunctions are liable to deepen young people's sense of alienation and antagonism towards officialdom, and exacerbate their sense that authorities and institutions are against them. They may reinforce the idea that their only hope of positive significance is by associating with those who are in opposition to those forces; those who, significantly, may not even know and are very unlikely to use their legal name (or 'gov' – the shortening some young people use to refer to their 'government name'). Considerable concern, then, should remain about both the efficacy and reasonableness of Gang Injunctions, given the potential effects they can have on both innocent and guilty parties.

Knife Crime Prevention Orders

Similar critiques can be made of Knife Crime Prevention Orders (KCPOs), which bear many similarities to Gang Injunctions. KCPOs are targeted not at gang crime per se, but more specifically at knife possession and 'knife crime'. Their legislative footing stems from amendments made to the Offensive Weapons Bill in February 2019. They have been piloted in London since May 2021 (Home Office, 2021b). The orders can be imposed on anyone over the age of 12 if, on the balance of probabilities, the person in question was deemed to be in possession of a bladed article in a public place without good reason, on at least two occasions.

Some of the provisions concerning KCPOs in the Offensive Weapons Bill necessitate a wide degree of discretion in interpretation. One potential condition of KCPOs, for instance, prohibits a young person from 'using the internet to encourage crime involving bladed articles'. What precisely ought to constitute 'encouragement'? Taking into account current police priorities, this condition has likely been designed to target the increasingly popular genre of rap music known as 'drill'. This genre involves, among other things, young people rapping about violence and other illicit activities in the areas in which they live (for further details see Fatsis, 2019; Lynes et al, 2020). To what extent, however, does rapping about violence further encourage it? This is a difficult empirical question to answer, but it is clear that many young people reject the proposition that drill encourages violence – instead, it is seen to simply reflect the serious violence already present in young people's lives (see Irwin-Rogers et al, 2020). As thousands of drill music tracks are produced and uploaded to internet platforms such as YouTube and Soundcloud every month, preliminary research indicates that 'there is no meaningful relationship between drill music and real-life violence' (Kleinberg and McFarlane, 2020). For many young people, producing drill music is one of the few viable and meaningful routes to feeling like a significant part of the world around them (see Thapar, 2019). Indeed, creating, performing and disseminating music enables young people to connect to their closest and extended peer groups, feel like part of a community and receive peer affirmation. It can provide a sense of agentic effectiveness that might otherwise be sorely lacking in their lives.[8]

Serious Violence Reduction Orders

There are similar issues, again, with the Serious Violence Reduction Orders (SVROs) brought in by the government through the Police, Crime, Sentencing and Courts Bill 2021. These orders can be imposed on any person aged 18 or over who has been convicted of an offence involving the use of a bladed article or other offensive weapon, or who had such a weapon with them when an offence was committed. They can also be imposed, moreover, on those convicted of an offence which did *not* involve his or her own use or possession of a bladed article or other offensive weapon, where it is found on the 'balance of probabilities' that the person knew or ought to have known that *another person* would use or be in possession of such a weapon in the commission of an offence (Bridges, 2021). This provision, that an individual could be punished when a court decides they probably knew about another person committing a weapon-enabled offence, brings with it all the well-established issues with 'joint enterprise' convictions (discussed later), and in fact may represent an exacerbation of them, given the looseness with which the phrase 'knew or ought to have known' may be interpreted (Bridges, 2021).

Young people subject to SVROs can be stopped and searched at any time and in any place, without the requirement for the police officer to have 'reasonable grounds'. SVROs can last for a minimum of six months and up to a maximum of two years, and be renewed and extended further on the application of the police. Those subject to SVROs are legally required to notify the police of any areas they move to or choose to reside in for more than a month, and failure to do so will itself constitute a criminal offence punishable by up to two years' imprisonment (Bridges, 2021).

In his summary of problems with SVROs for the Institute for Race Relations, Lee Bridges writes:

> SVROs will have the effect of severely restricting the freedom of movement of those who are made subject to them over extended periods, which may be considerably longer than the sentences they receive for the offences which made them liable for SVROs in the first instance. It will also put them at risk of persistent harassment by the police (from which there is no protection in the Bill) and of having their rehabilitation and reintegration into the community undermined, not least because of indirect effects of being legally labelled as 'persistent knife carriers' on their access to employment, education and other social opportunities. This will be particularly detrimental to those who are made subject to SVROs under the joint enterprise-type provisions of the Bill, who have not themselves been convicted of using or carrying a knife or other offensive weapon. And all of these consequences are likely to fall disproportionately on black people, something which the Government has admitted as likely to be the case. (Bridges, 2021)

Consistent problems in this succession of injunctions and court orders

All of these initiatives share similar harmful flaws. First, their reliance on the 'balance of probability' principle is a reduced burden of proof relative to that associated with the criminal law. This creates the significant possibility that some people will face severe incursions on their liberty without having undertaken the action(s) they are accused of. Second, they all rely on a simplistic notion of gangs, gang affiliation and gang culture, which feeds into provisions which can ban friends from meeting, sanction people for wearing certain clothes and punish individuals for the knowledge they are presumed to have of others' actions. Third, they all bear the markings of racialized criminalization. As has frequently been observed (for example, Williams and Clarke, 2018; Fatsis, 2019; Bridges, 2021), these forms of state retribution are highly likely – given substantial evidence of previous comparable state initiatives – to disproportionally affect young Black men in marginalized communities and to further deepen tensions between these communities and the police, as they become further 'sucked into a spiral of amplified contact and conflict' with the law (Webster, 2015, p 40). It is not hard to hear the echo of very old kinds of demonization, as discussed earlier, when looking at these measures, tied as they are to ideas of group pathology; the inherent criminality of 'subversive' cultural production; overweening peer influence; and the desperate need to tightly control those Others who are deemed a threat to social order.

For all those whom they affect, these suppression- and enforcement-based 'violence reduction' initiatives are also likely to erode young people's sense of mattering. It is reasonable to assume that they will intensify feelings on the part of many young people that state authorities are against them, and thus push them further away from legitimate means of achieving a positive sense of social significance and agency. The substantive content of these measures, which include a wide array of requirements and prohibitions that curtail young people's freedoms, strikes at the heart of some of the interpersonal relationships and social activities that play the greatest role in helping young people to develop a sense that they matter.

Joint enterprise, stop and search and the gangs matrix

> As Home Secretary, I will continue to listen to and back our police officers to make our streets safer. That's why we've made it easier for officers to use vital powers like stop and search, following a pilot programme, to make those who contemplate carrying weapons think twice. I listened carefully, and [the police] were very clear: stop and search is a vital tool in getting knives off our streets and saving lives.
>
> Priti Patel, Home Secretary, May 2022[9]

This array of court orders and injunctions expands and strengthens police powers in a manner which exacerbates a number of pre-existing issues, particularly (a) joint enterprise, and (b) stop and search. We briefly discuss each in turn in the following sections, as well as the compounding factor of London's 'Gangs Matrix'.

Joint enterprise

The legal doctrine of joint enterprise is a form of guilt by association, which means that a number of people can be held criminally liable for actions undertaken by another: for instance, if one member of a group (the principal party) uses a knife to kill or injure someone, other members of the group (the secondary parties) can, under the doctrine of joint enterprise, also be convicted of having caused the death or injury to that person (Bridges, 2021).

Use of the principle of joint enterprise has been criticized on a number of grounds. Firstly, it can lead to serious convictions 'on the basis of highly peripheral involvement in the criminal acts', using a very low evidential threshold (Jacobson et al, 2016, p iii) – the grounds used by courts to suggest associations between people, and joint involvement in crime, can seem questionable. This is closely tied to a second issue, the connection between the principle of joint enterprise and the dubious criteria for gang membership mobilized by the courts. A disproportionate number of young Black men have been affected by joint enterprise convictions due to their alleged involvement in gang-related violence, but the evidence advanced to prove their gang affiliation can be limited, in some cases, to a single music video (see Williams and Clarke, 2016, 2018; Fatsis, 2019; Conn, 2021). Thus, joint enterprise can drag large numbers of young people into the criminal justice system due to their social networks and loose associations, rather than any active involvement in violence or criminality (Jacobson et al, 2016, p iii; see Chapter 1).

A Supreme Court judgement in 2016 was highly critical of joint enterprise convictions and ostensibly brought in a strengthened legal test for them, but – according to recent analysis – this 'had no discernible impact on the numbers of people prosecuted or convicted of serious violence as secondary suspects'. The same analysis found, moreover, that the Black community continue to be 'consistently over-represented in joint enterprise prosecutions' (Mills, Ford and Grimshaw, 2022).

As with the court orders and injunctions already surveyed, joint enterprise can mean that – without a large or substantial body of evidence – young people can find themselves subject to substantial state sanction and control, or even imprisonment. Nijjar has described joint enterprise as a clumsy 'sledgehammer' for fighting gangs, whose impact is inevitably felt by young people who have only a very loose involvement with anything which could be described as a gang, let alone any direct involvement with violence (Nijjar, 2018, pp 153–8). Due to this, Nijjar has compared government 'anti-gang' measures – such as the use of joint enterprise and gang injunctions – to the schemes enacted by British authorities in India to control allegedly criminal groups. In particular, Nijjar draws attention to similarities between the demonizing and criminalizing ideas which underpinned the Criminal Tribes Act in colonial India, and the ways in which contemporary state initiatives rely on racialized notions of inherently dangerous populations (Nijjar, 2018, p 151; see also Moore, 2014). Similarly, Fatsis argues that the use of drill music in joint enterprise convictions is further evidence that, in today's Britain, 'black cultural life is patrolled' (2019, p 1311): rather than effectively responding to the perpetration of violence, or addressing its root causes, cultural expression associated with those deemed 'dangerous populations' is being criminalized.[10] The announcement in 2021 of £3.4 million being invested in 'work being carried out by the Metropolitan Police's Social Media

Hub to investigate online gang-related material and gather evidence for prosecutions' (Home Office, 2021a) strongly suggests an ongoing police focus on using music, videos and social media posts to 'prove' the gang affiliation of young people in London. These kinds of online surveillance are what Williams and Clarke (2018, p 11) have called 'ever-ready evidence gathering and guilt-producing devices'. Meanwhile, in Manchester, a 'super courtroom' opened in September 2021, allowing for trials of up to twelve defendants at once, explicitly designed to speed up the conviction of 'criminal gangs' (Ministry of Justice, 2021). Within a year of this gang-processing courtroom opening, ten young men from Manchester received sentences of between eight and twenty one years for conspiracy to commit grievous bodily harm and murder, in a case which attracted considerable controversy due to the prosecution's reliance on Telegram messages as evidence (Pidd, 2022).[11]

Particularly given the highly contentious nature of gang definitions mobilized by the police, and significant questions regarding the connection between gangs and violence, these developments are certainly cause for concern, when combined with the limited evidential requirements of the joint enterprise doctrine.

Stop and search

The threat to the public from violence and weapons plays a substantial role in government and law enforcement narratives about the powers of the police to stop and search people on the street (Shiner et al, 2018, p 2). In the Home Secretary's statement which opened this section, for instance, increased stop and search powers are directly connected to 'saving lives'. This idea, that stop and search is an effective tool for the reduction of violence, has been critiqued in many empirical analyses over the past few years (see Fatsis, 2019, p 1305 for a helpful summary). This is the first issue with stop and search that we discuss briefly in the following paragraphs, before moving on to two other closely entwined problems: disproportionality and community tension.

The vast majority of stop and searches lead to no further action on the part of the police. For instance, according to Metropolitan Police data, over 75 per cent (76.7 per cent) of searches undertaken over the two years 2019–21 led to no further action.[12] The majority (63 per cent) of further actions[13] taken following searches were due to drugs – though this still amounts to only 14.7 per cent of total search outcomes (when 'No futher actions' are included). The police do not keep data on the classification of drugs seized as a result of searches, but there has been considerable concern that many searches are occurring solely due to the smell of low-classification drugs, such as cannabis.[14] Only 1.7 per cent of stop and searches (10,351 out of 594,584 total) in London between July 2019 and July 2021 led to further action due to firearms offences or 'weapons, points and blades' offences (Figure 6.5).

Figure 6.5: Stop and search outcomes in London, July 2019–July 2021

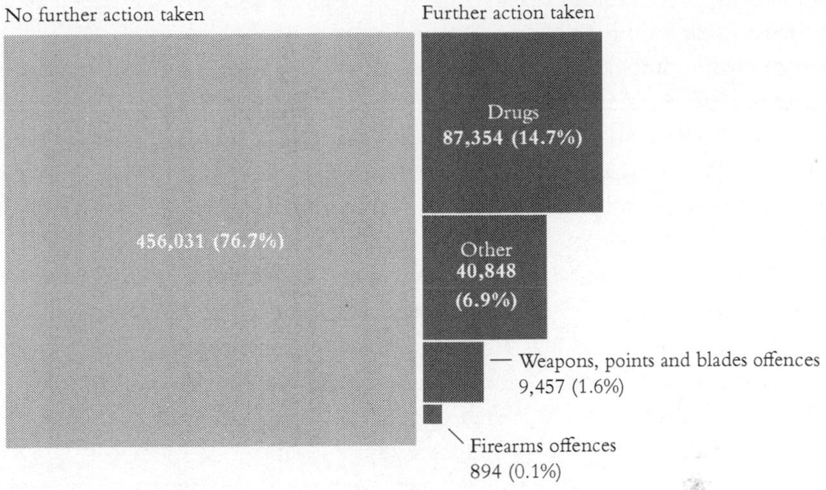

No further action taken   Further action taken

Drugs
87,354 (14.7%)

456,031 (76.7%)

Other
40,848
(6.9%)

— Weapons, points and blades offences
9,457 (1.6%)

Firearms offences
894 (0.1%)

Source: www.met.police.uk/sd/stats-and-data/met/stop-and-search-dashboard/

Over the course of the two years July 2019 to July 2021, then, less than 1 in 50 stop and searches in London found weapons. It is a common refrain among advocates of the practice that, regardless of statistics such as this, if stop and search tactics were successful in removing only one weapon from the street, it would be justified, as this might well be a life saved (see Williams and Squires, 2021, p 40). Notwithstanding substantial evidence that most young people carry knives due to fear or to status concerns, rather than intending to actually use them (see, for example, Squires, 2009, 2011; Brennan, 2019; Harding, 2020b), this line of argument could hold water only if unsuccessful stop and searches had negligible consequences – if all the searches which did not result in a weapon seizure did not have considerably adverse effects on young people's well-being, community relations and public safety.

There is a significant body of research, however, which suggests that stop and searches have precisely these negative effects. Firstly, a number of youth-led reports have highlighted how being stopped and searched impacts upon young people. A group in Camden (North London) made up of young people who have been affected by violence concluded that stop and search 'further alienate[s]' young people who may already have little hope or faith in state institutions (Lunghy et al, 2019, p 29). Similarly, the Reclaim group, based in Manchester, found that stop and search is experienced by young people as a profound kind of official 'disrespect', which can push them further from legitimate authority (Reclaim, 2020, p 22). In addition, a group of young researchers in Hackney (North East London) highlighted three major effects that experiences of stop and search were having on local young people: it caused trauma, it undermined

185

trust in state agencies and it reduced faith in police accountability (Account, 2020). Echoing this grassroots research, a number of studies have suggested that, in the way that it undermines community relations with and trust in the police, stop and search might in fact be criminogenic: far from reducing or preventing crime, it may encourage it (Keeling, 2017; Williams and Clarke, 2018, p 8; Brennan, 2019). One recent study of stop and search in England and Scotland made this claim as a key finding of their work: 'stop-and-search may damage trust in the police and perceptions of police legitimacy ... and this may result in increased offending behaviour' (Murray et al, 2021, p 263). This resonates with our discussion of 'violent emotions' in Chapter 5: experiencing an 'umpteenth public humiliation' (Jouai, 2018, p 95) at the hands of the police might well deepen the sense of personal diminishment which we know to be associated with the violent emotions of shame and rage. As Webster has put it, the 'sense of indignity, injustice and humiliation' from police labelling can 'propel rather than discourage repeated persistent offending' (Webster, 2015, p 41).

All of these effects are disproportionately felt, again, by Black young people from marginalized communities (Irwin-Rogers and Shuter, 2017; Irwin-Rogers, 2018). Metropolitan Police data for the two years July 2019 to July 2021 shows that, proportionally, most stop and searches tend to be in areas of London with the highest levels of poverty, and which are among the most ethnically diverse, such as Newham, Southwark, Tower Hamlets, Lambeth and Croydon.[15] People who had a Black 'ethnic appearance' (according to police records) were between two and five times more likely than those with a White 'ethnic appearance' to be stopped and searched between August 2019 and August 2021 (Figure 6.6).

Figure 6.6: London stop and searches, August 2019–August 2021, by 'ethnic appearance'

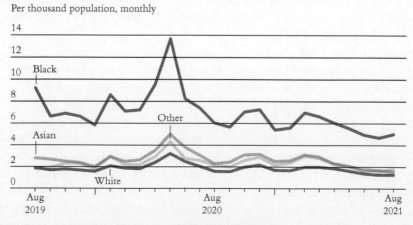

Source: www.met.police.uk/sd/stats-and-data/met/stop-and-search-dashboard/

Stop and search could gain additional legitimacy if – despite its negative effects, its disproportionality and the very small proportion of searches that result in weapon confiscation – it could be shown to reduce crime as a whole, as this would suggest it operates as an effective deterrent. This does not appear to be the case. A comprehensive review of this issue concluded that '[stop and search's] overall effect on crime is likely to be at best marginal' (Bradford and Tiratelli, 2019, p 1). This is substantiated by the government's own research: a Home Office-commissioned study of how Operation BLUNT 2 (which increased stop and search activity significantly in London) affected crime rates concluded that 'there was no discernible crime-reducing effects from a large surge in stop and search activity at the borough level during the operation' (McCandless et al, 2016, p 3). Ambulance call-outs actually fell faster in those boroughs that had smaller increases in weapons searches during the period of the operation, and reductions in knife homicides occurred evenly in boroughs which had very different levels of search activity, meaning that those reductions which occurred in boroughs prioritized by the operation cannot be attributed to increased searches (McCandless et al, 2016).

While it would be foolhardy to make any broad, generalized conclusions about stop and search tactics on the basis of this brief review, there do appear to be substantial grounds to question the effectiveness of stop and search as a violence reduction or a crime prevention measure. And there are certainly good reasons to question the wisdom of Priti Patel's decision, announced in May 2022, to expand section 60 powers – the powers through which the police can stop and search people within a given area without any grounds if they think there is a significant likelihood of violence. Patel's permanent changes to section 60 powers mean that more junior officers can authorise section 60, the powers can be in place for longer (up to 72 hours), they can be used when police anticipate that violence 'may' occur rather than 'will' occur, and there is no longer an obligation on the police to communicate to the public in advance when a section 60 authorization is occurring (Home Office, 2022). The reasons to fear the consequences of these changes do not need spelling out, given the wide-ranging problems with stop and search outlined above.

Gangs Matrix

These problems are exacerbated in London by the existence of the Gangs Matrix. Established in 2012 by then Mayor and current Prime Minister Boris Johnson, the Matrix is designed to be a risk-assessment tool, assessing and ranking London's suspected gang members according to their propensity for violence. Individuals on the matrix are known as 'gang nominals', and each is marked in a traffic-light scoring system as red, amber or green, according to their perceived risk of committing violence. A number of studies have found that the Matrix is hugely disproportionate in its labelling of young Black men as gang nominals, and that this labelling can have wide-ranging effects, deleteriously impacting upon young people's education, employment, immigration status and housing situation (Nijjar, 2018; Williams and Clarke, 2018; Wroe and Lloyd, 2020; Wroe, 2021). It has also been found to breach data protection laws by the Information Commissioner's Office (cited in Fatsis, 2019, p 1305), and to identify young people as gang members 'sometimes without any basis' (Fatsis, 2019, p 1305). At worst, in its constraining and limiting effects on young people's lives, the Matrix 'creates small lives and docile bodies' (White, 2020, p 36).[16]

All of this adds credence to the argument that marginalized and racialized communities are 'over-policed and selectively criminalised' (Shiner et al, 2018, p 2), forming 'a population of permanent suspects' (Webster, 2015, p 40). This can compound the other structural harms that they cumulatively encounter over the course of their lives, including those discussed in Chapter 4. Those young people who experience the most significant concentrations of harm from our nation's policies, systems and institutions are often the same young people who experience disproportionately assertive forms of state surveillance and control. Again, in whom they target and how they are justified, these modes of state surveillance and control seem closely tied to the kinds of youth demonization discussed in the previous section of this chapter.

Drugs policy

Lastly, we turn to drugs policy. Though it is a complex matter, there is a connection between young people's involvement in illicit drug markets and their propensity to become involved in violence, as either perpetrator or victim (see Chapter 5; Hales, 2021). Recent governments have certainly been keen to emphasize this connection, as evidenced, for instance, by the focus on this issue in the 2018 Serious Violence Strategy. It is thus useful to consider current state policies in relation to drugs – if such policies were to effectively and sustainably reduce the involvement of young people in dangerous drug markets, this would likely have a constraining effect on the prevalence of violence among them.

Unfortunately, this does not appear to be the case. Prohibitionist drug laws have generated a £7 billion illicit drug market in the UK, which interacts with various other social forces – such as poverty, consumerism and social media – to pull thousands of young people into a 'toxic trap' of dangerous drug dealing (Irwin-Rogers, 2019). This trap is made all the more enticing by structural features of the labour market outlined in Chapter 4, which have led to a proliferation of poorly paid and precarious jobs. This means that, for many young people, working in the illicit economy can seem far more accessible and appealing than legitimate forms of employment (Billingham et al, 2018, p 6; Reclaim, 2020, p 17). Koch has argued, along these lines, that exploitative working conditions in the licit job market, combined with an increasingly harsh regime of state social security, are 'structural conditions that drive young people into the illicit drugs economy' (Koch, 2019). This is not to downplay the relatively greater risks and harms present in illegal markets, of course: alongside the risk of violence, becoming involved in drug dealing can involve exploitative, coercive and abusive forms of relationship (Brierley, 2021, p 156). This is all the more reason why current prohibitionist approaches to drugs, which promote the development of illicit drug markets, need to be questioned, and why there is also an urgent need for more high-quality and meaningful legitimate job opportunities for young people.

The policing response to drugs markets can compound these harms. Mason (2020) analysed how one particular drugs crackdown operation had a variety of harmful effects which rippled out in a local community, causing (in his terms) relational harms, mental health harms and autonomy harms. Prohibitionist drug policy contributes significantly to the enticement of young people into clandestine drug-running arrangements, compounded by more localized criminal justice operations which generate a range of policing-derived institutional harms. For some young people, especially those alienated from mainstream institutions and legitimate work, immersion in the 'toxic trap' of the illicit drugs market can seem a more credible source of mattering – of respect, significance, competence and agency – than legal alternatives. This can be a fleeting, relatively inconsequential engagement, or it can be the weightiest decision a young person ever makes, resulting in the experience of substantial interpersonal harm.

Punishing and controlling responses to violence between young people

Responding to the issue of violence between young people entails difficult decisions for state decision makers and agencies about the balance of prevention and enforcement, and about the right approach to policing and punishment. We do not wish to present an overly simplified view of this complex problem. Its complexity is all the more reason to give it due consideration, however, including by examining the various harmful and counterproductive consequences that can flow from certain kinds of state policy and action.

As will be clear from the preceding discussion, we are concerned about a creeping punitiveness in the approaches that state agencies are pursuing to purportedly address the issue of violence between young people (welcome reductions in youth imprisonment notwithstanding). The measures discussed earlier share a number of problematic features, including: (a) the potential to criminalize and punish young people without substantial proof (due to the looseness of the 'balance of probabilities' test); (b) the potential to severely curtail young people's liberty – including the clothes they wear or the music they produce; (c) the potential to affect particular groups with a significant degree of disproportionality – particularly young Black men in marginalized communities; (d) a seeming over-reliance on the dubious old demonizing notion that certain kinds of cultural expression (particularly that which appears to be most associated with Black youth culture) are inherently pathological and criminogenic, or indeed criminal in and of themselves; and, lastly, (e) the potential to solidify young people's 'offender identity', to deeply exacerbate community relations with state agencies, and to undermine trust in the police, all of which can be directly criminogenic (see, for example, Motz et al, 2020 on the potency of criminal justice labelling; Brennan, 2019 on increased weapon-carrying among those who distrust police). It should go without saying, but due to these issues (among others), these measures can amount to structural harms, given that they derive from policies, systems and institutions, and that they can negatively affect young people's relationships, freedom, access to education and leisure, identity development and sense of recognition, and their mental health and well-being.

Any regime of policing and punishment is likely to entail some negative consequences for some people. But the extent and range of these consequences, and – in particular – their acute and potentially criminogenic concentration within particular communities, should raise profound doubts about the wisdom of our current regime. This is especially the case for those measures, such as stop and search, which have such a remarkably low rate of effectiveness as a tool to address violence and crime: given what we know about the many counterproductive effects of these searches, the government's recent insistence on expanding police stop and search powers should raise serious concerns.

These measures appear to follow the political logic outlined by Garland over twenty years ago, when explaining why harsh and ineffective enforcement policies are pursued by governments: '[They] can claim to "work" as a punitive end in themselves even when they fail in all other respects. ... [T]hey leave the fundamental social and economic arrangements untouched. Above all, they allow controls and condemnation to be focused on low-status outcast groups' (Garland, 2001, p 200). At worst, the initiatives discussed previously can leave young people – particularly young Black people from marginalized and poor communities – over-policed and under-protected: over-controlled and over-restricted by police and other state agencies; under-protected from interpersonal harm, due to their ineffectiveness in preventing violence; under-protected from the harms of the criminal justice system; and under-protected from the other structural harms which diminish their lives, due to the state's myopic focus on proximate rather than deeper societal correlates of violence. Implicit in this is a grim image: the adverse and marginalizing social conditions which predictably generate harm, crime and violence in communities remain 'untouched', while the state all too readily swings its punitive sledgehammer with the greatest vigour and nonchalance in those same communities, leaving young people structurally belittled, disproportionately punished and with precious little freedom – viewed as a 'dangerous and irredeemable class' undeserving of 'the liberties of free Englishmen' (Gilroy, 1982, p 92). We know many young people who would say that this is not some dystopian nightmare, but something close to the present reality. Its closeness to the old demonizing logics discussed in the previous section are also plainly apparent.

The Police, Crime, Sentencing and Courts Bill (2021) seems to reflect and perhaps worsen this picture. Alongside its particular provisions already discussed, it also betrays a governmental tendency to 'zoom in' on indicators of propensity for violence within individuals as if they are isolable, discrete features of young people's lives, separable from wider safeguarding and welfare concerns. As Firmin (2020, p 167) has highlighted, if we wish to ensure that young people are safe and well, we should not attempt to artificially atomize different risks that young people may face – of involvement in violence, of bullying, of criminal exploitation, of sexual exploitation, of intrafamilial abuse and so on – as if these often-related risks bear no connection to one another, have no common determinants and can be addressed independently. The Bill creates a new duty on professionals, led by police, to share information on and work together to address the conduct of any young person deemed at risk of involvement in violence – in language not dissimilar from the Prevent duty aimed at potential terrorists. Multiple agencies screening and intervening in young people's lives in this way often involves intense surveillance on the basis of (racialized) suspicion rather than substantial grounds (see, for example, Wroe and Lloyd, 2020), and appears to be in tension with the many other forms of multi-agency duty which are in place to address safeguarding and well-being concerns. As with Prevent, it risks labelling and stigmatizing individual young people due to stereotypes and demonologies as much as evidence, and, as with the Gangs Matrix, it has the hallmarks of a governmental obsession with rooting out and controlling potentially violent individuals, rather than addressing those inequalities in our society which predictably breed violence.

Save them

> We want to make sure that all young people across the country have access to good, rigorous, disciplined, socialised activities that teach them the way of truth and light.
>
> Kit Malthouse, Minister of State for Crime and Policing, House of Commons, March 2020[17]

Lastly, we turn with relative brevity to those responses to violence between young people which fit within the tradition of 'child-saving'. Originating in the late Victorian era, when there were increasing concerns both about the vulnerability of children and about the potency of pernicious influences on them – such as parental deficiencies and pathological cultures – 'child-saving' initiatives were aimed at rescuing young people from the threat of immorality, crime and violence (see Gillis, 1981; Wiener, 1994; Hendrick, 2015; Goldson, 2020; Muncie, 2021, pp 64–75). Through the course of the 20th century and into the 21st, this broad notion that children and young people need to be supported and saved rather than punished and condemned has lain behind a wide range of different practices – from highly individualized actions such as the removal of children from their families; to community-level initiatives such as the introduction of youth services; to a much wider concern with the social conditions that children live in, including an awareness that factors such as poverty, insufficient education and inadequate housing can have harmful effects. At best, this orientation towards children and young people leads to improvements in the fulfilment of their needs and their subjective well-being, and enhancements to their protection from crime. It can have deleterious consequences, however, when mobilized to instigate regimes of intrusive monitoring and surveillance, for instance, or when welfare objectives drive processes of normalization based on a particular White, middle-class ideal of childhood (see Muncie, 2021, pp 74–5; Williams and Squires, 2021, p 49).

In this section, we discuss a handful of tendencies which we believe can be harmful applications of 'child-saving' principles to the problem of violence between young people. We will explore four tendencies, which we have given stylized titles:

- remoralize them: fix their characters and remould them into ideal citizens;
- target the troublesome and enrol them on programmes that 'work';
- industrialize the problem, commodify those affected by it;
- sensationalize the issue, particularly if it earns donations and support.

For each, we will briefly describe (a) what it looks like, and (b) why it can be harmful. The word 'can' is important here: we do not wish to suggest that any and all initiatives which bear any resemblance to these four tendencies must be wholly bad or detrimental. As will be clear, we prefer to argue that there are cases in which these tendencies seem to have harmful effects, and that they are thus worth scrutinizing. Though analytically separable, the four tendencies are often entwined, as we will go on to discuss.

Remoralize them: fix their characters and remould them into ideal citizens

The idea of 'remoralization' goes back further than 'child-saving', to the earlier Victorian concern with inadequate character and wilful disobedience, but it was more reshaped than removed with the rise of later ideas about childhood vulnerability. To remoralize is to take an individual whom you deem to have deficient morality or character – due either to their chosen deviance or to iniquitous influences – and to somehow remould them into something closer to your ideal.

There is a subtle but vital distinction between remoralization socialization. Socialization is a general term for activities which help to induct children and young people into a particular society, familiarizing them with its norms and values, and supporting them to understand the forms of conduct which are (un)desirable within it. This process occurs, in some way, in every known society, especially within kinship groups such as families, and through educational practices. Remoralization is a form of socialization distinguished by two main features: (1) it entails a deficit view of the child or young person, as having developed negative character traits, including through previous socialization deemed wrong or inadequate; and (2) it is characterized by an assertive mode of socialization – a kind of didactic tutelage aimed at imposing certain habits and behaviours, as opposed to a more negotiated form of socialization which would place greater emphasis on young people's autonomy and agency (see Maynard and Stuart, 2018 for a discussion of approaches to work with young people specifically centred on empowerment and agency). In the terms of our concept of social harm outlined in Chapter 2, remoralization can be harmful in a number of ways: if it has a negative impact on young people's freedom, identity development, creativity, leisure or subjective well-being, for instance. As will be clear from the first feature of remoralization specified earlier, it can also entail a kind of demonization, and can thus carry with it all the attendant harms of demonization discussed in the first section of this chapter.

Researchers concerned with the history and trajectory of youth work have raised concerns about a growing governmental focus on remoralization since the New Labour years, particularly due to the government's regular rehearsal of fears about young people's declining morals, and about violence in particular. Remoralizing goals have a long history in youth-work practice: uniformed groups like the Boys Brigade were set up in the late 19th century to instil certain kinds of ideal values in young people, such as athleticism and nationalism; individualized 'case work' approaches have always contained elements of remoralization alongside respect for youth autonomy since their beginnings in the 20th century; and the thread of remoralization continues in many of the 'character-building', 'leadership' and 'service' initiatives of recent years (see, for example, Wallace and Kovatcheva, 1998, pp 63–77; Davies, 2019, pp 109–40). Most prominent among post-2010 schemes deemed by some to be 'remoralizing' is the National Citizen Service (NCS), a two-week programme for 16- to 17-year-olds designed to boost their citizenship and leadership skills (see Davies, 2019, pp 127–40 especially). In addition to skill and character development, NCS is intended to pull together young people from diverse backgrounds, whose paths would otherwise have been unlikely to cross. For this reason, proponents have described NCS as a way of creating a unified sense of 'us' in a society replete with fractures (Yates, 2021). For critics, however, NCS resurrects particular kinds of diagnoses about the need for 'active citizenship' among young people first popularized by the Conservative government of the 1980s (see Hendrick, 2015, p 12), and is inextricably entwined with a 'remoralizing' interpretation of contemporary youth problems. This is particularly due to the origin story of NCS, emerging as it did from David Cameron's view that Britain is broken; that the 2011 riots demonstrated untold depravity, disorder and violence among our youth; and that the solution is not to alter socioeconomic conditions – poverty, exploitative job markets or educational inequality, for instance – but to enrol young people on short-term projects which will reshape their character and turn them into better citizens (see, for example, Jensen, 2018, pp 115–16; Davies, 2019, pp 109–40; De St Croix et al, 2020). For detractors, the programme is based on a decontextualized and individualized approach to social problems, as if young people can be removed from their social context and rendered 'responsible future citizens' (De St Croix et al, 2020, p 464).

NCS has been subject to especially strong criticism for two main reasons: firstly, due to the extent to which it has been presented as some kind of panacea to youth issues by successive governments; and secondly – most importantly – due to the fact that the NCS scheme has received up to 95 per cent of central government funding for youth schemes since its introduction, at a time when community-based youth work and long-established youth centres (which provide broader support for a wider range of young people for a longer time period) have been extensively cut back (Davies, 2019, pp 127–40; see Chapter 4 on the latter point). Other government-backed initiatives, such as the #iWill campaign, which encourages community volunteering among young people, have received somewhat similar, though less widespread critique, for also receiving disproportionate government funds and focusing on a kind of remoralization (for example, Davies, 2019, pp 127–40).

At their best, both NCS and #iWill can be hugely beneficial to young people, supporting their subjective well-being and also helping to address the impact of structural harms in their lives. We know of one project supported through the #iWill fund, for instance, which enabled young people to campaign against precisely the kinds of over-policing discussed in the preceding section. Despite this, in much of their implementation, and certainly in the wider narrative about young people which they both draw upon and reinforce, they can exhibit harmful, remoralizing features, and have certainly consumed disproportionate government funding at a time of massive welfare cuts. This is compounded by the way in which they also adhere to some features of the second damaging form of 'child-saving' which we discuss in the following section – the tendency to focus on time-bound targeted programmes as the 'solution' to social problems involving young people, including violence.

Target the troublesome and enrol them on programmes that 'work'

> It seems easier to speak about specific projects and specific programmes than to raise fundamental issues of social inequality, racism and repressive state power ... to cushion the community against the impact of social problems, rather than dealing with the generative conditions of these social problems.
>
> White, 2013, pp 179–80

This quote from White neatly summarizes multiple problems with the tendency to believe that the solution to complex social problems such as violence can be found in the design and delivery of specific, targeted programmes. There is undoubtedly great value in specialized programmes which provide high-quality support to individuals and groups of young people when they need them and where they need them, particularly if these can contribute to permanent improvements to services and institutions. But, when tied to a simplistic approach to discovering 'what works', a superficial notion of innovation and with the decimation of long-term welfare provision, programmatic responses can amount to sticking plasters on gaping wounds, and can also serve a legitimizing function – drawing attention away from deeper-rooted social problems, to focus squarely on individualized risk factors, carrying the implication that the individual, far more than the historical and contemporary socioeconomic context, is the 'problem' (see White, 2013, p 180).

Thus, the issue here is one of emphasis and balance. We need good programmes for young people, and we need good evidence of their effectiveness, but an overweening focus on programmatic interventions can be to the detriment of recognizing that (a) there is a great need for improved social conditions, reduced structural harms and longer-term institutional support, as well as programmatic initiatives; and (b) any individual young person's life – let alone wider generational problems, community issues and the knotty matter of violence – is complex, and there are dangers and unintended consequences associated with attempts to place it in a Petri dish, in order to measure the apparent effects of individual variables. At worst, there is an analogous scenario to that already painted in relation to punitive policing, in which the structural conditions of many young people's lives steadily deteriorate; there is a dearth of 'essential institutions of care, nurturance and opportunity (Currie, 2020, p 15); but there abound a plethora of 'visible quick fixes', which apply a 'cost-benefits approach to remedying human misery' (Raventos and Wark, 2018, p 171).

There is a debate to be had about our current proximity to that undesirable scenario. There are certainly worrying signs. Kinsey, for instance, has highlighted the dangers of a burgeoning 'what works culture' in relation to 'knife crime' which 'oversimplifies the complex nature of youth crime', as well as the fact that many young people are critical of 'off the shelf', overly targeted interventions, because – among other things – they can inherently entail labelling and stigmatization (Kinsey, 2019, p 7; see also Reclaim, 2020, p 22). The government consistently highlight their £200 million investment in the Youth Endowment Fund (YEF) – a funder of programmes and 'what works' centre for interventions targeted at violence between young people – as a central plank of their approach to solving youth violence (see, for example, Home Office, 2021b). To its credit, YEF research (YEF, 2020, p 5) has identified the role of 'social and economic injustices' and criminal justice policies in exacerbating the issue of violence between young people, and the YEF has made clear its commitment to supporting social change. The manner of its presentation by government, however, at times implies that you can 'programme' your way out of complex social problems.

There has been a trend in recent years towards the 'programmification' of work with young people, and away from more long-term, relational kinds of support. As discussed in Chapter 4, a striking number of long-established youth and community centres have closed down since 2010 due to government funding cuts. Deeply embedded in their local neighbourhoods, often for many decades, these centres provided long-term support for children, young people and families, across all aspects of their lives, and were accessible for all. In many cases, due to the nature of their work, these centres' workers needed to be 'visible in the community for a number of years before they [could] become truly effective' (Seal and Harris, 2016, p 104). Today, a greater proportion of work with young people is delivered via targeted, time-bound projects, which come and go, focus on particular issues and do not enable young people to build sustained trusting relationships with professionals. We would argue that both these forms of youth work are valuable and needed, both have their inherent limitations and both can play a significant role in addressing social and biographical determinants of violence. It is thus detrimental if the former, community-embedded kinds of youth work are diminishing (for more on the role that youth work can play in addressing violence, see Seal and Harris, 2016; Pinkney, 2020; Smith, 2020).

Youth workers interviewed by Seal and Harris (2016, p 104), for instance, expressed concern about short-term targeting which meant they had to speed up their work, feeling that it eroded essential trust and relationships with young people, in service of the need to 'chase violence'. Youth Offending Team workers interviewed for a recent Inspectorate of Probation report similarly raised concerns about the short-term commissioning of third sector programmes, which resulted in 'short-lived projects, high turnover of staff, and practitioners not knowing what was available' (Phillips et al, 2022, p 35).

One driver of this issue is the growing fetishization of 'innovation' in the charity sector: as Hallsworth (2013, p 189) put it, 'the custodians of the money … expect to see innovation and novelty in the programmes they fund and, as such, generic long-standing interventions are not usually well looked-upon'. This leads us to our next theme: the increased marketization of 'solutions' to 'youth violence'.

Industrialize the problem, commodify those affected by it

The increasing marketization of the charity and voluntary sector intensifies the process of 'programmification' described earlier, encouraging a competitive kind of child saving. In our era of intense commodification and substantially market-driven politics (see Leys, 2003), industries can form around social problems. Societal ills can be monetized – you can make money from designing projects or whole organizations to address them. Arguably, one such industry is the 'youth violence industry' – made up of individuals, organizations, agencies and services who financially benefit from the extent of focus and funding which is dedicated to this particular issue (see Williams and Squires, 2021, pp 249–86 for their account of the more specific 'Knife Crime Industry'). As Rock (1995) put it, when the government endorses the importance of an issue, and begin to produce extensive data, reports and policy papers on it, this mass of information is pored over by other politicians and the media, but also, 'with peculiar intensity', by 'voluntary and statutory organisations continually hungry for money' (Rock, 1995, p 12).

There are signs of this process occurring in relation to violence between young people. After the government confirmed ongoing support for regional VRUs, for instance, one major national social enterprise produced a marketing brochure aimed at Police and Crime Commissioners which laid out its offer to manage local VRU delivery, promising to 'maximize local budgets to reduce violent crime'.[18] Competitive funding pots feed a marketplace of 'youth violence' projects in which different organizations vie to prove that they are uniquely well placed to address this social problem, and compete to keep costs low in order to secure resources.

A number of harmful consequences can flow from this. The overemphasis on competition between youth organizations can undermine their capacity to collaborate, can be hugely inefficient and can lead to young people being commodified. At worst, young people can be treated as little more than numbers or as 'good news stories' to showcase to funders. As De St Croix and colleagues put it, there is a growing risk of the 'datafication' of young people, in which they are valued as data points more than people (De St Croix et al, 2020, p 463). There is also a danger that organizations are incentivized to prioritize those young people who adhere to the ideals of funder-friendly evaluation, and to deprioritize those who are less attractive nodes for evaluation, such as those who are perceived to be too difficult to engage or overly resistant to change. At worst, we see 'young people's lives ... subordinated to outcome indicators' (De St Croix et al, 2020, p 467). Seal and Harris (2016, p 124) echo this, finding in their study of youth work that 'relationships were stifled by burdensome monitoring and evaluation regimes, and some "assessment" processes were acting to exacerbate a sense of detachment in young people's encounters with youth workers'. Youth workers, too, can be exploited, for simplistic stories of their impact, or in the more 'traditional' sense of exploitation: they can be overworked and underpaid. In the drive for cost-effectiveness, fostered by conditions of marketized scarcity, organizations can be led to keep employees' pay low and their contracts precarious. Lastly, if increasing proportions of state and philanthropic funding are tied to the issue of 'youth violence', it can pull organizations towards creating 'youth violence' interventions which they are not best placed to effectively deliver – everyone is incentivized to position themselves as a 'youth violence' specialist, even if they lack the requisite expertise (Peck, 2020, p 78). All of this is profoundly non-conducive to young people receiving the high-quality care, nurture and support that they need.

Sensationalize the issue, particularly if it earns you donations and support

The industrialization of any social problem can feed into exaggeration and demonization. Violence between young people is no exception. Competitive funding can incentivize a kind of 'race to the bottom' in how organizations describe their communities, as they compete to show that their problems with 'youth violence' are worse than any other area. They can be encouraged to exaggerate both the unique difficulties of their target young people and their 'uniquely enlightened' response (Muncie, 2021, p 78). If an organization relies upon public awareness – or public fear – of 'youth violence' for its funding and support, it can become dependent on the continuation of the problem. As Hallsworth (2013, p 194) put it, such organizations have 'a vested interest in discovering and maintaining precisely that which it ostensibly aims to expunge'. As we have stressed throughout this book, violence between young people is a serious problem which does require attention and action. All the more reason, though, to avoid misleading and perverse means to spread awareness of the problem, particularly where that involves exploiting young people, or exacerbating disproportionate or misplaced levels of anxiety and fear.

Perhaps the most notorious example of this came from within government itself. In 2019, the Home Office spent more than £57,000 distributing 321,000 chicken boxes to 210 chicken shops in England and Wales which bore '#KnifeFree' branding and contained stories deemed to illustrate the reasons why young people should stop carrying knives (Guardian, 2019; Williams and Squires, 2021). At the time, Policing Minister Kit Malthouse said: 'these chicken boxes will bring home to thousands of young people the tragic consequences of carrying a knife' (Demianyk, 2019). This 'insulting gimmick' (Dean, 2019) was broadly viewed as both utterly misguided and deeply offensive, relying on ideas about pathological Black youth culture: it's 'them' who eat chicken, it's 'them' who are violent (Dean, 2019; Demianyk, 2019; Guardian, 2019; Williams and Squires, 2021). It was also pointed out that the campaign was profoundly counterproductive, reinforcing the idea that knife-carrying is 'mainstream' and widespread (Dean, 2019). As the Reclaim youth group put it, such simplistic campaigns 'can feed fear and make weapon carrying seem more prevalent than the reality', particularly when they are 'based on stereotypes not evidence' (Reclaim, 2020, p 22).

The same year, a major national children's charity ran the fundraising gimmick captured in Box 6.1 – this text was accompanied by an image of a school-aged, Black young man wearing a stab vest with a cartoon sad face on it. This was part of a wider campaign which included other so-called 'essential items' for young people, such as a journal in which to express their emotional distress. A stab-proof vest is described as 'essential' for 'children aged 11–18', and the plea for donations includes the line: 'don't let stab-proof vests become part of the school uniform'. As well as an online 'shop' which 'sold' these items – that is, was a platform to encourage donations to the charity – they also had installations of the 'essential' items in a temporary pop-up shop in a wealthy area of central London (Lepper, 2019). Particularly given the use of a young Black male model, the campaign certainly seemed to run the risk of being precisely the kind of fear-mongering, stereotype-based initiative criticized by Reclaim and others, appearing to exploit the suffering of young people in order to attract donations. The web page included only a vague indication of what donations are spent on, and there were no links included to the charity's web pages on which information is provided about the detail of their work – which includes a number of well-regarded and high-quality programmes addressing different forms of exploitation. Neither did the 'online shop' contain links to the report that its pithy slogans were based on, which was a detailed, well-produced and valuable analysis of the problems facing young people in Britain in 2019. It appeared to be a simplistic and sensationalizing attempt at 'awareness

---

Box 6.1: Text from a national charity's 'stab-proof vest' fundraising campaign

Stab Vest

Does your child feel unsafe at school?

This essential stab-proof vest fits children aged 11 to 18.

With crime and violence on the rise, these vests are this season's must have item.

These vests aren't for sale because our shop isn't real. But the fear some young people are feeling is 100% genuine.

No young person should live in fear of crime – yet some tell us their fears are being ignored. It's time to listen.

Don't let stab-proof vests become part of the school uniform.

With a quick donation, you can help more young people feel supported and heard, not scared and alone.

Your donation could give more vulnerable children the support they need to heal and move on from criminal exploitation and abuse, so that they can look forward to a future free from fear and full of hope.

[This text is followed by donation buttons, with suggested donations of £12, £25, £50 or 'another amount'.]

Source: https://shop.childrenssociety.org.uk/stab-vest.html

---

raising' – at a time when lurid headlines about 'youth violence' and 'knife crime' were an almost daily occurrence in this country. As Williams and Squires (2021, pp 253–6) have pointed out, the currency of 'knife crime' in policy and the media has led to many unethical promotional practices from organizations keen to enter an 'attractive market', amounting to a 'multimillion-pound industry'.

Conclusion

> Part of our problem has been the tendency to grasp at some new youth program or police tactic as if it will somehow overcome the effects of generations of exploitation and dispossession and the absence of solid paths to a more secure and just future.
>
> Currie, 2020, p 16

This chapter is book-ended by quotes from Elliott Currie (2020) because he eloquently captures the fact that violence is a fundamentally historical problem. It is bound up with the historical accumulation of inequalities and social harms in particular communities, and any sustainable, long-term approach to addressing the problem of violence must reckon with this 'weight of the past' (Savage, 2021), rather than just reaching for a youth programme or police tactic to help prop up the present order of things. What unites harmful forms of demonization, punishment, control and 'child-saving' is that they do not address but, rather, obscure, the ways in which 'generations of exploitation and dispossession' have created the social conditions which predictably breed violence in British communities. The scale, severity and stubbornness of the structural harms discussed in Chapter 4 have become greater and more entwined through time – they are not ripe for plucking out of our society through some well-chosen programmes or draconian enforcement measures.

In how they shape perceptions and how they channel responses, the harmful tendencies explored in this chapter can turn attention away from historically accumulated, structural harms, onto a series of convenient 'bounded receptacles for blame': individual character flaws or feebleness; dysfunctional families; gangs and group savagery; and inherently criminogenic (Black) youth culture. This often involves disavowing the violence in our society: the idea that interpersonal violence belongs to those Others, who are not part of us, who are un-English, whom we disown. Violence is a property of the 'youth', especially those who, by virtue of poverty or 'race', can be deemed outcast, underclass, waste. They exhibit pathologies which we must treat with the most efficacious forms of programmatic and police response that we can devise. Their thoughts, emotions and actions are symptoms of these pathologies, rather than bearing any relation to how the structure of our society strips them of wealth, power, dignity, recognition and hope.

These harmful old ideas do not deserve any place in 21st-century discussion about the causes of, and responses to, violence between young people. Unfortunately, they seem to be alive and well in many of the contemporary policies, systems and institutions purportedly working to address 'youth violence'.

Conclusion: Towards a Less Harmful Society for Young People

Introduction

> Reforming the social, economic, and legal institutions that systematically humiliate people can do more to prevent violence than all the preaching and punishing in the world.
>
> Gilligan, 1997, p 239

If there is one central message of this book, it is this: we should not just aim for less violence between young people, we should aim for our society to be a far better and less harmful place in which to grow up. These goals are inseparable.

With that in mind, this conclusion is composed of three parts:

- First, we retrace our steps and summarize the main arguments of the book.
- Second, we indulge in a brief excursion into dystopian futurism, painting a grim picture of what the year 2030 could look like for our children and young people.
- Third, we describe some of the changes that we believe would help to make Britain a less harmful and a safer place for children and young people. We start this section by outlining the importance of addressing the maldistribution of four Rs: recognition, resources, risk and (state) retribution, building on many of the themes from earlier chapters of the book. We then move on to describe the more specific changes to policies, systems and institutions that we believe are needed to improve young people's lives.

We are conscious that much of this book has been written in a critical register, and so the vast bulk of this conclusion is dedicated to the third of the preceding points: to specific suggestions of the economic, political and social changes that our young people need. We do think it is important, however, to put this positive vision in the context of the more harmful future that we could be headed to, if certain tendencies discussed in this book continue, in order to further draw out the importance and urgency of significant social change – hence the dystopian excursion which makes up the second part of this conclusion.

The central arguments of this book: social harm, mattering and violence between young people

In the first chapter of this book, we laid out the latest statistical data available to us on the phenomenon of violence between young people. Inherent limitations to this data notwithstanding, it appears to show the following main trends:

- Taken as a whole, levels of interpersonal violence in England and Wales have been declining since the mid–1990s.
- The vast majority of interpersonal violence is committed by men.
- The vast majority of interpersonal violence involves a single perpetrator.
- Since 2015, adults (those aged 25 and over) have been responsible for a higher percentage of interpersonal violence in England and Wales than children and young people (those aged 24 and under).
- Since 2015, offences involving the use of knives in England and Wales have increased, as have hospital admissions for assaults involving sharp objects.
- In absolute terms, there are more victims and perpetrators of homicide in London aged over 20 than under 20, but under-20s as a group have a higher rate of homicide victims and perpetrators.
- There has been a general increase in the number of homicides in London since 2014, but the number of homicides in each of the six years from 2014 to 2020 remains below the previous peak in 2003.
- The vast majority of interpersonal violence in London is not flagged as gang related.
- Knife crime, gun crime and homicide are generally concentrated in the most deprived boroughs of London, and in the most deprived wards of these boroughs.

In the second chapter, we explained our approach to social harm, defined in reference to the concept of human flourishing: something is a social harm if it compromises human flourishing in a manner which could have been prevented. We suggested that a helpful notion of human flourishing draws together two related elements – need fulfilment and subjective well-being – and that it is possible to identify specific forms of harm which deny a person or people things that they need, or which undermine their well-being. We recognize that the two are often closely entwined in real-life experience: it is difficult to imagine a person's need for subsistence or affection going unfulfilled without this having a profound effect on how they think and feel about their life, for instance. We also introduced a distinction between interpersonal and structural harms, where the latter are those generated at the level of social structures such as policies, systems and institutions. This analytical distinction, though rarely clear cut in reality, was important for the discussion in later chapters.

The third chapter introduced the second key concept of the book: mattering. We argued that the drive to matter is a deeply significant psycho-social phenomenon, characterized by a need to feel that you are significant to others, and to feel that you have some effect on the world – to be recognized by others and to be a consequential force. We explored the cultural, emotional and psychological complexity of mattering, before outlining a number of global social processes which we believe may be making the quest to matter more complicated, difficult and ambiguous.

In the fourth chapter, we switched from the theoretical mode of the previous two chapters to a more descriptive and empirical one, as we examined some of the social harms which we believe are having the most significant effects on young people in today's Britain. We focused on poverty and inequality; declining welfare support; harms within the education system; unemployment and marginal work; and housing issues. We discussed how these forms of harm can affect young people's need fulfilment and subjective well-being, and the ways in which they can structurally belittle them – leaving them to feel inconsequential, insignificant and impotent: that they matter very little. We argued that the cumulative, grinding effects of these harms are felt as a daily pressure and pain by those affected by their intersecting influences. They may not be visible, they may be 'quiet', and they may thus be erroneously viewed as 'background', inert features of people's lives, but these harms disfigure days and alter life trajectories. They do not overwhelm individual agency, or remove the moral responsibility from young people for their actions, but we will have little hope of understanding or explaining those actions if we do not attend to the daily effects of these harms. They are not just impediments encountered in the temporal present: harms from earlier in life are carried by young people in their psychological architecture, and the anticipation of such harms in the future can be a significant influence on their choices and actions.

In Chapter 5, we pulled together the themes of the previous three chapters to discuss interpersonal physical violence between young people in the context of the social harms which disproportionately affect some communities and individuals. We suggested that the concentration of social harm in particular communities and biographies is incendiary: it reliably produces the kinds of violent emotion which we know to predictably precipitate physical interpersonal violence. This is a socio-historical problem: it is about the way that, over time, our nation's policies, systems and institutions have created a profound maldistribution of social goods (meaning that some communities lack the conditions for flourishing) and an equally marked maldistribution of social 'bads' (meaning that some communities encounter an accumulation of actively belittling and diminishing experiences). Drawing together our conceptualizations of structural harm and mattering, we endeavoured to show how structural features of society – such as policies, systems and institutions – can have a corrosive effect on young people's sense of mattering, in a manner which is likely to foster feelings of shame and humiliation which we know to increase a person's propensity to violence. The point is not that young people have no agency or choice, or that we should not hold a young person responsible for an act of violence: the point is that we cannot hope to understand the precipitation of that violence – and we certainly cannot hope to prevent further similar acts of violence across our society – if we do not attend to the diminishing, corrosive effects of structural harms, which can leave young people with intolerable, rage-inducing feelings of powerlessness, inadequacy, inferiority and indignity.

Lastly, in Chapter 6, we explored three kinds of response to 'youth violence' which we deem to be harmful: demonization, punitiveness and questionable attempts at 'child-saving'. We traced the historical origins of the demonizing tendencies which appear to be most potent in the present, focused in particular on various notions of individual or group pathology: the idea that certain kinds of people are inherently predisposed to crime and violence, or that certain kinds of family and culture are dysfunctional incubators of wickedness. In both cases, the 'certain kinds' are most often those drawn from poorer sections of society, young people and – most notably – racialized Others. We then switched to policing and the criminal justice system, examining the harmful effects of measures such as youth imprisonment, gang injunctions, joint enterprise and over-policing. We critiqued these on three main grounds: ineffectiveness (in some cases they can even be criminogenic); social harm (they can undermine need fulfilment and subjective well-being); and disproportionality (the effects of these measures are concentrated in precisely those communities which are already most affected by the issues described in Chapter 4). In our discussion of 'child-saving', we centred on those tendencies within the public and charity sector which (1) align with demonization, by concentrating myopically on individual moral character and seeking to address isolable 'pathologies', thus drawing focus away from wider social conditions; and (2) industrialize and sensationalize the problem of 'youth violence', often in a manner which both exploits and stereotypes young people. What unites the harmful forms of demonization, punishment, control and 'child-saving' explored in Chapter 6 is that they do not address, but rather obscure, the ways in which socio-historical conditions predictably breed violence in British communities.

Mobilizing the concepts of social harm and mattering, as we have done in this book, forces us to examine British society and the problem of interpersonal violence between young people from three different angles: to look up at the effects of powerful decision makers and social structures; to look back in time; and to look outward from the perspective of young people. We would argue that this is a more fruitful approach – or at least an important alternative approach – to the more popular angles from which the issue of 'youth violence' is examined: looking down at young people as a problematic mass; scrutinizing individuals as if detachable from their social context; or seeking bounded receptacles for blame in the form of one-word or one-phrase answers (it is all because of 'gangs' or 'troubled families' or 'Black youth culture'). Our society is not a pristine social order punctuated by inexplicable, criminogenic pathologies which must be rooted out. Instead, it is riven by historically entrenched structural inequalities and harms which are both damaging in themselves and predictable generators of increased physical interpersonal violence.

The accumulation over time of concentrated structural harms in particular places is like kindle, oxygen and heat which sets these places alight: the communities most harmed by the policies, systems and institutions of this country are on fire. Some young people and families in these areas are better insulated from the flames, and the blaze will manifest differently between people – sparking creative brilliance in some, but violent emotions in others. There is definite value in trying to work out how some young people stay safer from the fire than others; there is clear worth in examining why the flames have differing effects on people; and it is certainly fruitful both to train more 'firefighters' – those who support the young people experiencing most social harm – and to provide them with better equipment. But the most substantial positive change would come from better addressing the source of the inferno: the incendiary socio-historical predicament which far too many children and young people find themselves in.

In the following section, we first dramatize this socio-historical predicament – describing a dystopian near-future in which the damaging tendencies explored in this book have worsened – before then describing some of the changes which we think could substantially improve the circumstances experienced by our young people.

2030: a near-future dystopia

Britain's already hideous levels of inequality have worsened. There is a preponderance of gated communities, and of food banks. Those whose families have always amassed wealth are increasingly rich, and those whose families have never had much have increasingly little. The grip of wealth on power remains firm and stubborn. Money, influence, status and freedom are accumulated in gargantuan quantities among the tiny minority of ultra-privileged people, while the poorest accumulate only debt and fear.

There is much discussion about of what causes poverty, but it is treated as the product of individual fallibilities rather than societal structures. Personal decision making and stereotyped mothers receive most attention; the role of our political economy in systematically facilitating destitution is increasingly absent.

The richest 1 per cent continue to own a quarter of the country's wealth;[1] London's richest 10 per cent continue to own half of the city's wealth.[2]

The idea that Britain is a meritocracy still lingers. Its seemingly perpetual ideological power comes from the way in which it blends particular, contorted notions of individual freedom, equality and justice, in the context of entrenched hierarchy, inequality and disadvantage. The 'have nots' and the 'have yachts' are both encouraged to believe that they receive their just deserts.

Our economy is increasingly structured as an ultra-competitive, wholly rigged, individualized race for scarce resources, in which different people have hugely divergent starting positions. The prize for victory is ludicrous fortune, and the price of falling behind is punitive stigmatization, exclusion or institutionalization.

Those with bounteous capital, who accrue further earnings through various forms of rent, are able to evade the meritocratic principle – they amass ever-increasing money through nothing which could be conceivably described as 'merit'. With technology developed to measure their every motion, workers' 'merit', on the other hand, can be scrutinized down to each minute movement. Devices continuously monitor workers as they service mechanical processes: they are appendages of machines, fitted with machine-appendages to quantify their work. Even for the more white collar workforce, whether they work from home or in offices, the time they spend at their desks is recorded down to the last second.

The least fortunate are constantly compelled to exhibit their worth, to avoid being kicked from one precarious form of employment to another, or to nothing. The archetypal figure of our society is a social isolate, fending as an atomized individual for themselves (Marquand, 2015, pp 136, 142). There's little alternative to becoming a self-investing unit of human capital (Brown, 2017, p 33), measuring your skills, your health, your time, your wealth, perpetually networking and crafting your personal brand.

These conditions are found throughout much of the legitimate job market – the same job market which many young people are compelled to enter as early as they can. Rightly or wrongly, a significant number of young people feel that they can obtain work which is far better paid and attracts more dignity and respect by linking up with the local drug dealers than by going to a job centre.

Homes are commodified more than ever. Those who own multiple houses as investments, who exploit their occupants' need for shelter, are heralded as modern captains of industry – their wealth and power is celebrated in glossy magazines. Those who struggle to obtain any kind of humanly habitable home are deemed social pariahs, and are aggressively moved on from whatever temporary dwelling they can find in streets, parks and stations. Many families' housing conditions are squalid, but they are told to be grateful to have anything at all. Young people who stand to inherit property face fundamentally different life prospects to young people who do not.

The basic idea that every person is of equal worth has been almost entirely eroded. As in Victorian times, those with wealth and power look on the poor and the powerless as at once fascinating, intimidating and incomprehensible.

Children and young people from poorer and wealthier backgrounds often live within metres of one another, but a gulf separates their quality of life. Poorer students in state schools are overdisciplined and undersupported, while private education remains a passport to privilege.

The ubiquity of racial injustice is continually denied. Where it is 'addressed', it is through platitudes aimed at positive public relations, rather than policies designed to secure any genuine shift in power. People of colour – and people of African Caribbean heritage especially – continue to be overrepresented in the care system, alternative education, and the criminal justice system. The age-old notion that the 'problem' lies in the biology or culture of non-White people retains its hold on the public imagination – particularly among those who benefit most from it. It affects the experience of children and young people in all institutions of society.

A certain masculinity ideal continues to predominate. It holds that a man's significance to the world should be measured by what he has control over and can dominate. Women and girls of all ages suffer the consequences. Rates of violence against women and girls are not budging, but they receive relatively minimal coverage and concern, particularly when compared to more public and spectacular forms of violence. The daily violence occurring in homes across the country is treated as if mundane and banal – when it's on the street, it's of interest.

Charities are everywhere. Their adverts are all over public transport, all over roadside billboards. The children and young people that feature in them look vacant, helpless, a little bit grubby – but not too grubby. Similar portrayals of children and young people appear in some newspapers and government reports, in cases where the young people in question are deemed innocent.

In other publications, though, focused on those deemed deviant, young people are presented as chaotic, as dysfunctional, as a threat. Young people are patronized and demonized in equal measure.

Large charities rake in funding on the basis of evaluation reports which demonstrate that, for instance, if you put poorer, less well-nourished, traumatized young people through a particular charity programme when they're between the age of 14 and 16, it will have a small but statistically significant effect on a particular 'outcome'. There's precious little discussion of how our political economy systematically discriminates against and disadvantages huge swathes of children and young people. The bosses of well-resourced national charities have close personal connections with government ministers. There are plenty of charity dinners and fundraisers, but there aren't many youth or community centres. Young people are rolled out to tell their stories at these dinners. They aren't paid for it.

Local councils spend sizeable chunks of their budgets on consultants, who come in to teach them about systems change, service design, co-production, behavioural insights and agile leadership. None of the consultants seem able to help the councils to deliver high-quality and effective children's services with ever-diminishing government funding, though.

Every profession serving our most complex young people is increasingly underpaid, under-trained, under-supported and under-respected. People working in these professions are seen as the administrators of interventions, rather than skilled professionals developing caring relationships with young people.

There are more prisons than ever. More and more private companies and charities are running prisons, secure children's homes and young offender institutions. The distinction between the most financially successful charities and companies like G4S or Serco is becoming increasingly blurred. They compete in the same races for government contracts, on the basis of efficiency and cost savings. Punitive policies are profitable.

Among all this, violence between young people is still a major problem, its scale waxing and waning year to year according to various granular contingencies. It is still less common than violence between adults, or violence committed by adults against children and young people, but it continues to grab more headlines. Its presentation in the media and politics blends glamourization, stigmatization, exaggeration and sensationalism – British society seems both appalled and titillated by it. It remains concentrated in communities characterized by substantial poverty and inequality. There are countless programmes marketed as the solution, and politicians compete to appear most 'serious' in their response.

The academic world interacts in varying ways with the violence that occurs between young people. Compassionate voices are outnumbered by those who churn out subtle variations of theories centring on inadequate parenting, low aspirations and dysfunctional peer-group culture; by those who promote themselves as pre-eminent experts on the street brutality which they seem gratified to recount; and by those who produce glowing evaluations of the services provided by organizations which, coincidentally, fund those evaluations.

Young people are individualized, pathologized and scrutinized like never before, especially those from poorer backgrounds and those who are of colour. Government, the media, private companies and large charities all contribute to this, to their mutual benefit.

The changes that we need to improve life for Britain's young people

> Children should be treated as a crucial social resource and [should] represent for any healthy society important ethical and political considerations about the quality of public life, the allocation of social provisions, and the role of the state as a guardian of public interests.
>
> Giroux, 2010, p 93

The preceding section dramatized some harmful tendencies in contemporary British society, all of which have been touched upon in some way through earlier chapters of this book. In this section, we switch to a more positive tone, in order to outline various changes which we believe are necessary if our society is to become less harmful, and more conducive to the flourishing of children and young people.

The road to a safer and fairer Britain for all young people appears long and fraught with difficulty, but there are plentiful reasons for hope and optimism, as we seek to highlight in the following sections. We proceed from high-level, macro-scale matters of national political and economic orientation; through systemic and institutional issues affecting the general well-being of children, young people and families; before, lastly, addressing the more specific issues of crime, violence and criminal justice.

Recognition and resources, risk and retribution

> [Recent history] illustrates well the long-term inadequacy of policy initiatives that focus on the individual symptoms of social misery, such as low self-esteem, violent persona, or deficient academic skills, instead of addressing the material and political forces that generate the neglect, battery or hunger of children in economically fragile [places].
>
> Bourgois, 2003, p 325

We begin with our view on the macro-level changes that are needed to our society if it is to be made safer and less harmful for children and young people. Fundamentally, we need a more equitable distribution of four Rs: recognition, resources, risk and (state) retribution. This is the high-level political and economic orientation which we feel has the greatest hope of improving young people's lives across the country.

As we will show, these four Rs are closely connected to the themes of this book. Recognition and resources are centrally important goods which, as things stand, are highly concentrated among the most privileged individuals and communities in the country. These same people are also least exposed to significant risks and to state retribution. On the other hand, the most structurally marginalized communities in our country experience a scarcity of recognition and resources, and a disproportionately high level of significant risk and state retribution. This multifaceted inequality is unfair and unjust, and means that many children and young people are being exposed to profound adversity and harm: they dwell within an 'overall environment of danger' characterized by 'continuing marginality, neglect, and structural disadvantage' (Currie, 2020, p 8).

Recognition

> 'On the street' ... [there is] a profound preoccupation with the 'worth' of individuals at time when some individuals appear to be 'worth' less than others.
>
> Squires, 2009, p 260

Debates about the politics of recognition are long-running and extensive in political theory (see, for example, Taylor, 1992 and Honneth, 1996 for advocacy of such politics; Fraser, 2000 and McNay, 2007 for more critical views). At root, the politics of recognition is centred on three connected ideas: that we all deserve equal dignity and respect; that being recognized by others as having inherent worth is absolutely fundamental to human well-being; and that not being recognized in this way – suffering from 'misrecognition' or disrespect – is profoundly injurious to us (see Honneth, 1996, especially). On numerous occasions through the course of this book, we have referred to these arguments: recognition, status and belonging form the core of young people's identity needs (see Chapter 2); recognition is one of the two central components of mattering (see Chapter 3); and we have highlighted the stark inequality of respect, dignity and recognition in today's Britain (see Chapter 4). As alluded to by Squires in the quote at the beginning of this section, though the notion of recognition may seem abstract and somewhat intangible, it is perhaps at its most potent and its most dangerous on the streets of historically dispossessed communities, in which respect and 'worth' can be brittle and conflict over their distribution can be deadly. This was a prominent theme in our exploration of the social and psychological precipitators of violence in Chapter 5.

Greater equality of recognition in our society is sorely needed. Various forms of prejudice and Othering are deeply rooted in our culture and history. Institutionalized racist injustice remains a stain on our country's social fabric, as evidenced by stark racial inequalities in our education and criminal justice systems (see Chapters 4 and 6). Sexism is equally embedded in many societal structures – in the way that mothers are inadequately supported and all too readily stigmatized (see Chapters 4 and 6), for instance, but also within cultures of masculinity which continue to place great currency on the control of women (see Chapter 5).

Various writers have articulated the kind of egalitarian culture of recognition that our society needs: Sennet (2003, p 58) calls it 'inclusive mutual respect'; Millie (2009, p 267) 'mutual respect and empathy'; while Retzinger (1991) uses the single word 'solidarity'. Bourgois stresses the benefits of a more equitable distribution of recognition, particularly if it reaches those with the least wealth and power, referring to 'the respect that mainstream society needs to share with them for its own good' (2003, p 324). Those who experience the deepest forms of societal disrespect are often those who pose the greatest risks to public safety.

An egalitarianism of recognition at the level of sentiment is not enough, however. Too often, injustices are couched in terms of attitudes and interactions, rather than of power and social structure. Political philosopher Nancy Fraser has argued that fighting for mutual discursive respect is inadequate in the fight against prejudice and discrimination, writing that 'it is counterproductive to address [these injustices] through moralising condescension. ... That approach assumes a shallow and inadequate view of these injustices, grossly exaggerating the extent to which the trouble is inside people's heads and missing the depth of the structural–institutional forces that undergird them' (Fraser, 2019, p 19). The denigration and misrecognition of marginalized groups does not just spring from the will or whim of individuals: they are historically entrenched within consequential policies, systems and institutions. In Chapters 4 and 6 in particular, we explored many different ways in which racism and sexism manifest in children, young people and families' lives as structural harms – rectifying these injustices would require more than individualized attitudinal changes. Returning to Lebron's (2017) language from Chapter 3: any attempt to address entrenched racism, for instance, must attend to the structural 'disvaluation of black lives', which results in their being treated as 'inconsequential and disposable' (Lebron 2017, p 44). This would require changing the policies, systems and institutions which disproportionately damage the lives of Black people;

which are infused with racist cultures; and which continue to be marked by the lingering influence of colonialism and empire.

Redistribution of resources

As many political theorists and policy thinkers have argued, equality of respect is not compatible with gross inequality of resources – recognition must be tied to redistribution (Fraser, 2000; Lister, 2021, pp 217–21; Soliman, 2021, p 242). Savage (2021, p 201) goes as far as to argue that it is 'not analytically helpful' to treat redistribution and recognition as distinct political matters, given that 'issues of respect, worth, dignity and recognition' are inseparably tied to histories of immense material inequality. This aligns with our analysis throughout this book, particularly in Chapter 4, where we explored intersecting forms of material scarcity and misrecognition. The issue of redistribution is also closely tied to the fulfilment of many of the needs that form the basis of human flourishing outlined in Chapter 2, including subsistence, security, participation and leisure needs.

At worst, a nebulous culture of equal recognition can obscure fundamental disparities in the day-to-day quality of life experienced by different people, acting as a kind of ideological shroud which distorts perceptions of gargantuan economic inequality. Platitudinous assertions of equal worth are easier and cheaper than attending to the vast, systematically generated inequities within our political economy. Unfortunately, successive UK governments since the late 1970s have been far more likely to express the former than address the latter. Sayer (2005) articulated this brilliantly in a well-targeted attack on 'tokenistic' forms of recognition. His words are arguably even more apt today, and are worth quoting at length:

> An egalitarian politics of recognition at the level of professed attitudes is easier for the well-off to swallow than an egalitarian politics of recognition-through-distribution, and it suits them to regard the former as progressive and the latter as passé. ... In fact, it seems that in British political culture over the last three decades, the more everyone is discursively acknowledged as being of equal worth, the *less* pressure to change the distribution of material goods, because the inequality of the latter is increasingly seen as a separate matter. As culture has become more egalitarian, it has been supposed that economic equality matters less. (Sayer, 2005, pp 64–5, emphasis in original)

It would appear that this problem has deepened in the years since Sayer wrote these words reflecting on the Britain of the 1980s, 1990s and early 2000s. Economic inequality has worsened, and the notion that this is a profoundly serious, defining societal problem appears marginal to our politics. Our society continues to be marked by the '"feelgood" culture' which Sayer went on to critique, arguing that it is grounded in the dubious idea that marginalised people just need more self-esteem, 'as if, by an act of social levitation, they can free themselves from their lowly position, and without any redistribution of resources to them' (Sayer, 2005, p 226). Particularly when considering the lives of children and young people, to side-line the pivotal role of poverty and inequality in shaping today's Britain is a deep intellectual mistake at best, and an act of ideological distortion at worst. No meaningful form of equitable recognition can co-exist in the real world with either destitution or enormous inequality.

This point is crucial when considering the political ramifications of children and young people's subjective well-being and sense of mattering. There is a risk with any psychologically informed concepts that they will be deemed only an issue of individual cognition, emotions and interpersonal interactions. As with Sayer's earlier discussion of self-esteem, there is a risk that supporting more young people to feel happier, more satisfied with their lives, and to develop a meaningful sense of mattering, could be seen as soluble through some 'act of social levitation' – we just need to tell them they should be happy, that their lives have purpose, that they matter. As stressed throughout Chapters 3 to 5, a young person's sense of mattering is not just affected by how they feel they are perceived by others, or the extent to which they feel socially significant, but also by their sense of influence, potency and power. And, as demonstrated in Chapter 4 especially, both the sense of significance and of power are not just psychological issues, but psycho-social problems, shaped substantially by individual experiences of policies, systems and institutions. The struggle for high levels of subjective well-being and a sense of mattering is not just an ontological one related to questions of being and identity, but a material one, tied to inequalities of power and wealth, as well as of recognition.

A detailed discussion of policy measures that have the potential to radically reduce economic inequality is beyond the scope of this book. However, there are many comprehensive and compelling accounts that outline both the causes of severe economic inequality and potential solutions to it (see, for example, Baker, 2016; Brooks, 2014; Mazzucato, 2018). In short, such solutions typically involve a combination of rewriting the rules that underpin global markets and shifting the dial on taxation and transfer policies. As we have argued elsewhere (see Billingham and Irwin-Rogers, 2020, pp 59–60), redistributive measures such as Universal Basic Income (see, for example, Standing, 2017) could have a positive impact on well-being and mattering, in that they can reduce the kinds of precariousness, poverty, inequality and hardship which leave people feeling structurally belittled (see also Eisenstadt and Oppenheim, 2019, p 157).

In their real-world consequences on people's lives, then – including in relation to needs fulfilment, subjective well-being and mattering – recognition and redistribution are entwined. If we are to reduce harm and violence in young people's lives, we must address the 'vicious circle of subordination' which too many are caught within, in which 'the status order and the economic structure interpenetrate and reinforce each other' (Fraser, 2000, p 118), resulting in societal disrespect, material poverty and – ultimately – a deadening, dangerous, incendiary kind of structural diminishment (see Chapter 5).

Risk

The maldistribution of recognition and resources bears a close but complex relationship with risk. As Beck (1992, p 19) put it three decades ago, 'the social production of wealth is systematically accompanied by the social production of risk'. Risk is also associated with harm: if you are 'at risk', it tends to be some form of harm that you are at risk of. As will be clear from our arguments throughout this book (especially in Chapter 5), and from the preceding discussion, we would suggest that the maldistribution of recognition and resources is inherently harmful in its effects, and thus those who are most likely to be affected by disproportionate misrecognition and resource scarcity experience greater risk of harm, by definition.

We would also argue – again, in line with earlier arguments – that experiencing one form of social harm often heightens the risk of experiencing other harms. In some cases, for instance, experiencing one kind of structural harm, such as poverty, could increase the risk of experiencing another kind of structural harm, such as adverse treatment within the education system: we know, for instance, that there is a significantly higher rate of exclusion among poorer students (see Chapter 4). In other cases, it may be that experiencing structural harms increases the risk of experiencing interpersonal harms: as discussed at length in Chapter 5, the concentration of structural harms in particular communities makes it more likely that individuals within those places will become victims or perpetrators of interpersonal physical violence.

Thus, in different ways, both by definition and by causal association, there is a close link between the maldistribution of recognition, resources and risk. Those places which experience territorial stigmatization, whose occupants encounter higher rates of denigration, demonization and diminishment, and which are affected by significant poverty, also tend to be areas of heightened risk and danger. By contrast, particularly in an era of securitization, gated communities and 'panic rooms', those with the most wealth and prestige are usually those who are best protected from the most severe kinds of harm.

(State) retribution

Lastly, we turn to our fourth and final R: retribution. We can address this point with brevity, given the extensive discussion of this issue in Chapter 6.

As explained in that chapter, in today's Britain there is a marked disparity between those who are most and least policed and punished.

Our prison estate – both adult and youth – disproportionately houses those who experience the most material scarcity and misrecognition: it is most populated by people who are drawn from communities affected by both poverty and stigma (see, for example, Goldson, 2015; Scott, 2018). This is borne out by the latest statistics, which continue to show that people from poorer places, people of colour, care-experienced people and people with additional learning needs are hugely overrepresented in our prisons (see Prison Reform Trust, 2021). There are a number of reasons for this, including the fact these same people tend to be over-policed and punished more harshly than others (see, for example, Webster, 2015; Gunter, 2017; Williams and Clarke, 2018; Chapter 6), as well as being disproportionately affected by cuts to legal aid and by the enforcement of prohibitionist drug policies (see, for example, Stevens, 2011; Shiner et al, 2018; Duque and McKnight, 2019). Meanwhile, those with greater financial resources and status have a higher chance of evading state retribution: their activities are relatively under-policed, they have more money for expensive legal procedures and their cultural capital can affect sentencing (see, for example, Duque and McKnight, 2019).

★★★

These entwined, historically entrenched inequalities in the four Rs have a profound influence on the nature of our society. Indeed, they are among the most defining characteristics of contemporary Britain. If we want life to be much better for our young people, and we want there to be far less violence between them, these inequalities must be addressed. In the following sections, guided by this broad orientation, we identify some specific changes to policies, systems and institutions which could begin to take us in the right direction.

Schools and education

In our discussion of changes needed to schools and the education system, we will start with the specific issue of exclusions, before broadening out our focus in steps – first looking at inclusion and behaviour, then considering the fundamental question of what schools are for. None of the changes that we suggest in the following sections need detract from the central function of schools: to provide the best possible education to all. They are all measures which we believe would better equip schools to fulfil that role, as well as to achieve other, adjacent, complementary goals. There is a deeply damaging false dichotomy in debates about schooling, seemingly based on the idea that if you care about child welfare you cannot care about high-quality education, and vice versa. This is nonsense, as our discussion in this section should demonstrate.

Exclusions

As discussed in Chapter 4, there is compelling evidence regarding the damage that school exclusions can do. At a minimum, school exclusions need to be radically reduced; ideally, there should be more fundamental reform, so that nothing resembling the current system of exclusion exists. This is not to say that no student should ever move school, nor that there should be no specialist educational settings, but that how the former is done and how the latter are run could be made far more fair, equitable and effective.

In recent years a number of reports have outlined in detail the changes to policies, systems and institutions that are needed in order to substantially reduce exclusions. The RSA (Partridge et al, 2020), the Centre for Social Justice (2018), The Children's Commissioner (2019a), JUSTICE (2019) and the Timpson Review (HM Government, 2019) have all presented clear, evidence-based recommendations, covering school-level factors, society-level factors, the procedural (in)justice of the exclusions process and changes needed to the wider education system. Despite this, progress on this matter has been slow, resulting in the continuation of preventable harm to young people, including heightened risk of criminal exploitation and involvement in violence (see, for example, Temple, 2020).

Inclusive education, safeguarding and punitiveness

Beyond the issue of exclusions, there is of course a much wider discussion about the nature of schools as institutions, and the extent of their inclusiveness. These discussions are contentious and consequential because, as mentioned in Chapter 4, school is the only universal institution in society: the only institution that everyone is legally obliged to attend for over a decade (aside from the tiny home-schooled minority). It thus holds enormous practical, emotional and relational significance in young people's lives.

Schools are legally obliged to meet the needs of all their students, including making reasonable adjustments for particular students' complexities where required, and to safeguard their students. In our view, this requires them to provide both high-quality education and exemplary care. Schools should be specialists in both teaching their students and keeping them safe from harm – both within and beyond the school gates.

To do this requires additional resource (see Irwin-Rogers, Muthoo and Billingham, 2020): schools need adequate funding to provide inclusive education which enables our young people both to achieve brilliant academic results and to develop personally within a safe, nurturing environment.

It also requires sufficient recognition, training, status and reward for those staff members whose expertise most closely relates to inclusion and to young people's well-being: early years staff, support staff, Special Educational Needs staff, safeguarding leads, mental health leads, educational psychologists, speech and language therapists and so on. All of these roles are too often seen as supplementary or subsidiary, as compared to those more directly involved with teaching and learning, and they are frequently underpaid, under-trained and undersupported. In particular, Designated Safeguarding Lead and Special Educational Needs Coordinator roles are vitally significant leadership roles in schools, tasked with ensuring that students of all learning needs are educated to a high standard, and that students are kept safe, but – as mentioned in Chapter 4 – these roles are too often fulfilled on a part-time basis, by teachers who have a substantial teaching load. All of this is an enormous mistake, if we wish to see our schools protect our children from harm and support their well-being as effectively as they provide their education.

As discussed in Chapter 4, another significant mistake made by some schools is the adoption of cold, punitive approaches to discipline, which can undermine their capacity to safeguard children. Such regimes frustrate and anger precisely those students whom schools should be trying hardest to engage, causing some to emotionally divest from schooling, or (at worst) from any authority, agency or service, leaving them far more vulnerable to harm. Other professionals, such as youth workers, social workers and Youth Offending Team workers, can struggle to build trust with young people whose school experience has fundamentally alienated them from 'professionals', whom they suspect to be against them. Even more concerningly, some punitive practice puts young people directly in danger: as included in one of the Chapter 4 case studies, for instance, schools have sent students home for minor uniform issues without checking if a parent was home or if the student had keys to the house.

The movement towards 'zero tolerance' behavioural regimes in some English schools was substantially influenced by the example of a few particularly high-profile Charter School chains in the US. Two had an especially marked impact: KIPP and Uncommon. Both released statements in 2020, in light of the Black Lives Matter movement, to say that they are changing their whole approaches to discipline, in recognition of the fact that they had disproportionately negative effects on students of colour. Despite evidence that the adoption of similar approaches in English schools has had similar effects (see, for example, Thompson, 2021), there has not been a similar rethink in this country, and – in fact – the government policy of supporting 'Behaviour Hubs' has been seen as an entrenchment of 'zero tolerance'-style regimes (see, for example, Willow, 2021).

What are schools for? The potential of schools to support their communities

Alongside the culture of punitiveness which has swept over many English schools, another issue has been the tendency among some schools to retreat away from the wider community. As Harding (2014, p 274) put it, 'too often schools operate independently of other local agencies and isolate themselves within the community'. As this suggests, schools can fail to effectively engage with local organizations and youth professionals, who are frequently best placed to safeguard children and young people in the places outside of both home and school. Youth workers can build deep, trusting relationships, which can be vital for understanding the protective and risk factors in a young person's life, across all the social contexts they dwell in. Mohamed Abdallah, former safeguarding lead at Dunraven School in South London, made the point neatly by describing his work as a 'collaborative effort with local grassroots organisations' (Abdallah, 2019).

Some schools adopt a broad view of the role that they can play: woven into their local neighbourhoods, they invite the community into the school and reach out into it at every opportunity, seeking to maximize the positive impact that they can have on children, young people and families, supporting them far beyond the provision of education. From this perspective, schools are not just for education, but institutions that have an unmatched ability to address the social, cultural, emotional and economic complexities and difficulties of their young people, and of their local community. The power of schools' roles in their communities was seen clearly during the COVID-19 pandemic, during which schools distributed food, coordinated with other local agencies and provided wide-ranging support to their students and families.

There is a long-established (though never dominant) stream of educational thought and practice in this country which stresses the potential that schools have to support the welfare and development of their community, from the 'Village College' movement of the early 20th century to New Labour's 'Extended' school projects in the early 2000s (see, for example, Fisher, 1968; Dyson, 2011; Dyson et al, 2011; Rooney, 2013). In today's Britain, there is a nascent movement of schools – working within this broad tradition – who explicitly seek to adopt a 'community hub' role (see Hirst, 2020). Reach Children's Hub in South West London, for instance, attached to Reach Academy, is creating a cradle-to-career system of support for local children, young people and families which works closely with the school.[3] Manchester Communication Academy, similarly, engages in broad-ranging activities to support the health, prosperity and well-being of its local community.[4]

If they were given adequate political support, we could see many more such initiatives flourish across Britain. Depending on wider historical developments, they could of course become just another form of bruise cream applied to those communities left most devastated by our vastly inequitable political economy; yet another charitable endeavour to ease the suffering of the most marginalized. At worst, schools could be viewed as a panacea for social issues, despite ongoing funding crises, and in the context of further shrinkage in welfare provision. Dr Mary Bousted, joint general secretary of the National Education Union, has discussed the expansive role played by school staff in communities that experience significant disadvantage in these terms: 'They feed them, they clothe them, they're counsellors, they're supporters, they act as children's social workers. As the public realm has disintegrated, schools are one of the few public institutions left standing where families and children can get support' (Newsnight, 2021). Schools could continue to be left picking up the pieces of the 'disintegrating' public realm. Or, at best, if their potential to act as community hubs and to weave themselves into local support networks were to be realized – with adequate funding and policy support – they could do much more than that. They could become public institutions which do not limit themselves to teaching, disciplining and examining: they could be templates for a better society.

Support for young people before and beyond school: early years, children's social care and youth services

Early years

As discussed throughout this book (in Chapters 3 to 5 especially), the preschool years are a fundamentally important stage of children's lives, and an incredibly complex and difficult stage for parents and families. We do a remarkably bad job in this country of ensuring that all young children and their parents receive the support that they need. Childcare is extortionately expensive – recent analysis suggests that the UK has the third most expensive childcare system of OECD nations (Topping, 2021). Net childcare costs in this country amount to 30 per cent of the average parental wage, while in Denmark the figure is 9 per cent (Topping, 2021). As discussed in Chapter 4, SureStart and children's centre provision has been substantially cut, reducing the support available to parents in the communities which experience the highest rates of poverty. Lastly, there have been significant reductions to health visiting, which some argue leave young children at risk of harm in the first few years of their lives (see, for example, Lepper, 2021).

The early years are arguably the most important point at which support agencies can reduce the impact of poverty, inequality and adversity. Given all that we know about the potential long-term effects of childhood experiences, it is a remarkable political failure that we do not provide better social conditions for the first years of children's lives (see Billingham and Irwin-Rogers, 2020, p 61). At a minimum, central government should better subsidize childcare and should provide investment in all children's centres, in order to facilitate strong relationships between children, families and professionals. This would help to reduce inequalities, improve children's health and well-being and provide integrated services to children and their families (Irwin-Rogers, Muthoo and Billingham, 2020, p 63).

Children's social care

As discussed in some length in Chapter 4, there are fundamental problems with children's social care in this country, particularly due to the spiral of two interlinked problems: increased poverty and adversity (and thus increased demand for children's social care), and reduced funding (and thus reduced provision or 'supply' of children's social care). There is a clear case for government to dedicate substantial time and resources to addressing each of these problems.

One particularly acute issue for children in care (among many problems affecting this group) is their placement in un(der)regulated private accommodation. Urgent concerns have been raised about this, especially given the heightened vulnerability of such children to exploitation, and their well-known overrepresentation in the criminal justice system (see, for example, Butler, 2021b; Marsh, 2021). At worst, these children are both housed in unsafe settings and excluded from mainstream education, thus leaving them at substantial risk of harm. Our society must be better at preventing young people from reaching this incredibly vulnerable position and supporting those who are in it. Those whose nurture is entrusted to state agencies should be provided with the very highest standards of care. This would require a significant reform of care accommodation, in terms of both regulation and funding.

The UK Government's move in 2022 to withhold the entitlement to care from over-15s should be reversed urgently, given the acute vulnerability that it creates for a significant number of young people (Guardian, 2022). Beyond this, the dire state of children's social care – with its astronomic costs and poor outcomes for children and families – puts it in desperate need of enhanced funding and reform. This much was recognized by a government-commissioned review that reported its findings in May 2022 (MacAlister, 2022). The report forecast that without reform, the number of children in care would rise from almost 81,000 at the time of reporting, to over 95,000 by 2031–32. Among its key recommendations, the report urges government to commit to a five-year, £2.6 billion programme that invests in intensive, community-based services aimed at reducing both the number of children on the child protection register and placed in care.

While a one-off windfall tax on the 15 biggest companies in the children's social care sector was recommended to help fund this programme, critics have pointed out that this does nothing to change the profit-driven model that is now hard-wired into the sector: 85 per cent of children's homes, for example, are owned by private companies, and the market is advertised as a 'favourable demographic' to private equity investors (see also Jones, 2015, 2020, pp 376–80; Quarmby and Norris, 2022).

As critics including Professor Eileen Munro have highlighted, the review was subject to 'hobbling restrictions' from the outset, which inevitably led to its failure to adequately acknowledge the role of poverty and the crippling impact of a prolonged period of austerity on public services (see Butler, 2021a). Instead of isolated, short-term injections of money, a healthy and well-functioning system of children's social care will require a long-term commitment to substantial reinvestment and significantly better-funded public services, accompanied by a crucial strategic shift that re-establishes children as children, rather than as potential sources of profit over which private sector companies compete. Our chidlren's social care system would also benefit hugely from a reduction in child poverty: as Bennett and colleagues put it, 'national anti-poverty policies are key to tackling adverse trends in children's care entry in England' (Bennett et al, 2022, p 496).

Youth services

We discussed both cuts to youth services and the immense value of youth work in Chapter 4. Youth centres can significantly strengthen young people's sense of mattering, and can be places in which they find unconditional nurture, care and love, which may be lacking from other contexts in their lives. Such places are what Currie calls 'essential institutions of care, nurturance and opportunity' (Currie, 2020, p 15). Relationships with youth workers can be among the most profound and beneficial that young people experience (see the following section on one-to-one work). Youth services deserve considerable increases in both funding and political respect.

We will add two brief further points here, regarding the future shape of youth work. Firstly, alongside the issue of 'programmification' discussed in Chapter 6 (the sharp decline of youth centre institutions, and shift towards time-bound peripatetic youth programmes), there is the problem of mission creep towards the 'youth violence' agenda: organizations which may not be well equipped to directly address violence between young people are feeling themselves drawn towards it, particularly due to the relative availability of funding for that kind of activity. As Sherry Peck, the chief executive of Safer London, has put it:

> Many of those organisations who historically would provide essential youth provision or children or family centre spaces are having to attempt to move into the specialist 'youth violence' world to secure funding to continue to exist. This is wrong on a number of fronts and we would advocate both an increase in locally embedded youth work and support to ensure specialist services are funded to undertake the work that is still desperately needed. (Peck, 2020, p 78)

We concur: there is a pressing need for both community-based youth work and specialist support for those young people affected by violence – and for the two forms of provision to be joined up where needed – but a clear distinction between the two is important.

Secondly, in line with the heightened political respect which youth work deserves, there is a need for more thorough and creative thinking about the contexts in which youth workers can play a valuable role. Youth work takes place in dedicated centres, on streets, in schools, on estates, in parks, in primary healthcare settings, in hospitals, in youth custody settings, in shopping centres, within neighbourhood sports facilities and more. Too often, though, youth work is perceived as a kind of subsidiary add-on to other objectives in these places, such as educational attainment, crime reduction or the minimization of 'anti-social behaviour'. More strategic thinking is needed about the relationship that young people have with these different settings: the extent of freedom and agency they have in them; the network of peers and adults they interact with in them; the benefits and risks of each place; the fears and hopes young people bring to them; and so on, and thus about the particular value that youth work relationships can have in each setting, and the forms they can best take.

One-to-one support for young people: relationships that make a difference

> I hope those of us who have contact with [young people] create opportunities for them to fulfil their dreams, realize their hopes, and discover for themselves what it means to 'be somebody'.
>
> McIntyre, 2000, p 145

> The more mature human being seems to keep within their memories, to refer to in difficult times, the images of those people who have believed in them.
>
> May, 1998, p 139

> I think my presence as the one who had helped him be seen as an understandable human being by the people who made up his world had kept him alive. ... It is presumptuous to think that anyone can 'save' another person; the most one can do is to be present for them and encourage their ability and their motivation to live.
>
> Gilligan, 1997, p 266

As each of these quotes attests, in slightly different ways, supportive professional (and personal) relationships can make an enormous difference to young people: they can enhance well-being, reduce the impact of harm and – in some cases – may contribute to a reduced propensity for violence. Such relationships can also support a young person's sense of mattering – enabling them to feel that they are valued by others and that they can have a meaningful influence on the world.

Perhaps the most important effect of all the changes suggested in this section would be to increase the number of supportive relationships in young people's lives; especially those who face the greatest adversity and the most structural harm.

We have already alluded to the impact of such relationships in the early years, but they can also have profoundly positive effects on young people and young adults. At that stage, individuals are working out who they are, who and what is significant to them and who and what they wish to matter to. This is not easy – everyone makes mistakes in the course of this process, some with more terrible consequences than others. Supportive relationships with adults (as well as with peers) can be the single most important factor in guiding this process in positive directions. They can help young people to develop their spheres of competence and care – what they are good at and what they care about; to understand what makes for meaningful social bonds with others; support their academic and career progress, and much more – as McIntyre puts it, they can be invaluable aids in young people's quest to 'be somebody'.

This can be especially true for those young people and young adults who have experienced early adversity, or who have engaged in criminal activity, including violence. Research has highlighted the impact of trusted adults with such young people, and has identified key features of the most effective professional relationships. Brierley (2021, p 153) describes how, for those young people who need to process trauma, 'nurturing, caring, supportive adult relationships [can] help buffer the pain these reflections are likely to unearth' – supportive adults can help such young people to reflect and develop 'by walking alongside them through the complexities of human life'. Wong et al (2018) specify valuable features of such supportive professional relationships, finding that reciprocity, reliability, consistency and emotional pleasure were key to the success of the 'offender' engagement programme that they studied. Somewhat similarly, young people suggested to Seal and Harris that 'honesty, authenticity, trustworthiness, humour, understanding, loyalty and, notably, *passion*' were the most important qualities in youth workers seeking to reduce community violence (Seal and Harris, 2016, p 125, emphasis in original). Lastly, in his description of how 'Jim' worked with 'Daniel' (whose violence is discussed in Chapter 5), Harris (2017, p 528) writes that Jim allowed Daniel to perceive 'a more affirming standpoint of the generalised other towards himself' and to 'construct a subjectivity less centred on violence'. Harris concludes by arguing that: 'Empathic professionals who are able to contain young people's emotional affect and defensive projections without retaliating or retreating into their own defensive professional identities can begin to modify violent behaviour' (Harris, 2017, p 530). All young people benefit hugely from well-crafted supportive professional relationships, then, and there is evidence to suggest that this is particularly the case for those who have experienced the most significant complexities and difficulties. Such relationships can be found in all kinds of institutional setting and service, from schools to mental health agencies, and more must be done to provide conducive conditions for them to flourish. This is partly an issue of funding — effective relationship-building requires resources (see Chapter 4) — but also of organizational cultures: as discussed in Chapter 4 and earlier, some school cultures are not conducive to the development of positive student–staff relationships, for instance, and Harris (2017, p 530) suggests that 'cultures can quash good practice' across a range of welfare services and institutions.

Housing and local communities

Far too many children and young people are growing up in insecure or inadequate housing, with a variety of harmful effects (see Chapter 4). This is a fundamental societal failing and a profound barrier to their flourishing, and must be rectified: central government and local authorities should be doing all that they can to invest in genuinely affordable and social housing for those who need it most.

Too often, young people affected by the rapid pace of change in their communities are not informed about, involved in or benefiting from that change (see, for example, Billingham et al, 2018). If they are to be positively engaged in their local neighbourhoods, young people should have the opportunity to participate in helping to shape their futures (see Billingham and Irwin-Rogers, 2020, p 60). This is particularly important in those inner-city areas most profoundly affected by processes of gentrification.

There is also a great need for young people to have access to high-quality leisure facilities in their local areas. To focus briefly on a specific example, we would argue that too many hyper-local estate or neighbourhood-based facilities, such as ball courts (also known as 'cages' or 'Multi-Use Games Areas'), are both undervalued and inadequately inclusive, particularly those facilities which are most used by the least privileged demographic of young people. They are too often in poor condition or accessed only by some young people (football and basketball facilities tend to be dominated by teenaged boys, for instance). Much more could be done to enhance the quality and the safety of these places, given that they can be sites of both huge benefit and significant harm to young people (see Billingham, 2020).

The role that these kinds of facilities can play in enhancing both the mattering and the safety of young people has been eloquently articulated by Henry Giroux, based on his own personal experience:

> For many of the working-class youth in my neighbourhood, the basketball court was one of the few public spheres in which the kind of cultural capital we recognised and took seriously could be exchanged for respect and admiration. ... Nobody was born with innate talent. Nor was anybody given instant recognition. The basketball court became for me a rite of passage and a powerful referent for developing a sense of possibility. We played day and night. ... Basketball was taken very seriously because it was a neighbourhood sport, a terrain where respect was earned. It offered us a mode of resistance, if not respite, from the lure of drug dealing, the sport of everyday violence, and the general misery that surrounded us. The basketball court provided another kind of hope, one that seemed to fly in the face of the need for high status, school credentials, or the security of a boring job. It was also a sphere in which we learned about the value of friendship, solidarity, and respect for the other. (Giroux, 2012, pp 9–10)

Employment

Life for British young people would be far safer, more meaningful and more purposeful if there was more widespread availability of good-quality work-related opportunities. Employment can provide income, self-worth, dignity and a positive sense of the future, particularly if employers provide supportive working conditions, training and clear progression routes. In reality, too many work opportunities available to young people are poorly paid, exploitative and precarious (see Chapter 4).

Exploitation by adults or by peers is one of the most significant extra-familial dangers to our young people, and this is exacerbated by a lack of decent legitimate work opportunities (Pitts, 2013; Harding 2020a). Too many young people are faced with a legitimate economy which can seem just as grim and exploitative as illegal routes to income. For some, 'gig economy' work with poverty pay has precious little to recommend it over drug-running. We have an exploitative legal job market and a prosperous illegal drugs market: a dangerous, toxic combination (Koch, 2019). If they are to be kept safe, we need both better employment opportunities for young people and radically reformed drugs policies, which should focus on harm reduction (discussed further in the next section).

Government should both address the growing issue of insecure, low-quality and low-paid work among young people and invest in high-quality employment programmes, training schemes and apprenticeships, as well as better incentivizing businesses to invest in the progression of junior employees (see Irwin-Rogers, Muthoo and Billingham, 2020, p 63). The nature of the job market for adults requires urgent attention too, of course: even if we solely consider the impact on children and young people, parents working multiple, insecure, poorly paid jobs can have a profoundly damaging effect.

Criminal justice, youth justice and policing

Too often our criminal and youth justice systems are overly punitive and profoundly ineffective; and too often the nature of policing in this country stokes division and tension rather than supporting cohesion and peacefulness in our communities (see Chapter 6). As welfare provision has reduced and our political economy has become increasingly inequitable, we have become progressively more over-reliant on our justice systems and police to address social problems: our (adult) prison population has almost doubled since the 1990s (Prison Reform Trust, 2021), for instance, and police officers are increasingly called upon to address mental health issues and other forms of social crisis. This is reflected in the striking title given by Lane to her article exploring recent experiences of police officers in the UK (Lane, 2019): 'I'm a police officer not a social worker or mental health nurse'.

As will be clear from the arguments presented in this book, we would suggest that this under-provision of community support and over-reliance on policing and justice needs to be reversed. As Scott (2018, p 206) has highlighted, there is a general pattern discernible across nations where those who dedicate most resources to welfare provision spend the least on criminal justice, and vice versa: societies make decisions about whether to enhance the welfare of their most marginalized citizens, or instead control and punish them for their misdemeanours. We would support a shift towards the former: if the changes advocated for in previous sections were brought about, we would not need to rely so much on heavy-handed policing and justice strategies. We are thus aligned with what Edwards and Prins (2014, pp 68–9) describe as a 'transformative' approach to criminal justice, in which issues of crime and violence are viewed as 'problems of social and economic policy' more than of individual behaviour, and the most effective long-term solutions are seen as 'improved education, training, employment, housing, health, leisure and family support' as well as 'reducing gross inequalities of wealth and opportunity among urban populations'.

As for those who have committed harmful or criminal acts, there is a growing literature on desistance which aligns with many of our arguments in this book. In their summary of the findings from desistance research, for instance, Maruna and Mann state: 'People are more likely to desist when they have strong ties to family and community, employment that fulfils them, recognition of their worth from others, feelings of hope and self-efficacy, and a sense of meaning and purpose in their lives' (Maruna and Mann, 2019, p 7). These social conditions, which predictably foster desistance, bear a clear resemblance to the kinds of societal change we are outlining in this chapter, as well as to our conceptualization of mattering outlined in Chapter 3.

More specifically, in line with arguments throughout this book, we would advocate urgent reconsideration of our national drugs policy; significant reform to reduce racial discrimination throughout the criminal justice system; greater investment in diversionary schemes for all age groups; and a deep reconsideration of the role of policing, guided by the central importance of working in a mutually respectful manner with and for communities, as well as by an open exploration of what should and should not be within the remit of the police.

Violence Reduction Units and the public health approach to violence

Lastly, we turn more directly to the specific issue of violence. As the Youth Violence Commission (Irwin-Rogers, Muthoo and Billingham, 2020) made clear, the 'public health approach' to reducing violence has the potential to substantially improve life for children, young people and families, and to play a significant role in preventing harm (see also Fraser and Irwin-Rogers, 2021). The public health approach is in line with the analysis presented in this book, particularly due to its potential to address the social conditions which predictably breed violence: at its boldest, a public health approach to violence reduction is a socio-historical task, addressing the historical accumulation of adversity and harm in particular communities, as opposed to treating violence as an isolable social problem. As well as involving targeted interventions for those who are at risk of or who have perpetrated acts of violence, a public health approach should also involve more universal, population-level change, and a concerted effort to reduce structural harms affecting children and young people.

There are now 20 VRUs across England and Wales, which are – in various ways – institutional vessels for the implementation of a public health approach. These units require long-term funding and a clearly defined role (see Irwin-Rogers, Muthoo and Billingham, 2020). We would argue that, due to their inherently place-based approach, attending to the idiosyncrasies of the communities they operate within, VRUs have the potential to go far beyond the provision of targeted interventions and could play an important role in many of the changes discussed in this chapter. To take just three examples of the broader remit we think they could adopt (with sufficient funding and policy support):

- Working with other local agencies, VRUs can address the localized structural harms in their communities which contribute, directly or otherwise, to the problem of violence. For instance, they can play a leading role in examining and addressing issues of institutional racism within key local settings and services, such as schools and social care (see Mwale, 2020, pp 75–7).
- Relatedly, VRUs can avoid narrow and simplistic ways of understanding and responding to violence between young people, addressing the broad-ranging issues which both contribute to and stem from this form of violence. For instance, they can play a role in tackling cultures of masculinity which make violence more likely; can address the specific effects of this violence on young women (see Iyere, 2020, p 73); and can ensure that the mental health and well-being of young people affected by violence is supported in a culturally competent manner (see Williams et al, 2020).
- VRUs can avoid a myopic focus on street-based violence between young people, instead recognizing the importance of addressing other forms of violence, including violence between adults; violence affecting women and girls; violence against children by adults; and violence against parents and carers by their children. This is particularly important, given the interconnectedness of these forms of violence and more visible, more 'sensational' street-based forms (see, for example, Levell, 2022).

Personal responsibility, proportional demands on services and funding

There are a number of reasons why readers might object to the suggestions presented in this chapter. While it is not possible for us to foresee or to address them all, there are three particular objections which we expect to be most common, and so we address these briefly in turn in the following sections.

What about personal responsibility?

Given our focus on structural harm throughout this book, and our discussion of broad societal changes in this chapter, some may argue that we are denying the importance of personal responsibility. It is all very well to suggest changes to policies, systems and institutions – this argument can run – but individuals also need to take responsibility for their behaviour.

We have three responses to this. Firstly, the most extreme variants of this argument rest on a false dichotomy: it is not the case that individual actions are either entirely prompted by structural factors or wholly the result of the person's 'free' decision making. Any choice or activity is the outcome of a complex combination of the two. Nowhere in this book have we denied that individuals should be held responsible for their actions, and as we emphasized in the Introduction, explanation and exoneration are two separate endeavours: in seeking to explain why certain people may behave in certain ways, we do not morally exculpate them.

Secondly, in our discussion of mattering, we have attended to the development of subjectivity and agency, and thus to the ways in which individuals navigate the world and undertake actions: we have discussed the yearning to matter as a complex psycho-social process, involving substantial social influence but also allowing for individual reflection and agency.

Lastly, we would argue that, if our goal is to address the socio-historical factors which make violence more likely, and thus aim towards sustainable, long-term reductions in violence, emphasizing personal responsibility does not advance the cause very far. We need to examine and to change the conditions within which individuals are operating if we are to have any hope of affecting their thoughts, emotions and actions. Outlined in this chapter are the changes to policies, systems, institutions and cultures which we believe can positively alter the contexts within which personal responsibility is enacted, in a manner which has the potential to reduce the harmfulness and violence of our society.

Of course, none of this precludes the idea that there should also be measures undertaken – such as the one-to-one support already described – to help individuals address their harmful behaviours (see, for example, Seal and Harris, 2016, p 80, on 'constructive confrontations' with young people).

Many of the suggestions in this chapter place hugely unrealistic expectations and demands on important institutions and services

We can address this objection with greater brevity. Firstly, we have emphasized throughout the chapter that all of the institutions, services and organizations which provide much-needed nurture and care to our children and young people should be adequately funded and supported for the activities that they undertake. Secondly, we would argue that the structural changes to society which we have advocated – such as redistribution of wealth – would result in a reduction of the complex difficulties which these agencies are addressing. We need both less adversity in our society and enhanced resourcing for those agencies and individuals which support our communities, families, children and young people.

Demands placed on particular institutions and services should always be kept proportional, in light of the scale and the complexity of the issues they address, and the resources they have to do so. At the current time, we would argue that a wide range of institutions and services are being expected to meet demands and needs beyond their capacity – mental health services, schools, social care and police, for instance, are all facing immense strain, due to the combination of deepening social problems in our society and declines in funding.

It is a damaging mistake to adopt a simplistically 'blaming' attitude towards services, or to take a fine-toothed comb to their failings, without providing them with the resources that they need to operate more effectively, or while neglecting the social problems which are generating heightened demand for them.

All of these changes will be incredibly expensive to the taxpayer

Perhaps the most predictable objection is that all of the changes outlined in this chapter involve substantial state expenditure. We can respond to this through three lines of argument.

Firstly, we would argue that there is a powerful ethical case for the state to spend considerable resources on the changes discussed earlier, in order to reduce harm and violence in society. If the state's primary responsibility is the safety and security of its citizens, this provides a compelling justification for this expenditure.

Secondly, many of the changes outlined in this chapter would in fact rectify enormous state overspending and inefficiencies. The Youth Violence Commission found that the costs associated with responses to serious violence between young people were around £11 billion between 2009 and 2020 (Irwin-Rogers, Muthoo and Billingham, 2020). Within criminal justice, the punitiveness of current policies is considerably more expensive to the taxpayer than the more welfare-oriented measures which we advocate. Investment in high-quality early years provision would prevent far more expensive interventions at later stages of life. In addition – tied to our response to the objection already put forward – were we to have significantly less poverty and adversity in our communities, the state would not need to spend nearly as much money on remedial measures to reduce the hardship experienced by their inhabitants.

Thirdly, there are a number of measures which could be enacted to offset increased state spending. These include progressive changes to income tax rates, wealth taxes, and the closing of tax avoidance and evasion loopholes. As Streeck (2014, p 66) has shown, across the Global North, low tax receipts are a more prominent cause of government debt than high spending. Arguments that the country simply 'does not have the money' to enact the kinds of progressive social policies already outlined are fast being picked apart by proponents of Modern Monetary Theory (MMT), who explain that it is simply not possible for countries with monetary sovereignty to 'run out of money'. According to MMT, while substantial rates of inflation are a central risk to be mitigated against, large deficits should often be regarded as welcome and necessary components of a healthily functioning economy (see Kelton, 2020, pp 72–3).

Address harm, reduce inequality, enhance care

> Where people are well cared for, where they have something meaningful to do in their lives that brings them respect and a sense of contribution as well as a measure of economic security and well-being, where they are treated well and fairly by authorities, including those in the criminal justice system, and where they have the support of stable communities and nurturing families and can envision a future of the same kind for themselves and their progeny, they are unlikely to commit violence against one another.
>
> Currie, 2016, p 93

> Young Londoners are not the issue – the problem is the context in which they are trying desperately to create their lives.
>
> Peck, 2020, p 78

We have reached a point in our technological, cultural and economic development which should render social harm both a political priority and a key metric of our success – or our decency – as a society. There are some social harms which are more intractable features of the human condition than others, but we have the collective resources and capability to sharply, drastically reduce the amount of social harm inflicted on the most marginalized young people in our society.

One important step in this vital task is to stop holding up a magnifying glass to the harms that are committed by young people against one another, and instead turn more of our attention towards the structural aspects of our society that systematically generate harm, and thereby predictably increase the probability of interpersonal violence. Gilligan (1997, pp 236, 239) puts it beautifully: 'If we wish to prevent violence, then, our agenda is political and economic reform … reforming the social, economic, and legal institutions that systematically humiliate people can do more to prevent violence than all the preaching and punishing in the world.' He published that book

25 years ago. Our decision makers would do well to take its message more seriously today.

Ultimately, all of the suggestions outlined in this chapter relate to two broad social changes, which are needed in parallel. First, we need to reduce the vast inequalities in recognition, resources, risk and retribution which contort and diminish the lives of far too many children, young people and families. Second, we need to ensure that all children and young people have nurturing, consistent and caring adults in the many different contexts of their lives: this will require increased and more sustainable funding for the institutions in which such adults proliferate; enhanced levels of training and support for those adults; and – most importantly – far wider and better provision for parents, particularly when their children are young. These two changes are needed in tandem. The second without the first would amount to mere sticking plasters on gaping wounds; the first without the second would be a very cold kind of revolution.

Notes

Introduction

[1] We would hope, for instance, that the Youth Violence Commission presented a nuanced picture of violence between young people. It is partly our experience of undertaking extensive research for the Commission, however, that has made us more critical of the 'youth violence' label, for the reasons we outline in this section.

[2] If a word or phrase is morally dubious in itself, that may be sufficient grounds for disposal. If the issue with a word or phrase is the problematic connotations which have become attached to it, it will always be more difficult to establish the extent to which the word/phrase has a life beyond those connotations and can be salvaged, or has become irreparably tarnished by them.

[3] When undertaking the research captured in Billingham et al (2018), for instance, we asked some of our respondents what proportion of local young people they thought were involved in the criminal justice system. Answers tended to range between 10% and 60%. The actual figure, according to the local Youth Offending Team manager, was around 1%. There may be many reasons for these misconceptions, but the potency of 'youth violence' discourse certainly seemed to play a role.

[4] For a sophisticated and compelling account of the current moral panic surrounding 'knife crime' specifically, which is neither lazy nor simplistic, see Williams and Squires (2021).

Chapter 1

[1] We would like to thank Gavin Hales for compiling the data that underpins the charts in this chapter.

[2] Hoxton East and Shoreditch is something of an outlier, experiencing by far the highest levels of recorded knife crime, but also being one of Hackney's lesser deprived wards, according to the IMD. This may well be due to the particularly stark levels of inequality within the ward, with pockets of considerable wealth alongside neighbourhoods experiencing substantial poverty.

Chapter 2

[1] See Canning and Tombs (2021) for a more comprehensive discussion.

[2] While Sweden provides some good examples of relatively effective harm reduction social policies, it should nevertheless be noted that other policies, for example those relating to drug distribution and consumption, have been criticized as repressive approaches that increase harm (Transform Drug Policy Foundation, 2018).

[3] Maslow's original model of need developed in 1943 contained only five stages.

[4] In addition to needs fulfilment and subjective well-being, in some circumstances we think there could be value in considering a third approach to understanding human flourishing: the extent to which people exhibit good character. While the first needs-based approach to

thinking about human flourishing encourages a consideration of what people have in their lives and the second subjective well-being approach focuses attention on how people think and feel about their lives, this third approach would shift our analytic gaze onto what people are like and what people do, focusing in particular on the way in which people relate to one another as members of social groups. In short, human flourishing could also be conceptualized as the extent to which people within a particular society exhibit good character, such as being kind, compassionate, honest, loving, generous, acting with integrity and so on. While some people are likely to reject or be inherently sceptical of a character-based understanding of human flourishing, on the grounds that it represents an outdated relic of a bygone era, there are certain angles and approaches that social harm scholars could use to interpret and apply character-based thinking in pursuit of more radical and progressive agendas. It is possible, for example, to flip the traditional focus, by emphasizing the fundamental role of social structures in hampering or fostering good character, away from the individualizing approaches that tend to dominate much of the literature to date. Consider, for example, the virtues of compassion and humanity. Many social harm scholars, including Pemberton (2015) and Slapper and Tombs (1999), have explored the commodification process that occurs within capitalist societies – and in particular neoliberal capitalist societies – which distorts human relationships into mere transactions between objects or units. In short, people's propensity to feel and demonstrate compassion and humanity towards one another is drained away through the relentless commodification of all forms of human life. Conceptualized in this way, it is possible to make a strong case that competitive capitalist 'free-market' economies generate serious social harm through their tendency to undermine compassion and humanity in the societies in which they operate, hence compromising human flourishing at both an individual and collective level. In this book, however, we confine our conceptualization of human flourishing to need fulfilment and subjective well-being because, on this particular subject, we see these two ways of understanding human flourishing to be the most pertinent. We reached this conclusion after fiery inter-author debate that persisted over several weeks and months. Despite barbed comments and heated exchanges – and many arguments about Aristotle's intellectual credentials – the authors remain, broadly speaking, on cordial terms.

5   In recent years, however, a growing body of research has linked human activity such as hydraulic fracturing (fracking) to damage-causing earthquakes (see Booher, 2015).

6   There is of course profound difficulty in seeking to distinguish between interpersonal or structural harm in many cases, given that this necessitates an assessment of the extent to which an individual act was structurally determined or facilitated. An act of domestic violence, for instance, committed by a man against a woman, could be described simply as an interpersonal harm. Many have argued, however, that such acts are inextricably tied to patriarchal social structures (see, for example, Bettman, 2009). We cannot provide a definitive answer in the abstract as to what precisely distinguishes an interpersonal harm from a structural one, but we do explore the matter at length through examples discussed throughout the book (and in Chapter 4 in particular). Though in real life it may be difficult to draw a clear line between these two forms of social harm, we believe the distinction remains analytically and politically important, as it draws attention to the role that policies, systems and institutions play in making harm more likely or more frequent, rather than narrowing our focus solely to the level of individuals, as if their acts are wholly 'free' and the possibilities of their lives unstructured.

Chapter 3

1   There are of course differing interpretations of what a psycho-social approach entails (see Gadd and Jefferson, 2007; Seal and Harris, 2016, pp 30–2; Jones, 2020). Our

approach might be considered to stray from more conventional kinds of psycho-social approach, due to the limited extent to which we delve into psychoanalytical territory. We have restricted our engagement with psychoanalysis in this book, partly due to accessibility considerations and partly due to our theoretical orientations – we are keen to ensure that psychological depth is matched by due attention to macro-scale structural factors, for instance (see Chapter 4). Our approach could be described as small-p 'psycho-social' rather than big-p Psychosocial, hence our use of the former designation.

[2] Arguably, one significant limitation of criminological accounts which focus on the operation of cultural norms and social codes is that they can fail to fully incorporate the fundamental causal significance of human relationships, as they wax and wane, deepen and tear apart. Too often, relationships appear to be just a feature of social groups, or a relative afterthought when writers are analysing the reasons behind young people's actions. There are of course many exceptions to this – see Vigil, 1988; Alexander, 2000; Bourgois, 2003; Deuchar, 2009; Contreras, 2013; and Fraser, 2015, for instance. The importance of relationships for mattering is something we ourselves have certainly not accorded sufficient significance in our previous work (see Billingham and Irwin-Rogers, 2020, 2021).

[3] Later developments of Bourdieu's ideas by other writers, such as the concept of 'street capital', are discussed in following chapters.

[4] It is beyond our scope to delve into philosophical discussion about the fundamental nature of reality, or to engage in the epistemological debate about the nature of our access to it.

[5] Prilleltensky (2020, p 18) has suggested that the need to matter is 'almost as compelling' as the need for food.

[6] As we will go on to explore in more detail in Chapter 5, the risk of nihilism is inherent in this: worth, value and significance can drain from the self and from the world in tandem. If a person feels themselves to be insignificant and inconsequential, they can lose moorings in existence – how do you discern what is meaningful and forceful in the world, if your place within it feels vanishingly small?

[7] The language of narrative can help to explain why the feeling of not mattering is so deeply troubling. We're all the protagonists of our own narratives, but if we feel that we don't matter, we feel utterly inconsequential to the world around us – an incidental protagonist: an oxymoron which signifies a horrifying self-concept.

[8] 'Crisis' narratives are of course something of a sociological cliché, especially when applied to young people. Goldson (2011) is cutting about such narratives, stating that 'ill-defined, historically decontextualised and hyperbolic constructions of "crisis"' hugely underplay the complexity of young people's worlds – he argues that 'the realities of such worlds express a far greater sense of historical continuity and are profoundly more disorganised, localised, nuanced and complex than "crisis" discourses – underpinned by notions of unique temporal specificity, aberration and national uniformity – seem to assert' (Goldson, 2011, pp 11, 5). This critique is well made, and so we would not wish to overstate the crisis-of-mattering narrative – we present it more as a question and a provocation than as an assertion. Prilleltensky's (2020) idea of a *global* crisis of mattering certainly seems bold, given the stark differences in social experience in the Global South and the Global North, for instance. In his more recent work, the crisis narrative seems to have been toned down somewhat – in their book *How People Matter*, for example, Prilleltensky and Prilleltensky (2021) do describe apparent signs of mattering crisis in multiple countries, but suggest that the problem is worst in less equitable countries, such as the US (Prilleltensky and Prilleltensky, 2021, p 7). They still suggest that a 'profound sense of worthlessness' is 'affecting millions of people', and they call for 'nothing less than a mattering revolution' (Prilleltensky and Prilleltensky, 2021, p 7).

Chapter 4

1 Relative poverty levels are usually determined by reference to the median income, which is the income amount that divides a population into two equally sized groups: one with incomes below the median and one with incomes above the median.

2 Defined as living below the threshold of 60 per cent of the contemporary median income after housing costs.

3 Below 50 per cent of contemporary median income, before housing costs.

4 Ofcom (2020) estimated that between 1 million and 1.8 million children lack access to a laptop, desktop computer or tablet in their homes.

5 Of course, there are many people who are able to maintain pride rather than living in shame through adversity (see Savage, 2021, p 210), and there are many ways that those experiencing poverty assert their dignity, express their personhood and carve out their agency (O'Hara, 2020; Lister, 2021). They thereby establish themselves as people who are consequential and who matter in the world, but through a form of cultural, personal and political struggle which is rooted in resistance to structural inequality and harm.

6 Alternative Provision is a term that refers to institutions tasked with educating young people who have been excluded from mainstream schools in England and Wales.

Chapter 5

1 Gaskell (2005), interestingly, opts to use a hyphenated compound of the two: 'shame-humiliation'. Katz (1988, p 27), somewhat by contrast, suggests that shame is defined by a self-perceived inadequacy which feels visible to those you respect, while humiliation is a self-perceived inadequacy visible to people who you feel want to degrade you. On this view, shame is prompted by feeling that your deficiencies are seen by those who you hope could be 'for' you, humiliation by feeling that they are seen by those who seem to be 'against' you.

2 Of course, gender can affect the meaning that power holds for an individual, as well as the expectations that an individual has of their own power. In men, for instance, there can be a deeply held sense of entitlement to have power and control over women: see Rose (2020), and discussion in the following section of this chapter.

3 This is in keeping with the approach to action eloquently described by Young as 'Merton with energy, Katz with structure' (Young, 2007, p 54): we cannot understand complex social activities like violence with reference only to the 'cold' workings of structures, as Merton (1938) tends to do in his structural analysis of crime; but neither can we only rely on energetic accounts of their proximal emotional drivers, as Katz (1988) seems to do. Young uses the example of poverty, pointing out that the 'structural predicament' of the poor is not just 'a deficit of goods' – as Merton can seem to imply – but is also a 'state of humiliation' (Young, 2007, p 54). We expounded upon this point at length in Chapter 4, using the work of O'Hara (2020), Tyler (2020) and Lister (2021) in particular: the experience of poverty in British society is most certainly a state of humiliation, and to narrate this structural harm as solely a 'cold' material matter would be to fundamentally misconstrue the role that it plays in making certain forms of action – including violence – more likely. Equally, to narrate the driving emotions of a violent individual without making any reference to their experience of this structural diminishment, or to relegate this to some distant causal 'background', would be to make the opposite, similarly damaging mistake.

4 Studies also consistently describe a culture among young men in which insults have a kind of verbally belittling quality. For example, Ellis quotes a man insulting a combatant by calling him a 'little fucking prick … little cunt' (Ellis, 2016, p 87), while Wilkinson similarly ascribes significance to the terms 'little punk-ass' and 'little sorry-ass' (Wilkinson,

2001, p 256). This verbal diminishment can become physical, of course: Katz describes how public violence can be intentionally humiliating, driving victims 'down' so that they are 'suddenly made small' (Katz, 1988, p 27).

[5] Interestingly, Fraser (2015, p 100) points out the similarities between territorial violence among young people – aimed at crystallizing identity and affirming power in an 'uncertain and unsteady world' – and the process of nation-state formation.

[6] The issues with endemic conflict and violence found in some children's homes are made considerably worse by their under-resourcing and low status, and there can be similar problems in some other institutional settings such as AP (places of education for young people outside of mainstream schooling). As discussed in Chapter 4, though there are of course many high-quality children's homes and AP settings, both tend to be under-regulated, under-discussed and under-supported in this country, reflecting the extent to which their marginalized inhabitants are structurally devalued. Inequalities and flaws in our care and education systems, exacerbated by policies such as austerity, can breed deeply harmful institutional practices and cultures.

[7] On a slightly more quotidian level, sheer boredom can also play a role: if there are limited options available for enjoyable, exciting leisure activities, this can increase the likelihood of young people engaging in violence 'for the buzz' (see Corrigan, 1979; Fraser, 2015, pp 148–50).

[8] For more of Smith's thoughts on young people, mental health, violence and the police, see Account (2020).

[9] In an article which has a far broader scope than the localized worlds of gangs, Davies (2021) tracks the changing nature of recognition in both politics and everyday life, and suggests that the era of platform capitalism has brought about a new kind of reputational economy. In this new, platformed world, seeking reputation online may obtain greater prominence in some people's lives than warmer, deeper forms of social and political recognition. Davies argues that 'the quest for recognition is more exacting and slower than that for reputation' (Davies, 2021, p 99), and suggests that this may be one significant factor driving people's pursuit of instant online reputation over richer, less individualized kinds of recognition. These processes certainly seem to be having an impact on young people.

[10] Another area of agreement seems to be the influence of significant social changes, such as those explored in the second part of Chapter 3. Between Pitts (2013) and Hallsworth (2013), for instance, there seems to be substantial alignment on the growing influence of consumerism in young people's lives. Where Pitts sees this as part of the 'neoliberal gangland', Hallsworth views it as 'cultural imperative' of the street world in marginalized communities.

[11] This is not to say that it is not possible to incorporate relational, emotional and existential components of violence within a broad Bourdieusian framework – see Fraser's (2015) sophisticated Bourdieusian ethnography of gangs in Glasgow, and Weaver and Fraser (2022)'s approach to 'thick understanding of situated social relations', which integrates Bourdieu's concept of habitus with Donati's relational realist framework in order to go beyond either individualizing or 'gang' frames.

Chapter 6

[1] Our description of this harmonious organic order myth bears similarities to Chamberlen and Carvalho's (2022, p 93) discussion of hostile solidarity and the social body: they suggest that the 'hostile form of solidarity' which underlies punitiveness in Western liberal societies is grounded in 'an image of community in which individuals are bonded together through their vulnerability against crime and their antagonism towards criminals … the

parts of the social body that are identified as sources of [crime] become other to it, while the exclusion and removal of these "bad parts" becomes the main way to preserve and reinforce a sense of social integrity'.

2   It scans and analyses only publications which Google has access to, for instance.

3   See Jouai (2018, p 93) for similar reflections on the French state's treatment of colonies abroad and suburbs at home.

4   Ethnographies of youth subcultures and gangs go far beyond this binary distinction between 'conformist' and 'oppositional' orientations. Writers from the US such as Horowitz (1983) and Contreras (2013), for instance, have shown how young people's engagement in crime and violence can involve a complex mixture of cultural influences, including both conformist ideas about the 'American Dream' and profound rejections of mainstream values. Katz argued that a desire for rebellion is in fact, paradoxically, at the heart of conventional American materialism – a craving for deviance drives materialism, more than the other way round: 'materialism may be less essential to the motivation to become deviant than an association with deviance is essential to the motivation to be acquisitive' (Katz, 1988, p 358n).

5   Both of these quotes are from a debate on 'knife crime' which took place in the House of Commons on 25 March 2019. Full transcript available: https://hansard.parliament. uk/Commons/2019-03-25/debates/D6B4D711-F983-439F-A598-670CFE4D36B2/ KnifeCrime [Accessed 5 September 2021].

6   From a debate on 'knife crime' which took place in the House of Commons on the 23 March 2020. Full transcript available: https://hansard.parliament.uk/Commons/2020-03-23/debates/2C67C988-019B-4101-A52B-14286685B0A8/KnifeCrime [Accessed 6 September 2021].

7   This is despite the fact that policing has not been immune to funding cuts: post-2010 austerity policies significantly affected police officer numbers. Since Kit Malthouse's statement at the start of this section, made in 2020, police numbers have increased. But if they increase by 20,000 from their 2020 levels, as Malthouse suggested will happen, they will just return to pre-austerity, 2010 levels. See https://fullfact.org/crime/ police-numbers/.

8   Aside from all of these problems with KCPOs, there also appear to be more basic issues with their implementation: in the first six weeks of their being trialled in London, only two KCPOs were applied for by the police, and both were turned down by magistrates (see Sky News, 2021).

9   https://twitter.com/pritipatel/status/1526853266562228225?t=gL47QFdTMjeNVdje UJ887w&s=19

10   The Crown Prosecution Service is now reviewing the legal guidance for prosecutors on the way that drill music is used in trials, due to concerns it can unfairly prejudice some cases (Pidd, 2022).

11   The judge in this case said that the defendants were not in joint enterprise, but were all principal parties. Pidd (2022) highlighted similarities between conspiracy legislation and joint enterprise, however, and wrote that 'supporters say these men were found "guilty by association", some after taking part in a Telegram group chat ... weeks before any violence was carried out by some of the other defendants'. The local MP, Lucy Powell, has written to the justice secretary about the case, saying 'it was just the latest example of black youths in her constituency being unfairly drawn into a "gang" narrative because of the music they listen to and who they know' (Pidd, 2020).

12   All data in this paragraph is for between July 2019 and July 2021, and is publicly available at www.met.police.uk/sd/stats-and-data/met/stop-and-search-dashboard/ [Accessed 7 September 2021].

13 In police parlance these are called 'positive outcomes', and include arrest, penalty notice, postal charge requisition/summons, community resolution or caution.

14 For example, see Assembly Member Caroline Russell's question on this topic to the Mayor of London, Sadiq Khan, in a London Assembly meeting of 24 June 2021. Available online at: www.london.gov.uk/questions/2021/2300 [Accessed 7 September 2021].

15 All data in this paragraph is for between July 2019 and July 2021, and is publicly available at www.met.police.uk/sd/stats-and-data/met/stop-and-search-dashboard/ [Accessed 7 September 2021].

16 At time of writing (February 2022), the not-for-profit organizations Liberty and UNJUST are taking the Metropolitan Police to court over the Gangs Matrix. They are 'challenging the lawfulness of Matrix, arguing that it discriminates against people of colour, particularly Black men and boys, and breaches human rights, data protection requirements and public law principles' (from www.libertyhumanrights.org.uk/issue/liberty-challenges-met-poli ces-discriminatory-gangs-matrix/ [Accessed 6 February 2022]).

17 From a debate on 'knife crime' which took place in the House of Commons on 23 March 2020. Full transcript available: https://hansard.parliament.uk/Commons/2020-03-23/debates/2C67C988-019B-4101-A52B-14286685B0A8/KnifeCrime [Accessed 6 September 2021].

18 The brochure is publicly available: https://cdn.catch-22.org.uk/wp-content/uploads/2020/02/ViolenceReduction_Booklet_2020.pdf [Accessed 8 September 2021].

Conclusion

1 Credit Suisse, 'Global Wealth Databook', November 2016, available online at: http://publications.credit-suisse.com/tasks/render/file/index.cfm?fileid=AD6F2B43-B17B-345E-E20A1A254A3E24A5#page=147 [Accessed 4 September 2018].

2 www.trustforlondon.org.uk/data/topics/inequality/.

3 See www.reachchildrenshub.com/ [Accessed 13 February 2022]. Billingham worked for Reach Children's Hub between 2016 and 2021.

4 See www.communitymca.co.uk/ [Accessed 13 February 2022].

References

Abdallah, M. (2019) 'No school should see itself as an island', *Times Educational Supplement* [online] 15 October, Available at: www.tes.com/news/no-school-should-see-itself-island [Accessed 19 September 2021].

Account (2020) *Policing in Hackney: Challenges from Youth in 2020*, London: Hackney CVS.

Adshead, G. (2001) 'A kind of necessity? Violence as a public health problem', in S.L. Bloom (ed) *Violence*, London: Karnac, pp 31–56.

Alexander, C. (2000) *The Asian Gang*, London: Berg.

Alexander, G.S. (2018) *Property and Human Flourishing*, Oxford: Oxford University Press.

Allen, R. and Sims, S. (2018) *The Teacher Gap*, Abingdon: Routledge.

Anderson, E. (2000) *Code of the Street*, London: W.W. Norton and Company.

Andrew, A., Cattan, S., Costa-Dias, M., Farquharson, C., Kraftman, L., Krutikova, S., Phimister, A. and Sevilla, A. (2020) 'Learning during the lockdown: real-time data on children's experiences during home learning', *Institute for Fiscal Studies* [online], Available at: www.ifs.org.uk/uploads/Edited_Final-BN288%20Learning%20during%20the%20lockdown.pdf [Accessed 19 September 2021].

Apland, K., Lawrence, H., Mesie, J. and Yarrow, E. (2017) 'A review of evidence on the subjective wellbeing of children excluded from school and in alternative provision in England', *Children's Commissioner for England* [online], Available at: www.childrenscommissioner.gov.uk/wpcontent/uploads/2017/11/CCO-Childrens-Voices-Excluded-from-schools-and-altprovision.pdf [Accessed 19 September 2021].

Apouey, B., Roulet, A., Solal, I. and Stabile, M. (2020) 'Gig workers during the COVID-19 crisis in France: financial precarity and mental well-being', *Journal of Urban Health*, 97: 776–95.

Arendt, H. (1970) *On Violence*, New York: Harcourt.

Atkinson, R. (2020) *Alpha City*, London: Verso.

Baker, D. (2016) *Rigged: How Globalisation and the Rules of the Modern Economy were Structured to Make the Rich Richer*, Washington, DC: Centre for Economic and Policy Research.

Bakkali, Y. (2019) 'Dying to live: youth violence and the munpain', *The Sociological Review*, 67(6): 1317–32.

Barker, J., Alldred, P., Watts, M. and Dodman, H. (2010) 'Pupils or prisoners? Institutional geographies and internal exclusion in UK secondary schools', *Area*, 42(3): 378–86.

Batchelor, S. (2011) 'Beyond dichotomy: towards an explanation of young women's involvement in violent street gangs', in B. Goldson (ed) *Youth in Crisis?* London: Routledge, pp 110–27.

Bateman, T. (2015) 'Trends in detected youth crime and contemporary state responses', in B. Goldson and J. Muncie (eds) *Youth Crime & Justice*, 2nd edn, London: Sage, pp 67–82.

Baum, D. (1996) 'Can integration succeed? Research into urban childhood and youth in a deprived area of Koblenz', *Social Work in Europe*, 3(3): 14–21.

Bauman, Z. (2000) *Liquid Modernity*, Cambridge: Polity.

Baumer, E. (2002) 'Neighbourhood disadvantage and police notification by victims of violence', *Criminology*, 40: 579–616.

BBC (2019) 'Tory leadership: how much has social care been cut?', Available at: www.bbc.co.uk/news/health-48690733#:~:text=Spend ing%20on%20adult%20social%20care,cut%20since%202010%20to%20 5%25 [Accessed 5 March 2021].

Beck, U. (1992) *Risk Society: Towards a New Modernity*, London: Sage Publications.

Beck, V., Fuller, A. and Unwin, L. (2006) 'Safety in stereotypes? The impact of gender and "race" on young people's perceptions of their post-compulsory education and labour market opportunities', *British Educational Research Journal*, 32(5): 667–86.

Becker, E. (1973) *The Denial of Death*, New York: Free Press Paperbacks.

Belger (2021) 'Councils in deficit told to find SEND savings in exchange for £100m bailouts', *Schoolsweek* [online] 19 March, Available at: https://schoolsweek.co.uk/councils-receive-conditional-send-special-needs-school-funding-bailouts/ [Accessed 19 September 2021].

Bennett, D., Shluter, D., Melis, G., Bywaters, P., Alexiou, A., Barr, B., Wickham, S. and Taylor-Robinson, D. (2022) 'Child poverty and children entering care: a longitudinal ecological study at local area-level in England, 2015–2020', *The Lancet Public Health*, 7: 496–503.

Berg, M., Slocum, L. and Loeber, R. (2013) 'Illegal behaviour, neighbourhood context, and police reporting by victims of violence', *Journal of Research in Crime and Delinquency*, 50: 75–103.

Bettman, C. (2009) 'Patriarchy: the predominant discourse and fount of domestic violence', *Australian and New Zealand Journal of Family Therapy*, 30(1): 15–28.

Bhattacharyya, G., Elliott-Cooper, A., Balani, S., Nisancioglu, K., Karam, K., Gebrial, D., El-Enany, N. and De Noronha, L. (2021) *Empire's Endgame: Racism and the British State*, London: Pluto.

Bhopal, K. (2011) ' "This is a school, it's not a site": teachers' attitudes towards Gypsy and Traveller pupils in schools in England, UK', *British Educational Research Journal*, 37(3): 465–83.

Billingham, L. (2020) 'Sports cages: places of safety, places of harm, places of potential', online report for Hackney Quest, Available at: www.csnetwork.org.uk/en/resources/spotlight-features/sports-cages-places-of-safety-places-of-harm-places-of-potential [Accessed 19 September 2021].

Billingham, L. and Irwin-Rogers, K. (2020) 'Mattering and the violence in our cities', in J. Dobson and R. Atkinson (eds) *Urban Crisis Urban Hope*, London: Anthem Press, pp 55–62.

Billingham, L. and Irwin-Rogers, K. (2021) 'The terrifying abyss of insignificance: marginalisation, mattering and violence between young people', *Oñati Socio-Legal Series*, 11(5): 1222–124.

Billingham, L., Isaacs, J. and Oyeleye, R. (2018) 'Hackney Wick through young eyes', online report for Hackney Quest, Available at: www.hackn eyquest.org.uk/images/HWTYE.pdf [Accessed 19 September 2021].

Bloodworth, J. (2019) *Hired*, London: Atlantic Books.

Boateng, F.D. (2018) Crime reporting behaviour: do attitudes towards the police matter? *Journal of Interpersonal Violence,* 33(18): 2891–916.

Body-Gendrot, S. (2005) 'Deconstructing youth violence in French cities', European Journal of Crime, Criminal Law and Criminal Justice, 13(1): 4–26.

Bond, E. and Hallsworth, S. (2017) 'The degradation and humiliation of young people', in V. Cooper and D. Whyte (eds) *The Violence of Austerity*, London: Pluto, pp 75–84.

Booher, J. (2015) 'Fracking-caused earthquakes: how alleged threats could trigger the Corps of Engineers' section 10 jurisdiction', *Environmental Law*, 45(1): 235–55.

Bottoms, A.E., Mawby, R.I., Walker, M.A. (1987) 'A localised survey in contrasting areas of a city', *British Journal of Criminology*, 27(2): 125–54.

Bourdieu, P. (1979) *Distinction*, London: Routledge.

Bourgois, P. (2003) *In Search of Respect: Selling Crack in El Barrio*, Cambridge: Cambridge University Press.

Bowen-Viner, K. (2021) 'Education without a place to call home', in L. Menzies and S. Baars (eds) *Young People on the Margins*, London: Routledge, pp 156–77.

Bradford, B. and Tiratelli, M. (2019) 'Does stop and search reduce crime?', *UK Justice Policy Review Focus*, 4, Centre for Crime and Justice Studies.

Brennan, I.R. (2019) 'Weapon-carrying and the reduction of violent harm', *The British Journal of Criminology*, 59(3): 571–93.

Bridges, L. (2021) 'The Police Bill, SVROs and guilt by association', *Institute for Race Relations*, [online] 20 May, Available at: https://irr.org.uk/article/police-bill-svros-guilt-by-association/ [Accessed 7 September 2021].

Brierley, A. (2021) *Connecting with Young People in Trouble*, Hook: Waterside Press.

Briggs, S. and Cameron, F. (2012) 'Complex trauma: a composite case study exploring responses to complex trauma across a lifespan', in J. Anderson, B. Sapey and H. Spandler (eds) *Distress or Disability?* Lancaster: Centre for Disability Research, pp 43–8.

Brookman, F., Bennett, T. Hochstetler, T. and Copes, H. (2011) 'The "code of the street" and the generation of street violence in the UK', *European Journal of Criminology*, 8(1): 17–31.

Brooks, R. (2014) *The Great Tax Robbery*, London: Oneworld Publications.

Brotherton, D. (2015) *Youth Street Gangs*, London: Routledge.

Broucek, F. (1979) 'Efficacy in infancy: a review of some experimental studies and their possible implications for clinical theory', *International Journal of Psychoanalysis*, 60: 311–16.

Brown, W. (2017) 'A citadel that stormed itself', *New Humanist*, 132(4): 33–9.

Bullinger, M. (2002) 'Assessing health related quality of life in medicine. An overview over concepts, methods and applications in international research', *Restorative Neurology and Neuroscience*, 20: 93–101.

Butcher, M. and Dickens, L. (2016) 'Spatial dislocation and affective displacement: youth perspectives on gentrification in London', *International Journal of Urban and Regional Research*, 40(4): 800–16.

Butler, P. (2021a) 'Review of children's social care in England ignores role of poverty, expert says', *The Guardian,* [online] 26 April, Available at: https://www.theguardian.com/society/2021/apr/26/review-childrens-social-care-england-ignores-role-poverty-says-expert [Accessed 2 June 2022].

Butler, P. (2021b) 'Profits from English children's care homes indefensible, bosses to be told', *The Guardian*, [online] 9 June, Available at: www.theguardian.com/society/2021/jun/09/profit-levels-in-childrens-care-homes-in-england-indefensible-bosses-told [Accessed 14 August 2021].

Cachia, R., Ferrari, A., Ala-Mutka, K. and Punie, Y. (2010) *Creative Learning and Innovative Teaching: Final Report on the Study on Creativity and Innovation in Education in the EU Member States*, Seville: Institute for Prospective Technological Studies.

Canning, V. and Tombs, S. (2021) *From Social Harm to Zemiology*, London: Routledge.

Carr, R., Slothower, M. and Parkinson, J. (2017) 'Do gang injunctions reduce violent crime? Four tests in Merseyside, UK', *Cambridge Journal of Evidence-Based Policing*, 1(4): 195–210.

Centre for Social Justice (2009) 'Dying to belong', [online], Available at: www.centreforsocialjustice.org.uk/wp-content/uploads/2009/02/DyingtoBelongFullReport.pdf [Accessed 17 October 2021].

Centre for Social Justice (2018) 'Providing the alternative: how to transform school exclusion and the support that exists beyond', online report, Available at: www.centreforsocialjustice.org.uk/wp-content/uploads/2018/08/Providing-the-Alternative-Final-V.pdf [Accessed 18 September 2021].

Chamberlen, A. and Carvalho, H. (2022) 'Feeling the absence of justice: notes on our pathological reliance on punitive justice', *The Howard Journal of Crime and Justice*, 61: 87–102.

Chase, E. and Walker, R. (2013) 'The co-construction of shame in the context of poverty: beyond a threat to the social bond', *Sociology*, 47(4): 739–54.

Chatzidakis, A., Hakim, J., Litter, J. and Rottenberg, C. (2020) *The Care Manifesto: The Politics of Interdependence*, London: Verso Books.

Cheng, T.C. and Lo, C.C. (2019) 'Physical intimate partner violence: factors related to women's contact with police', *Journal of Comparative Family Studies*, 50(3): 229–41.

Child Poverty Action Group (2020) 'The cost of learning in lockdown: family experiences of school closures', online report, Available at: https://cpag.org.uk/sites/default/files/files/The-cost-of-learning-in-lockdown-UK-FINAL_0.pdf [Accessed 18 September 2021].

Children's Commissioner (2013) ' "They go the extra mile": reducing inequality in school exclusions', online report, Available at: www.childrenscommissioner.gov.uk/wpcontent/uploads/2017/07/They_Go_The_Extra_Mile-.pdf [Accessed 18 September 2021].

Children's Commissioner (2019a) 'Exclusions: children excluded from mainstream schools', online report, Available at: www.childrenscommissioner.gov.uk/wp-content/uploads/2019/05/Exclusions-cover-merged.pdf [Accessed 18 September 2021].

Children's Commissioner (2019b) 'Keeping kids safe: improving safeguarding responses to gang violence and criminal exploitation', online report, Available at: www.childrenscommissioner.gov.uk/wp-content/uploads/2019/02/CCO-Gangs.pdf [Accessed 1 August 2021].

Chiodo, D., Crooks, C.V., Wolfe, D.A., McIsaac, C., Hughes, R. and Jaffe, P.G. (2012) 'Longitudinal prediction and concurrent functioning of adolescent girls demonstrating various profiles of dating violence and victimization', *Prevention Science*, 13: 350–9.

Chua, A. (2003) *World on Fire: How Exporting Free Market Democracy Breeds Ethnic Hatred and Global Instability*, New York: Anchor Books.

Clark, M.E. (1990) 'Meaningful social bonding as a universal human need', in J. Burton (ed) *Conflict: Human Needs Theory*, London: Macmillan Press, pp 34–59.

Coleman, C. and Moynihan, J. (1996) *Understanding Crime Data: Haunted by the Dark Figure*, Buckingham: Open University Press.

Collins, R. (2008) *Violence*, Princeton: Princeton University Press.

Community Links (2019) 'Community conversations: unearthing community-led ideas for tackling youth violence', [online], Available at: www.community-links.org/wp-content/uploads/Community-Links-Community-Conversations-2018.pdf [Accessed 3 March 2021].

Conn, D. (2021) 'One death, 11 jailed teenagers: was a Moss Side murder trial racist?', *The Guardian*, [online] 5 June, Available at: www.theguardian.com/world/2021/jun/05/one-death-11-jailed-teenagers-was-a-moss-side-trial-racist [Accessed 23 October 2021].

Contreras, R. (2013) *The Stickup Kids: Race, Drugs, Violence and the American Dream*, Berkeley: University of California Press.

Cooney, M. (1998) *Warriors and Peacemakers: How Third Parties Shape Violence*, New York: New York University Press.

Cooper, V. and Whyte, D. (eds) (2017) *The Violence of Austerity*, London: Pluto Press.

Copson, L. (2016) 'Realistic utopianism and alternatives to imprisonment: the ideology of crime and the utopia of harm' *Justice, Power and Resistance*, 1: 73–96.

Copson, L. (2018) 'Beyond 'Criminology vs Zemiology': Reconciling crime with social harm', in A. Boukli and J. Kotzé (eds) *Zemiology: Reconnecting Crime and Social Harm*, London: Palgrave Macmillan, pp 33–56.

Corrigan, P. (1979) *Schooling the Smash Street Kids*, London: Macmillan.

Costanza, R., Fisher, B., Ali, S., Beer, C., Bond, L., Boumans, R., Danigelis, N.L., Dickinson, J., Elliott, C. and Farley, J., (2007) 'Quality of life: an approach integrating opportunities, human needs, and subjective well-being', *Ecological Economics*, 61: 267–76.

Cottrell-Boyce, J. (2013) 'Ending gang and youth violence: a critique', *Youth Justice*, 13(3): 193–206.

Cowburn, A. (2020) 'Home Office ministers admit knife crime "is back" amid rise in incidents in recent years', *Independent*, [online] 9 November, Available at: www.independent.co.uk/news/uk/politics/knife-crime-uk-home-office-kit-malthouse-b1719807.html [Accessed 23 October 2021].

Cox, K., Sullivan, C., Olshansky, E., Czubaruk, K., Lacey, B., Scott, L. and Willems Van Dijk, J. (2018) 'Critical conversation: toxic stress in children living in poverty', *Nursing Outlook*, 66(2): 204–9.

Craggs, H. and Kelly, C. (2017) 'School belonging: listening to the voices of secondary school students who have undergone managed moves', *School Psychology International*, 39(1): 56–73.

Crook, F. (2016) 'Secure schools are the wrong answer to the wrong question', *The Howard League*, [online] 13 July, Available at: https://howardleague.org/blog/secure-schools-are-the-wrong-answer-to-the-wrong-question/ [Accessed 7 September 2021].

Crossley, S. (2017) *In Their Place: The Imagined Geographies of Poverty*, London: Pluto Press.

Crossley, S. (2018) *Troublemakers: The Construction of 'Troubled Families' as A Social Problem*, Bristol: Policy Press.

Cummins, I. (2018) 'The impact of austerity on mental health service provision: a UK perspective', *Environmental Research and Public Health*, 15(6): 1145–56.

Cunningham, I., Lindsay, C. and Roy, C. (2021) 'Diaries from the front line – formal supervision and job quality among social care workers during austerity', *Human Resource Management Journal*, 31(1): 187–201.

Currie, E. (2016) *The Roots of Danger*, Oxford: Oxford University Press.

Currie, E. (2020) *A Peculiar Indifference*, New York: Metropolitan Books.

Cusset, F. (2018) *Le déchaînement du monde*, Paris: La Découverte.

Davies, B. (2019) *Austerity, Youth Policy and the Deconstruction of the Youth Service in England*, London: Palgrave Macmillan.

Davies, W. (2021) 'The politics of recognition in the age of social media', *New Left Review*, 128: 83–99.

Dean, B. (2019) 'The Home Office's chicken box campaign isn't just offensive – it's dangerous', *Huffington Post*, [online] 15 August, Available at: www.huffingtonpost.co.uk/entry/chicken-shops-home-office-knife-crime_uk_5d5538f5e4b0eb875f1fd8ea [Accessed 8 September 2021].

Demianyk, G. (2019) 'Diane Abbott leads backlash over 'offensive' anti-knife messages in chicken shops', *Huffington Post*, [online] 15 August, Available at: www.huffingtonpost.co.uk/entry/diane-abbott-leads-backlash-over-offensive-anti-knife-messages-in-chicken-shops_uk_5 d5474e2e4b08ed26723dfa3?utm_hp_ref=uk-homepage [Accessed 8 September 2021].

De St Croix, T., McGimpsey, I. and Owens, J. (2020) 'Feeding young people into the social investment machine: the financialisation of public services', *Critical Social Policy*, 40(3): 450–70.

Densley, J. (2013) *How Gangs Work*, London: Palgrave Macmillan.

Department for Education (2020a) 'LA and school expenditure: 2018 to 2019 financial year', [online], Available at: www.gov.uk/government/collections/statistics-local-authority-school-finance-data [Accessed 8 September 2021].

Department for Education (2020b) 'Permanent and fixed-period exclusions in England: 2018 to 2019', [online], Available at: www.gov.uk/government/statistics/permanent-and-fixed-period-exclusions-in-england-2018-to-2019 [Accessed 8 September 2021].

Department for Education (2020c) 'Pupil exclusions', [online], Available at: www.ethnicity-facts-figures.service.gov.uk/education-skills-and-training/absence-and-exclusions/pupil-exclusions/latest#full-page-history [Accessed 8 September 2021].

Department for Education (2020d) 'School workforce in England', [online], Available at: https://explore-education-statistics.service.gov.uk/find-statistics/school-workforce-in-england [Accessed 8 September 2021].

Department for Education (2021) 'NEET statistics annual brief: 2020', [online], Available at: www.gov.uk/government/statistics/neet-statistics-annual-brief-2020 [Accessed 8 September 2021].

Department for Work and Pensions (2020a) 'Households below average income: 1994/95 to 2018/19', [online], Available at: www.gov.uk/government/statistics/households-below-average-income-199495-to-201819 [Accessed 8 September 2021].

Department for Work and Pensions (2020b) 'Households below average income (HBAI) quality and methodology information report', [online], Available at: https://assets.publishing.service.gov.uk/government/uploads/system/uploads/attachment_data/file/875331/households-below-average-income-quality-methodology-2018-2019.pdf [Accessed 8 September 2021].

Deuchar, R. (2009) *Gangs, Marginalised Youth and Social Capital*, London: Trentham Books.

De Zulueta, F. (2001) 'Violent attachments and attachment to violence', in S.L. Bloom (ed) *Violence*, London: Karnac, pp 31–56.

Dobash, R.P. and Dobash R.E. (2020) *Male–Male Murder*, London: Routledge.

Dorling, D. (2018) *Peak Inequality: Britain's Ticking Time Bomb*, Bristol: Policy Press.

Dorling, D. (2020) 'Foreword', in M. O'Hara, *The Shame Game: Overturning the Toxic Poverty Narrative*, Bristol: Policy Press, pp xiii–xviii.

Duckworth, J. (2002) *Fagin's Children: Criminal Children in Victorian England*, London: Hambledon and London.

Duque, M. and McKnight, A. (2019) 'Understanding the relationship between inequalities and poverty: mechanisms associated with crime, the legal system and punitive sanctions', CASEpaper 215/LIPpaper 6, LSE Centre for Analysis of Social Exclusion, [online], Available at: https://sticerd.lse.ac.uk/dps/case/cp/casepaper215.pdf [Accessed 25 September 2021].

Dyson, A. (2011) 'Full service and extended schools, disadvantage, and social justice', *Cambridge Journal of Education*, 41(2): 177–93.

Dyson, A., Cummings, C. and Todd, L. (2011) *Beyond the School Gates: Can Full Service and Extended Schools Overcome Disadvantage?* London: Routledge.

Education Support (2019) *Teacher Wellbeing Index 2019*, London: Education Support.

Edwards, A. and Prins, R. (2014) 'Policing and crime in contemporary London: A developmental agenda?', *European Journal of Policing Studies*, 2(1): 61–93.

Edwards, A., Hughes, G. and Swann, R. (2015) 'Community safety and the policing of young people in austere times', in B. Goldson and J. Muncie (eds) *Youth Crime and Justice*, 2nd edn, London: Sage, pp 191–208.

Edwards, K.M. and Neal, A.M. (2017) 'School and community characteristics related to dating violence victimization among high school youth', *Psychology of Violence*, 7(2): 203–12.

Eid, M. and Larsen, R.J. (eds) (2007) *The Science of Subjective Well-Being*, New York: Guilford Publications.

Eisenstadt, N. and Oppenheim, C. (2019) *Parents, Poverty and the State: 20 Years of Evolving Family Policy*, Bristol: Policy Press.

Ekpoudom, A. (2020) 'Drillosophy: why UK rappers are teaching Plato in lockdown', *The Guardian*, [online] 5 May, Available at: www.theguard ian.com/music/2020/may/05/drillosophy-why-uk-rappers-are-teaching-plato-in-lockdown [Accessed 25 September 2021].

Elliott, G.C. (2009) *Family Matters: The Importance of Mattering to Family in Adolescence*, Chichester: Wiley-Blackwell.

Elliott, G.C., Colangelo, M. and Gelles, R.J. (2005) 'Mattering and suicide ideation: establishing and elaborating a relationship', *Social Psychology Quarterly*, 68(3): 223–38.

Elliott, G.C., Kao, S. and Grant, A., (2004) 'Mattering: empirical validation of a social-psychological concept', *Self and Identity*, 3(4): 339–54.

Elliott, G.C., Cunningham, S., Colangelo, M. and Gelles, R. (2011) 'Perceived mattering to the family and physical violence in the family by adolescents', *Journal of Family Issues*, 32(8): 1007–29.

Ellis, A. (2016) *Men, Masculinities and Violence*, London: Routledge.

Ellison, R. (2001[1947]) *Invisible Man*, Harmondsworth: Penguin.

Emsley, C. (2005) *The English and Violence Since 1750*, London: Continuum.

Eron, L. and Slaby, R. (1994) 'Introduction', in L. Eron, J. Gentry and P. Schlegel (eds) *Reason to Hope: A Psycho-social Perspective on Violence and Youth*, London: American Psychological Association.

Esping-Anderson, G. (1991) *The Three Worlds of Welfare Capitalism*, Princeton: Princeton University Press.

Eurostat (2020) 'Overcrowding rate by age, sex and poverty status – total population', EU-SILC survey, [online], Available at: http://appsso.eurostat.ec.europa.eu/nui/submitViewTableAction.do [Accessed 25 September 2021].

Evans J., Meyer D., Pinney A. and Robinson B. (2009) *Second Chances: Re-engaging Young People in Education and Training*, Barkingside: Barnardo's.

Fatsis, L. (2019) 'Policing the beats: the criminalisation of UK drill and grime music by the London Metropolitan Police', *The Sociological Review*, 67(6): 1300–16.

Firmin, C. (2020) *Contextual Safeguarding and Child Protection*, London: Routledge.

Fisher, N. (1968) 'Village colleges', *Periodicals Archive Online*, 1(4): 70.

Flett, G. (2018) *The Psychology of Mattering: Understanding the Human Need to be Significant*, London: Academic Press.

Flett, G. (2022) 'An introduction, review, and conceptual analysis of mattering as an essential construct and an essential way of life', *Journal of Psychoeducational Assessment*, 40(1): 3–36.

Flett, G.L., Goldstein, A.L., Pechenkov, I.G., Nepon, T. and Wekerle, C. (2016) 'Antecedents, correlates, and consequences of feeling like you don't matter: associations with maltreatment, loneliness, social anxiety, and the five-factor model', *Personality and Individual Differences*, 92: 52–56.

Ford, T., Parker, C., Salim, J., Goodman, R., Logan, S. and Henley, W. (2018) 'The relationship between exclusion from school and mental health: a secondary analysis of the British Child and Adolescent Mental Health Surveys 2004 and 2007', *Psychological Medicine*, 48(4): 629–41.

Foucault, M. (1977) *Discipline and Punish*, Harmondsworth: Penguin.

Fourcade, M. (2021) 'Ordinal citizenship', *The British Journal of Sociology*, 72(2): 154–73.

Franke, Hillary A. (2014) 'Toxic stress: effects, prevention and treatment', *Children,* 1(3): 390–402.

Fraser, A. (2015) *Urban Legends*, Oxford: Oxford University Press.

Fraser, A. (2017) *Gangs and Crime*, London: Sage.

Fraser, A. and Irwin-Rogers, K. (2021) *A Public Health Approach to Violence Reduction: Strategic Briefing*, Dartington: Research in Practice.

Fraser, N. (2000) 'Rethinking recognition', *New Left Review*, 3: 107–24.

Fraser, N. (2019) *The Old Is Dying and the New Cannot be Born*, London: Verso.

Fuller, A., Beck, V. and Unwin, L. (2005) 'The gendered nature of apprenticeship: employers' and young people's perspectives', *Education and Training*, 47(4/5): 298–311.

Gadd, D. and Jefferson, T. (2007) *Psycho-social Criminology*, London: Sage.

Galfalvi, E., Hooley, T. and Neary, E. (2020) 'Are young people aged 16–19 using or expecting to use the gig economy for their careers?' *Journal of the National Institute for Career Education and Counselling*, 45: 34–40.

Garland, D. (2001) *The Culture of Control*, Oxford: Oxford University Press.

Garthwaite, K. (2016) *Hunger Pains: Life inside Foodbank Britain*, Bristol: Policy Press.

Gaskell, C. (2005) ' "Fighting for respect": youth, violence and citizenship in East London', PhD thesis, Queen Mary, University of London, October.

Gazeley, L. (2012) 'The impact of social class on parent-professional interaction in school exclusion processes: deficit or disadvantage?' *International Journal of Inclusive Education*, 16(3): 297–311.

Gazeley, L. and Dunne, M. (2013) 'Initial teacher education programmes: providing a space to address the disproportionate exclusion of black pupils from schools in England?' *Journal of Education for Teaching: International Research and Pedagogy*, 39(5): 492–508.

Giddens, A. (1986) *The Constitution of Society: Outline of the Theory of Structuration*, Cambridge: Polity.

Giddens, A. (1991) *Modernity and Self-Identity: Self and Society in the Late Modern Age*, Cambridge: Polity.

Gilbert, J. (2006) *Common Ground: Democracy and Collectivity in an Age of Individualism*, London: Pluto.

Gilligan, J. (1997) *Violence: Reflections on a National Epidemic*, New York: Vintage.

Gillis, J.R. (1981) *Youth and History: Tradition and Change in European Age Relations, 1770–Present*, London: Academic Press.

Gilroy, P. (1982) *There Ain't No Black in the Union Jack*, London: Routledge.

Giroux, H. (2010) *Youth in a Suspect Society*, London: Palgrave Macmillan.

Giroux, H. (2012) *Disposable Youth*, London: Routledge.

Golding, P. and Middleton, S. (1982) *Images of Welfare*, Oxford: Martin Robertson.

Goldson, B. (2011) 'Youth in crisis?', in B. Goldson and J. Muncie (eds) *Youth in Crisis?* London: Routledge, pp 1–19.

Goldson, B. (2015) 'The circular motions of penal politics and the pervasive irrationalities of child imprisonment', in B. Goldson and J. Muncie (eds) *Youth Crime and Justice*, 2nd edn, London: Sage, pp 170–90.

Goldson, B. (2020) 'Excavating youth justice reform: historical mapping and speculative prospects', *Howard Journal of Crime and Justice*, 59(3): 317–34.

Golombok, S. (2000) *Parenting – What Really Counts?* London: Routledge.

Gove, W., Hughes, M. and Geerken, M. (1985) 'Are uniform crime reports a valid indicator of index crimes? An affirmative answer with minor qualifications', *Criminology*, 23: 451–501.

Graeber, D. (2018) *Bullshit Jobs: A Theory*, London: Allen Lane.

Gray, P., Smithson, H. and Jump, D. (2021) 'Serious youth violence and its relationship with adverse childhood experiences', HM Inspectorate of Probation Academic Insights 2021/13, Available at: www.justiceinspectora tes.gov.uk/hmiprobation/wp-content/uploads/sites/5/2021/11/Acade mic-Insights-Gray-et-al.pdf [Accessed 6 February 2022].

Griffin, C. (1993) *Representations of Youth: The Study of Youth and Adolescence in Britain and America*, Cambridge: Polity.

Groos, K. (1901) *The Play of Man*, New York: Appleton.

Gross-Manos, D. and Ben-Arieh, A. (2017) 'How subjective well-being is associated with material deprivation and social exclusion in Israeli 12-year-olds', *American Orthopsychiatric Association*, 87(3): 274–90.

Guardian (2019) 'Chicken boxes to return to Home Office with handwritten knife crime solutions', [online] 19 August, Available at: www.theguard ian.com/uk-news/2019/aug/19/chicken-boxes-home-office-knife-crime [Accessed 25 September 2021].

Guardian (2022) 'The Guardian view on the care-leaving age: teenagers are children too', [online] 31 January, Available at: www.theguardian.com/commentisfree/2022/jan/31/the-guardian-view-on-the-care-leaving-age-teenagers-are-children-too [Accessed 13 February 2022].

Gunter, A. (2017) *Race, Gangs and Youth Violence*, Bristol: Policy Press.

Gustafsson, M. (2020) 'Young workers in the coronavirus crisis', *Resolution Foundation*, [online] 19 May, Available at: www.resolutionfoundation.org/app/uploads/2020/05/Young-workers-in-the-coronavirus-crisis.pdf [Accessed 25 September 2021].

Habermas, J. (1987) *The Philosophical Discourse of Modernity*, trans. F. Lawrence, Cambridge: MIT Press.

Hales, G. (2021) ' "The marketplace is more volatile and violent than it has ever been": an exploration of the links between drug market and violent crime trends in England and Wales in recent years', London: Crest Advisory.

Hall, S. and Winlow, S. (2015) *Revitalizing Criminological Theory: Towards a New Ultra-Realism*, London: Routledge.

Hall, S., Critcher, C., Jefferson, T., Clarke, J. and Roberts, B. (1978) *Policing the Crisis: Mugging, the State, and Law and Order*, London: Macmillan.

Hallsworth, S. (2013) *Beyond Gangs*, London: Palgrave Macmillan.

Hallsworth, S. and Brotherton, D. (2011) *Urban Disorder and Gangs: A Critique and a Warning*, London: Runnymede.

Hamre, B.K. and Pianta, R.C. (2005) 'Can instructional and emotional support in the first-grade classroom make a difference for children at risk of school failure?', *Child Development*, 76(5): 949–67.

Hanushek, E.A. and Rivkin, S.G. (2012) 'The distribution of teacher quality and implications for policy', *Annual Review of Economics*, 4: 131–57.

Harding, S. (2014) *The Street Casino: Survival in Violent Street Gangs*, Bristol: Policy Press.

Harding, S. (2020a) *County Lines: Exploitation and Drug Dealing among Urban Street Gangs*, Bristol: Bristol University Press.

Harding, S. (2020b) 'Getting to the point? Reframing narratives on knife crime', *Youth Justice*, 20(1–2): 31–49.

Harker, L. (2007) 'The impact of housing on children's life chances', *Journal of Children's Services*, 2(3): 43–51.

Harris, P. (2017) 'Inter-subjectivity and worker self-disclosure in professional relationships with young people: a psycho-social study of youth violence and desistance', *The Howard Journal*, 56(4): 516–31.

Hart, T.C. and Rennison, C. (2003) 'Reporting crime to the police, 1992–2000', *Bureau of Justice Statistics Special Report*, Available at: https://bjs.ojp.gov/content/pub/pdf/rcp00.pdf [Accessed 23 October 2021].

Hastings, A. and Gannon, M. (2021) 'Absorbing the shock of austerity: the experience of local government workers at the front line', *Local Government Studies*, online preprint, Available at: https://www.tandfonline.com/doi/full/10.1080/03003930.2021.1889516?scroll=top&needAccess=true [Accessed 21 May 2022].

Havard, T.E., Densley, J.A., Whittaker, A. and Wills, J. (2021) 'Street gangs and coercive control: the gendered exploitation of young women and girls in county lines' *Criminology & Criminal Justice*, online preprint, Available at: https://journals.sagepub.com/doi/full/10.1177/17488958211051513 [Accessed 21 May 2022].

Hayes, D. (2018) 'Serious violence strategy: experts advocate earlier interventions', *Children and Young People Now*, May, pp 12–13.

Hendrick, H. (2015) 'Histories of youth crime and youth justice', in B. Goldson and J. Muncie (eds) *Youth Crime & Justice*, 2nd edn, London: Sage, pp 3–16.

Hillyard, P. (2019) 'Review of *Zemiology: Reconnecting Crime and Social Harm*', *Justice, Power and Resistance*, 3(2): 172–7.

Hillyard, P. and Tombs, S. (2004) 'Beyond criminology?' in P. Hillyard, C. Pantazis, S. Tombs and D. Gordon (eds) *Beyond Criminology: Taking Harm Seriously*, London: Pluto Press, pp 10–29.

Hillyard, P. and Tombs, S. (2005) 'Beyond criminology?', in D. Dorling, D. Gordon, P. Hillyard, C. Pantazis, S. Pemberton and S. Tombs (eds) *Criminal Obsessions: Why Harm Matters More than Crime*, London: Centre for Crime and Justice Studies.

Hillyard, P., Pantazis, C., Tombs, S. and Gordon, D. (eds) (2004) *Beyond Criminology: Taking Harm Seriously*, London: Pluto Press.

Hinds, D. (2019) 'Funding announced to train 900 new children's social workers', [online] 8 January, Available at: https://www.gov.uk/government/news/funding-announced-to-train-900-new-childrens-social-workers [Accessed 2 June 2022].

Hirst, V. (2020) 'How "cradle-to-career" schools provide all-round support and tackle inequality', *theconversation*, [online] 2 December, Available at: https://theconversation.com/how-cradle-to-career-schools-provide-all-round-support-and-tackle-inequality-150795 [Accessed 3 September 2022].

HM Government (2019) 'Timpson review of school exclusion', online report, Available at: https://assets.publishing.service.gov.uk/government/uploads/system/uploads/attachment_data/file/807862/Timpson_review.pdf [Accessed 18 September 2021].

Hobbs, D. (2013) *Lush Life: Constructing Organised Crime in the UK*, Oxford: Oxford University Press.

Holligan, C. and Deuchar, R. (2014) 'What does it mean to be a man? Psycho-social undercurrents in the voices of incarcerated (violent) Scottish teenage offenders', *Criminology & Criminal Justice*, 15(3): pp 361–77.

Home Office (2021a) '£130.5 million to tackle serious violence, murder and knife crime', [online] 8 March, Available at: www.gov.uk/government/news/1305-million-to-tackle-serious-violence-murder-and-knife-crime [Accessed 7 September 2021].

Home Office (2021b) 'Knife Crime Prevention Orders begin in London', [online] 7 July, Available at: www.gov.uk/government/news/knife-crime-prevention-orders-begin-in-london [Accessed 7 September 2021].

Home Office (2022) 'Home Secretary backs police to increase stop and search', [online] 16 May, Available at: https://www.gov.uk/government/news/home-secretary-backs-police-to-increase-stop-and-search [Accessed 21 May 2022].

Honneth, A. (1996) *The Struggle for Recognition: The Moral Grammar of Social Conflicts*, Cambridge: Polity.

Horowitz, R. (1983) *Honor and the American Dream: Culture and Identity in a Chicano Community*, New Brunswick: Rutgers University Press.

Humphreys, D.K., Esposti, M.D., Gardner, F. and Shepherd, J. (2019) 'Violence in England and Wales: does media reporting match the data?' *British Medical Journal*, 367: 1–6.

Ilan, J. (2015) *Understanding Street Culture: Poverty, Crime, Youth and Cool*, London: Palgrave Macmillan.

Institute for Fiscal Studies (2019) '2019 annual report on education spending in England: schools', Available at: www.ifs.org.uk/publications/14344 [Accessed 7 September 2021].

Intriligator, M.D. (2003) *Globalization of the World Economy: Potential Benefits and Costs and a Net Assessment*, Santa Monica: Milken Institute.

Irwin-Rogers, K. (2018) 'Racism and racial discrimination in the criminal justice system: exploring the experiences and views of men serving sentences of imprisonment', *Justice, Power and Resistance*, 2(2): 243–66.

Irwin-Rogers, K. (2019) 'Illicit drug markets, consumer capitalism and the rise of social media: a toxic trap for young people', *Critical Criminology*, 27(4): 591–610.

Irwin-Rogers, K. and Shuter, M. (2017) *Fairness in the Criminal Justice System: What's Race Got To Do with It?* London: Catch22.

Irwin-Rogers, K., Muthoo, A. and Billingham, L. (2020) 'Youth Violence Commission: final report', Available at: http://yvcommission.com/wp-content/uploads/2020/07/YVC-Final-Report-July-2020.pdf [Accessed 7 September 2021].

Irwin-Rogers, K., Decker, S., Rostami, A., Stephenson, S. and Van Hellemont, E. (2019) 'European street gangs and urban violence', in I. Vojnovic, A. Pearson, G. Asiki, G. DeVerteuil and A. Adriana (eds) *Handbook of Global Urban Health: The Metropolis and Modern Life*, New York: Routledge, pp 484–508.

Isenberg, B. (1991) 'Habermas on Foucault: critical remarks', *Acta Sociologica*, 34(4): 299–308.

Issit, M.L. (2020) *Opinions throughout History: Globalization*, New York: Grey House Publishing.

Iyere, E. (2020) 'Girls, young women and their unheard and unhealed trauma', in K. Irwin-Rogers, A. Muthoo and L. Billingham 'Youth Violence Commission: final report', pp 73–4, Available at: http://yvcom mission.com/wp-content/uploads/2020/07/YVC-Final-Report-July-2020.pdf [Accessed 7 September 2021].

Jacobson, J., Kirby, A. and Hunter, G. (2016) 'Joint enterprise: righting a wrong turn', *Prison Reform Trust*, Available at: www.prisonreformtrust.org.uk/Portals/0/Documents/Joint%20Enterprise%20Writing%20a%20Wr ong%20Turn.pdf [Accessed 7 September 2021].

Jasko, K., LaFree, G. and Kruglanski, A. (2016) 'Quest for significance and violent extremism: the case of domestic radicalization', *Political Psychology*, 38(5): 815–31.

Jayanetti (2021) 'Councils in England facing funding gaps plan to cut special needs support', *The Guardian*, [online] 15 May, Available at: www.theg uardian.com/education/2021/may/15/councils-in-england-facing-fund ing-gaps-plan-to-cut-special-needs-support [Accessed 7 September 2021].

Jensen, T. (2013) 'Riots, restraint and the new cultural politics of wanting', *Sociological Research Online*, 18(4): 36–47.

Jensen, T. (2018) *Parenting the Crisis*, Bristol: Policy Press.

Jones, D.W. (2020) *Understanding Criminal Behaviour: Psychosocial perspectives on criminality and violence*, London: Routledge.

Jones, R. (2015) 'The end game: the marketisation and privatisation of children's social work and child protection, *Critical Social Policy*, 35(4): 447–69.

Jones, R. (2020) *A History of the Personal Social Services in England: Feast, Famine and the Future*, London: Palgrave Macmillan.]

Jouai, E. (2018) 'Who is the subject of violence?', *Radical Philosophy*, 2(3): 93–97.

Joseph Rowntree Foundation (2022) 'UK Poverty 2022: the essential guide to understanding poverty in the UK', Available at: www.jrf.org.uk/report/uk-poverty-2022 [Accessed 25 January 2022].

Joseph-Salisbury, R. (2020) *Race and Racism in English Secondary Schools*, London: Runnymede.

JUSTICE (2019) 'Challenging school exclusions', Available at: https://files. justice.org.uk/wp-content/uploads/2020/08/06165917/Challenging-Rep ort.pdf [Accessed 7 September 2021].

Kashima, Y. (1997) 'Culture, narrative, and human motivation', in D. Munro, J.F. Schumaker and S.C. Carr (eds) *Motivation and Culture*, London: Routledge, pp 16–32.

Katz, J. (1988) *The Seductions of Crime*, New York: Basic Books.

Keeling, P. (2017) *No Respect: Young BAME Men, the Police and Stop and Search*, London, UK: Criminal Justice Alliance.

Kelton, S. (2020) *The Deficit Myth: Modern Monetary Theory and How to Build a Better Economy*, London: John Murray Publishers.

Kemper, T.D. (1987) 'How many emotions are there? Wedding the social and automatic components', *American Journal of Sociology*, 93: 263–89.

King, L.A. and Geise, A.C. (2011) 'Being forgotten: implications for the experience of meaning in life', *The Journal of Social Psychology*, 151: 696–706.

King, M. (2009) 'Clarifying the Foucault–Habermas debate: morality, ethics, and normative foundations', *Philosophy & Social Criticism*, 35(3): 287–314.

Kingdon, J.W. (1993) 'How do issues get on public policy agendas?', *Sociology and the Public Agenda*, 8(1): 40–53.

Kinsey, L. (2019) '"Youth knife crime" in context: adolescents beyond objects of concern', *National Association for Youth Justice*, [online] May 2019, Available at: https://thenayj.org.uk/wp-content/uploads/2019/05/ Youth-knife-Crime-Briefing-May-191.pdf [Accessed 23 October 2021].

Kleinberg, B. and McFarlane, P. (2020) 'Violent music vs violence and music: drill rap and violent crime in London' *arXiv*, preprint arXiv:2004.04598.

Koch, I. (2019) 'Who are the slave masters of today? County lines, drug trafficking, and modern slavery policies', *Centre for Crime and Justice Studies*, [online] 5 December, Available at: www.crimeandjustice.org.uk/resour ces/who-are-slave-masters-today-county-lines-drug-trafficking-and-mod ern-slavery-policies [Accessed 23 October 2021].

Kochel, T.R., Parks, R. and Mastrofski, S.D. (2013) 'Examining police effectiveness as a precursor to legitimacy and cooperation with police', *Justice Quarterly*, 30(5): 895–925.

Kolodny, N. (1996) 'The ethics of cryptonormativism: a defense of Foucault's evasions', *Philosophy & Social Criticism*, 22(5): 63–84.

Kotkin, J. (2020) *The Coming of Neo-Feudalism*, London: Encounter Books.

Kotzé, J. (2019) *The Myth of the Crime Decline*, London: Routledge.

Kruglanski, A., Gelfand, M., Belanger, J., Sheveland, A., Hetiarachchi, M. and Gunaratna, R. (2014) 'The psychology of radicalization and deradicalization: how significance quest impacts violent extremism', *Advances in Political Psychology*, 35(1): 69–93.

Kulz, C. (2015) *Mapping the Exclusion Process: Inequality, Justice and the Business of Education*, London: Communities Empowerment Network.

Kulz, C. (2017) *Factories for Learning*, Manchester: University of Manchester Press.

Lalander, P. and Sernhede, O. (2011) 'Social mobilization or street crimes: two strategies among young urban outcasts in contemporary Sweden', *EDUCARE* 2: 99–121.

Lane, R. (2019) '"I'm a police officer not a social worker or mental health nurse": online discourses of exclusion and resistance regarding mental health-related police work', *Journal of Community & Applied Social Psychology*, 29(5): 429–42.

Lauger, T. (2012) *Real Gangstas*, London: Rutgers University Press.

Lauger, T. and Densley, J. (2018) 'Broadcasting badness: violence, identity, and performance in the online gang rap scene', *Justice Quarterly*, 35: 816–41.

Lawson, J. and Silver, H. (2007) *A Social History of Education in England*, London: Routledge.

Lebron, J. (2017) *The Making of Black Lives Matter*, Oxford: Oxford University Press.

Lepper, J. (2019) 'Charity "sells" children's stab vests online', *Charity Digital*, [online] 29 August, Available at: https://charitydigital.org.uk/topics/topics/charity-sells-childrens-stab-vests-online-6045 [Accessed 7 September 2021].

Lepper, J. (2021) 'Health visitor cuts put children at risk of harm', *Children & Young People Now*, [online] 1 July, Available at: www.cypnow.co.uk/news/article/health-visitor-cuts-put-children-at-risk-of-harm [Accessed 7 September 2021].

Lepper, J. (2022) 'England's first Secure School gains royal assent', *Children & Young People Now*, [online] 5 May, Available at: https://www.cypnow.co.uk/news/article/england-s-first-secure-school-gains-royal-assent [Accessed 21 May 2022].

Levell, J. (2022) *Boys, Childhood Domestic Abuse and Gang Involvement: Violence at Home, Violence On-road*, Bristol: Bristol University Press.

Lewchuk, W. (2017) 'Precarious jobs: where are they, and how do they affect well-being?' *The Economic and Labour Relations Review*, 28(3): 402–19.

Lewis, D.M. (2017) 'A matter for concern: young offenders and the importance of mattering', *Deviant Behavior*, 38(11): 1318–31.

Leys, C. (2003) *Market-Driven Politics*, London: Verso.

Lister, R. (2021) *Poverty*, 2nd edn, Cambridge: Polity.

Littler, J. (2017) *Against Meritocracy*, London: Routledge.

Loopstra, R., Reeves, A., Taylor-Robinson, D., Barr, B., McKee, M. and Stuckler, D. (2015) 'Austerity, sanctions, and the rise of food banks in the UK', *British Medical Journal*, 350: 1–6.

Lunghy, E., Osman, A., M.K., Musa, A., Angel, Silva and Che (2019) *Insiders Looking Out: Solutions to Youth Violence from People Who Have Lived It*, London: The Winch.

Lynch, J.P. (2006) 'Problems and promise of victimisation surveys for cross-national research', *Crime and Justice*,34(1): 229–87.

Lynes, A., Kelly, C. and Kelly, E. (2020) 'Thug life: drill music as a periscope into urban violence in the consumer age', *The British Journal of Criminology*, 60(5): 1201–19.

MacAlister, J. (2021) 'The case for change', *The Independent Review of Children's Social Care*, [online] Available at: https://childrenssocialcare. independent-review.uk/wp-content/uploads/2021/06/case-for-change. pdf [Accessed 7 September 2021].

MacAlister, J. (2022) 'The independent review of children's social care: final report', [online] May, Available at: https://childrenssocialcare.independ ent-review.uk/wp-content/uploads/2022/05/The-independent-review-of-childrens-social-care-Final-report.pdf [Accessed 2 June 2022].

MacIntyre, A. (2007) *After Virtue*, 3rd edn, London: Bloomsbury.

Marquand, D. (2015) *Mammon's Kingdom*, Harmondsworth: Penguin.

Marsh, S. (2021) 'Thousands of children sent to unregulated care homes amid Covid', *The Guardian*, [online] 6 January, Available at: www. theguardian.com/society/2021/jan/06/thousands-of-children-sent-to-unregulated-care-homes-amid-covid [Accessed 7 September 2021].

Marshall, S.K. (2004) 'Relative contributions of perceived mattering to parents and friends in predicting adolescents' psychological wellbeing', *Perceptual and Motor Skills*, 99(2): 591–601.

Martin, K. (2008) *Hard and Unreal Advice: Mothers, Social Science and the Victorian Poverty Experts*, London: Palgrave Macmillan.

Maruna, S. and Mann, R. (2019) 'Reconciling "desistance" and "what works"', HM Inspectorate of Probation Academic Insights 2019/1, Available at: www.justiceinspectorates.gov.uk/hmiprobation/wp-content/ uploads/sites/5/2019/02/Academic-Insights-Maruna-and-Mann-Feb-19-final.pdf [Accessed 7 September 2021].

Marx, K. 1978[1852] 'The Eighteenth Brumaire of Louis Bonaparte', in R.C. Tucker (ed) *The Marx–Engels Reader*, New York: W.W. Norton and Company.

Maslow, A.H. (1943) 'A theory of human motivation', *Psychological Review*, 50(4): 370-–96.

Mason, W. (2020) '"No one learned": interpreting a drugs crackdown operation and its consequences through the "lens" of social harm', *The British Journal of Criminology*, 60(2): 382–402.

Matera, C., Meringolo, P. and Reino, M. (202[1]) 'Metastereotypes, perceived mattering, and well-being among minority groups', *Psychology, Health & Medicine*, 26(10): 1274–81.

Max-Neef, M. (1992) 'Development and human needs', in M. Max-Neef and P. Ekins (eds) *Real Life Economics*, London: Routledge, pp 197–214.

May, R. (1998) *Power and Innocence*, London: W.W. Norton and Company.

Mayhew, H. (2008 [1859]) *London Labour and the London Poor*, London: Wordsworth.

Maynard, L. and Stuart, K. (2018) *Promoting Young People's Wellbeing through Empowerment and Agency*, London: Routledge.

Mazzucato, M. (2018) *The Value of Everything: Making and Taking in the Global Economy*, Milton Keynes: Penguin Random House.

McAdams, D.P. (1993) *The Stories We Live By: Personal myths and the Making of the Self*, London: The Guilford Press.

McCandless, R., Feist, A., Allan, J. and Morgan, N. (2016) 'Do initiatives involving substantial increases in stop and search reduce crime? Assessing the impact of Operation BLUNT 2', Home Office report, [online] March, Available at: https://assets.publishing.service.gov.uk/government/uplo ads/system/uploads/attachment_data/file/508661/stop-search-operat ion-blunt-2.pdf [Accessed 13 February 2022].

McCluskey, G., Cole, T., Daniels, H., Thompson, I. and Tawell, A. (2019) 'Exclusion from school in Scotland and across the UK: contrasts and questions', *British Educational Ressearch Journal*, 45(6): 1140-59.

McDonald, K. (2003) 'Marginal youth, personal identity, and the contemporary gang: reconstructing the social world?', in L. Kontos, D. Brotherton and L. Barrios (eds) *Gangs and Society: Alternative Perspectives*, West Sussex: Columbia University Press, pp 62–74.

McGrath, L., Griffin, V., Mundy, E., Curno, T., Weerasinghe, D. and Zlotowitz, S. (2016) 'The psychological impact of austerity: a briefing paper', *Educational Psychology Research and Practice*, 2 (2): 46–57.

McIntyre, A. (2000) *Inner City Kids*, New York: NYU Press.

McNay, L. (2007) *Against Recognition*, Cambridge: Polity.

Merton, R.K. (1938) 'Social structure and anomie', *American Sociological Review*, 3: 672–82.

Messerschmidt, J.W. (2013) *Crime as Structured Action: Doing Masculinities, Race, Class, Sexuality, and Crime*, New York: Rowman and Littlefield.

Millard, W. (2021) 'Children who come in contact with social services', in L. Menzies and S. Baars (eds) *Young People on the Margins*, London: Routledge, pp 124–55.

Miller, J. (2008) *Getting Played: African American Girls, Urban Inequality, and Gendered Violence*, New York: NYU Press.

Millie, A. (2009) 'Conclusions: promoting mutual respect and empathy', in A. Millie (ed) *Securing Respect*, Bristol: Policy Press, pp 267–76.

Mills, H., Ford, M. and Grimshaw, R. (2022) *The Usual Suspects: Joint Enterprise Prosecutions Before and After the Supreme Court Ruling*, London: Centre for Crime and Justice Studies.

Ministry of Housing, Communities and Local Government (2019) *Indices of Deprivation*, ID 2019 for London, Available at: https://data.london.gov.uk/dataset/indices-of-deprivation [Accessed 23 October 2021].

Ministry of Housing, Communities and Local Government (2020) 'Live tables on homelessness', Available at: www.gov.uk/government/statistical-data-sets/live-tables-on-homelessness [Accessed 4 March 2021].

Ministry of Justice (2021) '"Super courtroom" opens in Manchester', [online] 10 September, Available at: https://www.gov.uk/government/news/super-courtroom-opens-in-manchester [Accessed 5 June 2022].

Mishra, P. (2018) *Age of Anger*, Harmondsworth: Penguin.

Mohan, J., Twigg, L. and Taylor, J. (2011) 'Mind the double gap: using multilevel modelling to investigate public perceptions of crime trends', *British Journal of Criminology*, 51(6): 1035–53.

MOPAC (2019) 'What Londoners tell us around knife crime and violence', *MOPAC Evidence and Insight*, Available at: www.london.gov.uk/moderngovmb/documents/s63353/Appendix%20B%20-%20MOPAC%20Surveys%20presentation.pdf [Accessed 23 October 2021].

Moore, J.M. (2014) 'Is empire coming home? Liberalism, exclusion and the punitiveness of the British State', *Papers from the British Criminology Conference*, 14: 31–48.

Mosher, C., Miethe, T.D. and Hart, T.C. (2010) *The Mismeasure of Crime*, London: Sage.

Motz, R., Barnes, J., Caspi, A., Arseneault, L., Cullen, F., Houts, R., Wertz, J. and Moffit, T. (2020) 'Does contact with the justice system deter or promote future delinquency? Results from a longitudinal study of British adolescent twins', *Criminology*, 58(2): 307–35.

Moxon, D. (2011) 'Consumer culture and the 2011 "riots"', *Sociological Research Online*, 16(4): 183–7.

MPS (Metropolitan Police Service) (2020a) 'Knife crime offences recorded within MPS geographical area', Available at: https://t.co/rLgMocG5QB?amp=1 [Accessed 23 October 2021].

MPS (2020b) 'People aged 10–19 proceeded against. 01/FOI/20/013470', Available at: www.met.police.uk/SysSiteAssets/foi-media/metropolitan-police/disclosure_2020/may_2020/youth-offenders-aged-10-19-in-london-2015-20192 [Accessed 23 October 2021].

MPS (2021a) 'Met Crime Data Dashboard', Available at: www.met.police.uk/sd/stats-and-data/met/homicide-dashboard/ [Accessed 23 October 2021].

MPS (2021b) 'Teenagers charged with homicide. FOI/21/017659', Available at: www.met.police.uk/cy-GB/SysSiteAssets/foi-media/metropolitan-police/disclosure_2021/february_2021/teenagers-charged-with-murder-2017-20202 [Accessed 23 October 2021].

Muncie, J. (2021) *Youth and Crime*, 5th edn, London: Sage.

Munro, D. (1997) 'Introduction', in D. Munro, J.F. Schumaker and S.C. Carr (eds) *Motivation and Culture*, London: Routledge, pp vii–2.

Murray, C. (1999) *The Underclass Revisited*, New York: American Enterprise Institute.

Murray, H.A. (1938) *Explorations in Personality: A Clinical and Experimental Study of Fifty Men of College Age*, London: Oxford University Press.

Murray, K., McVie, S., Farren, D., Herlitz, L., Hough, M. and Norris, P. (2021) 'Procedural justice, compliance with the law and police stop-and-search: a study of young people in England and Scotland', *Policing and Society*, 31(3): 263–82.

Mwale, T. (2020) 'Rethinking peace and justice: addressing structural violence and institutional racism', in K. Irwin-Rogers, A. Muthoo and L. Billingham, 'Youth Violence Commission: final report', pp 75–7, Available at: http://yvcommission.com/wp-content/uploads/2020/07/YVC-Final-Report-July-2020.pdf [Accessed 7 September 2021].

Nastic, D. (2012) 'Why we need a relative income poverty measure', *Poverty*, 143: 14–17.

National Education Union (2018) 'Teachers' pay: shining a light on pay', Available at: https://neu.org.uk/media/471/view [Accessed 31 May 2022].

Newburn, T., Jones, T. and Blaustein, J. (2018) 'Framing the 2011 England riots: understanding the political and policy response', *The Howard Journal of Crime and Justice*, 57(3): 339–62.

Newsnight (2021) [Online] Available at: https://twitter.com/BBCNewsnight/status/1364717183947993088 [Accessed 10 January 2021].

Nijjar, J.S. (2018) 'Echoes of empire', *Social Justice*, 45(2/3): 147–62.

Nixon, R. (2013) *Slow Violence and the Environmentalism of the Poor*, Cambridge: Harvard University Press.

NOMIS (2021) 'Census 2011 tables', Available at: www.nomisweb.co.uk/census/2011/data_finder [Accessed 23 October 2021].

Nussbaum, M. and Glover, J. (1995) *Women, Culture, and Development: A Study of Human Capabilities*, Oxford: Oxford University Press.

Obsuth, I., Murray, A.L., Malti, T., Sulger, P., Ribeaud, D. and Eisner, M. (2017) 'A non-bipartite propensity score analysis of the effects of teacher–student relationships on adolescent problem and prosocial behavior', *Journal of Youth and Adolescence*, 46(8): 1661–87.

Odling, G. (2021) 'A quarter of London's gang murders are linked to violent "drill" rap music that glamourises violence, study shows', *Daily Mail*, [online] 10 October, Available at: www.dailymail.co.uk/news/arti cle-10078383/One-four-London-gang-murders-linked-drill-rap-music-glamourises-violence-study-shows.html [Accessed 23 October 2021].

OECD (2013) *OECD Guidelines on Measuring Subjective Well-being*, Paris: OECD Publishing.

Ofcom (2020) 'Connected nations 2020', [online], Available at: www.ofcom. org.uk/__data/assets/pdf_file/0024/209373/connected-nations-2020.pdf [Accessed 15 April 2021].

Office for National Statistics (ONS) (2010) 'Overcrowded households by borough', Available at: https://data.london.gov.uk/dataset/overcrowded-households-borough [Accessed 15 April 2021].

ONS (2013) 'CT0109 – sex by age by ethnic group – London to London Boroughs', Available at: www.ons.gov.uk/peoplepopulationandcommun ity/culturalidentity/ethnicity/adhocs/000109ct0109sexbyagebyethnicgrou plondontolondonboroughs [Accessed 23 October 2021].

ONS (2015) 'Persistent poverty in the UK and EU: 2008–2013', Available at: www.ons.gov.uk/peoplepopulationandcommunity/personalandhouseh oldfinances/incomeandwealth/articles/persistentpovertyintheukandeu/ 2015-05-20 [Accessed 15 April 2021].

ONS (2017) 'Public perceptions of crime in England and Wales – Appendix tables', Table A2, Available at: www.ons.gov.uk/peoplepopulationandco mmunity/crimeandjustice/datasets/publicperceptionsofcrimeinenglandand walesappendixtables [Accessed 23 October 2021].

ONS (2020) 'Child physical abuse – Appendix tables', Available at: www. ons.gov.uk/peoplepopulationandcommunity/crimeandjustice/datas ets/childphysicalabuseappendixtables [Accessed 12 February 2022].

ONS (2021a) 'Crime in England and Wales: year ending March 2021', Figure 7, Available at: www.ons.gov.uk/peoplepopulationandcommun ity/crimeandjustice/bulletins/crimeinenglandandwales/yearendingmarch2 021#types-of-violence [Accessed 23 October 2021].

ONS (2021b) 'Homicide in England and Wales', Available at: www. ons.gov.uk/peoplepopulationandcommunity/crimeandjustice/datasets/ appendixtableshomicideinenglandandwales [Accessed 23 October 2021].

ONS (2021c) 'Offences involving the use of weapons: data tables', Available at: www.ons.gov.uk/peoplepopulationandcommunity/crimeandjust ice/datasets/offencesinvolvingtheuseofweaponsdatatables [Accessed 23 October 2021].

ONS (2021d) 'EMP17: people in employment on zero hours contracts', Available at: www.ons.gov.uk/employmentandlabourmarket/peopleinw ork/employmentandemployeetypes/datasets/emp17peopleinemploymento nzerohourscontracts [Accessed 15 April 2021].

O'Hara, M. (2020) *The Shame Game*, Bristol: Policy Press.

O'Laughlin, B. and Sloam, J. (2022) 'Cycles of insecurities: understanding the everyday politics of young Londoners', *Cities*, [online] 12 May, Available at: https://doi.org/10.1016/j.cities.2022.103743

Pager, D. and Karafin, D. (2009) 'Bayesian bigot? Statistical discrimination, stereotypes, and employer decision making', *The Annals of the American Academy of Political and Social Science*, 621(1): 70–93.

Pantazis, C. and Pemberton, S. (2009) 'Nation states and the production of social harm: resisting the hegemony of "TINA"', in R. Coleman, J. Sim, S. Tombs and D. Whyte (eds) *State, Power, Crime*, London: Sage, pp 214–33.

Partridge, L., Landreth Strong, F., Lobley, E. and Mason, D. (2020) 'Pinball kids: preventing school exclusions', *RSA*, [online] Available at: www.thersa. org/reports/preventing-school-exclusions [Accessed 18 September 2021].

Pearlin, L.I. and LeBlanc, A.J. (2001) 'Bereavement and the loss of mattering', in T.J. Owens, S. Stryker and N. Goodman (eds) *Extending Self-esteem Theory and Research: Sociological and Psychological Currents*, Cambridge: Cambridge University Press, pp 285–300.

Pearson, G. (1983) *Hooligan*, London: Palgrave Macmillan.

Pearson, G. (2011) 'Perpetual novelty: youth, modernity and historical amnesia', in B. Goldson (ed) *Youth in Crisis?* London: Routledge, pp 20–37.

Peck, S. (2020) 'To safeguard young people we must tackle inequality and social injustice', in K. Irwin-Rogers, A. Muthoo and L. Billingham (eds) *Youth Violence Commission: Final Report*, pp 78, Available at: http://yvcom mission.com/wp-content/uploads/2020/07/YVC-Final-Report-July-2020.pdf [Accessed 7 September 2021].

Peelo, M., Francis, B., Soothill, K., Pearson, J. and Ackerley, E. (2004) 'Newspaper reporting and the public construction of homicide', *British Journal of Criminology*, 44(2): 256–75.

Pemberton, S. (2015) *Harmful Societies: Understanding Social Harm*, Bristol: Bristol University Press.

Phillips, J., Whitfield, K., Hamilton, P., de Hoog, F. and Coleman, C. (2022) 'Promising approaches to knife crime: an exploratory study', *HM Inspectorate of Probation Research & Analysis Bulletin 2022/03*, [online], Available at: https://www.justiceinspectorates.gov.uk/hmiprobation/wp-content/uploads/sites/5/2022/05/RAB-2022-03-Promising-approac hes-to-knife-crime-v1.1.pdf [Accessed 5 June 2022].

Phillips, T. (2018) '"This is black children killing black children": former Equality Commission chairman Trevor Phillips says white liberals need to "tell the truth about violence in UK semi-ghettos"', *Mail on Sunday*, [online] 11 November, Available at: www.dailymail.co.uk/debate/arti cle-6376287/Former-Equality-Commission-chairman-TREVOR-PHILLIPS-black-children-killing-black-children.html [Accessed 23 October 2021].

Pidd, H. (2022) 'Manchester MP to write to minister over 'guilty by association' verdicts', *The Guardian*, [online] 4 July, Available at: https://www.theguardian.com/law/2022/jul/04/manchester-mp-to-write-to-minister-over-guilty-by-association-verdicts [Accessed 24 July 2022].

Pinkney, C. (2020) 'Responding to youth violence through youth work', *National Youth Agency*, [online], Available at: www.nya.org.uk/static/93bd3700a201b0f74bd1daaa0f78b6eb/Responding-to-Youth-Violence-Through-Youth-Work-final.pdf [Accessed 18 September 2021].

Pitts, J. (2013) *Reluctant Gangsters: The Changing Face of Youth Crime*, London: Willan.

Pitts, J. (2020) 'Black young people and gang involvement in London', *Youth Justice*, 20(1–2): 146–58.

Prilleltensky, I. (2014) 'Meaning-making, mattering, and thriving in community psychology: from co-optation to amelioration and transformation', *Intervención Psicosocial*, 23(2): 151–72.

Prilleltensky, I. (2020) 'Mattering at the intersection of psychology, philosophy, and politics', *American Journal of Community Psychology*, 65(1–2): 16–34.

Prilleltensky, I. and Prilleltensky, O. (2021) *How People Matter*, Cambridge: Cambridge University Press.

Prison Reform Trust (2021) *Bromley Briefings Prison Factfile Winter 2021*, London: Prison Reform Trust.

Purdam, K., Garratt, E.A. and Esmail, A. (2016) 'Hungry? Food insecurity, social stigma and embarrassment in the UK', *Sociology*, 50(6): 1072–88.

Putnam, R. (2001) *Bowling Alone: The Collapse and Revival of American Community*, London: Simon and Schuster.

Quarmby, K. and Norris, S. (2022) 'Children's social care cannot be reformed without recognising the impact of poverty and austerity', [online] 25 May, Available at: https://bylinetimes.com/2022/05/25/childrens-social-care-cannot-be-reformed-without-recognising-the-impact-of-poverty-and-austerity/ [Accessed 02 June 2022].

Radford, L., Corral, S., Bradley, C. and Fisher, H. (2011) *Child Abuse and Neglect in the United Kingdom Today*, London: National Society for the Prevention of Cruelty to Children.

Ransby, B. (2018) *Making All Black Lives Matter*, Oakland: University of California Press.

Raque-Bogdan, T.L., Ericson, S.K., Jackson, J., Martin, H.M. and Bryan, N.A. (2011) 'Attachment and mental and physical health: self-compassion and mattering as mediators', *Journal of Counseling Psychology*, 58(2): 272–8.

Rashid, S. and Brooks, G. (2010) *The Levels of Attainment in Literacy and Numeracy of 13–19 Year Olds in England, 1948–2009*, London: NRDC.

Raventos, D. and Wark, J. (2018) *Against Charity*, London: AK Press.

Ray, L., Smith, D.B. and Wastell, L. (2003) 'Understanding racist violence', in E. Stanko (ed) *The Meanings of Violence*, London: Routledge, p 112–29.

Raymen, T. (2019) 'The enigma of social harm and the barrier of liberalism: why zemiology needs a theory of the good', *Justice, Power and Resistance*, 3(1): 134–63.

Reclaim (2020) *Listening to the Experts: Getting Behind the Headlines to Hear What Young People Want and Need to Stay Safe from Violent Crime*, Manchester: Reclaim.

Reece, J (2021) 'New narratives: reaching young people and families or colour affected by serious violence', *Mind in Mind,* [online], Available at: https://mindinmind.org.uk/thought-pieces/new-narratives-reaching-young-people-families-of-colour-affected-by-serious-violence/ [Accessed 18 September 2021].

Reiman, J. (1998) *The Rich Get Richer and the Poor Get Prison*, 5th edn, Boston: Allyn and Bacon.

Renold, E. and Barter, C. (2003) '"Hi, I'm Ramon and I run this place": challenging the normalisation of violence in children's homes from young people's perspectives', in E. Stanko (ed) *The Meanings of Violence*, London: Routledge, pp 90–111.

Retzinger, S.M. (1991) *Violent Emotions*, London: Sage.

Reyes, D. (2013) 'A composite case study of a woman with human immunodeficiency virus: integration of nursing research and theory with practice', *International Journal of Nursing Knowledge*, 24(1): 59–62.

Roberts, J. and Hough, M. (2005) *Understanding Public Attitudes to Criminal Justice*. Maidenhead: Open University Press.

Robinson, R. and Ryder, J. (2013) 'Psycho-social perspectives of girls and violence: Implications for policy and practice', *Critical Criminology*, 21: 431–45.

Rock, P. (1995) 'The opening stages of criminal justice policy making', *British Journal of Criminology*, 35(1): 1–25.

Rodd, H. and Stewart, H. (2009) 'The glue that holds our work together: the role and nature of relationships in youth work', *Youth Studies Australia*, 28(4): 4–10.

Rooney, D. (2013) *Henry Morris: The Cambridgeshire Village Colleges and Community Education*, Cambridge: The Henry Morris Memorial Trust.

Roorda, D.L., Koomen, H.M.Y., Spilt, J.L. and Oort, F.J. (2011) 'The influence of affective teacher–student relationships on students' school engagement and achievement: a meta-analytic approach', *Review of Educational Research*, 81(4): 493–529.

Rose, J. (2020) *On Violence and On Violence against Women*, London: Faber.

Rosenberg, M. and McCullough, B.C. (1981) 'Mattering: inferred significance and mental health among adolescents', *Research in Community & Mental Health*, 2: 163–82.

Royce, P. (2015) *Poverty and Power*, 2nd edn, London: Rowman and Littlefield.

Rucman, A.B. (2019) 'What is crime? A search for an answer encompassing civilizational legitimacy and social harm', *Crime, Law and Social Change*, 72: 211–26.

Sammons, P., Day, C., Kington, A., Gu, Q., Stobart, G. and Smees, R. (2007) 'Exploring variations in teachers' work, live and their effects on pupils: key findings and implications from a longitudinal mixed-method study', *British Educational Research Journal*, 33(5): 681–701.

Sandberg, S. and Pederson, W. (2011) *Street Capital: Black Cannabis Dealers in a White Welfare State*, Bristol: Bristol University Press.

Sanders, B. (1994) *Gangbangs and Drive-bys: Grounded Culture and Juvenile Gang Violence*, New York: Aldine de Gruyter.

Santanello, A.P. (2011) 'A composite case study of an individual with anger as a presenting problem', *Cognitive and Behavioral Practice*, 18(2): 209–11.

Sartorius, N., Ustun, T.B., Costa e Silva, J.A., Goldberg, D., Lecrubier, Y., Ormel, J., von Korff, M. and Wittchen, H.U. (1993) 'An international study of psychological problems in primary care: preliminary report from the World Health Organization collaborative project on "Psychological Problems in General Health Care"', *Archives of General Psychiatry*, 50: 819–24.

Savage, M. (2021) *The Return of Inequality*, Cambridge: Harvard University Press.

Sayer, A. (2005) *The Moral Significance of Class*, Cambridge: Cambridge University Press.

Sayer, A. (2015) *Why We Can't Afford the Rich*, Bristol: Policy Press.

Scheff, T. and Retzinger, S. (1991) *Emotions and Violence*, New York: Lexington Books.

Schelhase, M. (2021) 'Bringing the harm home: the quest for home ownership and the amplification of social harm', *New Political Economy*, 26(3): 439–54.

Schieman, S. and Taylor, J. (2001) 'Statuses, roles, and the sense of mattering', *Sociological Perspectives*, 44(4): 469–84.

Schlossberg, N. (1989) 'Marginality and mattering: key issues in building community', *New Directions for Student Services*, 48: 5–15.

Scott, D. (2018) *Against Imprisonment*, Hook: Waterside Press.

Scott, J.C. (1990) *Domination and the Arts of Resistance*, New Haven: Yale University Press.

Seal, M. and Harris, P. (2016) *Responding to Youth Violence through Youth Work*, Bristol: Policy Press.

Seligman, M.E.P. (2011) *Flourish: A Visionary New Understanding of Happiness and Well-being*, New York: Free Press.

Sender, H., Hannan, M.A., Billingham, L., Isaacs, J. and Ocitti, D. (2020) 'Rethinking prosperity: perspectives of young people living in East London', *Institute for Global Prosperity*, [online], Available at: https://discov ery.ucl.ac.uk/id/eprint/10100056/7/Sender_Rethinking%20Prosperity. pdf [Accessed 18 September 2021].

Sennett, R. (2003) *Respect*, Harmondsworth: Penguin.

Seymour, R. (2014) *Against Austerity*, London: Pluto Press.

Sharpe (2016) *A Fiery and Furious People: A History of Violence in England*, Harmondsworth: Penguin.

Shaw, B. (2021) 'Special educational needs and disabilities', in L. Menzies and S. Baars (eds) *Young People on the Margins*, London: Routledge, pp 32–50.

Shichor, D. (2018) 'Thinking about punishment (or the lack of it): the case of the economic meltdown', *Journal of Business Ethics*, 147: 185–95.

Shiner, M., Carre, Z., Delson, R. and Eastwood, N. (2018) 'The colour of injustice: "Race", drugs and law enforcement in England and Wales', *StopWatch, Release and LSE*, [online], Available at: www. release.org.uk/publications/ColourOfInjustice [Accessed 7 September 2021].

Shute, J. (2016) 'Hunting Gruffalo with a blunderbuss: on the ethics of constructing and responding to English youth gangs', in J. Jackson and J. Jacobs (eds) *The Routledge Handbook of Criminal Justice Ethics*, London: Routledge, pp 370–88.

Sibley, D. (1995) *Geographies of Exclusion*, London: Routledge.

Sites, P. (1990) 'Needs as analogues of emotions', in J. Burton (ed) *Conflict: Basic Human Needs*, New York: St. Martins Press, pp 7–33.

Skinner, G. and Bywaters, P. (2022) 'The relationship between poverty and child abuse and neglect: new evidence', Child Welfare Inequalities Project Final Report, University of Huddersfield, [online], Available at: https:// research.hud.ac.uk/media/assets/document/hhs/RelationshipBetweenPo vertyChildAbuseandNeglect_Report.pdf [Accessed 24 July 2022].

Skogan, W.G. (1977) 'dimensions of the dark figure of unreported crime', *Crime and Delinquency*, 23: 41–50.

Sky News (2021) 'Met Police knife crime reduction trial yields just two court orders in first 10 weeks', Available at: https://news.sky.com/story/ met-police-knife-crime-reduction-trial-fails-to-result-in-a-single-court-action-12412643 [Accessed 26 September 2021].

Slapper, G. and Tombs, S. (1999) *Corporate Crime*, Harlow: Longman.

Slater, H., Davis, N. and Burgess, S. (2012) 'Do teachers matter? Measuring the variation in teacher effectiveness in England', *Oxford Bulletin of Economics and Statistics*, 74: 629–45.

Smith, A. (1776) *The Wealth of Nations*, London: W. Strahan and T. Cadell.

Smith, N. (2020) 'Securing a brighter future: the role of youth services in tackling knife crime', Report for the All-Party Parliamentary Group on Knife Crime and Violence Reduction, [online], Available at: www.preven tknifecrime.co.uk/wp-content/uploads/2020/03/Securing-a-brighter-fut ure-the-role-of-youth-services-in-tackling-knife-crime-v.2.pdf [Accessed 26 September 2021].

Smith, R., Aston, H. and Pyl, K. (2012) 'NFER teacher voice omnibus November 2012 survey: school exclusions', *NFER*, [online], Available at: www.nfer.ac.uk/publications/99930/99930.pdf [Accessed 26 September 2021].

Soliman, F. (2021) 'States of exception, human rights, and social harm: towards a border zemiology', *Theoretical Criminology*, 25(2): 228–48.

Sollner, A. (2014) 'Globalization, greed and exploitation: how to break the baleful path?', *Journal of Business and Economics*, 84: 1211–35.

Söllner, M., Dürnberger, M., Keller, J. et al (2022) 'The impact of age stereotypes on well-being: strategies of selection, optimization, and compensation as mediator and regulatory focus as moderator: findings from a cross-sectional and a longitudinal study', *Journal of Happiness Studies*, 23: 635–5.

Somerville, P. (2009) '"The feeling's mutual": respect as the basis for cooperative interaction', in A. Millie (ed) *Securing Respect*, Bristol: Policy Press, pp 139–70.

Soppitt, S., Oswald, R.J. and Walker, S. (2021) 'Condemned to precarity? Criminalised youths, social enterprise and the sub-precariat' *Social Enterprise Journal*, [online] 28 December, https://doi.org/10.1108/sej-06-2021- 0044.

Spigner, C. (1998) 'Race, class, and violence: research and policy implications', *International Journal of Health Services*, 28(2): 349–72.

Spruyt, B., Van Droogenbroeck, F., Siongers, J. and Bradt, L. (2021) 'When individual differences meet society: on the complex relationships between boredom proneness, material deprivation, and aspects of subjective well-being among young adolescents', *Youth & Society*, 53(7): 1111–31.

Squires, P. (2009) '"You lookin' at me?" Discourses of respect and disrespect, identity and violence', in A. Millie (ed) *Securing Respect*, Bristol: Policy Press, pp 239–66.

Squires, P. (2011) 'Young people and "weaponisation"', in B. Goldson and J. Muncie (eds) *Youth in Crisis?* London: Routledge, pp 144–60.

Standing, G. (2017) *Basic Income: And How We Can Make It Happen*, Harmondsworth: Penguin.

States of Mind (2020) 'Schools are prioritising academic achievement over wellbeing and growth: young people want to know why', [online], Available at: www.statesofmind.org/journal/2020/11/04/academic-over-wellbeing-young-people.html [Accessed 26 September 2021].

Steger, M.B. (2020) *Globalization: A Very Short Introduction*, Oxford: Oxford University Press.

Stevens, A. (2011) *Drugs, Crime and Public Health: The Political Economy of Drug Policy*, London: Routledge.

Stone, A.A. and Mackie, C. (2013) *Subjective Well-being: Measuring Happiness, Suffering, and Other Dimensions of Experience*, Washington: National Academies Press.

Storer, R. (2020) 'Unicef to feed hungry children in UK for first time in 70-year history', *The Guardian*, [online] 16 December, Available at: www.theguardian.com/society/2020/dec/16/unicef-feed-hungry-children-uk-first-time-history [Accessed 26 September 2021].

Storrod, M. and Densley, J. (2017) '"Going viral" and "Going country": the expressive and instrumental activities of street gangs on social media', *Journal of Youth Studies*, 20: 677–96.

Streeck, W. (2014) *Buying Time*, London: Verso.

Streeck, W. (2016) *How Will Capitalism End?* London: Verso.

Tarling, R. and Morris, K. (2010) 'Reporting crime to the police', *British Journal of Criminology*, 50(3): 474–90.

Taylor, B. (1983) 'Does higher socio-economic status increase risk of violent victimisation or simply its reporting in crime surveys?', paper presented at the annual meeting of the American Society of Criminology, Denver, November.

Taylor, C. (1992) *Multiculturalism and the Politics of Recognition*, Princeton: Princeton University Press.

Taylor, J. and Turner, J. (2001) 'A longitudinal study of the role and significance of mattering to others for depressive symptoms', *Journal of Health and Social Behavior*, 42(3): 310–25.

Taylor, K-Y., (2016) *From #blacklivesmatter to Black Liberation*, Chicago: Haymarket Books.

Temple, A. (2020) 'Excluded, exploited, forgotten: childhood criminal exploitation and school exclusions', *Just4Kids Law*, [online] Available at: www.justforkidslaw.org/sites/default/files/fields/download/JfKL%20school%20exclusion%20and%20CCE_2.pdf [Accessed 26 September 2021].

Thapar, C. (2021) *Cut Short*, Harmondsworth: Penguin.

Thompson, I. (2021) 'Zero tolerance policies, a tool that entrenches anti-Blackness in UK schools', *BLAM Charity*, [online], Available at: https://blamuk.org/2021/08/20/zero-tolerance-policies-a-tool-that-entrenches-anti-blackness-in-uk-schools/ [Accessed 26 September 2021].

Tillson, J. and Oxley, L. (2020) 'Children's moral rights and UK school exclusions', *Theory and Research in Education*, 18(1): 40–58.

Toch, H. (1972) *Violent Men*, London: American Psychological Association.

Tombs, S. (2016) 'Better regulation: better for whom?' *Centre for Crime and Justice Studies*, [online] 20 April, Available at: www.crimeandjustice. org.uk/sites/crimeandjustice.org.uk/files/Better%20regulation%20brief ing%2C%20April%202016_0.pdf [Accessed 26 September 2021].

Tombs, S. (2018) 'For pragmatism and politics: crime, social harm and zemiology', in A. Boukli and J. Kotzé (eds) *Zemiology: Reconnecting Crime and Social Harm*, London: Palgrave Macmillan, pp 11–31.

Tomsen, S. (2008) 'Masculinities, crime and criminalisation', in A. Thalia and C. Cunneen (eds) *The Critical Criminology Companion*, London: Hawkins Press, pp 94–104.

Topping, A. (2021) 'How do UK childcare costs stack up against the best?', *The Guardian*, [online] 12 September, Available at: www.theguardian.com/ money/2021/sep/12/how-do-uk-childcare-costs-stack-up-against-the-best [Accessed 26 September 2021].

Totten, M. (2003) 'Girlfriend abuse as a form of masculinity construction among violent, marginal male youth', *Men and Masculinities*, 6(1): 70–92.

Transform Drug Policy Foundation (2018) 'Drug policy in Sweden: a repressive approach that increases harm', Available at: https://transformdr ugs.org/blog/drug-policy-in-sweden-a-repressive-approach-that-increa ses-harm [Accessed 26 September 2021].

TUC (2021) 'Insecure work: special edition of the TUC's jobs and recovery monitor', [online] Available from: www.tuc.org.uk/sites/default/files/ 2021-07/insecurework2021.pdf [Accessed 26 September 2021].

Turner, A. (1972) *The San Jose Methods Test of Known Crime Victims*, National Criminal Justice and Statistics Service, Law Enforcement Administration, Washington, DC: U.S. Government Printing Office.

Tversky, A. and Kahneman, D. (1971) 'Belief in the law of small numbers', *Psychological Bulletin*, 76(2): 105–10.

Tyler, I. (2013) *Revolting Subjects*, London: Zed.

Tyler, I. (2020) *Stigma*, London: Zed.

United Nations (2018) 'Youth 2030: working with and for young people', Available at: www.un.org/youthenvoy/wp-content/uploads/2018/09/ 18-00080_UN-Youth-Strategy_Web.pdf [Accessed 26 September 2021].

Vigil, J.D. (1988) *Barrio Gangs*, Houston: University of Texas Press.

Vigil, J.D. (2003) 'Urban violence and street gangs', *Annual Review of Anthropology*, 32(1): 225–42.

Vita, G., Hertwich, E.G., Stadler, K. and Wood, R. (2019) 'Connecting global emissions to fundamental human needs and their satisfaction', *Environmental Research Letters*, 14(1): 1–16.

Vorobej, M. (2008) 'Structural violence', *Canadian Journal of Peace and Conflict Studies*, 40(2): 84–98.

Wacquant, L. (2008) *Urban Outcasts*, Cambridge: Polity.

Wallace, C. and Kovatcheva, S. (1998) *Youth in Society*, London: Macmillan.

Walsh, D., McCartney, G., Smith, M. and Armour, G. (2019). 'Relationship between childhood socioeconomic position and adverse childhood experiences (ACEs): a systematic review', *Journal of Epidemiology and Community Health*, 73: 1087–93.

Weale, S. (2020) 'Youth services suffer 70% funding cut in less than a decade', *The Guardian*, [online] 20 January, Available at: www.theguardian.com/soci ety/2020/jan/20/youth-services-suffer-70-funding-cut-in-less-than-a-dec ade [Accessed 26 September 2021].

Weaver, B. and Fraser, A. (2022) 'The social dynamics of group offending', *Theoretical Criminology*, 26(2): 264–84.

Weber, M. (2010 [1905]) *The Protestant Ethic and the Spirit of Capitalism*, London: Routledge.

Webster, C. (2015) '"Race", youth crime and youth justice', in B. Goldson and J. Muncie (eds) *Youth Crime & Justice*, 2nd edn, London: Sage, pp 31–48.

Westergaard, J. (1999) 'Where does the Third Way lead?', *New Political Economy*, 4(3): 429–36.

White, J. (2020) *Terraformed*, London: Repeater.

White, R. (2013) *Youth Gangs, Violence and Social Respect*, London: Palgrave Macmillan.

Wiener, M. (1994) *Reconstructing the Criminal*, Cambridge: Cambridge University Press.

Wilkinson, D. (2001) 'Violent events and social identity: specifying the relationship between respect and masculinity in inner-city youth violence', *Sociological Studies of Children and Youth*, 8: 235–69.

Wiliam, D. (2016) *Leadership for Teaching Learning: Creating a Culture Where All Teachers Improve So That All Students Succeed*, West Palm Beach: Learning Sciences International.

Williams, E. and Squires, P. (2021) *Rethinking Knife Crime: Policing, Violence and Moral Panic?* London: Palgrave Macmillan.

Williams, E., Iyere, E., Lindsay, B., Murray, C. and Ramadhan, Z. (2020) 'Therapeutic intervention for peace (TIP) report: culturally competent responses to serious youth violence in London', *Power the Fight*, [online], Available at: www.powerthefight.org.uk/wp-content/uploads/2020/09/ TIP-final-report.pdf [Accessed 26 September 2021].

Williams, P. (2015) 'Criminalising the Other: challenging the race-gang nexus', *Race & Class*, 56(3): 18–35.

Williams, P. and Clarke, B. (2016) 'Dangerous associations: joint enterprise, gangs and racism', *Centre for Crime and Justice Studies*, [online] January 2016, Available at: www.crimeandjustice.org.uk/sites/crimeandjustice.org. uk/files/Dangerous%20assocations%20Joint%20Enterprise%20gangs%20 and%20racism.pdf [Accessed 23 October 2021].

Williams, P. and Clarke, B. (2018) 'The black criminal Other as an object of social control', *Social Sciences*, 7(11): 234–52.

Willis, P. (1977) *Learning to Labour*, London: Ashgate.

Willow, C. (2021) 'After a year of Covid, a behaviour crackdown is an insult to England's children', *The Guardian*, [online] 9 April, Available at: www.theguardian.com/commentisfree/2021/apr/09/covid-behaviour-england-children-schools [Accessed 26 September 2021].

Winlow, S. and Hall, S. (2013) *Rethinking Social Exclusion: The End of the Social?* London: Sage.

Wolf, S. (2010) *Meaning in Life and Why It Matters*, Princeton: Princeton University Press.

Wong, K., Kinsella, R. and Meadows, L. (2018) 'Developing a voluntary sector model for engaging offenders', *The Howard Journal of Crime and Justice*, 57: 556–75.

Worth, J. (2020) *Teacher Labour Market in England: Annual Report 2020*, Slough: NFER.

Wortley, E. and Hagell, A. (2021) 'Young victims of youth violence: using youth workers in the emergency department to facilitate "teachable moments" and to improve access to services', *Archives of Disease in Childhood – Education and Practice*, 106: 53–9.

Wright, C. (2010) 'Othering difference: framing identities and representation in black children's schooling in the British context', *Irish Educational Studies*, 29 (3): 305–20.

Wright, L., Head, J. and Jivraj, S. (2019) 'What moderates the scarring effect of youth unemployment on later life mental health?' *Journal of Epidemiology and Community Health*, 73(1): 6.

Wroe, L. (2021) 'Young people and "county lines": a contextual and social account', *Journal of Children's Services*, 18(1): 39–55.

Wroe, L. and Lloyd, J. (2020) 'Watching over or working with? Understanding social work innovation in response to extra-familial harm', *Social Sciences*, 37(9): 1–16.

Wroe, L. and Pearce, J. (2022) 'Young people negotiating intra- and extra-familial harm and safety: social and holistic approaches', in D. Holmes (ed) *Safeguarding Young People*, London: Jessica Kingsley, pp 83–110.

Yar, M. (2012) 'Critical criminology, critical theory and social harm', in S. Hall and S. Winlow (eds) *New Directions in Criminological Theory*, London: Routledge, pp 52–65.

Yates, J. (2021) *Fractured: Why Our Societies Are Coming Apart and How We Put Them Back Together Again*, Manchester: Harper North.

Young, J. (1999) *The Exclusive Society*, London: Sage.

Young, J. (2007) *The Vertigo of Late Modernity*, London: Sage.

Young, T. (2011) 'In search of the "shemale" gangster', in B. Goldson (ed) *Youth in Crisis?* London: Routledge, pp 128–43.

Young, T., Hulley, S. and Pritchard, G. (2020) 'A "good job", in difficult conditions: detectives' reflections, decisions and discriminations in the context of "joint enterprise"', *Theoretical Criminology*, 24(3): 461–81.

Youth Endowment Fund (YEF) (2020) 'What works: preventing children and young people from becoming involved in violence', Available at: https://youthendowmentfund.org.uk/wp-content/uploads/2020/10/YEF_What_Works_Report_FINAL.pdf [Accessed 26 September 2021].

Žižek, S. (2000) *The Ticklish Subject: The Absent Centre of Political Ontology*, London: Verso.

Žižek, S. (2008) *Violence: Six Sideways Reflections*, London: Verso.

Žižek, S. (2009) *Violence*, London: Profile Books.

Index

References to figures appear in *italic* type;
those in **bold** type refer to tables.